D1566812

Autocracy in the Provinces

Autocracy in the Provinces

THE MUSCOVITE GENTRY AND
POLITICAL CULTURE IN THE
SEVENTEENTH CENTURY

Valerie A. Kivelson

STANFORD UNIVERSITY PRESS 1996
STANFORD, CALIFORNIA

Stanford University Press
Stanford, California

© 1996 by the Board of Trustees of the
Leland Stanford Junior University

CIP data are at the end of the book

Printed in the United States of America

Stanford University Press publications are distributed exclusively by
Stanford University Press in the United States, Canada, Mexico, and Cen-
tral America; they are distributed exclusively by Cambridge University
Press throughout the rest of the world.

To Tim, Rebecca, and Leila

Acknowledgments

After such a long process of writing and rewriting, I have collected such a debt of gratitude to so many people and organizations that my acknowledgments threaten to rival the book itself in length. I have been fortunate in having colleagues, friends, and family around me, both in Russia and in this country, who have made the project interesting and enjoyable from beginning to end.

I would like to express my gratitude first of all to the organizations that have supported my work along the way. For the last five years, the History Department of the University of Michigan has provided a congenial and challenging home for me. A postdoctoral fellowship from the Joint Committee on Soviet Studies of the Social Science Research Council allowed me some time to revise the manuscript. This book evolved from my doctoral dissertation at Stanford University, and I completed the bulk of the archival research for it in the (former) Soviet Union under the auspices of the International Research and Exchanges Board. I am grateful to IREX and to the U.S. Department of Education, which supported my work in the Soviet Union with a Fulbright-Hays Doctoral Dissertation Research award. I also received generous support from the SSRC, Stanford University, and a Whiting Fellowship in the humanities. Two years at the Stanford Humanities Center gave me an opportunity to encounter new ideas from many disciplines. I am extremely grateful to all of these foundations and institutions for supporting my work and for giving me encouragement with their votes of confidence.

The staffs of various Russian and American libraries and archives have been very helpful to me in compiling material for this work. I would like to express particular thanks to Wojciech Zalewski at Stanford's Green Library, Alan Polard at the University of Michigan's Harlan Hatcher Library, and the informed and obliging people in the Russian Reading Room at the University of Illinois, Urbana. In Russia, the staff of the Central State Archive of Ancient Acts (now the Russian State Archive of Ancient Acts) in Moscow has been consistently helpful and efficient. In recent years, Andrei Bulychev has been extraordinarily obliging in tracking down sources and illustrations for me. The people at the Manuscript Division of the Saltykov-Shchedrin State Public Library in Leningrad (as they were known before the change of regimes, and names) were particularly kind and obliging. The staff of the Archive of the Leningrad Section of the Institute of History of the USSR of the Academy of Sciences and the staff of the Lenin Library were also helpful.

To my colleagues and friends I owe immeasurable gratitude for inspiration, ideas, challenges, criticism, and enthusiasm. I was extraordinarily fortunate that Nancy Shields Kollmann came to Stanford the same year that I did and that she was willing to assume the burden of a fresh graduate student along with all of the other trials of a new assistant professor. I could not have found a better adviser or friend. She guided me skillfully through graduate school, and she has remained an inspiration for me and for the entire field. Terence Emmons and Hal Kahn read my work in its early form and gave me erudite and insightful commentary. To the Stanford crew of commuting historians, Phil Ethington, Estelle Freedman, Hal Kahn, Patty Seleski, and John Smail, a carpool of articulate and argumentative scholars, I send nostalgic thanks for years of discussion and comradeship.

At Michigan, the list of colleagues who have read my work and given me helpful comments and criticism is long, so I cannot give each one the special thanks merited. I would like to single out a few to whom I am particularly indebted. David Bien helped me immeasurably with the comparative aspects of the book and lugged my manuscript across the Atlantic several times. Laura Lee Downs seems to think I have written a comedy, and her evident enjoyment of the chuckles hidden in the text cheered me greatly. Vic Lieberman posed the hardest questions in the kindest way imaginable. David Scobey helped me grapple with difficult theoretical issues in his inimitable manner and pushed me to areas that I otherwise would have avoided. Ron Suny has been an exemplary friend and colleague. I would also like to thank the Early Modern Reading Group and other colleagues in my department for their attention to my work: Marvin Becker, Miriam Bodian, Jane Burbank, Geoff Eley, Tom Green, Susan Johnson, Sue Juster, Michael MacDonald, Jonathan Marwill, Kathy Oberdeck, Bill Rosenberg, Tom Tentler, and Hitomi Tonomura.

My interest in medieval Russian history was originally sparked by the incomparable lectures of Edward Keenan. He has continued to be a challenging and erudite critic. For their helpful readings I would like to thank Samuel Baron, Ann Gorsuch, Ken Lockridge, Cathy Potter, and Dan Smail. Michael Khodarkovsky and Edward Ponarin helped me to refine the translations of several passages. A number of research assistants made my job easier: Diahanna Lynch, Rebecca Friedman, Liz Pascal, and Amy Clark. Amy is responsible for the beautiful graphics on the genealogical charts. Liz saw me through the final stages, going through a voluminous amount of tedious bibliographic work efficiently and with good humor.

Two friends and colleagues have helped me immeasurably with their rigorous criticism. Dan Kaiser has slogged through every word of this work in multiple forms and has not allowed shady logic, over-enthusiastic interpretation, or even mistakes in the notes to slip by unnoticed. My good friend Phil Ethington has kept me thinking throughout.

Finally I want to thank my kinship group, whose support has been constant. My parents, Daniel and Margaret Kivelson, and my aunt Nina Auerbach stood by me in spite of lengthy delays. My father, incredibly, read the final draft, a task above and beyond the call of parental duty. My daughters, Rebecca and Leila, have been more or less patient. Tim Hofer has gone through every step of the way with me and has always provided affection, enthusiasm, and clarity.

V.A.K.

Contents

8. The Year 1648 and Beyond: The Transformation of Muscovite
    Political Culture   241

Conclusion   266

16 pages of illustrations follow p. 180

Tables, Maps, and Figures

Tables

Figures

Maps

Preface

This is a book with a clear agenda: to explore and display the possibilities for social, cultural, and political development under the rule of an autocratic state. The problems set forth in this book respond to two sets of literature: the State School of Russian history, which posits the complete, controlling power of the absolutist tsarist (or authoritarian Soviet) state over a passive, anarchic, or broken society; and the more recent Western literature on civil society, which analyzes autonomous spaces in the public, nongovernmental sphere. In general, historians of this latter bent follow Jürgen Habermas in applying the concept of civil society exclusively to modern, literate print-cultures. Although seventeenth-century Muscovite society was theocentric, highly traditional, largely illiterate, and deeply dependent on the state in all aspects of life, and therefore does not at all fit the Habermasian prerequisites for forming a civil society, Muscovites nonetheless found interstitial spaces in the overarching autocratic culture in which to conduct their own affairs. This arena of early-modern social autonomy is the central topic under investigation in this work. In this study of the Vladimir-Suzdal' region in the seventeenth century, I set out to determine the nature and limits of autonomous activity among a small but important group in Muscovite society, the provincial gentry. Using the theoretical concept of political culture to bridge the two areas of central interest to me—politics and culture—I seek to explore the interactions between state and society and the changing ways in which a common culture both united and divided Muscovite attitudes and practices.

Spanning the entire seventeenth century, the book examines changing practices and ideological understandings of tsarist rule across a period of tremendous but effectively masked transformation. Exploring the meaning of autocracy (*samoderzhavie*) to the people concerned, I have tried to take seriously the varied representations of "the political" that Muscovite culture itself produced, representations that ranged from the most standard visions of Orthodox patrimonialism to hypertrophied despotic centralism, to consultative governance, to collective, kinship-based consensus rule. Into this complex brew increasingly intruded, during the course of the seventeenth century, an element of bureaucratic regulation and impersonal legalism. The gentry's interactions with these disparate conceptions of political propriety, and the ever-changing balance among them, form another theme of this book.

Autocracy in the Provinces also pursues a comparative approach, situating Muscovite political culture in a Western European context and, to some extent, decentering the traditional comparative framework by viewing Western Europe in a Muscovite context. Overall, the purpose of the comparisons included in this book is to understand and appreciate what it was that the members of the gentry of the Muscovite provinces (and by extension, of gentries of other early-modern monarchies) were doing and how they were thinking and to avoid more invidious questions about what they were *not* doing. Comparative analyses traditionally have cast the Russian gentry in a very negative light, condemning it for passive acceptance of the intrusive control of an autocratic state. The primary response by those seeking to defend the much-maligned gentry from such charges has been to dig for (somewhat artificial) evidence of the gentry's organized politics of resistance to such interference. My goal in this book is not to provide an apology for the members of the provincial gentry, whose violent and litigious exploits pepper the text, but rather to turn the comparative lens around and to see in what ways the Muscovites may have typified early-modern petty nobilities, whose efforts tended far more towards reaching accommodations with rising centralizing states than toward opposing them, and toward carving out autonomous spaces within and beneath state control rather than wresting control away from monarchical regimes.

If this book occasionally adopts a defensive line toward the gentry, this tone arises not because I envision for myself a mission of championing this long-gone group but instead because the gratuitous charges of passivity leveled against it carry weighty implications for current understandings of both Muscovite autocracy and of later Imperial and Soviet political developments. A "real" nobility (as in France or England), the line goes, would have coalesced as a proper corporate estate and would have served as a foundation for democratic development, would have stemmed the tide of rising absolutism (and later authoritarianism?). On this larger, metahistorical level, my contention is that such arguments do not hold water. While the Muscovite tsarist regime was indeed a truly autocratic state, as far as such ideal types can exist in real societies, its power and success rested upon forms of negotiation and toleration of areas beyond its control, which were as genuine and significant as those worked out in legal terms by corporate bodies and legislative houses in the West. Furthermore, to hold as normative the forms of political resistance familiar and glorified in Western European history is to invalidate the quite different goals and aspirations of other societies and other nobilities. Accommodation with the Orthodox tsarist state was, for the Muscovite gentry, not only desirable but necessary, from both practical and theological points of view, while accommodation with the gentry meant for the state not compromising its absolutist control but rather bolstering its power and securing its extension into the countryside. This book thus combines a close local study of politics in five particular provinces with a broader analytical task of understanding the practical workings of early-modern autocratic monarchies.

A Note on Sources

This investigation of the gentry of the Vladimir-Suzdal' region is based on information compiled on 4,100 individuals, from 977 families (surnames), from five provinces: Vladimir, Suzdal', Lukh, Iur'ev Pol'skii, and Shuia. Approximately half of these surnames (527) appear only once or have only a single representative in the documents I have accumulated from the region. The remaining 450 surnames (accounting for 3,573 individuals), however, appear repeatedly in the sources during the seventeenth century, and these families form the core of this study. Because of the nature of the sources and the society that produced them, only 210 of the individuals mentioned in the sources were women.

The source base for this study is quite varied. Most of the documents cited I found in Russian archives, at the Russian State Archive of Ancient Acts (*RGADA*), the St. Petersburg Branch of the Institute of History (*SPbFIRI*), and the manuscript divisions of the Russian National Library in St. Petersburg (*RNB*) and the Russian State Library in Moscow (RGB). In the 1850s V. A. Borisov published two collections of source materials specifically from the Vladimir-Suzdal' area, and the Soviet Academy of Sciences published another in 1984.[1] Other relevant documents are scattered in larger collections with no particular regional focus.[2] Publications of law codes and edicts furnish the legal framework in which the machinations of local politics transpired.

In establishing a list of residents of the five provinces, military muster rolls (*desiatni*) provided a chronological framework and cast of characters. Muster rolls list each servitor in a district in hierarchical order descending from those of highest rank and with the largest land allotment to those of lowest rank and smallest allotment. Muster rolls exist for all of the towns from the beginning of the seventeenth century until the 1670s or 1680s.[3] Somewhat to my surprise, I found that the muster rolls represent only about one-quarter of the regional servicemen who appear in other local documents. To the basic lists compiled from the muster rolls, I added information culled from legal cases, mostly concerning land disputes, complaints about threats, violence, and damage of property, and dishonor suits.

Petitions serve as the major source of information on provincial life, although official reports filed by town governors or other town authorities and repetitive orders from the capital, which recapitulated all prior transactions involved in any given case, also provide a great deal of information. Decrees, rescripts, and copies of official documents given to private parties to prove various claims supplement these kinds of sources. Petitions to the *Razriadnyi prikaz* (Chancellery of Military Affairs) and the *Pomestnyi prikaz* (Chancellery of Service Lands) reveal a great deal about attitudes toward service and material wealth. Marriage contracts, wills, and a few communications with the ecclesiastical authorities about donations, burials, and admission to monastic orders add a slightly more human note to the documentation. A handful of private letters survive from late in the century, and occasionally a published version of a literary tale or poem contributes to the information available about the provincial gentry of the Vladimir-Suzdal' region. Collective petitions, in which the gentry of the entire realm banded together to request major reform, provide information on the most overtly political aspects of the gentry's behavior. Many of these have been published.[4]

Information on the titles, positions, and career advancement of individuals derives from data I collected from archival and published sources, which I supplemented by using a number of invaluable indices and compilations. Publications of *razriadnye knigi* and *dvortsovye razriady* (service registers with meticulously compiled indices) make information on service assignments reasonably accessible. A. P. Barsukov's catalog of seventeenth-century town governors and an alphabetic guide to *boiarskie knigi* (rosters of high-ranking servitors) from 1853 assist in reconstructing the service titles of some individuals. E. D. Stashevskii's book on the landholding of Moscow gentry adds to the information available on men of Moscow rank. Veselovskii's roster of state secretaries and clerks in the official bureaucracy is the most helpful source of data on administrative personnel.[5]

Records on the Kablukov family and their neighbors in Shuia survive in the Kablukov Collection (*SPbFIRI*), an unusually complete family archive by Muscovite standards. Another even larger group of documents on the Kablukovy was assembled by V. A. Borisov, a history buff of the mid–nineteenth century, and is preserved as the Borisov Collection (also at *SPbFIRI*). (For descriptions of documents that were denied me from the Borisov and Kablukov collections, I relied on M. G. Kurdiumov's description of the documents in the archives of the Imperial Archeographic Commission.) These two treasure troves, supplemented by documents in the collection of Suzdalian Acts at *SPbFIRI* and scattered references in documents in Moscow archives, permitted me to reconstruct a sketchy account of the Kablukovs' interactions with their neighbors and with the state.

Technicalities

Because Russian spelling was far from standardized in the seventeenth century, I have had to make decisions along the way about how to render names and terms. I have generally used modernized spelling of Russian terms but have maintained the original spellings of first names. Thus the use of the letters "o" and "a" alternate according to the preference of the scribe (Afanasii can become Ofonasii). Use of soft and hard signs and of the letters "sh/shch" was also

much less regularized than in modern Russian. I have used the modified Library of Congress system of transliteration, which explains
(for those who do not read Russian) the generous sprinkling of apos-
trophes throughout the text.

Patronymics also pose a problem. Members of the gentry very
often identified themselves with a patronymic in addition to a first
and last name, but the forms they used varied. Instead of the higher-
class usage that has become standard—the "ovich" form—most of the
lesser gentry employed a more complicated patronymic: Ivan, Vasilii's son (Ivan Vasil'ev *syn*). For the sake of simplicity I have used the
possessive form of the father's name but have omitted the word son
(or daughter). Thus Ivan Vasil'ev *syn* appears in the text as Ivan
Vasil'ev. When individuals attained higher standing or rank, they
switched to the "ovich" patronymic, so both forms occur in the text.

Finally, not even dates allow for simple translation. The Russian
calendar dated events from "the creation of the world," which theo-
logians set at the year 5508 B.C. Thus, the year 1648 would be the
year 7156 in the Russian dating system. However, to complicate
matters further, the Russian year began on September 1, so the year
7156 would span the time from September 1, 1647, to August 31,
1648. When no month is indicated, therefore, translation of a Russian calendar year is ambiguous and is represented with a slash: 7156
= 1647/48.

Autocracy in the Provinces

Introduction

> The Russian system of government . . . is what political thinkers call "a dominating and despotic monarchy." After he inherits the crown, the Tsar, or Grand Prince, alone rules the whole country; all his subjects, the noblemen and the princes as well as the common people, townsmen, and peasants, are his serfs and slaves, whom he treats as the master of the house does his servants.
> —Adam Olearius, 1647[1]

According to the image traditionally presented in the historical literature, Muscovite Russia of the seventeenth century, ruled by the Romanov tsars, was the epitome of an absolutist, autocratic state. Dominated by a single, divinely sanctioned ruler, controlled at all levels by an omnipresent and intrusive state system, the Muscovite population acknowledged in writing and in action the unrestricted authority of the tsar. At every significant point in their lives, Muscovite subjects encountered representatives of the tsar's unlimited power. Yet in the interstices of the autocratic state, society developed many spheres of autonomy, and people conducted their lives in ways quite unconnected with the controlling agenda of the tsarist regime.

In many ways, the absolutist image of tsarist rule reflects and was reflected in actual Muscovite political practice, but until recently historians have left unexplored the meaning of autocratic rule and its variations in different countries, on different classes, and at different times. In an effort to understand the ways in which the state system operated beneath the elaborate language and ritual enactment of Romanov absolutism, this study examines the community and political culture of the gentry, called at the time "provincial service people," in five provinces of the central Russian region (Vladimir, Suzdal', Lukh, Iur'ev Pol'skii, Shuia). The study analyzes the ways in which ostensibly unlimited autocratic power touched the lives of the gentry and how these people, in turn, shaped the relationship to suit their interests and fit their needs. Although it was a small segment of the population, the provincial service class occupied a position of social, economic, and political significance far beyond its limited numbers.[2] The state relied on gentry servicemen to fill the ranks of its cavalry brigades, to serve in provincial administrative posts, and, increasingly through the course of the seventeenth century, to supervise and discipline the peasantry. The gentry comprised the lowest tier of the personally privileged elite. Below them, the majority of the population was more or less enserfed, at least after the middle of the seventeenth century.

By and large the gentry has escaped the notice of Muscovite historians, although some studies have examined the gentry's corporate identity. Most historians have preferred to concentrate on either the aristocratic boyars in Moscow or the exploited peasantry. A number of recent works on the boyar elite have substituted for the old idea of unmitigated tsarist tyranny a much needed sense of the collective, consensual nature of political decision making in court circles.[3] These important reinterpretations have described the workings of a small but influential circle around the tsar in Moscow. Only by extending the scope of inquiry from the court to the provinces, however, can we hope to understand the Muscovite political system as a functioning whole. Through an examination of the provincial gentry and its interactions with the state, this study addresses the question of how the Muscovite autocracy, with its seemingly impracticable combination of absolutist pretensions and chronic shortages of bureaucratic and disciplinary might, managed to govern its vast and ever-growing territories so successfully. The participation of the provincial gentry made that success possible.

Autocracy West and East

In recent reexaminations of early modern absolute monarchies, historians have questioned the plausibility of the idea that any single man could rule an entire state at his whim. Constraints of distance, diversity, and limited resources, not to mention the limited efficacy and energy of any single person, diluted even the most exemplary absolutist regimes. Customary law, divine order, and traditional values undercut absolutist aspirations. In the West, established corporate bodies—guilds, estates, and parliaments—also stood their ground against the unlimited exercise of monarchical power. Even the routinization of procedure essential to a centralizing regime threatened a ruler's unconditional power by solidifying the arbitrary into predictable norms. Both in Western Europe and in Russia, monarchs had to cultivate symbolic authority so as to extend their control of society far beyond the capabilities of their actual coercive power. Scholars of Muscovite history have added their voices to the effort to peel off the veneer of absolutism in order to reveal the "true" structure of limited rule hidden beneath.

Viewed cumulatively, these new investigations of absolutism force a reassessment of the very definition of autocracy as denoting the unlimited rule of a single monarch. The limits and constraints placed upon autocrats, the importance of symbolic sources of legitimacy, the involvement of elites, and the compliance of the governed did not necessarily signify a breakdown or inadequacy of autocracy. Autocracy was, in practice, a much richer political system than standard, blanket definitions allow. Within all absolute monarchies, individuals and groups retained or created for themselves areas of autonomy, independence, and empowerment. Yet absolutism retained a distinctive quality that distinguished it from other forms of rule: in codified political theory, in prescriptive legislation, and in articulated intent, autocratic rulers expressed a universalizing claim to unlimited power and untrammeled authority, derived from divine right. As defined by Nicholas Henshall in his survey of the topic, in principle absolutism is despotic, crushing the rights and privileges of individuals and collective bodies. It is autocratic, eschewing consultation with traditionally constituted bodies, and it is bureaucratic, reliant on powerless functionaries to carry out the monarch's whims, regardless of society's response.[4]

In order to learn more about the nature of autocracy in the Muscovite tsardom, the present study examines the ways in which tsarist autocracy operated outside of the Kremlin in Moscow and how its precepts were put into effect in the provinces. Study of the provincial gentry provides an avenue for examining both the direct impact of the official system on provincial society—for the members of the gentry participated in the state on a daily basis in every facet of their lives—and the areas of autonomous social interaction which the state left unregulated and unimpeded.

Localism and the Provincial Servitors

A discussion of the significance of local ties in shaping Muscovite political culture requires some preliminary definition and explanation of the central terms *localism* and *community* in the Muscovite context. Familiar as the idea of gentry communities with strong local affiliations may be from the Western European experience, scholars have disputed their very existence in Muscovite Russia.[5] Ferdinand Tonnies's concept of *Gemeinschaft*, community, has become part of the common vocabulary of scholarship on premodern societies. The term denotes "an organic social relationship characterized by strong reciprocal bonds of sentiment and kinship within a common tradition."[6] As employed in traditional anthropological studies, the term *community* connotes various permutations of an isolable, clearly demarcated group of people, usually united by residence in and allegiance to a particular territorially bounded area.[7] Some recent studies of community depart from this classic paradigm and emphasize the flexibility of identification of villagers or community members within a larger society in which loci of loyalties, affiliations, and interests vary.[8] In the case of the Russian provincial gentry, the latter, more flexible sense of community applies, although perhaps tending to an even looser sense of collective affiliation.

Muscovite gentry servitors knew and proclaimed their identity as servitors of a particular province. Most official communiqués identified the parties involved according to social rank and regional affiliation: "I, Ivashko, Suzdalian rank-and-file gentry servitor"; or "we, gentry servitors of all ranks from Vladimir." Individually and collectively, members of the gentry identified themselves as members of a particular local community. To some extent this territorial identification derived from and was imposed by the state. The state conferred land and rank on newly risen gentrymen and in return demanded military service. Surveillance of service obligations took place in provincial capitals, according to lists preserved in provincial archives. Provincial gentrymen were "inscribed into the lists" of a particular town, and only in exceptional cases could they alter their official regional affiliation. So, in addition to granting men land in a particular region, the state nurtured regional ties among its military servitors by keeping track of town affiliations and forming cavalry regiments from servitors of separate towns.

On the other hand, local allegiances were not merely artificial constructs imposed from above. Whatever the distant origins of local identities, by the seventeenth century the gentry had not only accepted its regional status but had elaborated upon official designations with its own concepts of community and localism. The gentry of Vladimir or Suzdal' or Lukh formed separate communities in the

sense of "a solidary body made up of persons who have a set of interlocking attachments that give primary direction to a substantial
proportion of their acts."[9] This open-ended definition proves particularly appropriate to the Muscovite setting. Gentry servitors defi-
nitely shared interlocking attachments. They shared fundamental
concerns over the distribution of land in their vicinity, over the level
of taxation and additional exploitation of their peasants by state officials, over the allocation of intangibles such as prestige and authority
within their ranks, and over a wide assortment of other issues relating to what Prasenjit Duara dubs "the cultural nexus of power."[10]
Interlocking interests, of course, do not necessarily imply harmony
or unity of goals. In many cases, local gentry locked horns as their
interests clashed. They shared concern over property and prestige,
each convinced that he deserved the lion's share of both. Thus the
very intensity with which the Vladimir-Suzdal' gentry engaged in
a common set of local concerns produced conflict rather than con-
cord. The strength of community feeling emerges as much from the
level of discord—seen both in unending litigation and in physical
brawls—as from any perceptible idyllic harmony of *Gemeinschaft*
community.[11]

In interaction with the state, the gentry both accepted and im-
proved upon official designations of regional affiliation. While calling themselves Suzdalians or Iur'ev-Pol'skians, servitors also functioned within a somewhat broader conception of local community.
Their primary interests did not stop short at the meandering borders
of their official provinces. Interests in land and in marriage links
crossed provincial boundaries. They were limited more by distance
than by administrative divisions.[12] Thus the gentry worked out its
own definition of local community in the face of official administrative designation.

Muscovite servitors demonstrated little of the boosterish team
spirit that local studies so often discover.[13] Where some communities display fierce local loyalty and pride, whether to their mountain
town in the Spanish Sierra or to the local football team, Muscovite
gentrymen left no trace of any such spirited attachment. Instead,
their localism, as glimpsed in surviving documents, revolved primarily around their own particularistic interests, especially concerning their families and estates. When the gentry of a particular region
shared common interests, the community provided a felicitous solidarity base from which to formulate demands addressed to the state.

Using the collective identity foisted on them by official regulation, provincial servitors formulated collective pleas in the name of all those serving by the muster rolls of particular provinces. "We, the poor servitors of Suzdal', request that additional monetary grants be given to us, or else we cannot serve in your Sovereign service." "We, servitors of all rank of Shuia, request that we be allowed to operate a mill on the River Teza." Such requests carried additional weight when they expressed the wishes of the entire community and therefore had to be taken seriously by Moscow officialdom.

Muscovite gentry displayed a variant of community feeling both more and less localized than that of the prototypical *Gemeinschaft*. A more narrowly focused, more particularized sense of community emerges from the servitors' fixation on matters concerning their own material and social standing, matters which involved them in tight solidarities of family, friends, and followers, forming subgroups within the gentry residing in the province. Rather than forming corporative groups, voluntary associations, or estate-representative bodies, the gentry clustered into small, intimate, interdependent circles. A less localized sense of community is evident in the tendency for gentry alliances to cross provincial boundaries and in the absence of elaborate local regalia or ritual.

Under the overarching framework of autocratic rule, the gentry's activities within the semiautonomous social spaces provide a distant parallel to the workings of a "public sphere" or "civil society" as described by Jürgen Habermas for Western Europe, and yet in fundamental ways they diverge from Habermasian and general western understandings of what constitutes a public sphere. Civil society is generally defined as a "realm of commodity exchange and social labor governed by its own laws," in other words, an arena of economic transactions autonomous from the control of the state.[14] The "liberal" or "bourgeois" public sphere is "a sphere between civil society and the state, in which critical public discussion of matters of general interest was institutionally guaranteed."[15] Integral to both concepts is the insistence on institutionalized practices and corporate bodies, and on autonomy from the state. The notion of a developing civil society poses a useful antidote to the assumption that society in Russia was inert, backwards, and inchoate, and that the state was the only dynamic force in Russian history. Although Habermas's terms, developed to describe eighteenth-century England, naturally do not apply neatly to seventeenth-century Muscovy, the concept of a civil society with its own sphere of interests and activity, apart from those of the state, offers a promising route for gaining access to the social half of the state-society dichotomy.

In the Muscovite case, it is difficult to distinguish areas of economic or social life that were completely apart from state regulation or untouched by service or status considerations related to official hierarchies. Every aspect of provincial life, from rank to landholding to inheritance, was in some way regulated or determined by state policy. It is even impossible to establish a clear line between state and society at all, as boundaries blurred and individuals could act simultaneously as state agents and social actors. Nor does the Muscovite case offer parallels to the institutionalized voluntary associations or literate print cultures that form the core of the public sphere as defined in Western development. The critical discussion and oppositional politics central to Habermas's definitions assumed such different forms in Muscovy that the parallel can be made weakly at best. The terms, then, have little direct application to Muscovite gentry communities, but the general notion of a civil society or a public sphere in which premodern people could function apart from autocratic regulation is an extremely important one and informs my approach throughout this book. They are concepts that allow a certain degree of independence and agency to early-modern actors in a society without the identifiable benchmarks of opposition offered by a free press, literate culture, or institutional autonomy. One key arena in which the Muscovite variant on civil society developed was within the local community.

The conduct of the gentry as a whole in 1613 after the election of Mikhail Fedorovich, the first Romanov tsar, dramatically demonstrated that its primary concern lay in the small, local politics of the provinces, not in the grander spheres of national events. After mobilizing militias of gentry and townspeople from all over the realm and fighting to rid the land of foreign invaders, the middling ranks of Muscovite society gathered together to select a new tsarist dynasty (the old one having died out) but then returned to their homes in the provinces. At a time when Western European nations were developing radically new concepts of citizenship and sovereignty, and when in neighboring Poland the nobility already governed the king, the Muscovite gentry quietly turned over power to the new tsar and went home.

The gentry's consuming interest in local issues exercised a powerfully formative influence on the nature of Muscovite politics. Its deliberate disengagement from matters of central-state politics gave free rein to the bureaucratic forces of the centralizing state. Its inward-turning orientation actively, rather than passively, contributed to the rise and legitimation of absolutist rule. Policymakers and political theorists have traditionally viewed localism and regional power bases as enemies of centralized absolutism.[16] In the Muscovite case, however, the two complemented and reinforced each other. Each had its own sphere of activity, and each by and large left the other in peace. Provincial servitors quite literally kowtowed to tsarist authority because they had no reason to do otherwise. The political culture left them ample latitude for pursuing their own interests outside of the boundaries of tsarist space. At the same time, gentry localism furnished an important source of stability on which the state rested, and it provides a key to understanding the Romanovs' enduring success.

A broader notion of community, one based on a grander conception of the unity of all of Orthodox Rus' united by faith under a divinely selected tsar, linked provincial gentry to each other and to the rest of the Muscovite tsardom. The image of a Russian Orthodox community served a unifying function in Muscovy and in significant measure determined the outlines of Muscovite political culture. Muscovy occupied an anomolous position in the Christian world in that its particular variant of Christianity was more or less contained within its own national borders, although some pockets of Russian Orthodox believers lived in neighboring lands. Confronting heathen forces of Islam to the south and east and heretical armies of Catholicism and Protestantism to the north and west, Muscovites found in religion a rallying cry and a spur to patriotic nationalism.[17] This dual identification with a religious and national community resounds most clearly during the period of self-definition forced by the Time of Troubles (1605–13), a period of tsarlessness, foreign invasion, and domestic disorder. In 1609, in a congratulatory decree issued to the people of Vladimir for their defense of the Muscovite state, the tsar of the moment, Vasilii Shuiskii, exhorted the Vladimirites to continue the good work, saying "you have stood up together with us against those of other faiths; and whomever God might will to die in this [battle for] truth, will become a true martyr."[18] The same dual religious and national identity resounds throughout the indignant reply of the monk Avraamii Palitsyn, besieged within the walls of the Trinity–St.

Sergei Monastery outside of Moscow, to a Polish-Lithuanian offer of surrender in 1609:

> Let it be known to your dark majesties, O proud leaders Sapieha and Lisowski, and to all your warriors that in vain you are tempting us, Christ's flock of Orthodox Christians. O opposers of God and abomination of dissolution! Let it be known to you that even a ten-year-old Christian child . . . would laugh at your madness and advice. . . . For what good is there for a man to love darkness more than light and to exchange the truth for a lie, and honor for dishonor, and freedom for bitter slavery? So how could we abandon our eternal, holy, Orthodox Christian faith of the Greek confession and subordinate ourselves to new heretic confessions of those who dropped out from the Christian faith? . . . Or what is the gain and the honor for us to abandon our Orthodox sovereign tsar and in subordinating ourselves to an impostor, enemy and a criminal?[19]

Palitsyn's choice of imagery suggests the ways in which absolute subservience to an Orthodox tsar could translate, in contemporary terms, into the ultimate freedom. As part of an Orthodox community, provincial gentry, too, envisioned service to the tsar as service to God and religion. Local communities, with their conflicts and solidarities, made sense only within the context of the broader nation of true Christians and subjects of the tsar. Local autonomy within an Orthodox order defined two opposed but complementary aspects of Muscovite political culture.

Muscovite Political Culture

Political culture, like any catchphrase, has been defined in a variety of ways and employed with a wide range of goals and outcomes.[20] I use it in this work as a descriptive device and shorthand term to indicate the zone of intersection between political practices and structures and cultural expectations, norms, and values. Political culture should not be viewed as a reified, static, or defining quality of a people or a state, but rather as a heuristic tool for examining political and cultural characteristics and directions of change. The label serves as a reminder of the sometimes intractable quality of custom and the weight of cultural baggage that a society in transition must drag at least part way along its new route. The definition of political culture that I find most congenial recognizes the existence of overarching structures, such as language and established institutions and traditions, that set the parameters of thought and behavior within a

society, but it also concedes to individuals and groups the power continually to reshape those structures and modify them in the course of
practice.[21] It allows for change originating both within a society and
through interactions with other cultures. Political expectations and
concepts may change and evolve over time, whether under pressure
of foreign influences or in response to internal developments and
changes. In the Muscovite case, both sources of innovation affected
the political culture.

Muscovite political culture operated according to its own internal
logic. Western travelers to Muscovy noted the exaggerated, slavish
subordination of the service population to the tsar. They explained
this abject groveling as a result of brutal coercion on the part of the
state and a natural cringing cowardice on the part of the people.
Adam Olearius, emissary from the Duke of Holstein, wrote in the
1640s that the Russian state banned foreign travel for its people,
"so that they might remain tranquil in slavery and terror."[22] This
kind of observation set the tenor of discussion in much historical
work ever since. In scholarly writing as well as in popular interpretations, historians frequently blame the Russian people for their
own subordination to tyrants. Instead of attributing the docility of
the masses to either false consciousness or spiritual weakness, it
seems more fruitful to attempt to understand the compliance (or
noncompliance) of the governed within a many-sided relationship
between dominant power structures and the subordinate population.
Following the lines of argument raised by recent work in cultural
history, I assume significant reciprocity within systems of domination and see power as to some extent a negotiated relationship, not a
simple, unilateral imposition by the strong on the weak.

Nancy Kollmann and others have productively employed Max Weber's definition of patrimonial rule—growing out of the ruler's household authority and "intermingling . . . courtly life and governmental
functions"—to describe the tsardom.[23] As envisioned in Muscovite
historical commentaries and as presented in petitions and judicial-
administrative records, the tsar ruled as a stern yet merciful father in
a patriarchal household. The notion of the state as an extension of
the ruler's household and of the nation as family continued to shape
Muscovite politics long after the administrative bureaucracy had far
outgrown the personalized sphere of the tsar's household. Long after
the state administration had grown into a large, impersonal appara-

tus, Muscovite political rhetoric maintained that the tsar's righteous wrath kept order and upheld a high religious timbre in the land, while his mercy and personal intercession protected the people, his children, from harm. According to both religious and secular commentaries, the tsar's own virtue and faith played a crucial role in Muscovite religious-political ideology. The tsar's personal piety figured centrally in maintaining the stability of the tsardom. In turn, the people's orthodoxy and their advice, voiced through ritual ceremonies of affirmation, kept the tsar himself on a godly course.

Interactions with the state were almost always framed as supplications for mercy.[24] From the most pathetic appeal for a tax exemption to the most workaday request for authorization to build a new town hall or to order more paper and ink for the governor's office, communications with the central administration were formulated as petitions for mercy and addressed directly to the tsar himself. After enumerating the troubles at hand, an official request very often closed with the words "Sovereign, Tsar and Grand Prince! Have mercy on me!" with no particular course of action (such as sending office supplies or approving the construction of the new building) mentioned. In the formulaic salutations used in addressing the tsar, his subjects acknowledged their status as children and perpetuated their ruler's absolute, paternal position. The lower social orders—peasants, conscripted military servitors, and townspeople—appealed to the tsar's parental protection as his *siroty* (orphans). Members of the privileged elite of the hereditary service classes called themselves the tsar's *kholopy* (slaves) when they begged for his mercy. The usual translation of the term *slaves* stresses the servile content of this salutation to an autocratic monarch, but Richard Hellie's work on slavery allows for a different interpretation: *kholopstvo* was a form of social welfare that allowed society's down-and-out members to indenture themselves to a patron in return for sustenance and protection.[25] For the elite "slaves," however, appeals to the tsar's mercy did not reflect economic or social poverty. When members of the boyar aristocracy and the gentry called themselves slaves of the tsar, they invoked his protection just as the lower-ranking "orphans" did in their imagery of dependency.

God and tsar stood together at the apex of the established order. Olearius noted this merger of earthly and divine leadership in his learned commentary on the Russian state in the seventeenth century. He wrote, perceptively, that "the Russians imagine that the Grand Prince does everything according to the will of God."[26] He writes further:

> The Russians exalt their Tsar very highly, pronouncing his name with the greatest reverence at assemblies, and they fear him exceedingly, even more than God. . . . Beginning very early, they teach their children to speak of His Tsarist Majesty as of God, and to consider him equally lofty. Thus they often say, "God and the Grand Prince [alone] know that." The same idea is expressed in others of their bywords: they speak of appearing before the Grand Prince as "seeing his bright eyes."[27]

Of course, the West, too, knew a natural hierarchical order ordained by God, a Great Chain of Being. Russia's theocentric political cosmology had much in common with equivalent currents in the West, which survived to the French Revolution and beyond. By the seventeenth century, however, God's intentions had come under revisionist scrutiny in the West. Newton, Hobbes, and Locke were published and read; the Netherlands threw off their monarchs; the English Parliament beheaded the king. The French aristocracy rebelled against the crown for a good part of the century and, even when not rebelling, insisted on the legality and inviolability of their provincial rights. Muscovite political culture, by contrast, remained on the surface committed to a static, divinely ordained political order, in spite of the changes in administrative practice brewing domestically and the radically new international setting in which they found themselves participating. Whereas in England, France, or even Poland a monarch distinguished and legitimated him- or herself as much by the cultivated and sophisticated milieu of the royal court as by statemanship and ceremony, Muscovite tsars gained popular reverence by ringing church bells and standing for endless hours in bone-chillingly cold stone churches.[28] If they had any inclination to indulge in Western-style pleasures, they had to hide these nasty habits behind the closed doors of the Kremlin. Prince V. V. Golitsyn, the favorite of Regent Sophia in the 1680s, accumulated an impressive collection of western-style clothing, which he could wear only for private hunting parties, since western clothing was banned by law.[29] In the sixteenth century, while Shakespeare enjoyed the sponsorship of Queen Elizabeth, the operator of Russia's first printing press was driven out of the court of Ivan the Terrible and fled the country.

In Muscovy, moreover, no other conceptions of sovereignty exerted cultural force equal to that of the stern yet beneficent, divinely anointed father-tsar. Other theoretical sources of legitimacy, such as ancient lineage or the voice of the people, surfaced in Muscovite rhetoric and ritual, but they were consistently assimilated to divine and paternalistic understandings of authority. Thus, for example, when the ancient line of Riurikovich grand princes and tsars died out in 1598, a motley array of pretenders to the throne justified their candidacies on the basis of a complicated set of interrelated ideological claims, involving divine choice, popular election, and kinship links. The Romanov tsars, enthroned in 1613 to replace the defunct ruling dynasty of Riurikoviches, played up their kinship links to the extinct line by a roundabout genealogical calculation (Mikhail was the great-nephew of the first wife of Ivan the Terrible). Furthermore, with the accession of the Romanovs popular acclaim became a regular part of the coronation proceedings. Official publicity as well as popular formulations stressed that Mikhail Romanov was chosen "by God and all the people."[30] Indeed, Mikhail was selected by the decision of an Assembly of the Land, attended by a broad cross-section of society. Yet, as described in the tales and other documents from the time, popular approval of a tsar symbolized not elective choice or democratic process, but rather the confirmation of God's choice by the Orthodox community. In 1611, two years before the selection of Mikhail Romanov to fill the empty throne, messengers brought to Moscow oaths of loyalty from the people of Kazan' who gravely sealed their oaths by kissing the cross to "whomever God should give us as tsar."[31] In effect, they issued a blank check to whoever should emerge as the leading candidate, assuming that the political world worked according to divine laws. Later chroniclers asserted that Mikhail himself had not in fact been chosen by a popular assembly, but had instead been selected by God while still in the womb.[32] Muscovy had developed a noninstitutional political culture in which popular will and organizational procedure entered political discourse as important legitimating factors but served as vehicles for expressing and confirming God's will rather than as a rival basis for political initiative. Thus, God's will served as the primary legitimizing force. Even when the popular will apparently exerted itself through quasi-institutional forms, Muscovites viewed these as manifestations of a divine plan communicated to the human realm through the pious vessel of the Orthodox community, attuned and responsive to God's intensions.

This vision of Orthodox piety and social harmony shaped Muscovite understandings of political life in significant ways, but this ideological system did not by any means translate into an actual reality of unrelenting harmony and piety. Provincial servitors devoted most of their time to thinking and acting on quite a different level. They turned their attention to climbing the local social ladder, increasing their landed and monetary fortunes, marrying off their sons and daughters advantageously, and undercutting their rivals. Greed and competition over prestige and leadership produced friction under autocratic rule as in any other system. Nonetheless, Orthodox principles and patterns of viewing the world governed the ways in which Muscovites *conceived* of their political universe. Symbolic vocabulary and forms of conflict and political interaction necessarily were adapted to the prevailing cultural framework.

Muscovite political culture proved to be a flexible one, able not only to incorporate competition and greed into its overarching framework but also to adapt to radical changes in the nature of government in the seventeenth century. In the first century of Romanov rule, administrative regulation gradually encroached on the tradition of personalized rule. The state grew increasingly distanced, depersonalized, and bureaucratized. Instead of personal mercy from the tsar, the mass of people began to encounter abstract justice meted out by bureaucratic officials according to general rules.[33] This depersonalization created some dissonance, but local communities and individual relationships proved powerful enough to assimilate central officials to local customs, patronage, friendship, and power dynamics and to recast the institutional process into a bureaucracy with a human face. The provincial gentry was able to refashion central official procedures along more comfortable, personalistic lines while avoiding direct conflict with the controlling intent of the central state.

For all the rise of bureaucracy and the gentry's evident ability to use it advantageously, belief in and hope for a harmonious Muscovite political family continued to provide a powerful unifying myth to all levels of society until Peter the Great wrenched the political theory of the country more into line with its evolving bureaucratic realities. The two systems, although seemingly diametrically opposite, worked together for centuries, one the undercurrent and the other the dominant, acknowledged discourse. Even before Peter, in the second half of the seventeenth century, Muscovite society had come to recognize the strength and importance of regularized, bureaucratic process, but the sharp edges of routinized procedure had generally been softened through traditional means, by personal connections with tsarist administrators, by gift-giving, exceptionalism, and mercy. Peter's revolution inverted the value hierarchy, standing the customary, divine, personalized cosmology on its head but not by any means eliminating it from either political ideology or practice.[34] As the semioticians Jurij Lotman and Boris Uspenskij explain, Peter shifted the positive and negative value indicators, switching plusses to minuses, lauding the cool, impersonal, incorruptible processes of faceless institutions over the warmer loyalties and obligations among individuals, subordinating his stern and benevolent authority as father of orphans to his role as energetic first servant of the state. Yet his reversal of signs did not remove the personal, nor was he blind to the continuing power of the newly discredited forms of personalized politics.

The Personal Is Political: Political Culture in Muscovy and the West

The interplay of privileged and suppressed conceptions or modes of politics offers a useful angle of comparison with Western states. In contrast to Muscovy, already during the sixteenth century both Western and Eastern European societies had developed intellectual traditions that elevated principles of abstract law and justice and placed high value on the impersonal functioning of a regularized, uniform administrative system.[35] The Polish-Lithuanian Commonwealth took this tendency to an extreme, so that the king himself was elected and upon assuming office was subject to the laws of the land and bound by solemn contract to observe a set of rights and privileges belonging to the nobility. Nobles had formal, institutionalized forums for deliberation of policy issues. Provincial assemblies met regularly and sent delegates to the national Diet with emphatic instructions about their provinces' wishes. According to the vocabulary and theoretical constructs of political life in the Commonwealth, all nobles were equal. They boasted of their "golden liberty," and all understood the power of the *liberum veto*, the right of any individual nobleman attending the Diet to veto the deliberations of the rest. Of course, in practice some nobles were more equal than others. Patronage networks bound together by personal favor and personal obligation formed around the few truly powerful magnates of the land, while the rank-and-file nobility, the crown, and, most severely, the peasantry, all suffered at the expense of the personal and arbitrary power of the magnates. But practical function aside, by the sixteenth and seventeenth centuries the vocabulary of rights and legalism dominated in Polish-Lithuanian political culture.[36]

West of Poland, legal consciousness was equally or more developed. Olearius's account of his journey to Russia as emmissary of the Duke of Holstein reflects the intellectual standards of his day and testifies to the status of law among the educated in the German states. In describing the Russian system of governance, Olearius quotes Aristotle's distinctions between legitimate and tyrannical regimes: "The first subserves the welfare of the subjects and the second the personal wants of the sovereign." Olearius relegates Russia to the latter category, among other reasons because the tsar "is not subject to the law and may, as he desires and deems fit, publish and establish laws and orders."[37] In these two lines, Olearius reveals three important aspects of his own cultural environment. First, scholars such as he understood political theory per se as a branch of thought separate from theology. In Muscovy political theory did not diverge from theology until the late seventeenth century, under the influence of Polish and Ukrainian thinkers.[38] Second, he held a concept of rule legitimized through the well-being of the people, what Ernst H. Kantorowicz entitles "polity-based kingship." Third, he placed high value on the rule of law, binding even upon the sovereign. In Muscovy, as is shown below, the political order was decisively God-based, law could be contravened by the tsar at will, and political theory did not yet exist, except as litanies of pious devotion to God and tsar.

In France, a complex and highly articulated set of provincial institutions gave provincial nobles and merchant classes a sense of entitlement about territorial rights and privileges and a self-righteousness regarding traditional autonomy and customary practices. In his study of Languedoc, William Beik describes the formalized practices of the many institutionalized bodies that participated in governing Languedoc: the *parlements*, the Estates, the *comptes*, each of which had its own charter, protocols, rituals, jurisdictions and subcommittees. Local leaders discussed their provincial rights and demonstrated their determination to protect established privileges from the incursions of the crown. In spite of this language of institutions and rights, however, the politics of Languedoc functioned in a very traditional mode, by personal connections both within the province and between the province and influential people at court in Paris or Versailles. Politics was conducted in at least two registers: a legalistic, institutional one and a personal, customary one. The personal, customary mode appears to have been the more effective one. In order to accomplish anything at all, Languedocians (and presumably other subjects of the French crown) had to curry favor with important individuals, had to give gifts and trade favors, and ultimately had to give way to the unquestionable finality of the personal wishes of the king.[39] Recent work on criminality and the courts in England reveals a similar pattern of highly articulated laws, procedures, and institutions of justice paired with a flexible disregard for all of the formalistic rules when particular circumstances made them irrelevant. The law was designed to uphold morality, and "criminal law as written worked as an ideal, as a moral standard that was enforced or waived as seemed appropriate."[40] As in France, English justice spoke a formalized, institutional language but functioned in informal, personalistic ways. As all of these works demonstrate, Western societies did not abandon overnight their premodern, customary practices, expectations, and value systems in favor of coolly rational or strictly constitutional calculations. In Perry Anderson's description, absolutist monarchies were "exotic, hybrid compositions whose surface 'modernity' again and again betrays a subterranean archaism."[41]

In spite of powerful continuities of more traditional practices, however, early modern European cultures experienced the impact of jurisprudential, constitutional discourse very profoundly. In the West during the early modern period a vocabulary of institutions, procedures, and legal rights delimited the terms of debate about proper political activity. In the sixteenth and seventeenth centuries, a discourse of the public, political sphere was emerging as the privileged one in Western Europe, while the politics of personal mercy and particularism still continued to exert its powerful influence underneath or alongside the newer, explicitly acknowledged realm of rational jurisprudence. The two spheres of discourse mutually affected each other, shaped and influenced each other, so that neither one existed in a pure, unadulterated form, and the language and practice of politics produced an amalgamation of mutually contradictory and yet somehow compatible forms and compromises.

In Russia, by contrast, the privileged sphere of discourse was the personal, the arbitrary, the merciful. Use of personal ties and appeals to the tsar's sense of pathos and clemency were viewed as the correct ways of conducting business. There was little articulated conception of a public, political sphere in which different rules applied from those governing personal, private life, although concerns about fairness and unbiased justice did arise both in popular complaints and in official law codes. There also was no explicit sense of a division between the concerns of private and public life. Parentage, clan links, birth order, strategic marriage, all served as the basis for status, advancement, and prospects, making the personal the essence of the political. The personal was political, but in quite a different sense from that in which feminist theorists of the last few decades have used the phrase. The novel discovery in Muscovy in the late seventeenth century would not have been that private life had its political aspects (which everyone knew, and which was formalized in the system of genealogical ranking known as *mestnichestvo*), but rather that there could be a meaningful distinction between public politics and family or private politics at all. As the words and actions of the servitors of the Vladimir-Suzdal' region demonstrate, demands, needs, privileges, and goals were all viewed in terms of personal relations and family advancement. The personal shaped every interaction among these people and every encounter they had with the state, which was always itself personified in the very human and individual figure of the tsar or in the generally evil incarnation of one of his officials.

In each of these societies the privileged tradition or set of values overshadowed a suppressed tradition, an unstated, or sometimes decried and derided, current that ran parallel to the dominant strain and shaped it in unacknowledged or unrecognized ways. The less acknowledged mode of political conduct could work just as powerfully as the one publicly touted, but its functioning tended to be covert. In Poland-Lithuania, the suppressed aspect included magnate domination, inequalities among the nobles, and the importance of personal connections and patronage. In France, the two discourses seem to have functioned simultaneously in the seventeenth century, eventually mingling as the personal aura of the king became diffused in the practices of the state.[42] England developed its own peculiar ideology of a virtuous community of involved (and manly) citizens, a rational discourse based on personal, moral concerns. In Muscovy, that less acknowledged side was the impartial, impersonal public sphere, the rule of law and bureaucracy of which the West was and is so proud.

The routinizing, impartial side of Muscovite political administration was certainly not altogether invisible, however, and as the seventeenth century progressed it even received significant acclaim in certain spheres, particularly in the courts and the law codes. The seventeenth century in Muscovy was one of tremendous, rapid change. The territory of the state tripled over the course of the century, and the number of administrative personnel increased ten-fold. The crazy quilt of laws, decrees, edicts, and customs accumulated since the last brief codification of laws in the mid–sixteenth century was rationalized, published (in one of the earliest efforts at large-scale official printing), and disseminated with some fanfare throughout the country. Bureaucratic staff throughout the vast and growing realm increasingly relied on the law as a generalizing guide to administrative practice. In the second half of the seventeenth century even the pretense of personal connection with the tsar was dropped in many interactions. The 1649 law code eliminated the traditional role of the tsar as final instance of legal appeal, and late in the century central chancelleries discontinued the practice of sending communications to provincial governors in the name of the tsar.[43] Even in physical terms, the traditional intimacy of the service elite with the tsar dramatically diminished during the seventeenth century as the numbers of noblemen at court and in Moscow grew beyond the capacity of the Kremlin and the capital city to accommodate them. In 1685/86, an official decree sent the surplus nobility out into the provinces, away from the "shining eyes of the tsar," signalling the conversion of close proximity to the tsar into distant, impersonal, official relations with the sovereign and his state administration.

In the early seventeenth century, the gentry responded to this depersonalizing trend and to the routinization and bureaucratization of relations with outrage, but with time it showed an ability to adapt to the inevitable. Members of the gentry proved adept at referring to legal statutes or technicalities in order to strengthen appeals for justice, yet in language and practice the gentry continued to invoke justifications of mercy and piety. Throughout Russian society suspicion of impersonal, institutional relations was so persistent that when Peter the Great unveiled the well-known secret that Muscovy had indeed become a routinized administrative state, he inverted the value structures of traditional Muscovite culture. When he began to speak in glowing terms of the virtues of impersonal, regularizing administration and law, his lack of tact called forth a deep, emotional backlash and left a lasting scar upon Russian cultural memory.

This observation about the inversion of Western norms of privileged and suppressed political traditions offers a productive way of looking at Muscovy in its own right and of comparing it with other early modern political cultures. Study after study on Western European states in the early modern period reveals that, behind facades of institutionalization and centralization, the practices associated with personal connections and patronage continued to determine how things actually were accomplished. If that is so, then what difference, if any, did all of the complicated institutional forms and the discussions of rights and law in Western states make? Was Muscovy, with its ideology of an all-powerful and all-merciful tsar and its reliance on personal connections and patronage, identical to Louis XIII's France, Stuart England, or the German principalities, which, after all, relied as much on personalized patronage networks as Muscovy, in spite of all their institutional sophistication? Instinctively, the student of Muscovy would have to answer in the negative: the institutions and traditions of French jurisprudence, for example, did make a significant contribution to political and social development, regardless of the particularistic and personalized elements that survived. However, in order to answer these questions on the basis of more than vague intuition, this work is structured as a focused case study that moves from the specifics of seventeenth-century Muscovy toward comparison with other states in an attempt to answer questions about early modern political culture and the nature of autocracy.

The tremendous contributions of Western scholars to the study of absolutist states provide a clear and accessible basis for comparison with Muscovy. For instance, direct comparison indicates that both France and Muscovy operated according to the rules of influence and patronage and that in both cultures the sovereign's position as ultimate arbiter whose whim could not be crossed was unquestioned. However, the similarities should not obscure the differences. Muscovy and France were and would remain very different societies. One of the key differences lies in their choices of which set of symbolic representations to exalt. If early modern France was not yet functioning according to modern rules of rationalized, bureaucratized, impersonal justice and administrative regulation, it nonetheless valued those principles and paid lip service to them. The existence of formal, chartered institutions, even if they were devoid of much real power, was something more than window dressing in French politics: it created the basis for future development and it located the impersonal as an ideal toward which to strive. This difference in attitudes toward public/political and private/personal spheres contributed to significant practical differences between the two societies, in spite of the fact that both spheres and both discourses actually existed and ran concurrently in both societies.

Local Focus: The Vladimir-Suzdal' Region

Five adjoining *uezdy* or provinces form the focus of this local study of the Muscovite provincial gentry. The five provinces, located about 200 kilometers north and east of Moscow, are Vladimir, Suzdal', Iur'ev Pol'skii, Lukh, and Shuia. (See Maps 1 and 2.) The chosen area serves as an appropriate basis for a local study for several reasons.[44] First, a central Russian focus complements the growing literature on the militarized southern and eastern borderlands, Siberia, and the north.[45] Although scholars of the borderlands frequently compare their subjects to the central regions as if the latter were a known quantity, the central provinces have actually received less attention than the periphery. Surprisingly little work has been done on the central Russian heartlands since Iu. V. Got'e's 1906 monograph, *Zamoskovnyi krai*. The major work of note in this category is Iu. G. Alekseev's local study of Pereiaslavl' in the sixteenth century, although a number of Russian scholars have produced local studies of other provincial "corporations."[46]

Second, the focus on the Vladimir-Suzdal' region provides a rare opportunity to study gentry communities in a fairly tranquil setting, since the development of many other gentry communities in central Muscovy was influenced by particular local variations in political and social history. For instance, the western portions of Muscovy abutted enemy territory and were sporadically conquered by Swedes and Poles. The Novgorodian and Pskov lands, in contrast, were conquered by Muscovy itself: their landlords were deported and an entirely new set of service-landholders was then created in those territories by Ivan III and Ivan IV. The Vladimir-Suzdal' provinces' eastern location sheltered them from the worst effects of invasion during most of the seventeenth century, although Vladimir itself was

MAP I. The Central Muscovite Lands in the Seventeenth Century (showing 1667 borders). Dotted rectangle shows area of Maps 2 and 3. Adapted from Allen F. Chew, *An Atlas of Russian History: Eleven Centuries of Changing Borders*, revised ed. (New Haven, 1970), p. 45; Iu. V. Got'e, *Zamoskovnyi krai v XVII veke* (Moscow, 1937), map enclosure; M. K. Liubavskii, *Obrazovanie osnovnoi gosudarstvennoi territorii Velikorusskoi narodnosti* (Leningrad, 1929; reprint Gulf Breeze, Fl, 1969), map enclosure; E. Ia. Vodarskii, *Naselenie Rossii v kontse XVII-nachale XVIII veka* (Moscow, 1977), pp. 248–49.

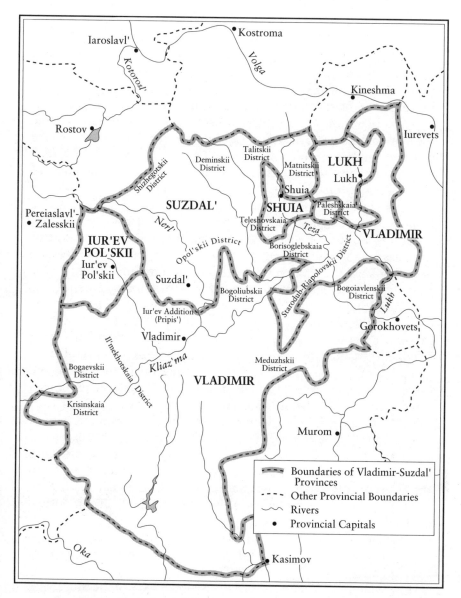

MAP 2. The Vladimir-Suzdal' Region in the Seventeenth Century. Adapted from E. Ia. Vodarskii, *Naselenie Rossii v kontse XVII-nachale XVIII veka* (Moscow, 1977), pp. 248–49, by permission of the author, with additional information from M. K. Liubavskii, *Obrazovanie osnovnoi gosudarstvennoi territorii Velikorusskoi narodnosti* (Leningrad, 1929; reprint Gulf Breeze, Fl, 1969), map enclosure.

a contested region during the Time of Troubles at the beginning of the century and all five provinces suffered serious damage at that time.[47] In provinces farther east, non-Russian people formed a significant part of the population base and altered community life. The incorporation of non-Russian peoples, such as Tatars, altered the dynamics of gentry communities in the areas where they settled in large numbers.[48] In terms of religion, too, the Vladimir-Suzdal' region was quite homogeneous. Neither converts nor members of other faiths left much trace in the documentary record, so Muscovite patterns emerge as they evolved internally, without an identifiable "other" in the neighborhood. To the north, social development followed yet a different course. There, until the seventeenth century, free peasant smallholders cultivated most of the land in the absence of gentry landlords, so the northern gentry communities existed as recent grafts onto an established society of freeholders. Proximity to the capital and the court presents yet another source of possible distortion of the configuration of local gentry society. Landowners in Moscow province by and large outranked those in the more distant provinces.[49] Gentrymen who lived close to Moscow generally devoted their political and social energies to events in the capital and therefore did not develop much in the way of distinct provincial communities. The Vladimir-Suzdal' provinces were far enough away from the magnet of Moscow to devise their own community structure without bending towards its attractive force. In his extensive study of gentry landholding throughout Muscovy in the seventeenth and eighteenth centuries, Ia. E. Vodarskii finds consistent patterns in the kinds of land and the distribution patterns in ownership of land and peasants in all of the "non–black soil" provinces of central Muscovy except those immediately around Moscow itself. His results suggest that a close study of a few of the central provinces may provide general insights into the internal lives of the other provinces of the region.[50]

How typical the Vladimir-Suzdal' provinces were of the Muscovite tsardom as a whole is more difficult to say. The borderlands all had distinctly different social and economic profiles, which no doubt affected their political configurations, yet the gentry from "all the land" shared common concerns and on occasion banded together to present their shared grievances and demands. They operated within a single political universe and understood the set of same rules. They spoke the same language, served together in the cavalry militia, and shared a common religion and a common tsar. Petitions, wills, and administrative memoranda from all over the country display similar or identical format, and very often identical content. The strong evidence of commonalities among the gentry of different regions suggest that some degree of generalization may be possible. In light of all of the various regional variations that characterized the Muscovite lands, the centrally located, predominantly Slavic provinces around Vladimir may approximate a kind of cultural common denominator, displaying patterns which typified to greater or lesser extent most of the other areas of the realm without many of the particular regional influences that affected development in the peripheries or at the very center.

Of the central region in the seventeenth century, the five provinces of the Vladimir area proved good candidates for study because of their integrity as a geographic (although not administrative) unit and because of the availability of published, as well as archival, sources. Not incidentally, the great beauty of the two major towns, Vladimir and Suzdal', as well as the possibility of visiting them under the rules of Intourist (in the days before *perestroika*), predisposed me to select them as the focus of my research.

Localism and autocracy have generally been viewed as antagonistic forces, battling to the death in the early modern period. Yet the imaginary dividing line between state and society does not withstand scrutiny. State officials often belonged to local society, whether by birth, landholding, marriage, or other affiliation. If they did not have immediate ties on their arrival in a locale, they would be swiftly absorbed into the currents and flows of community relations, so that their identities as state officials and as local patrons or clients became inextricably entangled. That understanding illuminates the more complex relationship between centralism and localism, between control and autonomy, in quite a different light, dissolving the sharp divisions and clarifying the compatibility of two apparently opposing systems. As the seventeenth century and the process of administrative growth progressed, the blurred and negotiated relationship between an increasingly institutionalized but persistently personalized state administration and the gentry landlords who both staffed and obeyed that administration continued to shape the nature of autocracy in the provinces.

CHAPTER I

The Outlines of a Gentry Class

Social Structure

In 1648 a memorandum from the tsar and boyars reported that "the Moscow gentry, and *zhil'tsy*, and [provincial] gentry, and lesser gentry of various towns, and foreigners, and leading merchants, and . . . all other merchant guilds, and trading people of the urban neighborhoods" had submitted a petition to the tsar requesting the summoning of a council of all the land.[1] The memorandum's careful enumeration of ranks, set in their invariable order, exemplifies Muscovite conceptions of the constituent parts of society. Sometimes such lists are more inclusive or more detailed, sometimes less, but always the order and the sense of ranking are clearly articulated. The provincial gentry comprised the lowest rung of the privileged elite within a highly stratified, explicitly ordered society. Its place within the hierarchy was clearly delimited.

The category of gentry landowners was in part created and in part consolidated by the grand princes of Moscow toward the end of the fifteenth century. Under Ivan III, the state, rich in land but poor in cash and in constant need of mounted soldiers, began to grant plots of land to able-bodied men on the condition that the new landholders perform military service. These landlord–militia men were known as *pomeshchiki*, holders of *pomest'ia* (conditional land grants). By the mid–sixteenth century, *pomeshchiki* had grown into a sizable class of small landholders who depended on the state for land grants and monetary subsidies and who held privileges conditionally on the fulfillment of service obligations. Along with their land, these militia men received some of the defining privileges of the Muscovite elite. Like members of the boyar aristocracy, *pomeshchiki* received their rank and land on an individual basis according to the circumstances of their birth and service. This placed them among the elite group of families who served by patrimonial right (*po otechestvu*), not by mass conscription (*po priboru*). They were entitled to receive justice from the highest-level courts, hold demesne land untaxed, and serve in the tsar's cavalry militia. The *pomest'e* system underlay the formation of the petty gentry class and secured its subsistence and its loyalty to the state.

Provincial gentrymen held three different titles, signifying descending status: *vybornye dvoriane* (literally, selected courtiers) were the highest-ranking members of the provincial gentry, selected by their peers or by the local governor to serve in regimental service; *dvorovye deti boiarskie* (literally, courtier sons of boyars) were middle-ranking members of the provincial gentry, serving by the court lists; and *gorodovye deti boiarskie* (literally, boyars' sons of the town) were the lowest-ranking members of the provincial gentry, serving by the town lists. The terms themselves suggest the various origins of the *pomeshchik* class. The word *dvoriane* derives from the root meaning "court" and could be most literally translated as "courtier," but in the sense of one who serves the tsar's court in any of a number of military or administrative capacities rather than in the more refined "courtly" sense. *Deti boiarskie* means "boyars' children," but the origins and significance of the term remain uncertain. The original *deti boiarskie* may have been literally the children of boyars, later augmented by "all service people of the lesser sort." Over time, the numbers of *pomeshchiki* grew along with the government's need to defend newly conquered territories, as the state inducted into the service class formerly landless people, displaced servitors from the lower ranks of former appanage princely courts, taxpayers, and "even armed slaves from boyar households."[2] Requiring armed men to defend its borders, the state accepted recruits from various social origins, including virtually any man who was willing to bear arms in return for a plot of land.

Cavalry service remained the defining condition of membership in the provincial gentry until the mid–seventeenth century. In the sixteenth and early seventeenth centuries, rank-and-file provincial

TABLE I.I
Theoretical Land Allotment in 'Cheti,' 1609–68
(No. of cases in parentheses)

Town	Selectmen	Dvorovye	Gorodovye
Iur'ev	488.4 (49)	391.6 (56)	268.5 (145)
Lukh	628.9 (19)	473.5 (17)	344.0 (50)
Suzdal'	517.1 (337)	369.7 (274)	264.6 (463)
Vladimir	465.8 (136)	371.4 (84)	233.4 (412)

SOURCES: *RGADA, f. 210, opis' 4, Dela desiaten', books 299, 302, 304; opis' 10, Vlad. stol, books 4, 15, stlb. 11, 40, 72, 82, 101, 115; Stolbtsy Moskovskogo stola Razriada, no. 22, pt. 1, pp. 1–161, no. 106, pt. 3, pp. 1–54; RNB, Ermitazhnoe sobranie, no. 343/2.*

gentry served in military regiments, predominantly in the cavalry militia. Cavalrymen were organized in units of tens, hundreds, and thousands. The smaller units were composed of men from a single province who served together in a group.[3] The lowest ranks of gentry enrolled for service in the registers of their home town, their *gorod*, and received their monetary grants and land entitlements from the town authorities (in contrast to men of higher rank, whose payments came from the territorial chancelleries, or *chetverti*). Thus, the rank-and-file provincial servitors went by the title "gentrymen serving by the town list" (*deti boiarskie po gorodovomu spisku* or *gorodovye deti boiarskie*). Servicemen received cash and land allotments from the state to support their service. The size of monetary and land grants promised by the state correlated strictly to rank, diminishing with each step down the ladder. For example, among the Vladimir-Suzdal' gentry in the seventeenth century, *vybornye* received an average cash allotment of 13.2 rubles, *dvorovye* an average of 10.3, and *gorodovye* an average of 8.7.[4] Land allotments also declined with rank, although average holding varied significantly by province. Table 1.1 gives the theoretical allotments of land granted to servitors in the Vladimir-Suzdal' region according to rank, showing one-third of total holdings based on a three-field crop rotation system. Note that these numbers reflect theoretical entitlements rather than actual grants given. The state was notoriously derelict in distributing salaries, and land holdings generally reached only about half the size of the theoretical allocation.

Campaign service demanded a certain degree of material security, because cavalrymen provided all of their own equipment, food, and supplies. Mobilization orders specified that men should "prepare themselves, feed their horses and stock up on supplies."[5] Because of their relative poverty, the lowest-ranking *gorodovye deti boiarskie* could rarely afford to equip themselves fully for military combat. If too poor to serve on campaign, gentrymen stayed at home and served in the towns' siege units, patrolling the town walls at night and ostensibly protecting the town from brigands' raids. According to one count, of 27,433 provincial *dvoriane* and *deti boiarskie* in 1630, 11,583 served in the town garrisons and 15,850 in regiments.[6] Most young men in the provinces began their service as *gorodovye deti boiarskie*, and some worked their way up the hierarchical ladder.

A few fortunate youths skipped the initial step, courtesy of their fathers' privileged positions, and entered service at the second rung, as *deti boiarskie po dvorovomu spisku* (or *dvorovye deti boiarskie*), meaning gentrymen serving by the "court" list. More commonly, however, men earned this higher rank after decades of meritorious, or at least reliable, service. *Dvorovye deti boiarskie*, endowed with more generous land and money service compensation rates than those received by *gorodovye*, more often managed to fulfill their service obligations as fully equipped cavalrymen in the campaign regiments of the tsar's army. Still, many complained of poverty or failed to appear for service "due to poverty." Other poor men promised to serve "on a nag . . . , but with a monetary grant [from the Military Chancellery] could serve on a fine horse."[7]

From these two lowest categories, a favored few were chosen as "select gentrymen," *vybornye dvoriane*. The practice of *vybor* or selection seemingly evolved in the first half of the sixteenth century. The practice was consolidated in the 1550s, when Ivan IV ordered that 1,000 of the best, most reliable, and most prosperous provincial landowners be selected locally and sent to Moscow to expand the corps of servicemen in the capital.[8] In military service selectmen were assigned as captains of cavalry units. Unlike the poorer *gorodovye* and *dvorovye deti boiarskie*, who performed local service in siege regiments or on short campaigns, selectmen were expected to perform full military service on distant campaigns with full armor, fine Asian steeds, weapons, and accompanying military slaves. Even among the select corps, individuals pleaded for service exemptions due to material hardships. For example, Savva Zakhar'ev Iazykov, a selectman from Lukh, although in good health had "a poor *pomest'e*, without inhabitants since the Lithuanian devastation. No *votchina*. He lives on his relatives' money . . . and would serve on a horse with a matchlock and bow and arrows, but without a grant from the sovereign he cannot serve."[9] It is difficult to know what to make of the constant refrain of poverty; it was one of the few legitimate excuses for avoiding military service, but it also reflected the marginal economic status of the gentry and the harsh conditions of provincial life.

A group of servitors called *zhil'tsy* occupied a transitional status between Moscow and provincial ranks.[10] In the seventeenth century they acted as lower-echelon military and administrative personnel. They served from their own *zhiletskii* list, which until the end of the sixteenth century was appended to the end of lists of Moscow-rank servitors on service rosters. In the seventeenth century the *zhil'tsy* were shifted down to head the town lists instead. In a system where order of precedence strictly indicated hierarchy, the placement of *zhil'tsy* between provincial and Moscow lists confirms that group's intermediate status between provincial and Moscow ranks.[11] *Zhilets* was strictly an entry-level rank. Highly placed provincial servitors with impressive service records could not enter the transitional *zhiletskii* ranks themselves, but they could launch their sons' careers there, and thus set the young men off on a path toward advancement into Moscow ranks.

Above the provincial gentry on the service and status hierarchy were the *dvoriane moskovskie*, or Moscow gentry, comprising the lowest rung of the Moscow-based elite. Because their names were inscribed in the service rolls of the city of Moscow rather than in the lists of provincial towns, they occupied a far more prestigious position than their provincial juniors. Grigorii Kotoshikhin, who wrote a systematic description of the Muscovite state and society in the 1660s, explained that "such [Moscow] gentry are assigned to various duties, as governors, and to embassies as ambassadors, and to conduct investigations and as officials in the chancelleries in Moscow, and as commanders of [regiments of] serving men, and as colonels and heads of musketeers."[12] They were entitled to land in the immediate environs of Moscow as well as in the provinces, but many made their homes on their provincial estates when not in service. Of the Moscow gentry, distinguished, titled figures appear in the sources as active members of local communities. *Stol'niki* and *striapchie*, men of the second tier of Muscovite aristocracy, just below the highest-ranking members of the duma, maintained an active presence in the provinces where they held their estates. These men filled a variety of prestigious administrative and military functions such as town governors or military commanders, as the frequent conjunction of titles *stol'nik-voevoda* indicates.

TABLE I.2

Percentage of Service Population by Rank in Vladimir-Suzdal', 1621–1700

Ranks	1621–40	1641–60	1661–80	1681–1700
Moscow rank	9.9%	3.6%	21.0%	47.9%
Zhil'tsy	0.4	2.6	30.6	14.8
Selectmen	17.0	20.3	3.9	1.8
Dvorovye	15.4	16.1	9.5	20.1
Gorodovye	57.3	57.3	35.0	15.4
TOTALS	100%	99.9%	100%	100%

SOURCES: Author's compilation, based on archival and published documents identifying servitors by rank.

During the course of the seventeenth century, the relative number of Moscow gentry in the Vladimir-Suzdal' provinces rose dramatically, while the fraction of landowners in the region who served from the provincial lists decreased. The prestigious categories of *zhil'tsy* and higher Moscow ranks among the Vladimir-Suzdal' gentry grew, with a general inflation of honors that occurred in the latter part of the century. At the same time, the percentage of men serving at the lowest gentry rank, *gorodovoi syn boiarskii*, shrank markedly, as men either rose into the higher strata of the service gentry or sank into the lower service class. (See Table 1.2.)

This shift in the relative presence of various rank categories most likely resulted from changes in land distribution policy and service demands. At the beginning of the seventeenth century, following the Time of Troubles, the new Romanov government under Patriarch Filaret made a concerted effort to distribute land to landless and impoverished members of the gentry militia. Special distributions on a mass scale allotted lands to young men who had come of age during the confusion of the Time of Troubles, and so had not received their allotments, and to older cavalrymen who had served in the victorious militia against invaders but held little or no land for their own support. Filaret decreed that estates that had been temporarily seized by invading forces be returned to their former owners, and people who had held property in areas that were still under enemy control should be compensated with new lands. His policy showed a serious concern with securing the material viability of the gentry militia forces by guaranteeing them a minimum amount of arable land.[13] After Filaret's death in 1634, the prudent policy of land distribution gave way to an unrestrained distribution of lands and privileges to court favorites. As landholding became increasingly a source of wealth in and of itself, rather than a by-product of service, the poorer gentry lost out in the scramble for land. The great law code of 1649 prohibited further distribution of court lands to private landholders, and a general ban on alienation of court lands was enforced through the 1650s and 1660s. Under Tsar Fedor Alekseevich and into the 1680s, distributions of lands once more increased, this time with an even more blatantly elitist character: great boyars and royal favorites enjoyed the benefits of the state land fund, while ordinary gentrymen received little or nothing. As the state placed less and less value on the old gentry militia it not coincidentally lost interest in providing material support to its gentry servitors. Although gentrymen could still scramble for land made available for reassignment by the death of the former owner, by confiscation or forfeiture, or through purchase, marriage, or inheritance, no new mass distributions of state lands augmented these splintered holdings. At the same time, great landlords and owners of *votchiny*, lands held in outright tenure, tended to consolidate their holdings through the century.[14] Changing military requirements also drove many of the lower-ranking provincial servitors out of the gentry class and into the less prestigious infantry ranks. These developments help to explain the bifurcation of the gentry class in the seventeenth century and the virtual disappearance of the lowest-ranking *gorodovye deti boiarskie*, who sank out of the gentry class and into the non-noble category of peasantless landowners (*odnodvortsy*).

Because Muscovites themselves ordered their society so clearly by rank, status, and precedence, historians have followed their lead. Scholars have enumerated distinctions among the three groups of provincial gentry and have assumed a clear-cut, almost impenetrable divide between the provincial ranks and the Moscow-based elite. Life in the provinces, however, observed no such sharp distinctions. Moscow-rank servitors settled in the provinces and intermingled to such an extent with local *zhil'tsy* and *dvoriane* that a division between provincial and Moscow ranks makes little sense in studying the gentry as a group. Moscow- and provincial-rank people worked together on local affairs, submitting petitions together, such as a 1656 petition in which Moscow-rank men, transitional *zhil'tsy*, provincial-rank servitors, and generally all landholders of Suzdal' Province jointly requested official authorization for a town hall clerk so that their business could be properly registered.[15] Hierarchical status was carefully observed among provincial residents, as the tiered listing of petitioners in this request illustrates, but the distinctions marked differences within a single community, not between Moscow and provincial communities. The different ranks and titles are most useful as indicators of stratification within a single social group or community. Mandatory sequential passage through the ranks required that every *vybornyi* had at one time been a *gorodovoi syn boiarskii*, and most *zhil'tsy* and many Moscow gentry had risen from provincial families. All of these ranks could coexist within a single nuclear family. While some families never or rarely rose above the lowest or the middle rank, many could claim at least a distant relative in the highest echelons. Because the provincial landlords themselves appear largely to have ignored distinctions between Moscow and provincial rank in their relations with each other, I have included under the rubric "provincial gentry" not only provincial servitors whose names appeared on the muster rolls of provincial towns but also Moscow-rank servitors who lived on their provincial estates and participated in local affairs. Thus I use place of residence and daily affiliation instead of nominal rank as criteria in delimiting the group. Where previous studies suggest serious fragmentation within the service elite along lines of rank, this approach allows an analysis of the landlords of a given province as a community, riven by its own conflicts and united by its own solidarities. It allows for the possibility that communities formed and functioned in Muscovy across and around limits and categories established by the state.

Gentry communities in the provinces were broader and more inclusive than has been thought, drawing in men of court rank as well as impoverished provincial *deti boiarskie*. One group, however, remained aloof from provincial affairs and concerned itself strictly with grander matters. This was the small group of great boyars, high court officials and church magnates, the group known to the provincial landlords as the corrupt, exploitive "strong people," or *sil'nye liudi*. A small group of high-born clans, court favorites, and chancellery heads clustered around the tsar at the very peak of society. Boyars were the leading aristocrats, generally the senior males from the most influential ancient clans, their numbers augmented and replenished by the tsar's current favorites and in-laws. A consultative duma, or council, met to approve laws, advise the tsar, and to judge legal cases. The four top secular ranks—boyars, *okol'nichie*, *dumnye dvoriane* and *dumnye d'iaki*—composed the duma or council ranks. People of this caliber mingled very little with the provincial gentry. They usually ran their estates in the provinces with the casual indifference of absentee landlords and interacted with local gentry communities either indirectly, through their local overseers, or directly in their official capacities as governors, judges, or military commanders rather than as neighbors.[16]

The gentry and the Moscow-rank elite together formed the top layers of servitors in the Muscovite military and administration. Beneath these illustrious ranks served men of the lower service class or servitors by contract or by collective conscription (*po priboru*). These men formed the tsar's infantry regiments and new formation regiments based on Western European models. They served as musketeers, Cossacks, artillerymen, soldiers, dragoons, lancers, and as members of a nonelite cavalry (*reitary*). By the mid–seventeenth century, these lowly regiments still occupied positions of far lower prestige than their outmoded, high-status superiors but were a far more effective military force. In peacetime they acted as a local constabulary and filled positions as jail guards and court bailiffs. Others served auxilliary functions, working as state bricklayers, masons, messengers, gunsmiths, and postmen. Like the gentry, the lower service class owed compulsory, lifelong service to the tsar. In contrast to the gentry classes, which served by birthright and were assessed and remunerated individually for their service, lower-level servitors enrolled by contract (although many were sons of lower-level servitors) and were rewarded by collective grants given to entire companies. They settled en masse in assigned neighborhoods in towns and, when not engaged in active service, supplemented their meager governmental salaries in the manner of townspeople, with artisanal crafts and market stalls.

The lower service class grew during the seventeenth century as Muscovy came to rely increasingly on modern infantry to fight against Western foes. Ivan the Terrible created the first regiment of musketeers in the mid–sixteenth century, but the first conscription of common taxpayers to fill new formation regiments took place in the mid–seventeenth century. New formation regiments grew rapidly, reaching 60,000 men in 1663 and 100,500 in 1681. The state encouraged, and at times forced, sons of gentry servitors to join new formation regiments (discussed in more detail below) instead of joining their fathers' militia units. With transfers from the gentry cavalry augmenting the growing number of foreign mercenaries and peasant and urban draftees, the size of the new formation regiments grew rapidly at the expense of the old style cavalry militia.[17]

Administrators and chancellery personnel occupied an awkward position in society. Their status is not easily defined. At the bottom of the administrative hierarchy, town-square clerks and lesser secretaries in provincial governors' offices occupied a social position equivalent to that of taxpaying townspeople. At the top, the state secretaries and powerful clerks of central chancelleries mingled easily with boyars and the other duma ranks. Chancellery people often purchased estates in the provinces in the second half of the seventeenth century in an effort to secure their privileged status by obtaining the appropriate appurtenances. Top-ranking chancellery secretaries (*d'iaki*), like the boyars they emulated, rarely spent time on their provincial estates, but second tier clerks (*pod'iachie*) behaved more like Moscow gentry and took more active interest in their properties.

Thus a complex hierarchy of service ranks surrounded the provincial gentry, reaching up to the highest echelons of the Muscovite boyar aristocracy and down to the lowliest state bricklayer. All of these people together, however, comprised only a tiny percentage of the general population. The privileged, landowning classes were situated at the top of a social pyramid with a sharply widening base. Peasants made up the vast majority of the population. Provincial gentry devoted much time and energy to finding, recruiting, and maintaining a peasant workforce. Until the middle of the seventeenth century, peasants retained some rights of voluntary movement and could sell themselves into slavery or bind themselves to landlords through contract agreements. From midcentury on these legal rights disappeared, although illegal peasant flight perpetuated traditional movement patterns, and hired labor continued to play a significant role in gentry farming.

Gentry or Not?

Was the Muscovite *dvorianstvo* a real "gentry"? In describing the Muscovite elite, translation poses difficult problems. Many Western historians have felt uneasy borrowing the terms *nobility* or *aristocracy* for the boyar elite, because the boyars lacked the regional power bases that gave Western aristocracies their strength relative to the king.[18] Even more difficulties plague the translation of the terms for Muscovite *dvoriane* and *deti boiarskie*. I have chosen to use the old-fashioned translation *gentry* in this study despite the fact that most recent scholarship has rejected the term because of the heavy freight of inappropriate connotations that it drags with it, carried over from the English manorial gentry. The English gentry and the Muscovite *dvorianstvo* could hardly be more different. Two fundamental sets of characteristics define the ideal English gentleman: possession of landed estates and of a degree of gentility. Sir Thomas Smith, writing in England in the 1560s, insisted that a gentleman must act like a gentleman. "He must shew a more manly courage and tokens of better education, higher courage, more liberalitie than others, and keep about him idle men who shall doe nothing but waite upon him."[19] William Harrison defined gentlemen as titled nobles, knights, esquires, and "last of all they that are simplie called gentlemen," including "those whome their race and blood or at least their vertues doo make noble and knowne."[20] Keith Wrightson writes that "Gentility was based on landed wealth, a wealth conspicuously displayed in the superior houses, diet and clothing of gentlemen, in the leisure which they enjoyed, in the number of servants they employed and in the memorials which they erected to perpetuate their memory after death."[21] Although British country squires included a good share of ruffians and crude yokels, at least in the ideal, English gentlemen lived in manor houses inherited from their fathers and left to their sons, serving as local patrons and justices of the peace, collecting rents from their tenants, and cultivating a style of civility and respectability. Their distinction from the yeoman farmers around them derived from a combination of factors, including wealth and birth, and from a genteel cultural ambience, which they carefully nurtured.[22]

On all of these counts, Russian *dvoriane* and *deti boiarskie* followed a course quite distinct from that of their English counterparts. Their economic marginality often made it difficult for them to distinguish their manner of life from that of the peasants around them, and they complained constantly about a shortage of servants and staff. Muscovite landholding tended to be fragmented rather than consolidated into a single manorial estate. The market in land in Russia was extremely active, and plots changed hands continuously, so that the nostalgic attachment of a gentleman to his ancestral lands did not develop, either as a literary image or, as the rapid turnover of properties shows, in practice.

If the manorial tradition had only limited resonance in the Muscovite provinces, the cultured, polite aspect of English gentle life made an even weaker showing. At the beginning of the seventeenth century, few of provincial landlords could sign their own names on official documents. By the 1670s almost all could sign their names in seemingly practiced hands, but few owned books or displayed any literary interests. Very rarely would a gentryman put a cultured gloss on his miserable situation. The extraordinary Ivan Funikov, for example, described his imprisonment and torture at the hands of the brigands of the Second False Dmitrii (one of the pretenders to the throne during the Time of Troubles) in humorous, rhythmic verse.[23] Such instances, however, are extremely rare. Much more representative are the countless pages of testimony about one provincial landlord beating up another "until his face was swollen and blue," or others drinking themselves into a stupor. A seventeeth-century satirical poem entitled "Tale of Luxurious Life and Pleasure" describes the ideal life of a small *pomest'e* landlord as one of feasting, music, and drunken delight:

> And whoever wishes to drink and drinks himself drunk, he may sleep as much as he wants without interruption; there are many beds there, soft feather mattresses, pillows, cushions, blankets. And for those who are hung over, there are salty foods all prepared, cabbage in big pots, pickles and mushrooms, and pears, and turnip, garlic, onion, and other food for hangovers.
>
> And there is also a great lake filled with wine of double strength. And whoever feels like it, have no fear! Drink it up, even two cups in a row. And nearby is a pond of mead. And whoever comes here, God help you, have a drink in whatever manner, with the ladle or dipper, bend and drink, or scoop [it] with your hand. And nearby is a whole swamp of beer. And whoever comes there, drink and pour it on your head! Wash your horse, and bathe yourself, and no one will reprimand [you], nor say a word. Because there is plenty of everything there, and everything grows by itself. Everyone may drink and eat at will there, and sleep aplenty, and rest at his leisure.[24]

The gentry paradise may represent what Muscovite provincials dreamed of, but the "Tale of Foma and Erema" sticks closer to their lived experience. This tale describes the lot of two impoverished gentry brothers who find themselves in one scrape after another. Their adventures inevitably conclude with angry crowds forcing them to flee out of windows and over fences. "Once upon a time, in some place or other, lived two brothers, Foma and Erema, like one person. Their faces were identical, but their traits were different: Erema was hunch-backed, and Foma had a cataract. Erema was bald, and Foma was mangy." After wandering through a provincial marketplace, hungrily eyeing food they cannot afford, the brothers decide to crash a party uninvited:

> Erema had a *gusli* [a stringed instrument similar to a dulcimer], and Foma had an organ.
> They smoothed their mustaches and went to a feast. They took a drink of beer:
> Erema pours and Foma brings it over.
> As much as they drink, even more they pour out onto the ground; they don't care about [wasting] other people's goods.
> Erema plays and Foma sings,
> and the people at the feast got angry at Erema and Foma.
> [They beat] Erema with a club, Foma with a board.
> Erema they beat on his bald pate, and Foma on his.
> Erema cries out and Foma squeals:
> "Masters, neighbors, Stop!"
> Erema left; Foma ran away,
> Erema into a barn, and Foma under a barn.[25]

These literary examples accurately reflect the image of provincial landowners' lives that emerges from documentary sources. The picture displays almost unrelieved rudeness and coarseness, with a frequently repeated motif of drunkenness and violence. If "gentlemanly" civility is a necessary part of defining a gentry, then the Muscovite *dvoriane* scarcely qualify.

Because of the poor fit of Western terminology to the Muscovite case, English and American historians have been receptive to the alternate vocabulary of Muscovite society proposed by Richard Hellie, who substitutes the categories of upper, lower, and middle service classes for more Western terms such as aristocracy, gentry, and common infantrymen. I am reintroducing the old-fashioned term *provincial gentry*, despite its Western, manorial connotations and its admittedly incomplete fit, primarily to emphasize my own divergence from previous historiography on the Muscovite *dvoriane* and *deti boiarskie*. Where many historians have stressed the centrality of the state in forming the class, and of service to the state in maintaining the class, my research indicates that the concerns of landholding and estate management formed a much more central concern for these people than did state service. Although to readers primarily familiar with Western European history the boorish Muscovites may seem a far cry from a recognizable gentry, to me what is striking about the *dvorianstvo* is that it was in fact a local landed elite, in many ways more similar to its Western counterparts than has been acknowledged. The provincial landlords of Russia did live in a very different culture from that of the English gentry, so many of the cultural indicators of "civilized" gentry are absent. On the other hand, many of the social and economic traits of a local landholding elite are present: Russian provincial landlords held land, often over a span of generations, within a particular region; they resided on their estates and worked to build and maintain them; and they used local peasant labor to farm their lands. Very often petitioners identified themselves as landowners of a given province (*pomeshchiki* and *votchinniki* of Iur'ev Pol'skii, for instance), mentioning no service rank at all and thereby stressing their status as landlords over their status as servitors.

Thus, in spite of glaring differences between English and Muscovite provincial landowners, I have chosen to resuscitate the term *gentry* for polemical reasons, in order to counteract the historical tendency to picture Muscovite society as one defined solely by service to the all-powerful state. Although the ideals of the British gentleman and Muscovite gentryman may have been worlds apart, these men resembled each other in their roles as provincial notables and landlords.[26] The argument for similarity of role seems to me to be a meaningful one, in that it challenges the view of Russian society as "inchoate," or enslaved to the state through an all-embracing system of service obligation. The language and culture of service formed an extremely important axis of Muscovite political culture and social order, but it was not the only axis of people's lives. The provincial gentry, with their ancestral affiliation with particular provinces and their manifest interest in building and maintaining their local estates and stature, provide a significant corrective to the notion of Muscovy as a nation of domesticated, dependent slaves of the tsar.

Service Structures and Rewards

The soldiers of Russia are called syny [deti] boiarskie or the sons of gentlemen, because they are all of that degree by virtue of their military profession. For every soldier in Russia is a gentleman, and none are gentlemen but only the soldiers that take it by descent from their ancestors, so that the son of a gentleman (which is born a soldier) is ever a gentleman and a soldier withal and professeth nothing else but military matters.[27]

Giles Fletcher, an Englishman, wrote this tortuous description of the Russian gentleman-soldier after his visit to the court of Tsar Fedor Ivanovich, son of Ivan the Terrible, at the end of the sixteenth

century. Although incorrect on a few details, Fletcher captured a
sense of the inextricable relation between "gentle" birth and military
service.[28] Service to the sovereign was the burden and privilege of
hereditary membership in the gentry class.

The limited research that has been published on gentry service
tends to focus on determining the relative contributions of birth,
service, and wealth as bases of social superiority and status in Muscovite society. Most interpretations stress the primacy of service
over birth. Kliuchevskii emphasized service as the central factor in
the provinces when he concluded that the highest court (duma) ranks
were assigned "by heritage, Moscow ranks by heritage and service,
provincial ranks by service alone."[29] From the premise that service
was the sole source of status or advancement for the gentry, historians frequently draw derogatory conclusions about the inefficacy of
the gentry class. N. P. Pavlov-Sil'vanskii, for example, wrote that
Muscovite gentry servitors failed to consolidate as a nobility because
the indissoluble link between state service and privileged status kept
them in a dependent position relative to the state, the primary source
of wealth and privilege:

> Service to the state determined the entire organization of the gentry class.
> Bonded dependency upon the government vitiated its independent signifi-
> cance, [and] did not allow the development in its midst of corporate goals
> or of a conception of the honor of a gentry estate. In a minor gentryman
> (syn boiarskii) of Muscovite times, the "service man" dominated over the
> "gentryman."[30]

Roland Mousnier's description of Muscovy as a "liturgical," or
service, society similarly stresses service as the crucial ordering
principle.[31]

Service inarguably provided one of the pivotal axes of gentry estate
formation. Service obligations entitled the gentry to its privileged
status and provided a framework and set of standards for organizing
gentry life. In calculations of merit, in determining who deserved promotion, a man's service record and particularly the number of years
in service figured prominently. In principle, advancement through
the ranks followed sequential order rigidly. Multiple decrees emphasized the illegality of skipping stages: "Do not register in *vybor* before
dvorovoi."[32] Exceptions did occur, but local communities kept careful track of the progress of their members and protested any violations of the proper order of advancement. The gentry servitors of
Uglich lodged a complaint in 1639 in which they collectively de-

nounced the registration of several local men above the rank they deserved. They complained that two men had been undeservedly registered as selectmen, "neither for service nor for participating in the siege of Smolensk, nor were they wounded; and we, your slaves, have served you, Sovereign for 30 or 40 years, and we never have falsely petitioned you about elections of selectmen. Merciful Sovereign . . . order them, Boris and Bogdan, written out of the select list, so that we in the future shall not live in ignominy because of them."[33]

Service brought promotions and rewards. Many men received bonuses simply for serving with their regiments as assigned. In 1637/8, Iakov Miachin was promoted to *dvorovoi* from *gorodovoi syn boiarskii* and was granted a 100-*cheti* (135-acre) addition to his service compensation rate for his service, for wounds he received, and for the death of his slave in battle at Serpukhovsk. For participating in a battle against the Cossacks he received 50 *cheti* more.[34] In constructing compelling cases for promotion or grants, Muscovite servicemen frequently relied on the strength of their service records alone.[35] Along with service, however, birth also played an important role in calculations of worth. The expression "service people by patrimony" (*sluzhilye liudi po otechestvu*) paired service with birth as equal and complementary contributors to defining gentry status. A series of seventeenth-century decrees affirmed that men were to be recorded "among the selectmen or on the *dvorovoi* list *by birth and for service*, whoever has served for a long time, and novices are ordered not to be registered among the selectmen or on the *dvorovoi* list."[36] Only those who were born into appropriately well-placed families could rightfully receive posts in which they could perform the service which would in turn advance them and qualify them and their offspring for further service and advance. Seventeenth-century officials in charge of assigning service rank (*okladchiki*) were instructed to consider the service capability (i.e., health and wealth), heritage, and service record of each servitor when assigning service ranks. Officials noted each of these factors and weighed them in various ways when doling out rewards. The service records of a man's kinsmen could weigh as heavily as his own in determining his service standing. In June of 1648, Semen Ivanov Shafrov, a *dvorovoi syn boiarskii* from Iur'ev Pol'skii, requested a raise in his rank from the Chancellery of Military Affairs. He listed his father's patriotic death in battle and his relatives' service status as well as his own service record, including dates, places, and concrete tasks completed:

I, your slave, was in Karpov with Boyar Vasilii Petrovich Sheremetev and I piled up earthen ramparts and dug ditches and built forts and stayed there until I was dismissed. I have no *pomest'e* or *votchina* and not a single miserable cottar (*bobyl'*), and my father was killed in service by Lithuanians near Moscow during the reign of Tsar Vasilii Ivanovich, and my relatives serve by the Moscow lists. Please inscribe me in the lists of selectmen.[37]

Boris Koisarov entered service as a novice in 1636/37 and received his father's entire, large service compensation award of 500 *cheti* "for his father's service and wounds and for his uncles' and brothers' deaths."[38] A heritage of paternal service and suffering thus served to justify a son's advancement.

Dvoriane and *deti boiarskie* in the sixteenth and seventeenth centuries performed compulsory service in the tsar's army and administration. They registered for service, upon reaching the age of fifteen, in the principal town or *gorod* of the province where they lived. They then maintained their affiliation with the town from which they served.

The mechanics of service within provincial gentry communities prove quite complicated. All members of the service classes had to appear periodically for military inspections. No dispensations were allowed. In A. A. Novosel'skii's words, "All of these decrepit, weakened and broken paralytics dragged themselves from distant provinces to Moscow: there were cases when they were brought in wagons, and long lines passed before the state secretaries."[39] Recruitment took three forms: *verstanie* for gentrymen serving by hereditary right, *verbovka* or *pribor* for lower service class recruits by contract, and forced conscription for the peasant infantry. As Brian Davies defines it:

> In its narrow sense, *verstanie* designated the process by which a middle service class novitiate (*novik*) of fifteen years of age or older was assigned to a service capacity order (*stat'ia*) calculated according to his hereditary lineage rights (*otechestvo*) and means, and officially enrolled in service with the cash, grain, and service land compensation rates (*oklady*) to which his service capacity order entitled him.[40]

Officials from the Chancellery of Military Affairs (*sborshchiki* or *razborshchiki*) assigned service capacity orders and remuneration rates to provincial servitors with the assistance of local witnesses who testified under oath. The local service population selected men to serve as witnesses (*okladchiki*).[41] *Okladchiki* presented to the officials from Moscow a roster of the gentrymen of the town and added pertinent information on each individual's mental and physical capacities ("in good condition" or "in good physical and mental condition") and how he would serve, with what armaments, horses, and bondsmen. Peter Vasil'ev Zaitsov, a selectman from Lukh with a theoretical entitlement of 900 *cheti*, was listed in the 1626 muster roll as follows:

> Himself capable. And according to the report of the *okladchiki* and the account of all the [gentry servitors of the] town he has an average quality *pomest'e* of 231-1/8 cheti. He has 20 peasants and cottars and receives 41 rubles in cash from the regional chancellery. He arrives for service on time and never runs from service prior to dismissal. And he serves on a good horse with a bow and arrows and a sword. And now he can serve from that *pomest'e* as previously without a grant, but if the sovereign grants him a monetary grant he could add armor and a spiked helmet and with him a man on a good horse with a matchlock. But Peter himself said about his *pomest'e* and about money and about service the same as the *okladchiks'* report, except that he has 18 peasants and 4 cottars.[42]

Okladchiki testified under oath, with threat of "great disgrace, cruel punishment, and eternal devastation in everything, without mercy," if they testified dishonestly or favored anyone in their reports.[43]

Gentry servicemen were assigned by the *okladchiki* to one of four categories; *nedorosli* (boys under fifteen years of age and not yet eligible for service); *verstannye* (enrolled in active service); *otstavlennye* (officially retired from service for extreme old age, incapacitating infirmity or dire poverty); or *v netchikakh* (absent from service without leave). Those who failed to appear for service were threatened with "heavy fines and punishments" and their people and peasants could be imprisoned until the masters fulfilled their obligations.[44]

In part because of absenteeism, but more because of the evident obsolescence of the traditional, haphazard militia, the state grew increasingly dissatisfied with the cavalry's martial performance during the seventeenth century. As a consequence, far more effective "new formation regiments" were created, modeled on Western European infantry. As the old-style cavalry militia became outmoded, the state had little use for traditional cavalry service and attempted to force insolvent members of the provincial gentry into the lower service classes and new formation regiments.[45] In 1664, for instance, the governor of Iur'ev Pol'skii submitted a list of *dvoriane* and *deti boiarskie* "who had been [taken off] the Iur'ev lists and allowed [to register] in other ranks by order of the Grand Prince."[46] Those who retained their gentry status served with increasing frequency as part of mixed units composed of both cavalrymen (called *reitary*) and infantrymen. As John Keep reminds us, "hard pressed provincials had no choice but to soldier on. It must be stressed that the decline of the levy did *not* mean a diminution of the ordinary gentryman's military role, since he was called on to fight in other capacities."[47] On the other hand, peasant conscription and the rise of new formation regiments did lessen the time demands on gentry servitors. A series of decrees reduced stints of service. One decree in 1632 reduced terms of active duty from six months a year to four, and in 1653 another decree reduced the term to three months, leaving these soldiers three-quarters of the year to spend at home running their estates.[48] In the first half of the seventeenth century, old or sick gentrymen won the right to send relatives in their places. If they had no available kinsmen to replace them, they could send taxpaying men as proxies.[49] In exchange for modifications in service requirements, the gentry shouldered increased responsibilities in supervising the peasantry. The formal enserfment of the peasants in 1649 indirectly granted provincial landholders new importance as masters of fully dependent serfs. The gentry welcomed this new role, one it had been requesting for years. The interests of the central administration and of the landholding elite solidified around the issue of controling and policing the peasantry.[50]

A sizable body of literature on the military reforms of the second half of the seventeenth century has demonstrated that the gentry militia essentially disappeared as a military force in the 1650s and 1660s.[51] By midcentury, engagements with the infantry-based armies of Poland and Sweden and advances in the technology of warfare had left the gentry militia, with its lack of discipline and primitive spears and swords, far behind. The cavalry's decline is evident both in the decreasing numbers of gentry cavalrymen recorded at military engagements and from more impressionistic accounts of the slovenly, unreliable behavior of gentry servitors. In 1647, with the goal of creating a more orderly, modern, Western-style infantry, Boris Morozov, Tsar Aleksei Mikhailovich's brother-in-law and chief adviser, introduced a limited draft of recruits from the taxpaying population on the basis of one man per ten or twenty households.[52] Ten years later the government institutionalized conscription as an annual levy. A series of decrees issued from the 1650s through the 1680s encouraged sons, brothers, and nephews of *deti boiarskie* who had not yet registered for service to enlist in lower-service-class regiments, in new formation cavalry units, or among the regular infantry soldiers.[53] After the Treaty of Andrusovo with Poland in 1667, according to M. M. Denisova's figures, gentry cavalrymen accounted for less than half of a total cavalry force of 42,500. P. I. Ivanov finds only 13,973 men in the *pomest'e*-based gentry militia in 1681. This figure indicates that of 70,000 gentry servitors, only one in five was actively engaged in cavalry service by the end of the century.[54]

The demise of the gentry cavalry militia, however, did not entail the disappearance of the gentry itself. While numbers from military musters reveal a marked decline in the old-style cavalry corps, the provincial landowning class continued to grow, albeit slowly. It grew through natural increase and also through the flow of Moscow-rank servitors who settled in the provinces when the capital could no longer house all of its service population. Spilling out from the capital in the late 1660s and throughout the 1670s, these emigrés from Moscow replenished the depleted provincial population and forged links with their new home communities. Together, natural increase and relocation from the capital explain the revival of provincial populations in the 1670s.[55] The obsolescence of the cavalry militia affected gentry servicemen in two ways: the amount of time demanded of them by state service obligations decreased, freeing them to stay home and manage their estates; and the nature of service gradually shifted from the battlefield to the administrative office.

The Gentry as Landlords

Social and service aspects of gentry life were inextricably interconnected, and both were related to gentry landowning. The state regulated all ownership of land, decreeing who could own land, how much they could own, and under what conditions. The state land fund served as the primary source of land given out to gentry, although an extremely active market and constant trades and gifts of land provided important secondary sources. Furthermore, the state set limits to the amount of land each individual landowner could possess, and if someone accumulated more than his or her allotment, the surplus could be confiscated.

Pomeshchiki bore responsibility for many aspects of their peasants' lives. When landlords assumed title to young, unmarried peasants, they assumed an obligation to arrange marriages for them. A memorandum transferring ownership of a peasant girl to a new land-lord asserts, "and it is up to Semen [the new master] and his wife and their children, to give her out in marriage while keeping her within their household, or wherever outside the house they wish to give her."[56] Peasants needed their master's permission to marry, particularly to marry a peasant of a different landlord. This is evident in marriage agreements such as the following, drawn up in 1679 by the peasant father of the bride to be: "In this 187 year (1679), on the 13th day of February . . . I, Andrei, gave him, Ivan, an agreement document, saying that I would give that daughter of mine, Agrepina, to him, Ivan, in marriage . . . and that I would bring and give to him, Ivan, a manumission document from my master, Stefan Ostaf'evich Zinov'ev, one week before the date of the marriage."[57] In other agreements, peasant fathers or brothers stipulated what would happen if the master refused to grant permission, indicating that the permission involved more than routine approval. When a peasant woman married a man belonging to a different master, her former master often lost all rights and privileges over her. In spite of this apparent disincentive for masters to allow marriage off the estate, such marriages were apparently quite common. Church dictates required local priests to determine that between the potential spouses there was no relationship of "family nor clan, nor godparenthood, nor intermarriage," and on small estates with few peasant laborers this regulation effectively required marriage outside of the estates.[58] The church exerted pressure on landlords to arrange timely marriages for their peasants in order to prevent them from falling into sin outside of marriage.[59]

A provincial landlord was responsible not only for ensuring the lawful marriage of his dependents; he also acted as primary judge and tax collector. Demesne land belonging to military servitors was exempt from taxes in the seventeenth century, but taxes were assessed on each peasant household. The state expected taxes to be paid in a lump sum by all of the peasants of an individual estate, and the landlord was responsible for collecting and handing over revenues. The landholder might have to make up any shortfall from his own purse, but he could use his position to bind his peasants all the more closely to him through a cycle of indebtedness. Disagreements within an estate fell within the jurisdiction of the landlord. The law code of 1550 stated that "boyars and petty boyars [gentrymen] who have full jurisdictional grants shall administer justice. . . ."[60] In disputes with people from outside the estate, external courts held jurisdiction, although often the landlord joined the other judges in resolving such cases. A charter granted by Patriarch Filaret to a Fedor Ragozin, a Vladimir *syn boiarskii* in his service, affirms the autonomy of a landlord within the borders of his holding:

> Whatever peasants and slaves live on Fedor's *pomest'e* should continue to live there, and our [patriarchal] district officials and bailiffs should not judge his people and peasants in anything . . . but should let him, Fedor, supervise and judge them himself or let his bailiff [judge them], but in mixed cases involving [other patriarchal people] and his people and peasants, let our [patriarchal] bailiffs and district officials judge, and Fedor will judge with them. And if anyone lodges charges against Fedor himself or against his bailiff, either I, the Great Sovereign most Reverend Filaret, Patriarch of Moscow and all Russia, or my boyars will judge him.[61]

Responsible for administering justice and collecting taxes from his own dependents, a provincial landlord had to participate actively in the life of his estate. Wealthy landowners conducted their estate business through overseers and bailiffs, but petty gentrymen commonly lived on their estates and worked closely with their overseers. Court cases and petitions show landlords' intense concern with augmenting their properties with even small slivers of land, with consolidating properties, and with converting as much as possible of their estates to *votchina* status. Documents reveal landlords' involvement with the actual cycle of production on their estates, their concern for the rye or barley harvest, for the collection of honey and beaver skins, for the fate of the berries in their woods. Frequent complaints in trial records involved charges that a neighbor trampled fields, chopped down trees, or injured livestock on a gentry landholder's estate. Wills record each bushel of rye, wheat, or oats borrowed or lent to be collected by or repaid to the deceased's estate.[62] As actively involved landlords, tax collectors, money lenders, and administrators of local justice, the provincial *dvorianstvo* may reasonably be said to resemble a gentry class.

The Agrarian Economy of the Vladimir-Suzdal' Region

Lying due east of Moscow, Vladimir province bordered on Moscow and Pereiaslavl'-Zalesskii provinces to the west and reached down to Kasimov in the south (see Map 2). Along the eastern edge of the province lay Murom and Gorokhovets provinces. Suzdal' ran along most of Vladimir's northern border, and the small Iur'ev Pol'skii Province nestled against its northwestern corner. A finger of Iur'ev Pol'skii Province at one time reached in between the Suzdal' and Vladimir provincial lines, but by the seventeenth century that outcropping had been incorporated administratively into Vladimir as the Iur'ev Addition (pripis').[63] As can be seen in the map, eccentrically shaped Suzdal' snaked around the other provinces, enveloping tiny Shuia and nearly encircling Lukh.

The five provinces formed a contiguous whole, with pieces woven together and islands of one dotting the others. The complexity of regional divisions and the proximity of territories of one province with those of its neighbor led to a certain degree of cross-settlement and joint administration among them. Families indigenous to one of the provinces often had scions in a neighboring one. Although the majority of families settled, married, and owned property within a single district, intermarriage and land purchases frequently took place across provincial boundaries within the five-province bloc.[64] Thus the five provinces formed a fairly cohesive unit in terms of population, administration, and geography.

Describing the area between Moscow and Nizhnii Novgorod—that is, the region of this study—the seventeenth-century German traveller Adam Olearius wrote, "The [River] Kliazma . . . runs from Vladimir. Here the terrain on the right begins to rise, making a very high bank that continues at about the same height for almost a hundred leagues along the Volga. From the river below, it looks like a series of contiguous heights. Above, however, it is even, flat country, bare of forest, and good for agriculture."[65]

The five provinces of this study lie in the non–black earth region of central Russia and so had far less fertile soil than the rich steppe lands. Of the non–black earth areas, however, the Vladimir Plain was favored with relatively advantageous conditions. The soil of the region has a moderately fertile upper layer of loam. The forests, where they had not been devastated by overuse, were mixed in type, with "mosaic stands of coniferous trees, such as pine, and broad-leaf deciduous species (lime, oak, elm and maple)," the same beautiful mixed forests that characterize the area today.[66]

For a central Russian region, the Vladimir-Suzdal' area enjoyed a relatively kind natural environment. As S. B. Veselovskii wrote:

The conjunction of soil conditions favorable to cultivation with convenient communication routes was the reason that the so-called Vladimir-

Suzdal' Plain was one of the most ancient and most important locations of settlement of Slavs in north-east Rus'. The River Kliaz'ma made a convenient communication route between the Volga and Oka. In addition to the Kliaz'ma, another important water route [the Kotorosl' and Nerl' Rivers] led into the Suzdal' area, joining it with the upper Volga. . . . The absence in the plain region of forests and swamps and the relatively good soil favored . . . the development of agriculture.[67]

Nature's blessings could be considered generous only in a relative perspective, however. Because of either the natural characteristics of the soil or its exhaustion, farming was difficult.[68] In the late seventeenth century an overseer of an estate wrote to his master from Shuia, saying, "There are few cattle here, my lord, and [so] there is no manure, and the land here, my lord, does not produce without manure. Where there is manure, there it grows, but without manure, there nothing grows and nothing will come up, but on the neighboring fields where, my lord, there is manure, there the grain is robust."[69] The landowner in this case, *stol'nik* A. I. Bezobrazov, followed the general economic trend when he largely ignored his estates in the central provinces, instead building up his holdings in the south and transferring his peasants from the "infertile central Russian villages to the southern black-earth lands," where their labor would yield far richer returns.[70] The steppe lands and the Volga basin, with their famous black earth and longer growing seasons, produced far better yields. For that reason, landlords maneuvered land trades, when they could, to exchange central brown- and grey-earth properties for holdings in the black-earth zones.[71] Laws passed in the seventeenth century limited the rights of nonresidents to purchase lands in the southern border areas, but the wealthier and more influential members of Muscovite society managed to circumvent the regulations. In general, wealthy landlords with diversified holdings farmed their southern lands and exploited their more centrally located properties for natural resources other than field crops. They devoted those lands to hayfields, forest resources, and fishing.[72]

Members of the gentry who held land exclusively in the central zones tended to be a middling sort who could not manage to obtain more fertile properties in the south but who succeeded in maintaining viable estates within the relatively densely settled Muscovite heartland.[73] The exodus of peasants to the south enfeebled the poorer members of gentry society, who could neither entice nor force their peasants to stay with them. According to calculations by A. Iakovlev and Veselovskii, gentry landlords who owned serfs at all throughout the tsardom averaged only five or six peasant households in their possession.[74] In the central Russian provinces, the average was slightly higher. According to my data on the five provinces of the Vladimir-Suzdal' region, a sample of 194 gentry landholders (including servitors' widows and orphaned children and landlords with no peasants) between 1626 and 1699 reported an average of 7.6 peasant households each, with a range of zero to 60 households. Both Iakovlev's sample and my own reflect marked regional variation, although the sample sizes become quite small and the results less meaningful when subdivided for such finely tuned results. Vladimir and Suzdal'/Shuia displayed the highest average holdings in both Iakovlev's tabulation and in my own. According to my calculations, between 1626 and 1699, 96 Suzdalian landlords held 918 households, averaging 9.6 each, while 60 Vladimir landlords averaged 6.9 households each. The smaller number of gentry landlords in Iur'ev and Lukh trailed those in the other provinces: 16 landlords in Lukh averaged 5.8 households each, while the 22 Iur'ev landlords held on average a minuscule 2.2 households.[75]

The law acknowledged that a minimum of fifteen peasant households was required to support the service of one fully equipped cavalryman or peasant recruit.[76] By this standard, most landowners in Vladimir-Suzdal' lacked even the minimum number of households necessary to support their service and purchase food, supplies, and equipment.

Not only the small number of peasants but also the small real estate holdings of many gentry cavalrymen made the *pomest'e* system a precarious way of supporting the cavalry forces. The state expected each cavalryman to possess a minimum of 100 *cheti* of land and to provide one additional fully armed and mounted soldier for each additional 100 *cheti*.[77] In the seventeenth century, middle-level servitors in Vladimir and Suzdal' averaged 161 *cheti* in one field (of a three-field system), a fully adequate amount of land. However, the large standard deviation, 116, reveals that a sizable number of these servitors had minuscule landholdings or none at all, thus destroying the initial impression of comfort and prosperity.[78] Furthermore, acreage without resident laborers had little value. Vodarskii observes that in the Vladimir region *pomest'e* tenure and small to medium estates clearly predominated over *votchina* tenure and great estates. The former accounted for 67 percent of all identifiable estate land in the 1680s and 87 percent in 1700. In contrast, great boyars and large latifundia monopolized most of the peasant laborers, holding 65 percent of the peasants of the region in 1700.[79] With this imbalance in the distribution of peasants and the ratio of workers to land, it is not surprising that the gentry of Vladimir-Suzdal' owned a large number of *pustoshi*, untenanted plots. Thus even in the central provinces, where economic extremes were less polarized than elsewhere in the realm and where petty *pomeshchiki* held most of the land, many gentrymen had to find ways to hire laborers (which they evidently did), or else were forced to live almost in the manner of peasants, possibly even performing the manual labor of farming their lands themselves.

As measured by the number of untenanted plots and peasantless lords, depopulation of the countryside in the central Russian area reached its worst in the first two decades of the seventeenth century, following the Time of Troubles. According to Iu. V. Got'e, the taxpaying population of the center rose rapidly in the next two decades, both through natural increase and by the return of refugees who had been displaced by chaotic times.[80] In the Vladimir-Suzdal' region, in keeping with the general trend of the broader central Russian region, the numbers of landlords who reported owning only one or two peasant households or none at all peaked in the 1620s and then receded. However, demographic trends were less extreme in the Vladimir-Suzdal' region and other central areas than in regions harder hit by the devastation and invasions of the Time of Troubles. Throughout the century, a sizable fraction of the properties in the region was described by its owners and by state surveyors as uninhabited, but populated villages were by no means a rarity even in the 1620s and 1630s. The rather equal balance between tenanted and untenanted plots held by gentry of the Vladimir-Suzdal' regions suggests a middling economic status, neither wealthy nor destitute.

In the Vladimir-Suzdal' area, the position of the service gentry was more secure than it was in the southern borderlands, where peasantless landlords predominated. Nonetheless, poverty was a familiar specter in the five provinces of the region. In 1626, for instance, 30 out of 77, or almost half, of Lukh servitors reported at the annual muster that they owned not a single peasant.[81] Other cases from Lukh illustrate the extreme poverty that could afflict members of the service community. Ivan Petelin, newly enrolled for service upon reaching the age of fifteen, held no *pomest'e*. He had not yet entered service and lived, "because of poverty, with his uncle, the clerk

Semen Sobakin."[82] One young Suzdalian described how he had wandered from house to house in desperate poverty and had fed himself by charity "in Christ's name," until a Moscow gentryman had trapped him in slavery by secretly writing up a binding slavery contract for him.[83]

Political geography thus contributed to shaping the social and economic environment in which the service gentry of the Vladimir-Suzdal' region built its homes and communities. Fairly fertile soil, scattered forests, and harsh but not unbearable weather conditions made the Vladimir-Suzdal' area a decent but not prime location for agricultural enterprises. Great secular and clerical magnates scrambled for properties in the warmer and more fertile south, and poor, lower-level servitors faced the dangers of military service and Tatar raids in the south and east, while the gentry of the Vladimir region had enough to support itself in shabby sufficiency most of the time.[84]

Corporate Identity as a Facet of Political Culture

In petitions and other interactions with the state, the *dvoriane* and *deti boiarskie* represented themselves in their various capacities as cavalrymen, servitors, or gentry landlords, but the question of how they viewed themselves collectively remains to be discussed. Muscovites' own representations of their social order suggest that horizontal solidarities, both of what would now be called estate (juridically defined status) and class (defined by economic status and relation to the means of production), were recognized as important forces, while significant vertical linkages simultaneously bound various strata together into pyramidal unions. Muscovites themselves saw their society as one ordered on hierarchical and categorical principles, and horizontal interests forged explicit, powerful solidarities.

More or less closed, hereditary estates were institutionalized by law and custom. Legal definitions and administrative practice contributed significantly to defining and hardening the differentiation among various strata. Tax status depended upon social status, as did other rights and privileges, with monastic authorities and elite military servitors enjoying a number of immunities. Only members of the service elite had the honor of taking their legal cases to the boyars' courts in Moscow as the court of first instance. Lesser people argued their cases in local courts. Such cases were transferred to Moscow only on appeal. Land ownership, control of peasant labor, trading rights, and alcohol production also pertained only to the service and merchant elite.

Not only in regulations from above but also in documents generated from below, all levels of society employed such estate terminology. Whether petitioning jointly or individually, gentrymen, boyars, townspeople, or peasants labeled themselves appropriately and used the formulaic address specific to their social conditions. In 1653, for instance, the townspeople of Shuia identified themselves by social category and rank when they addressed the tsar: "To Tsar, Sovereign, and Grand Prince Aleksei Mikhailovich of All Russia: your orphans, the little townspeople of Shuia and tax elder [*zemskii starosta*] Ivashko, son of Pavel Smolianin, and all of the little townspeople of Shuia petition you."[85] Members of the clergy called themselves "your pilgrims" in petitions to the tsar, and then specified their rank and monastic affiliation in some detail. Gentrymen called themselves "your slaves" (*kholopy tvoi*), and usually further detailed their rank and town affiliation, as for example, "We, your slaves, *dvoriane* and *deti boiarskie* of Lukh." Women of all social categories called themselves the sovereign's slaves, but they employed a different word (*raba*) from that used by the gentrymen and identified their social and marital standing as well: "I, your slave, Anis'ia, Ivan's daughter, widow of Iakov Sud'ev, townsman of Vladimir."

Among the gentry, as with the rest of the population, awareness of common class interest was promoted not only by official usage but also by the unofficial tensions and rivalries within an economically stratified society. Collective complaints by members of the gentry about abuses inflicted upon them by "the strong people" and by peasants reveal that the petty gentry felt its "otherness" from the social groups above and below it. The provincial gentry campaigned throughout the century to stop the depredations of "the strong people," ecclesiastical and boyar magnates, on its vulnerable labor supply and small estates.[86] In 1638 a group of provincial landlords charged that "strong people break into our estates and steal our bare necessities and beat our poor slaves to death and take our peasants away from us by force."[87] Other provincial servitors informed the tsar that people of high Moscow ranks were commiting violence, causing them losses, killing their people, and carrying off their slaves and peasants.[88] In 1623, a gentry landholder even went so far as to threaten vengeance against "the strong people": "Whoever takes peasants from us, we will burn their *votchina* estates."[89]

While complaining of pressure from above, the gentry simultaneously insisted upon its superiority to the peasantry and demanded
that the peasants be disciplined. The gentry's own marginal status is
evident in complaints formulated against the peasants: "[They] ran
away from many of us, having devastated our little homes, this winter and spring. . . . And now we, your slaves, in comparison with
previous years, suffer cruel destruction from our slaves and peasants."[90] The gentry perceived its vulnerability to those below and
wanted to make sure they stayed in their place. As evident in the
collective petition campaigns of the entire seventeenth century, the
gentry was acutely aware of the need to shore up its privileges and to
underscore its social differentiation from lower social groups.

Little consensus obtains among historians about the significance
of horizontal social stratification in Muscovy. Most Soviet and post-
Soviet scholars and some Westerners accept the existence of strong
horizontal estates or classes, which played active political roles in
defining themselves against each other and the state.[91] In this light,
Russian historians have developed the terms *gentry corporation* and
service city to describe what they see as semi-institutionalized provincial gentry associations, which derived their strength and significance in part from regional service lists and local mustering practices
but functioned as local bases of power and influence in negotiating
status and privilege with the centralizing state. According to this
model, gentry corporate estate organizations, along with other "estate representative institutions" such as Assemblies of the Land and
locally elected officials, reached their golden age in the late sixteenth
and early seventeenth centuries. Gentry corporations were protected
from outside incursions when, in response to their requests, decrees
by the tsar outlawed entrance to gentry status by men of lower ranks
and upheld local landholders' monopolistic right to land in their districts by formally excluding Moscow-rank servitors. Provincial selectmen voiced regional interests, or at least the interests of local
oligarchies, in Moscow and at Assemblies of the Land, and *okladchiki*, the local experts sworn to testify about the holdings and service capacity of each servitor in their districts, exerted a significant
degree of local discretionary authority in assigning town servitors
to ranks and compensation rates. Evidence of a collective identity
shared by the gentry servitors of a single town is found in group
petitions defending the honor of the town from various assaults, such
as the registration of unworthy members or the order of listing of

town militias. The Vladimir gentry, for instance, enjoyed the privilege of being listed "before all borderland and central towns, and at
musters it is ordered to review the Vladimirite *dvoriane* and *deti
boiarskie* before all other towns," while the gentry from the town of
Meshchera had to protest to gain the honor of serving at a level equal
to the gentry of other towns.[92]

According to this line of analysis, at the same time that local gentry organizations solidified their gains, the gentry as a whole began to
manifest a new, articulate corporate identity and to express its estate
interests vociferously, sometimes even belligerently. Emerging tri-
umphant and with enhanced self-consciousness after its leadership
role in the liberation of the Muscovite realm from foreign invaders
during the Time of Troubles, the gentry consolidated its position in
the first half of the seventeenth century by choosing and then closely
collaborating with the new tsar through its participation in the Assemblies of the Land held almost constantly in the first decades of
Romanov rule. The entire gentry estate voiced its interests in a wave
of collective petitions during the 1630s and 1640s. Taking advantage
of a wave of urban riots in 1648–50, the gentry reached its zenith in
the middle of the century, the argument continues, when it achieved
its long-desired aim of enserfing the peasantry.

Soon thereafter, according to this view, corporate unity faded, and
gentry status declined. Some argue that gentry interests melded entirely with the interests of the state after the regime bought serf
owners' loyalty and bound them to dependency on and acquiescence
to the coercive regime that guaranteed their control over their labor
force. Others attribute the decline of the gentry class to the disintegration of local "service corporations," which were undermined by
the loosening of restrictions on landownership, the influx of outsiders and Moscow-rank landlords into the provinces, and the lure of
the bright lights of Moscow. A third school of thought looks to military technology as the root of the gentry's collective decline: as old-
fashioned cavalries faded into obsolescence, the gentry inevitably
lost its corporate leverage. One way or another, then, those who see a
strong sense of corporate or class unity among the gentry perceive a
serious decline in the second half of the century.[93] While agreeing
with the general outline of this overview of the gentry's collective development, I stop short of endorsing the idea of gentry corporations.
This anachronistic terminology exaggerates the degree of formal corporate institutionalization present in the Muscovite provinces.

Many historians in the West have emphasized, on the contrary, the absence of identifiable estates and consequent absence of class mobilization or advocacy. Scholars as varied as Antonio Gramsci, Richard Pipes, and Hans-Joachim Torke state that precisely the lack of estate institutions and corporate bodies distinguished Muscovy's inert society from the more structured and hence more dynamic society of Western European countries. "In Russia the State was everything, civil society was primordial and gelatinous."[94] Such evaluations, however, overstate the case in the opposite direction. As discussed above, the juridical and social categories enforced by the Muscovite state as well as the self-defining language employed by various social groups demonstrate clearly that Muscovites perceived themselves as united into horizontal solidarities with others of their ilk, unified against the insolence and discontent of those below them and the arbitrary exactions, abuses, and unfair privileges of those above them. A melange of informal and noninstitutionalized class and estate, horizontal groupings played an important role in the politics and culture of Muscovy.

Not only horizontal but also vertical linkages crisscrossed the society in important ways, through local affiliations and through networks of patronage and clientage. As Daniel Rowland writes,

> The political divisions of the country were vertical as much as horizontal . . . these divisions consisted of groups each comprising some members of all politically active classes with an aristocratic family or two at the top rather than one class struggling against another. In sociological terms, this arrangement might be described as a web system of group relationships which cut across class lines and served to strengthen the social system by blurring class antagonisms.[95]

Rowland's balanced formulation captures the multiplicity of possible allegiances that shaped intergroup dynamics. Meaningful forms of assistance passed up and down, building another form of *Gemeinschaft* community along the vertical social axis. Neither vertical nor horizontal affiliations alone determined the collective identity of a Muscovite servitor. Rather, he operated in a grid of intersecting vertical and horizontal affinity lines. Collective identities did not remain constant but shifted according to the situation.

Social solidarities assumed particular forms and meanings in a society bonded together by a shared national myth of hierarchical harmony and by a common political culture that emphasized consensus over conflict. Muscovite notions of class were constructed out of cultural materials that stressed harmony within the social order far more than ascent of that order. The representations of class aims in the various gentry petitions show that material self-interest formed but one part of the vocabulary of the culture. Thus, during times of discontent, protesters articulated their anger at administrators and bureaucrats in moral as well as economic terms. The judges and chancellery personnel were "unjust" and should behave "righteously." Administrators stepped out of line when they built themselves "indescribable" stone palaces, "which did not happen under former sovereigns." When the tsar's kinsman, boyar Nikita Romanov, provoked gentry landholders in Elets by raiding their peasants and seizing their estates, the gentry asserted that "with such a great boyar it is impossible to live in neighborliness."[96] Protest against material exploitation had no meaning unless framed as protest against improper, impious, and disorderly behavior. The language of harmony and status quo in no way precluded expressions of self-serving agendas. It could accommodate extremely concrete, practical proposals of measures and solutions. It was more than a high-toned gloss on the "real" business of politics; instead it was an all-encompassing, flexible way of conceiving of interest-group maneuvers in terms created by and adapted to the cultural nexus of politics.[97]

With certain caveats and qualifications, the term *gentry* thus adequately describes the Muscovite *dvorianstvo*. Situated at the lowest edges of the hereditary elite, preoccupied with local concerns including landholding and agricultural labor, cognizant of its precarious status between the high nobility and the insubordinate masses, the *dvorianstvo* paralleled its Western counterparts in many ways. Service constituted a primary but not an exclusive dimension of the life of the *dvorianstvo*, and as the seventeenth century progressed, it played a diminishing part in constituting and defining *dvorianstvo* status. Acting at times in concert with local gentry communities and at times as a united gentry with clear common interests, the *dvorianstvo* constituted a particular class within Muscovite society. Class allegiance, however, remained contingent, attenuated by intersecting and competing vertical, familial, and religious bonds, and situated within a religiously rather than materially based understanding of society and human relations.

CHAPTER 2

Community and the Provincial Gentry

The Russian knows little of that deep attachment to one's patrimony which is as strong among the Germanic aristocracy as among the Germanic peasantry. With indifference he sees it pass into the hands of strangers. In Moscow a Mr. S., an intelligent man of excellent character, explained to me that he had sold an estate which bore his name and (what is highly uncommon in Russia) the estate had been in the family for two hundred years. In reply to my reproach, he said, "We do not have a western European attachment to our heritage!"
—August von Haxthausen[1]

Historiographic Background

As the emphatic tone of the Baron von Haxthausen in his 1843 description of the Russian provincial landowners illustrates, a discussion of gentry communities in Muscovy necessarily begins with a theoretical defence of the fundamental concepts involved. Most historians have denied or, more pointedly, not even considered the very existence among the Muscovite gentry of coherent and stable social bodies worthy of the name "community." Haxthausen's authoritative foreigner's assessment, like Tocqueville's of America, profoundly affected subsequent historical interpretations, both within Russia and abroad. Among his near contemporaries, Haxthausen's views found particularly forceful expression in the work of A. Romanovich-Slavatinskii, author of a much respected book about the Russian gentry from the time of Peter the Great until the emancipation of the serfs. "It has been noted by our researchers," Romanovich-Slavatinskii writes, "that until the time of Peter the Great, service people did not *have the significance of a local landowning class,* that they did not comprise *local gentry societies.* Service people were drawn to Moscow, and on their estates they were temporary guests. . . . Under such circumstances, local corporate ties among them were impossible, as were local gentry societies."[2]

Entrenched among pre-Revolutionary Russian scholars, this view continues to dominate among those held by Western historians, who commonly assert that Muscovite gentry cavalrymen lived peripatetic lives, riding from one military posting to the next and having only a minimal association of the concept of "home" with their fragmented and impermanent landholdings. The assumed feebleness of gentry regionalism has broad ramifications in explaining the perceived deficit of corporatism and independence characteristic of the Russian gentry.[3] Marc Raeff writes, "It was precisely this attachment to a specific locality, and the bonds of group and corporate loyalty it nourished, that had paved the way for the formation of estates in the West and given them a solid foundation for their privileged political role. Russia had either missed this development completely or experienced it in a very atrophied form."[4] In this analysis, the Russian elite failed to gain an independent power base in the provinces and therefore remained completely dependent on the tsar and on service to the tsar for financial and political security. From a putative lack of local roots these scholars infer a lack of political potency. In this historiographic context, gentry settlement patterns assume central importance for understanding the contours of Muscovite political life.

However, the Muscovite provincial gentry do not fit well in preestablished categories and must be characterized within a different framework. Like their Western counterparts, many gentrymen identified strongly with their native regions, but unlike Western nobilities, they did not associate their regionalism with a certain plot of land or ancestral manorial home. Instead they exhibited enduring affiliations to the area as a whole, to the province or cluster of provinces in which their families held land and from which they customarily entered the sovereign's service. They lived in relatively stable communities, with local kinship lines spanning the entire seventeenth century, many of them reaching back into the previous century and forward into the next.

Longevity of Family Lines within a Single Province

After enumerating six generations of Suzdalian ancestors, the Golenkin clan genealogy, submitted to the Ministry of Heraldry in 1686, concludes, "And our Golenkin clan is nowhere else other than Suzdal' and serves by no other town's lists."[5] The genealogy records that, by order of Tsar Ivan IV, Petr Fedorov Golenkin had received a grant of *pomest'e* land in Suzdal' in the year 1577/78, over a century prior

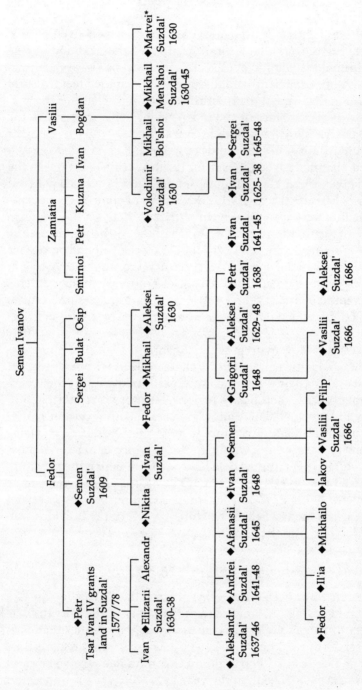

FIG. 2.1. Golenkin family genealogy. Individuals marked with a diamond (◆) have been documented in Suzdal'. Individuals marked with an asterisk (*) are not found in the archival genealogy. From *RGADA, f.* 210, *opis'* 18, *Rodoslovnye rospisi,* no. 54; *opis'* 10, *Vlad. stol, stlb.* 40, *l.* 123.

to the date of submission of the genealogical text. For evidence of their long Suzdalian affiliation and service, the Golenkins refer to the muster rolls compiled under Tsars Ivan IV, Fedor Ivanovich, and Mikhail Romanov. The genealogy emphasizes the Golenkins' long duration of settlement and localism, characteristic of many provincial families (see Golenkin genealogy, Figure 2.1).

The Golenkins' family history displayed a quite typical chronology. The mid– to late–sixteenth century, the latter half of Ivan IV's reign, was a formative period for central Muscovite provincial communities, a time of massive recruitment of new cavalry servitors by the state and of widespread resettlement of gentry landholders. Research into gentry genealogies points to the period between the mid–fifteenth and late–sixteenth centuries as a common moment of formation.[6] Profound dislocation of indigenous families occurred when the principality of Suzdal' was fully incorporated into Muscovy in 1451. At that time, many Suzdalian nobles moved to Moscow, and others shifted to different provincial locations. Having gained control of Suzdal', the Muscovite grand princes began distributing land as *pomest'e* estates in the second half of the fifteenth century. In a close study of the landholding families of Suzdal' province from the fifteenth century through the 1580s, N. K. Fomin uses census books and genealogical records to identify 200 landowning families active in Suzdal' during those years.[7] He establishes a group of families that were probably indigenous landowners, but he finds that most of the Suzdalian gentry families of the sixteenth century were not native families. Rather, the majority migrated to Suzdal' in clusters from Lithuania, Novgorod, Tver', and Moscow, beginning in the first half of the sixteenth century. A second major distribution of *pomest'e* estates occurred in the 1550s, when Ivan the Terrible granted estates both to newly arrived servitors from abroad and to Moscow servitors looking to the provinces for land to support themselves. Some new families moved into the region in conjunction with Ivan's creation of a special military unit of 1,000 cavalrymen registered in the famous *Thousand Book*.[8] Settlement was again disrupted in the 1560s and 1570s by Ivan the Terrible's peculiar *Oprichnina* policy, which divided the country in two parts, the *Oprichnina*, or Ivan's special lands and the people who lived on them, and the *Zemshchina*, or the rest of the tsardom. Members of the *Oprichnina* received full license to prey upon the *Zemshchina*. Of the gentry and noble families in Suzdal', 48 disappeared from local records during this period while 56 other families replaced them and settled in Suzdal' as members of the *Oprichnina* itself.

Following on the heels of the *Oprichnina*'s disruptions came several devastating famines, and then, if that was not enough, the "Evil Years," the Time of Troubles, with waves of foreign invasions and domestic unrest. Relatively high rates of continuity of settlement of Fomin's families through the rest of the sixteenth and into the seventeenth century testify to the tenacity of localism among the Muscovite gentry, as the period in question brought one form of devastation after another and was the most disrupted in Muscovite history. Some families appear to have left the region during the height of the troubles but returned to their ancestral home after the disruptions were over. Of Fomin's 200 sixteenth-century family names, 71 or 72 (36 percent) reappear or continue to appear in Suzdal' in the following century. Another 27 to 33 (approximately 15 percent) appear in the seventeenth century in one or more of the neighboring provinces, bringing the regional continuity to approximately 50 percent.[9] Taking a long-term perspective, 43 percent of the families that survived the *Oprichnina* era remained in the region for an entire century, with descendants still in the region in 1675.[10]

To put these various figures in perspective, M. L. Bush provides a wide range of family survival rates in his general study of European nobilities from medieval to modern times, concluding that an average of various nobilities at various times "furnishes a generally agreed extinction rate of around fifty per cent each century and a family life expectancy of no more than three generations."[11] Lawrence Stone in his study of the English peerage from 1558 to 1634 finds a persistence rate of 60 percent per century, with extinctions resulting primarily from "the natural erosion of families by the failure of the male line."[12] The Suzdal' gentry, then, while not as stable as the British peerage, fell only just short of the general European pattern of survival. Comparisons of this sort naturally raise problems of dissimilarity. For instance, Muscovite families extended beyond the nuclear family and so family names often survived due to the presence of extended clans. This would not have been as clear an option for the British aristocracy, with its strict rules of primogeniture, although it may have been the case for some of Bush's continental nobilities. In contrast, Stone's analysis, and any standard calculation of family longevity, takes into account the continued *existence* of the family line, not its continued residence in a given region, so the standard used here for persistence in the Suzdal' region is more stringent in that regard. The British peerage, traditionally considered a stable, ancient group, turns out to have been only slightly more stable than the Russian *dvorianstvo* with its reputation for inconstancy.

Continuity of settlement was not peculiar to the Vladimir-Suzdal' region. V. M. Vorob'ev and A. Ia. Degtiarev find substantial stability of settlement in the Novgorod region from the late sixteenth to the early eighteenth centuries. They have discovered a pattern, similar to that of the Vladimir-Suzdal' gentry, of dispersal during the *Oprichnina* of Ivan IV and during the Time of Troubles and return of former residents beginning after the Time of Troubles and continuing for the rest of the century. The turn-of-the-century dispersal was transitory, while the ancestral region exerted its attractive force on fugitives for the rest of the century. These findings for gentry landlords from Novgorod parallel Iu. V. Got'e's earlier discoveries about patterns of resettlement among peasants and townspeople, who also tended to return to their home provinces from the 1620s onwards. In his local study of the Pereiaslavl' Zalesskii province in the sixteenth century, Iu. G. Alekseev refines this pattern of settlement and resettlement with the information that many families forced out of their homes during the *Oprichnina* settled in neighboring provinces, as close to their native regions as possible.[13] The Vladimir-Suzdal' gentrymen who were scattered by the turn-of-the-century upheavals similarly gravitated back home.[14]

Since biological extinction of individual families was unavoidable, induction into elite ranks had to occur in order to maintain the numbers of the group. New families constantly moved to the area. The *Oprichnina* brought significant numbers of newly created service landholders to the region. In the late sixteenth century, with the growth of the army and the expansion of the tsardom, the state conferred gentry status on large numbers of lower-ranking men. Again, after the Time of Troubles, an influx of new gentry families moved into the Vladimir-Suzdal' area, some transferring from other regions, others newly promoted to gentry status. During the rest of the seventeenth century, massive-scale induction to gentry ranks slackened in the central provinces, but new men still managed to climb into the landholding elite. In 1635/36, 35 town clerks in Vladimir simultaneously received promotions into the ranks of lesser gentry, *gorodovye deti boiarskie*. Some of them may have come from families of gentry origins who had sunk into the mass of townspeople and lesser clerks after the *Oprichnina*, but others may have had no prior claim at all to gentry status. How successfully these newcomers established themselves as members of the gentry elite remains subject to doubt. Few of them managed to found a lasting gentry line; 20 of their names never reappeared among the Vladimir gentry after their initial elevation.[15] Promotions from below into the gentry appear to have effected little change in the generally stable composition of the local community. More influential in their presence were the increasing numbers of Moscow-rank gentry who made their homes and centered their lives in the provinces after moving there from the capital during the 1670s and 1680s. Established local families easily accommodated this highly esteemed group of newcomers and welcomed them into their communities as neighbors and marriage partners. All of this admixing from above and below notwithstanding, significant continuity of settlement characterized the seventeenth century.

The period of stabilization following the Time of Troubles constituted one formative movement for the provincial gentry, during which much new settlement and distribution of land occurred. Therefore it is interesting to trace continuity of families from that period of stabilization toward the beginning of the seventeenth century until the end of the seventeenth century. To conduct such an analysis I turned to the 4,100 individuals who constitute my index of the gentry population of the Vladimir-Suzdal' region in the seventeenth century. The first step in this analysis was to establish what constituted a family. Using surname as an identifier, I grouped the 4,100 individuals into 977 families. However, surnames do not provide an entirely reliable indicator of kinship, and in conducting any test of family duration and provincial affiliation, a potential difficulty arises in determining whether two people bearing the same last name were actually related. Genealogical records help to solve some of the puzzles. Analysis of 41 published and archival genealogies, along with another 40 partial genealogies constructed from bits of information culled from a wide variety of documents, establishes that most of the individuals with a common surname in the Vladimir-Suzdal' region were related by blood, but inevitably a group of individuals remains uncharted.[16] Of course, the sample families for which I am able to construct genealogies cannot be considered random: the fact that genealogical records of one sort or another survive a priori tips the scales toward evidence of kinship within surnames. Thus, the suspicion remains that the bulk of surnames may have been shared by several unrelated families.

The justification for assuming kinship on the basis of last name is reinforced, however, by the discovery that as a rule gentry "families" in the Vladimir-Suzdal' region tended to congregate within a single province. Defining affiliation with a province is not an entirely clear-cut issue either. Documents frequently identify people by their service affiliation, as "*suzdalets*" or "*suzdal'skii syn boiarskii,*" in which case affiliation is straightforward. Moscow-rank people were sometimes officially categorized by their provincial affiliations, particularly in their capacity as landholders. In 1649, for instance, the governor of Vladimir was ordered to assemble Moscow-rank servitors for military duty. He was to summon all "*stol'niki* and *striapchie* and Moscow gentry and *zhil'tsy*, [who are] Vladimir *pomeshchiki* and *votchinniki.*"[17] Not all documents utilized these convenient labels, however. When documents do not directly state a service or landholding affiliation, I have used evidence of landholding within a province, residence, or extensive court or administrative transactions in the provincial governor's office to determine links with the various provinces. Using this standard to establish the affiliations of a surname group, I find that most of the important families clustered all members of a surname group in a single province. This holds true not only of small surname groupings, such as Gavrilo Zhadovskii and his two sons, who lived in Suzdal' between 1647 and 1678.[18] The name compact residential pattern characterizes some of the largest families. For instance, without exception all 27 Kablukovs, 27 Oshanins, 26 Tregubovs and 20 Kozynskiis lived and served in Suzdal'. All eleven members of the Kipreianov family served from and held land in Iur'ev Pol'skii. This residential clustering is particularly helpful in sorting out kinship relations among people with extremely common last names. Karpov, for example, is a very widespread last name. However, when all 22 of the Karpovs in the region maintained Suzdal' service affiliations, and none had any affiliation with the other provinces, the evidence suggests (but cannot prove) kinship rather than coincidence.[19] On the basis of such corroborating evidence of genealogical linkages and provincial correspondence, I have assumed a person's surname as a rough indication of kinship among the Vladimir-Suzdal' gentry in tracing surnames through the seventeenth century.

Based on this assumption, an analysis of family duration in the seventeenth century shows two distinct patterns. First, of the 977 surnames that occur, 501 (or 51 percent) disappear after one mention or within one year, therefore indicating no measurable continuity

TABLE 2.1

Documented Length of Family Duration in the Vladimir-Suzdal' Region, 1600–1700

Duration in years	No. of surnames	Pct. of surnames	Duration in years	No. of surnames	Pct. of surnames
1–15	70	15.6%	61–75	56	12.5
16–30	64	14.2	76+	88	19.6
31–45	69	15.4	TOTAL	449	100.0%
46–60	102	22.7			

SOURCE: Author's compilation, based on archival and published documents.

NOTE: This table excludes those surnames represented by a single member and those with less than a year's duration in the region.

of stay in the region. Second, a large though less pronounced cluster of surnames register quite a long duration (46–60 years) in the Vladimir-Suzdal' area. The distribution of surnames that occur in more than one year is shown in Table 2.1.

These two patterns are not random. The low-duration peak is attributable in large part to a number of families and individuals who had only casual connections with the Vladimir-Suzdal' region, perhaps owning a single plot of land there. This group includes slightly more of the lowest ranking *gorodovye deti boiarskie* than the general gentry population as well as slightly more of the lofty Moscow ranks. These people's rapid disappearance may be explained by a fall into the lower service ranks, clerkdom, slavery, or banditry for the former and a disengagement from the region in the interests of advancement in the capital or affiliation with other provinces in the case of the latter. The second peak, in the 46–60 year range, reflects the period covered most extensively by surviving sources and suggests that actual duration of stay may well have been significantly longer.

When the large group of surnames that appear only once in all of the collected documents, or that have only a single representative in the region during entire century, is excluded from the calculations, the longevity of the remaining group becomes more apparent (see Table 2.1). The average length of stay for this group of families was 67 years, an impressive average in light of the limitations of source materials available for the beginning and end of the century.

The bimodal distribution of family durations, with peaks at both short and long durations, suggests that different families pursued different strategies or diverged in their attitude toward the Vladimir-Suzdal' provinces. Genealogical trees confirm the differences in practice. Certain families, particularly those with established roots in the area, centered their family existence within the confines of one or several of the Vladimir-Suzdal' provinces. These families congregated, reproduced, and stayed in their traditional homelands (see Kashintsov genealogy, Figure 2.2).

A number of local families grew into rather large clans, all or most of whose members remained in the home territory. The Obukhov family of Iur'ev Pol'skii provides a clear example of this pattern. Six generations of Obukhovs served from Iur'ev, from 1577 or earlier until 1698. Even after some members of the fourth generation achieved Moscow rank in the 1660s, they and their descendants continued to hold their estates in Iur'ev and to begin their service from the local Iur'ev muster rolls.[20] With their extended clan and tradition of service and residence in Iur'ev, the Obukhovs typify the rooted, local clans of the area (see Obukhov genealogy, Figure 2.3).

A second large, highly localized clan, the Kozlovs, illustrates an additional aspect of Muscovite gentry clan settlement patterns. Strongly rooted and established in Suzdal', they outdid the Obukhovs by one tier, with seven generations documented in Suzdal' by the end of the seventeenth century. A senior branch split off from the Suzdalian kin and began a separate line in Kazan' (see Kozlov genealogy, Figure 2.4). These individuals never again entered the documentary record of Suzdal' and had no further documented dealings at all with their Suzdalian relatives. Although family members certainly knew the relationships within the broader clan well enough to submit a complete, inclusive genealogy to the Heraldic Chancellery in 1686, the far more relevant kinship group apparently was the one operative within the provincial borders. Excluding the Kazan' branch, at least 47 of the 67 Kozlovs listed in Rummel' and Golubtsov's genealogy had clear Suzdal' service and land affiliations. Of those not clearly linked to Suzdalian service, some were still children and so had not established service records when the genealogies were drawn up in the 1680s, and others died young. The Kozlov genealogical table illustrates visually how the small senior rivulet flowed off to Kazan', while the main river of Kozlovs stayed in Suzdal'.[21] The Lazarevs, another ancient local family, claimed a tradition in Iur'ev dating back to the fourteenth century and land in Suzdal' documented since 1547. With a direct line continuing in Suzdal' from 1547 until 1687, the Lazarevs, too, lost a bit of their local strength to a stream heading off toward other provinces. (See Lazarev genealogy, Figure 2.5.)

Naturally, the Vladimir-Suzdal' region not only lost servitors as

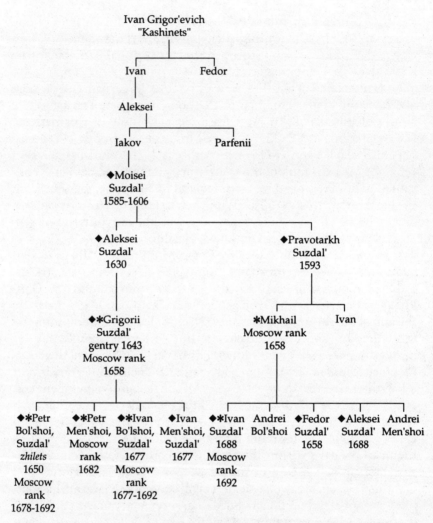

FIG. 2.2. Kashintsov family genealogy. Individuals marked with a diamond (♦) have been documented in Suzdal'. Individuals marked with an asterisk (*) are of Moscow rank. From Dolgorukov, *Rossiiskaia rodoslovnaia kniga*, pt. 4, pp. 115–17.

lines branched off to other regions, it also gained similar small trickles or streams from other families and clans in other regions. The Chelishchev and Voeikov families exemplify this phenomenon. A single family group from each of these settled in the region, while the main clan maintained its base elsewhere.[22]

The demographic tendency of extended clans to stay rooted in a traditional region while certain nuclear family groups split off and established themselves in new areas also helps to explain the bimodal duration pattern demonstrated by the Vladimir-Suzdal' gentry. Families with extensive representation in a given province had both a better biological chance of survival and a stronger bond to the area, while those with just one or two individuals divided off from their clans had less chance of surviving in the province on both scores.

Family names persisted within a single province not only through the seventeenth century but also through the eighteenth and nineteenth and into the twentieth century. Evidence of continual provincial affiliation is found in an index to the Vladimir gentry, published for antiquarian interest in 1905 by the Vladimir *guberniia*. A full 40 percent (105 out of 263) of the surnames of Vladimir gentry clans of the seventeenth century correspond with the surnames listed in the 1905 list.[23] Over and above the 40 percent of seventeenth-century Vladimir clans that survived in the province in the eighteenth and nineteenth centuries, many of the families prominent in neighboring Suzdal', Iur'ev, and Lukh in the seventeenth century had transferred to Vladimir *guberniia* by the time of the survey and were registered as nobles there. The Kablukovs, Kashintsovs, Koisarovs, Tregubovs, Bludovs, Alalykins, Stromilovs, and Sekerins all had descendants who had relocated to and were recorded in Vladimir in subsequent centuries. By the mid–nineteenth century, when "nests of gentlefolk" on their provincial estates become well known to us through the prism of fiction, the depth of local roots within an ancestral region is no longer subject to question.

Case Studies: Two Suzdalian Clans

Histories of particular families not only provide stories to personify statistics but also give meaning to them. Regional affiliations and loyalties had particular connotations in the Muscovite provincial settings, which a few family portraits help to clarify.

The most imaginative family legend from the region appears in the

(continued on p. 76)

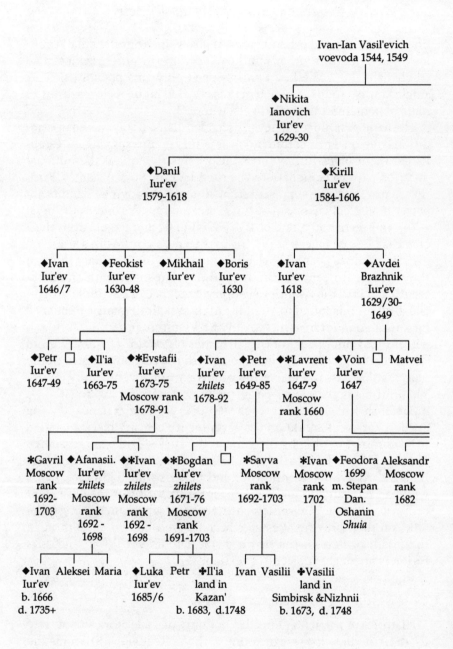

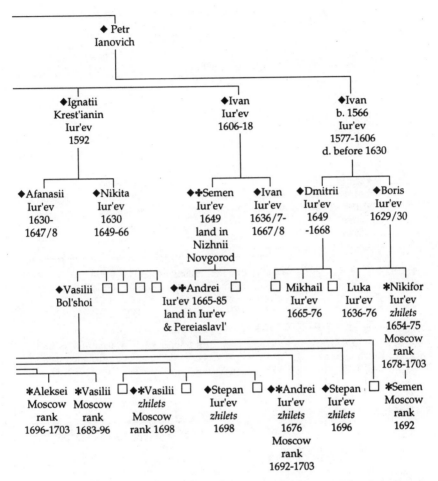

FIG. 2.3. Obukhov family genealogy. Individuals marked with a diamond (♦) have been documented in Iur'ev Pol'skii. Individuals marked with an asterisk (*) are of Moscow rank. Individuals marked with a club (♣) have been documented in other provinces. Individuals marked with a box (□) have no documented regional affiliation. From Rummel' and Golubtsov, *Rodoslovnyi sbornik*, 2: 194–205.

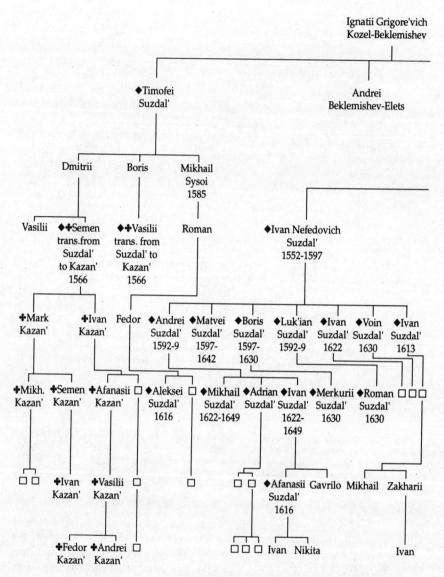

F I G . 2 . 4 . Kozlov family genealogy. Individuals marked with a diamond (♦) have been documented in Suzdal'. Individuals marked with a club (♣) have been documented in other provinces. Individuals marked with a box (□) have no documented regional affiliation. From Rummel' and Golubtsov, *Rodoslovnyi sbornik*, 1: 393–98.

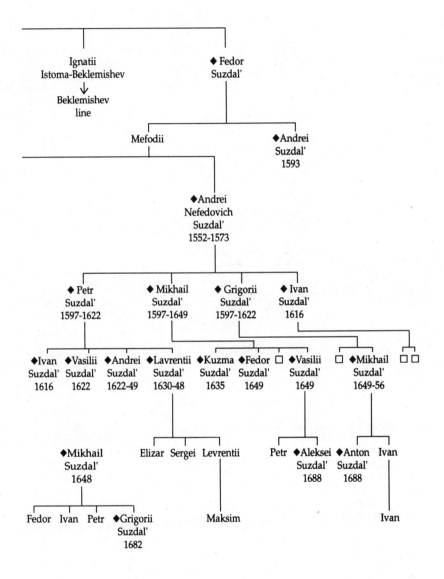

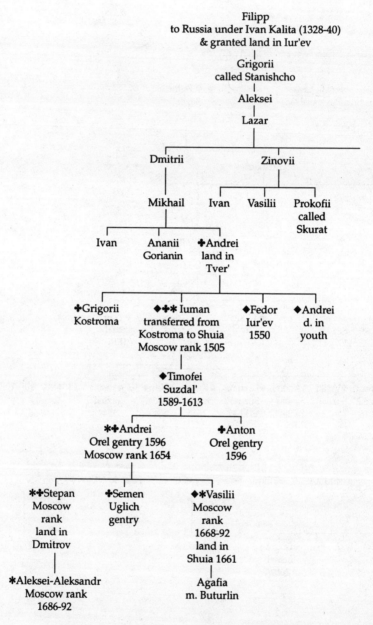

FIG. 2.5. Lazarev family genealogy. Individuals marked with a diamond (♦) have been documented in Suzdal' or Iur'ev. Individuals marked with an asterisk (*) are of Moscow rank. Individuals marked with a club (♣) have been

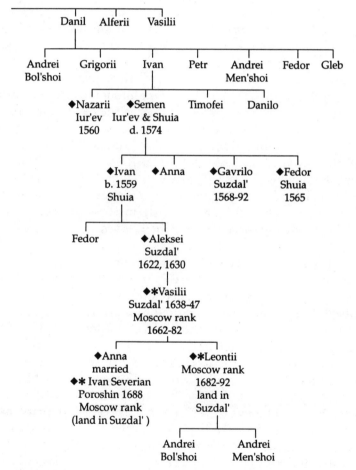

Danil   Alferii   Vasilii

Andrei   Grigorii   Ivan   Petr   Andrei   Fedor   Gleb
Bol'shoi   Men'shoi

◆Nazarii   ◆Semen   Timofei   Danilo
Iur'ev   Iur'ev & Shuia
1560   d. 1574

◆Ivan   ◆Anna   ◆Gavrilo   ◆Fedor
b. 1559   Suzdal'   Shuia
Shuia   1568-92   1565

Fedor   ◆Aleksei
           Suzdal'
           1622, 1630

◆✳Vasilii
Suzdal' 1638-47
Moscow rank
1662-82

◆Anna   ◆✳Leontii
married   Moscow rank
◆✳ Ivan Severian 1682-92
Poroshin 1688   land in
Moscow rank   Suzdal'
(land in Suzdal')

Andrei   Andrei
Bol'shoi   Men'shoi

documented in other provinces. From Rummel' and Golubtsov, *Rodoslovnyi sbornik*, 1: 503–19.

historical genealogy of the Bludov family, a text submitted to the
authorities in the 1680s when the Chancellery of Heraldry embarked
on a massive project to register the lineages of all major service families.[24] In their foundation legend, the Bludovs traced their origin
back to an eponymous progenitor, Bluda, who, according to the Primary Chronicle, served as a general in Kiev under Iaropolk Sviato-
slavich in 973. Leaping across centuries from this single Kievan reference, the account claims that members of the Bludov clan were
granted holdings in Suzdal' among other places in the time of Ivan
Kalita (1328–41) and served from there. Fomin unmasks this tale
as a fraud. The Bludovs, he found, arrived in the area along with a
large group of immigrants from Lithuania in the first half of the
sixteenth century.[25] After the fictitious introductory tale, the genealogy moves to firmer soil in tracing Bludov clansmen through
the sixteenth and seventeenth centuries as they served in Kozel'sk,
Kashira, Vorotynsk. With a cold deliberateness, the seventeenth-
century Bludovs omitted their Suzdalian kinsmen from the record:
"And our relatives who descended from Aleksei and from Fedor, sons
of Boris Bludov, were granted *pomest'e* lands in Meshcherskii and
Kozel'sk and Suzdal' provinces and their names are not recorded on
this list because they are not currently in Moscow. And they will
bring a listing of their generation themselves."[26] This list, if ever
compiled, is not extant.

The Suzdal' branch of the Bludovs experienced a singular fate in the
seventeenth century and was scarcely in a position to submit its genealogy in the 1680s and 1690s. Their criminal propensities and com-
promised social standing explain their Moscow relatives' reluctance
to include them in the family chronicle. Of the fourteen Bludov men
mentioned in the Suzdalian muster rolls of the seventeenth century,
only one served above the lowly category of *gorodovoi* or regular
town servitor. The one Bludov who made good, Roman Minin, entered service at the rank of *zhilets*, serving from the Suzdalian list, in
1685. Four of the Bludovs were locked up in prison in the early part of
the century, three for banditry and one for "tongue wagging" or
slander.[27] Several others failed to appear at military musters and were
recorded as no-shows (*netchiki*). Two of them were absent because
they had run off and become bandits. Another two had been ruined by
their bandit brothers' raids. Yet another sold himself into slavery.
Continuing the family tradition in the later part of the century, two
Bludov brothers set upon a neighboring landlord in Shuia province
and, according to the neighbor's deposition, tried to kill him.[28]

The Suzdalian Bludovs' connection to the genealogy submitted by the more upright branches of the Bludov line has particular interest because families of lowly status rarely left such complete accounts. Through their distant connection with the more respectable branches of their clan, the hooligan Bludovs testify to the fact that families of even their caliber could boast ancient roots and continuous lines in the Vladimir-Suzdal' area. The sons of Boris Bludov from whom the local line descended lived seven generations before those Bludovs who submitted the genealogy, indicating that the Suzdalian Bludovs could claim to trace their ancestry back at least that far.

The Kablukov family of Suzdal' and Shuia trod a far more successful path than the lawless Bludovs. They merit more than a passing mention, because throughout the seventeenth century they dominated the Suzdal' and Shuia regions economically and politically, and their history, richly documented in surviving collections in St. Petersburg, lends coherence and personality to this entire study.[29] The genealogy that they submitted in 1686 traced their ancestry back to the principality of Uglich in the time of Dmitrii Donskoi (1359–89), but their concrete documentation began in 1460, when Grand Prince Vasilii II granted Aleksei Semenovich Krasnolep, a distant ancestor, a *votchina* in Deminskii township of the Shuia Province, the core of the Kablukov estate for centuries to come.[30] In 1576 two cousins, Afanasii Fedorovich and Vasilii Semenovich, held tax-exempt land in Shuia. Vasilii's son Fedor inherited land not only from his father but also from his aunt, Fedos'ia. In 1614 Fedor married the daughter of another Suzdal' landlord, Osip Kuz'mich Tepritskii, and they had a son, Aleksei, who in turn would cut an important figure in Suzdal' for much of the seventeenth century.[31] The irascible and litigious Aleksei Fedorovich Kablukov consolidated and developed the family's local power (see the Kablukov genealogy, Figure 2.6). Aleksei Fedorovich wrangled all his life to build his estate in Shuia Province. From his first appearance in the sources in 1631/32, his constant preoccupation remained the enlargement of his landholdings. In 1642 he initiated a suit against his uncle Obrazets Afanas'evich over control of lands, finally settling out of court in 1645. A few years later he again troubled the courts about registering lands which were granted to him in 1645/46 but which were never officially recorded as his. The new additions brought his total holdings up to 240 *cheti*, over half his allotment of 400 *cheti*. Never missing an opportunity, he plunged into court again in 1656/57 to claim the estate of his late cousin Afanasii Il'ich, who had died that year without direct heirs.[32]

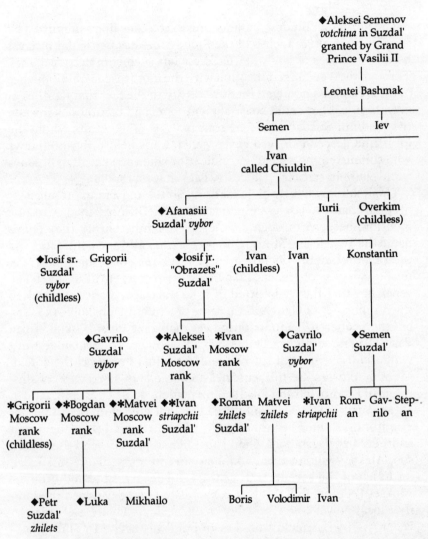

FIG. 2.6. Kablukov family genealogy. Individuals marked with a diamond (♦) have been documented in Suzdal'. Individuals marked with an asterisk (*) are of Moscow rank. From *RGADA, f. 210, opis' 18, Rodoslovnye rospisi*, no. 53; Ikonnikov, *Noblesse de la Russe*, vol. Y, pp. 235–37.

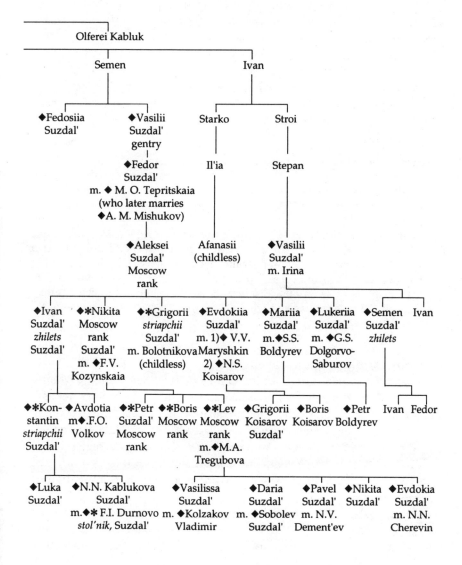

Aleksei Fedorovich did not limit his sights to his kinsmen's properties. He feuded constantly with members of the Tepritskii family, his
mother's relatives, as well as with a large number of unrelated neighboring landlords.[33]

When Aleksei's stepfather, Abram Makar'evich Mishukov, died
in 1657, Aleksei and his mother struggled for years in court to deprive Fedor, Mishukov's son by his first marriage (Aleksei's step-
brother) of his paternal inheritance and to secure it for the Kablukov
line instead.[34] The mother, Maria, launched the campaign alone,
couching her requests in pathetic phrases. She opened her petition
with the formulaic salutation appropriate to her status: "Your slave
Maritsa, widow of Avram Makar'evich Mishukov petitions." She
continued:

> In this year 7165 (1657), my husband died leaving behind me and his son
> Fedor, my stepson, and *pomest'e* lands in Shuia and Suzdal' Provinces
> totalling 398 *cheti* and 37 peasant households, and 30 1/8 *cheti* of un-
> tenanted demesne land. And I petitioned for all of this as my dower's
> portion, but by your decree, Great Sovereign, from my husband's allot-
> ment I received only 50 *cheti*, while my stepson received 343 *cheti* and
> with those *cheti* more than 30 peasant households. . . . Please order that
> half of my estate be given to poor me, because I have so little land and so
> few peasants and from these few *cheti* I cannot feed myself, and so that,
> wandering sadly from house to house, I will not die of hunger. And my
> stepson, Sovereign, has enough to serve your service even without my
> little share.[35]

According to 1649 Law Code, the widow of a service man who died
at home, while not actively engaged in the tsar's service, legally received only 10 percent of her husband's *pomest'e* holdings.[36] Mishukov's widow, nonetheless, pleaded successfully for half of her late
husband's estate. Once the widow Maria won her case, the true recip-
ient of the lands stepped forward to claim his gains: Aleksei Fedorovich petitioned to have his mother's dower's portion reregistered in
his name. Within three years of the legal victory, Aleksei committed
his twice-widowed mother to a convent as a nun, under the religious
name Marfa.[37]

Kablukov's land acquisition program made him a rich man. His
accumulated wealth helped him rise in the official hierarchy as well.
As a young man, probably still under twenty, he was promoted to
dvorovoi rank. Ten years later he was selected as a "selectman." In
1662 he served briefly as town governor of nearby Lukh. By the end of
his life he had achieved the rank of Moscow gentryman. On Octo-

ber 21, 1658, Aleksei's *votchina* in Davydova in Suzdal' Province burned, destroying his house and a cottar's cottage along with all the standing grain and livestock.[38] An official inquiry confirmed his report on the disaster, so he probably gained some kind of exemption in taxes or service dues for a period. The devastation did not jeopardize his economic status: at the time of his death in 1688, he left an estate large enough to encourage his son Nikita and his grandson Konstantin Ivanovich to feud over it.[39]

Capitalizing on his wealth and title, Aleksei bolstered his family's position through strategic marriages. Twice he married his daughter Evdokia advantageously, first to Vasilii Vasil'evich Naryshkin, a prosperous *dvorovoi syn boiarskii* from a large Vladimir clan, and in 1659/60, after Naryshkin's death, to Nikita Semenovich Koisarov, a member of the second leading family of Suzdal'. Soon after his promotion to Moscow rank, he orchestrated a union between his daughter Maria and Semen Stepanovich Boldyrev, who also held Moscow rank. According to the marriage agreement, because Aleksei Fedorovich "himself doesn't know how to write," his son signed the marriage contract in his place. The family patriarch may or may not actually have been illiterate: ten years earlier Aleksei Fedorovich himself signed a land division agreement in place of his son Grigorii.[40] In a further move to solidify local dynastic ties, this same son Grigorii married the widow of a Bolotnikov, another important Suzdalian clan with local roots reaching back to the *Oprichnina*. A daughter or granddaughter married Danilo Fedorovich Mishukov, grandson of Aleksei's stepfather, in 1677, presumably tying up some of the loose ends left over from the disputed inheritance of 20 years earlier.[41]

Throughout his life, Aleksei donated money periodically to the Shuia Trinity-Savior Monastery "to pray for the souls of his relatives. And when it comes time for him to be tonsured as a monk, he will come to us to be shorn, and the brothers will feed and care for him, and when he dies according to God's will, for endless eternity we, the Archmandrite and the brethren, will keep his name recorded honorably in the litany and in the synodicon on the wall and will remember him."[42] In the 1680s he also patronized local religious establishments, giving a series of monetary gifts for the construction of the Church of the Virgin of Kazan' in Shuia.[43] In a plaintive petition written shortly before his death, the old man begged the Metropolitan of Suzdal' and Torusa to allow him to take monastic vows at his local parish church of Saints Ioakim and Anna because he was too ill and feeble to travel to a monastery. Despite his history of generous support to that church, as well as to the monastery, the dying man's request was denied. Presumably he died untonsured, in his own home.[44]

In Aleksei Fedorovich's old age and after his death, his son Nikita assumed the role of clan patriarch and local magnate. Starting with an advantaged position due to his father's success, Nikita's career began easily, but did not progress particularly quickly or far. With the prerogatives deriving from his father's position, he entered service as a novice at the transitional *zhiletskii* level, probably in the early 1660s. Despite his prominence in Suzdal' and Shuia, he remained at that level for several decades. In 1682 he begged for a temporary release from service because of severe wounds inflicted upon him by unknown people while traveling on the road to Shuia. By 1691/92 he had at last been promoted, for his name appears in a *boiarskaia kniga*, or list of upper-level servitors, among the Moscow gentry.[45] Official records from Suzdal' and Shuia are liberally peppered with his name. He participated in disputes of all kinds. He foreclosed on loans to poor relatives, took possession of mortgaged estates, trampled his neighbors' fields, and sued for dishonor compensation.[46] For three years after his father's death Nikita fought the terms of Aleksei Fedorovich's will, attempting to deprive his brother's sons of their rightful inheritance. Konstantin Ivanovich Kablukov complained in court that his uncle Nikita would not abide by the will or by previous court rulings. Nikita had failed to sign over title to Konstantin's share within half a year of the old man's death, as stipulated by the will. "And he, Nikita, gave out those uninhabited fields for rent and allowed his various people and peasants to chop down the woods and rented them out to other people and collected fees from Konstantin's uninhabited fields and woodlands. And he, Nikita, sent his son Petr to Biakova [one of the disputed villages] and took from Konstantin's peasants their seed grain." The two generations finally made peace in 1689/90, when Nikita signed the third or fourth arbitration agreement with his nephew, apparently the first signed in good faith.[47]

Nikita continued his father's policy of strategic marriage alliances, constructing links with local magnates. He chose as his bride Fekla Vasil'evna Kozynskaia, a daughter of the wealthy Kozynskii clan, with whom his family had been feuding for years, and received a generous dowry from her father.[48] For his son Lev, he arranged an advantageous marriage with a daughter of Moscow-rank *striapchii* Andrei Ivanov Tregubov, from another large and highly placed Suzdal' family.[49] He matched his sister Lukeria with a Moscow-rank member of the Suzdalian Dolgovo-Saburov family.[50] In a most intriguing incident of abduction and "forcible matchmaking," he coerced his sister-in-law, Natal'ia Kozynskaia, to marry a local man, perhaps a protege, Sergei Sadykov. Natal'ia's brothers contested the marriage, but too late; she was already wed.[51]

Aleksei and Nikita built their careers within their provincial social milieu. Only at the ends of their lives did their local status receive commensurate recognition at the Moscow level. Yet, without Moscow rank and without significant marital or kinship ties outside of the Suzdal'-Shuia vicinity, they assumed the position of powerful magnates and local bosses. Echoed in their real estate preferences and in their marital choices, the Kablukovs' focus on their local provincial region, rather than on distant lands or Moscow, exemplifies the focus of provincial gentry life.

Nikita was the most dynamic but not the sole heir to Aleksei Fedorovich. Marfa Kablukova, a nun at the Shuia Savior Convent, lived up to the Kablukov tradition by carrying the family's characteristic aggressive traits into the convent. In 1689, the widowed Princess Tatiana Gundorova filed a series of complaints with the Metropolitan of Suzdal' and Iur'ev claiming that the nun Marfa had appropriated the "wretched" cell that she had purchased for herself in good faith the year before. Marfa countersued, calling Princess Tatiana's allegations false. After investigation, the Metropolitan ordered Marfa evicted from the cell. At that point, according to the princess's glum account, Marfa successfully bribed the local priest to reverse the judgment and find in her favor. "But," wrote the princess, "I bought it and paid money for it. Do not let them take it away from me without cause."[52] The resolution of the case remains unknown, but the typical Kablukov machinations were clearly at work, and successfully so, within the world of religious women as in the secular world of the men outside the convent walls.

On the male side, Nikita's brothers, Grigorii and Ivan, lived lives that closely paralleled Nikita's, but they took less active roles in local events. Very likely both brothers predeceased their father.[53] Ivan's son, Konstantin, however, emerged as the energetic rival to Nikita in family affairs who battled against his uncle in court for many years over his grandfather's estate. In Konstantin's generation, he and his brother Roman and their cousins, Petr, Lev, and Boris Nikitich, Matvei and Bogdan Gavrilovich, and Semen Grigor'evich all enjoyed the fruits of their predecessors' ambitions: they all were privileged with wealth and high title. Several if not all of them entered service from more prestigious *zhiletskii* lists rather than town rolls (Matvei Gavrilovich and Roman Ivanovich by 1675/6, Boris Nikitich by 1694/5), and ascended into the upper service ranks in Moscow.[54] The younger generation's rise into the higher Moscow ranks set them apart from their parents, whose influence and status remained essentially local. Their sisters continued to marry advantageously both within the community and upward into Moscow circles. Only with this fourth generation of the century, on the eve of the 1700s, did the Kablukovs establish significant ties with the Moscow elite, but still their new connections did not cause them to renounce their Suzdalian localism. Kablukovs continued to take an active part in Suzdalian affairs in the late seventeenth and early eighteenth century, holding land in the province and continuing their tradition of marrying into leading local families.[55]

Surviving sources document in fine detail the careers and financial strategems of this domineering and ambitious family. Very little survives of their emotional make-up or their more human characteristics. Marriage emerges from the sources as tactical maneuvering, religious donation as an insurance policy for old age, and family as a means toward advancement or as an obstacle to undivided inheritance. Only in their complaints about poverty and illness can we see these people as anything but cunning, crude, and climbing, and even then they expressed themselves in calculated formulae. This is the limited picture that emerges for the best documented family in the district; it is not surprising that virtually nothing can be derived about the emotional lives of the mass of provincial servitors.

Fragmentation of Landholding

The fragmentation of gentry landholding has traditionally provided the strongest argument against the existence of settled gentry communities, and hence against the possibility of local bases of power. The general view in historical literature maintains that in pre-Petrine Russia "The aristocracy was devoid of local power and bereft of consolidated landholdings because of an inheritance system which subdivided patrimonial estates, . . . and a tsarist policy dating from the late fifteenth century which compensated nobles for their service by grants of conditionally held estates in widely scattered areas."[56]

Most research on landholding has concentrated on the richest and most influential elites, Muscovite boyars and other members of the sovereign's court, who actually did hold lands in dispersed plots throughout the vast Russian empire, as studies of several individual boyars of the seventeenth century and broader studies of elite land-holding confirm.[57] Generalizing from the real estate portfolios of the rich and famous to the rank and file, however, has led to signifi-cant misunderstanding of gentry landholding. While it is true that provincial service gentry did not possess consolidated estates in the Western European sense, neither did they own bits of land separated by hundreds of miles as the great boyars did. Instead, throughout their lifetimes they generally gathered up pieces of land in their im-mediate vicinity, within their native province or in the surrounding provinces.

The process by which gentrymen acquired land reinforced the ten-dency to obtain parcels in close proximity to previous holdings. At ir-regularly conducted military reviews, government officials assigned each servitor a rank and an allotment of land to which, in principle, he was entitled. This theoretical allotment was called an *oklad*. Ini-tiative in locating available real estate subsequently rested upon the individual servitor. He could submit a request to have a given piece of land registered in his name and counted toward his allotment if he could find an area that was not already claimed by another ser-viceman, a monastery, or the crown. The land a man actually pos-sessed was called his *dacha*, or grant, and was marked off against his entitlement on the books of the Chancellery of Service Lands.[58] *Stol'nik* N. I. Akinfov, for example, applied to the Chancellery of Service Lands in 1673 requesting various unpopulated plots scattered throughout the Bogoliubskii district of Vladimir Province. He ex-plained that he already owned 255 *cheti* in Vladimir and lacked 575 of his entitlement of 830 *cheti*. In this case, other landlords contested some of the plots, insisting that they already owned the land.[59] In a more straightforward case, Aleksei Nagoi petitioned for registration of 113 new *cheti* in *pomest'e* to add to his prior 300 *cheti*, toward his 800 *cheti* entitlement.[60]

The likelihood of learning about available acreage in familiar haunts far exceeded the chances of hearing about land in distant regions. For this reason alone, most petty provincial servitors owned land within a narrowly prescribed area. Word of mouth could serve the same function as local knowledge, so occasionally documents state that trades of land took place between men of different provinces while they were in service together.[61] Far more commonly, however, trades, purchases, and claims on unclaimed land took place within the servitor's home province. Edicts on landholding further enforced localization of property. In the first half of the century, a number of decrees specified that provincial servitors should hold land only within their primary province and banned Moscow-rank people from acquiring properties in the provinces.[62] Throughout the course of the century these limitations were relaxed, but they complemented existing trends toward locally focused landholdings.

Establishing figures on landholding within and outside a given province proves exceedingly difficult. Among the 4,100 individuals in this study, complete landholding information is available on only 353. I consider data complete only when individuals listed their entire holdings and stated that they held land "in no other towns anywhere," or indicated in some other way that the lands listed represented the sum total of their holdings. Reports on landholding were required in many contexts in Muscovite bureaucratic procedures, so these data come from disparate sources. At military reviews, *okladchiki* reported on the economic status of each individual in the province, frequently including detailed descriptions of land distribution. For instance, *okladchiki* in Lukh reported that a servitor from their province held "*pomest'ia* in Lukh and in Kineshma—130 *cheti*, and this was given to him as *votchina* this year for [serving at] the siege of Moscow. He also has a *pomest'e* in Vologda, also 130 *cheti*."[63] Many others were recorded as having land exclusively within the home district, such as O. I. Aigustov, about whom the overseers of the 1648 muster in Lukh noted, "By decree of the sovereign tsar . . . it is ordered to give to Ostashka Ivanov Aigustov his father's *pomest'e* in Lukh of 111 and one-eighth and one-half of one-half of one-third *cheti*. Ostashka is now one and a half years old, but when he is fifteen and enters service he should serve the sovereign's service from that land and register in the Lukh service rolls as an adolescent."[64]

Other sources include reports to various ministries in conjunction with requests for promotions or supplementary grants or requests for land. In 1699, Petr Nikitich Kablukov testified before the Vladimir Judicial Chancellery that he owned nineteen peasant households in Suzdal' and Shuia, "and other than these he has no peasants, cottars,

TABLE 2.2
Concentration of Landholding by Landlord's Rank

| Landlord's rank | Landlords with holdings in | | | | | | | |
| | One province | | Vladimir-Suzdal' | | Multiple provinces | | Totals | |
	No.	Pct.	No.	Pct.	No.	Pct.	No.	Pct.
Moscow	24	12%	7	3%	173	85%	204	100%
Provincial	108	73	17	11	24	16	149	100
Aggregate	132	37	24	7	197	56	353	100

SOURCES: Moscow ranks derived in part from Stashevskii, *Zemlevladenie moskovskogo dvorianstva*; remaining data from author's compilation.

or household slaves acquired by purchase or gift or by any contract, in any other towns."[65] Marriage contracts often included transfer of dowry lands from the bride's father to her husband. When the Chancellery of Service Lands formalized these transactions, the rescript would occasionally enumerate the father's complete holdings, with the reminder that he had voluntarily parted with his lands and so should not receive more from the state.[66] The bridegroom, too, would file an official request to register the new lands, asking to have them added to his previous holdings. Legatees had to register whatever lands they inherited, adding them to their prior possessions. In this way, Boris Gavrilov Bitiagovskii left a record in 1684, when he inherited some land from his father, that he wished to add his father's properties in Vladimir, Oleksino, and Kashira Provinces to his own previous holdings in Bologotovsk and Oleksino.[67] Such listings, unfortunately rare, constitute full disclosure. Another major source for this compilation, accounting for 172 of the 353 complete accounts, is Stashevskii's listing of holdings of Moscow gentry based on reports filed in the year 1632/33. This treasury of information heavily weights my sample towards Moscow gentry and toward the first half of the century.

The landholding profile differs so radically between landlords of Moscow rank and provincial rank that providing aggregate figures makes little sense. The significant finding is the strong skew among provincial-rank proprietors to hold land within a single province (73 percent) or within a short radius of their home base (within the Vladimir-Suzdal' provinces), whereas among landowners of Moscow rank widely scattered holdings were the norm (85 percent) (see Table 2.2).

Establishing the typicality of the Vladimir-Suzdal' case study pre-

sents some difficulties. Scholarly literature on the subject is contradictory and inconclusive. Vorob'ev and Degtiarev find that in the
Novgorodian lands a startlingly small 2.5 percent of the real estate
owned by Novgorodian servitors lay outside that province's borders.
Novgorod may well have continued its exceptional status into the
seventeenth century, maintaining its regionalism to a degree un-
matched elsewhere in Muscovy. Ia. E. Vodarskii, on the other hand,
concludes from his analysis of *pomeshchiki* in 89 provinces, based on
personal statements collected in 1700, that gentry holdings concentrated within a single province were the rare exception rather than
the norm.[68] In 83 percent of the provinces he studies, landowners
collectively owned fewer than 50 percent of their peasant households within their own province. In his work on "service towns" in
the central Russian provinces, A. A. Novosel'skii argues that the integrity of local landholding had all but disintegrated by the mid–
seventeenth century: "In the ancient cities (Vladimir, Suzdal', Dmitrov, and others) landowning in the XVII century had already reached
such a level of dispersion that the functioning of the town mechanisms was paralyzed to a significant degree."[69] He concludes that
landowning and service assignments were so scattered by the second
half of the century that servitors could not return from remote estates for musters or even to receive their pay. Local witnesses could
no longer provide reliable details about the quantity and quality of
landholdings of town servitors, and they often testified that people
owned land "in various distant towns." Although this may be a question of a glass being "half full or half empty," my findings suggest a far
greater degree of territorial integrity in the landholding patterns of
the Vladimir-Suzdal' provincial-rank gentry than either Vodarskii's
or Novosel'skii's, while still falling far short of the regional exclusiv-
ity shown by the Novgorodian landholders. In my sample, six out of
ten seventeenth-century Vladimir-Suzdal' provincial servitors held
all of their land within the confines of their own province throughout
the century, while Moscow-rank landholders looked farther afield for
land acquisitions, perhaps making use of the broader connections
available to them.

As Table 2.2 makes clear, the two groups, those who owned land in
one province and those who owned land in several, displayed quite
distinguishable status profiles. Beyond rank alone, however, an element of regional orientation, perhaps a component of choice, also
entered into the equation. Among the group with widely scattered
holdings, length and depth of affiliation with the Vladimir-Suzdal'

region were generally slight. Those with dispersed holdings usually came from families that settled late in the area, most commonly as part of the Moscow-rank diaspora. Their ambitions focused on rising in the official governmental hierarchy, and they displayed little interest in provincial politics even after settling onto provincial estates. *Okladchik* reports on several of them included the information that they lived in Moscow and never had served with the town militia.[70] Because they figure so rarely in the documents from the Vladimir-Suzdal' region, their history receives little attention in this account, although following their alternative course would provide an interesting counterpart to the path of those members of the gentry who centered their lives around provincial affairs.

Another category of men in the multiple-province group received lands in distant provinces because their families' estates were too small to support all of the sons. These unfortunates were registered "*v otvode*" (by separate assignment) wherever land was available. Thus, the young boy Fedor Vasil'ev Nashchokin inherited a small estate in Suzdal' from his father, but his older brother Petr, who entered service before their father's death, had been granted 50 *cheti v otvode* in Mosal'sk province to support his service.[71] Although sons of poor fathers requested registration *v otvode* and needed it to support themselves, the connotation of the term was negative, particularly when the separate land assignment was far from the family home. Families preferred to serve together, as evident in a series of petitions from all over the country requesting reregistration of sons from separate service to the same lists as their fathers. For instance, Ivan Dmitriev Redrikov, a man from the Pereiaslavl'-Zalesskii branch of a family also based in Suzdal', petitioned in June 1648 to serve with his family, not from the province where he held land:

> I, your slave, was granted your sovereign *pomest'e* grant in Rostov Province after the death of my uncle, Ivan L'vov Redrikov, and from this *pomest'e* I was inscribed in the service lists of Rostov. . . . Order me, Sovereign, to serve from Pereslavl', where my father and my relatives serve you. . . . Order, Sovereign, my miserable little name crossed off the Rostov lists.

The authorities granted Redrikov's plea.[72] Other petitions show the reasons, both pragmatic and emotional, that families wished to serve together:

> To Tsar, Sovereign and Grand Prince Mikhail Fedorovich! Your slave Stepanko Krushchov petitions you. You, Sovereign, ordered that I should be

on your sovereign service in Kazan', but my little sons, Sovereign, Tro-
fimko and Sen'ka, were to be in your sovereign service in Tula, and my
men, Sovereign, are all in service with them. Merciful Tsar, Sovereign and
Grand Prince Mikhail Fedorovich, favor me, your slave. Order, Sovereign,
one of my little sons to be released to me in Kazan' because of my old age,
and my other little son order, Sovereign, released from Tula to Moscow for
a set time to bid me farewell, because of the distant separation. Tsar,
Sovereign, have mercy![73]

In ancient Kievan times, one of the most wretched categories of
people were the *izgoi*, that is, those not belonging to any identifiable
clan or group, falling between the cracks of society.[74] Some of the
same pathos emerges in the petitions of men torn apart from their
families and communities. The pitiable aspect of men forced by poverty to accept land away from home underscores the normative value
of holding land within the family's primary province.

In contrast to the people with scattered holdings, the families with
concentrated holdings within a single province or pair of neighboring
provinces were the same families that tended to maintain close family units in a single region, regardless of rank. The same families of
high provincial and Moscow rank that took the leading roles in local
politics, real estate markets, and litigation also generally held all of
their land in their home province. Lesser families such as the Golenkins, who were consistently associated with the region, also held all
of their land in their home district.[75] The contribution of personal or
family orientation is evident in the conduct of families with strong
local traditions who attained Moscow rank at some point in the seventeenth century. Very few of these families severed their links with
their home communities even when offered the fruits of the capital.
Like the Kablukovs, such families continued to hold all or most of
their land in their home provinces and to participate on the local
scene (see Ianov genealogy, Figure 2.7).

Almost without exception, scholars of Muscovite landholding
have emphasized the destructive effect of scattered landholding
upon the gentry. Historians have used scattered landholding patterns to explain a multitude of inadequacies of the Russian gentry.
Fragmented properties diminished gentry wealth, precluded the development of local power bases, and impeded the formation of corporate organizations or solidarity. All of these factors, in turn, rendered them helpless before the all-powerful tsar-autocrat. Departing
sharply from the general historiographic line, however, the evidence
from Vladimir-Suzdal' suggests a very different view of gentry land-

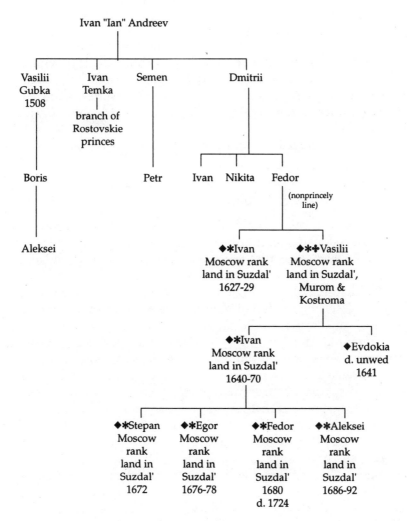

FIG. 2.7. Ianov family genealogy, from the line of Rostovskii princes. Individuals marked with a diamond (♦) have been documented in Suzdal'. Individuals marked with an asterisk (*) are of Moscow rank. Individuals marked with a club (♣) have been documented in other provinces. From Petrov, *Istoriia rodov*, 1: 100.

holding and its impact on gentry political culture. Property was far less scattered than has been commonly assumed, and more often than not gentrymen held all of their land within a single province, or even within a single district within a province. Although not consolidated into compact manorial estates, gentry real estate holdings, like gentry families, generally displayed distinct and lasting localism. The effects of such localism have yet to be considered in evaluations of Muscovite political culture and relations between gentry and autocrat.

The Real Estate Market and Consolidation of Holdings

Given the conditional nature of *pomest'e* land tenure, gentrymen always risked losing their property. The state could, and did, repossess land it had originally bestowed. In 1694 Iakov Il'in's Vladimir *pomest'e* "was taken away" by sentence of a high court.[76] A servitor from Lukh forfeited 50 *cheti* of land and 5 rubles from his cash allotment for deserting to the Poles during the "King's Son's Campaign" in 1618.[77] In addition to the threat from the state, foreclosure was quite common among the gentry, showing their active participation in a marketplace of debts and loans. In a clear example of appropriation through foreclosure, a court decision granted Aleksei Zabolotskii's *votchina* in Vladimir to a clerk, Leontei Grigor'ev Protopopov, on the grounds that Zabolotskii had borrowed 50 rubles and put up his *votchina* as collateral. When he failed to repay the loan by the date agreed upon in the contract, he forfeited his property.[78] Trickery and brute force also came into play in the transfer of property rights. Grigorii Bolotnikov complained when his first cousins abruptly altered the terms of an exchange of villages that he had negotiated with them. He had duly given them possession of his villages as expected, but they had demanded more. They had seized his peasants' houses and silos and had refused to release his peasants after beating them almost to death and breaking their legs.[79] In another case, a tale of extraordinary ineptitude, a pathetic Vladimir servitor complained that his own relatives had not once but twice had the audacity to seize and then sell his patrimonial *votchina* out from under his nose, thus making a double profit themselves and depriving him of his livelihood. He begged the tsar to intervene, "so that I, with my poor little wife and children, won't suffer torture by righter [beating about the shins for debt] and be entirely destroyed."[80]

Short of such blatant force or fraud, various other difficulties per-
suaded petty landowners to part with their property. The unique
correspondence between *stol'nik* A. I. Bezobrazov and his estate
overseers in the 1680s reveals the kinds of pressures that could be
brought to bear. One of Bezobrazov's overseers wrote to his master in
1680/81, explaining that some local smallholders "petition to you,
lord, to release them from service as soldiers and to let them serve
as previously among the horse guards and they will give you their
land in entirety." Others turned over land as collateral for loans
they would never repay. Another overseer wrote to Bezobrazov that
neighboring landholders "gave me their land because they borrowed
money . . . from the priest Trofim Potapovich, and I paid that money
back for them."[81]

While poor families frequently had to sell or trade their holdings
in difficult periods, wealthier families could better afford to keep a
given piece of land long-term, and property law allowed them to bequeath both *pomest'e* and *votchina* land to their heirs. However, rich
and poor alike bought, sold, and traded land at an impressive rate.
Nikita Kablukov bought or traded at least 21 pieces of land in the
space of twenty years, mostly with social equals within the same two
areas of Suzdal' and Shuia. The majority of these exchanges and sales
occurred with family members and in-laws. Kablukov engaged in
land deals with his brothers-in-law and their families (Dolgovo-
Saburov, Koisarov, Kozynskii, Mishukov, Volkov), with his grandmother's family (Tepritskii), and with his own sister, the widowed
Lukeria Dolgovo-Saburov. Other exchanges took place between long-
time Suzdal' neighbors and close associates, such as the Kolobovs
and Vysotskiis.[82]

Other gentry servitors maintained a similar pace of land turnover.
The histories of particular plots show the brisk pace of exchange
in land that characterized the Muscovite provinces in the seventeenth century. In 1672/73 the Chancellery of Service Lands granted a
votchina to State Secretary (*d'iak*) Andrei Iakovlev. A brief three years
later Iakovlev traded the *votchina* to Aleksei Zakharin, who held onto
it for another three years before trading it to *stol'nik* Sava Alekseevich
Shepelev.[83] In a very complex and disputed case, Mikhail Tiuchev and
his stepson, Fedor Korobov, each inherited a piece of *pomest'e* land
from Mikhail's wife (Fedor's mother) after her death. Before Fedor's
death a decade later, bits of those properties had been traded to at least
five different parties.[84] Everyone sold and traded land: widows, or-

phaned girls, boyars, Moscow-rank servitors, clergy, state secretaries, lesser clerks, lowly service gentrymen.[85] In principle *pomest'e* land could not be sold, and as *pomest'e* far predominated over *votchina* among provincial landholders, trades greatly outnumbered outright sales of land. Although sales of *pomest'e* did occasionally occur, the more legally correct route involved exchanging plots of service land that were nominally equivalent in quantity and quality. The booming land market reinforces George G. Weickhardt's contention that private, heritable property had become a commonplace concept among the Muscovite landholding classes by the seventeenth century.[86]

Rapid "mobilization" of land inspired the historians' axiom that the time gentrymen spent serving the tsar away from home eliminated any emotional attachment to the land they owned.[87] Land did change hands at a rapid rate, and previous scholars accurately represented this phenomenon. Significant from the point of view of community survival and integrity, however, is the addendum that most land transactions occurred between residents of the same area. Consequently, property did not leave the community's control. Many trades reflect efforts to consolidate fragmented plots. Established families such as the Kablukovs, Koisarovs, Kazimerovs, Lazarevs, Tregubovs and others built small empires in compact corners of particular provinces. The Kablukovs consolidated their holdings in Deminskii district (*stan*) in Suzdal' and Teleshovskaia district (*volost'*) in Shuia. Of their numerous exchanges and purchases of land through the seventeenth century, all but a few were concentrated in those two districts.[88] Several members of the Kablukov family did hold land outside these two districts. Aleksei Fedorovich had some villages in Opol'skii *stan* in Suzdal', which he left to his son and grandsons. Aleksei also inherited his cousin Afanasii's land in Talitskii *stan*, Suzdal', but he had parted with this outlying plot by the time of his death. Nikita Alekseevich held property in Suzdal' in Starodub-Riapolovskii *stan*, which he traded away. Other families, too, consolidated their holdings in particular corners of provinces when possible. The Kudriavtsevs and Nesvitaevs built their stronghold in Il'mekhotskii *stan* in Vladimir, and the Kazimerovs centered their operations in Opol'skii and Matnitskii *stany* in Suzdal'. The Khmetevskiis concentrated their property in Suzdal' Province, Opol'skii *stan*, traceably from 1592/93 until 1678/79. Between 1636 and 1688, the Lazarevs built their territorial base in one district of Shuia, Borisoglebskaia *volost'*, and in one of Suzdal', Matnitskii *stan*. The large, wealthy Oshanin family held almost all of their extensive properties in Shizhegottskii *stan* in Suzdal' and Meduzhskii *stan* in Vladimir (see Map 3).

Consolidation of property can been seen most clearly as a goal in wills or land division settlements, which occasionally specified that properties should be divided in coherent segments, not splintered into irrational strips. Prokofii Izmailov's heirs, for instance, asked that their late cousin's 440 *cheti* of *votchina* land be apportioned between them in discrete units, without splitting apart villages and fields.[89] Whoever composed a petition for five-year-old Danilo Afanas'ev Bologovskii and his three-year-old brother Iakov specified that in the division of their late father's property the authorities should "leave all [strips] adjoining each other and not in various [places]."[90]

The provincial gentry, ostensibly so callous about fragmenting and scattering their properties, displayed some efforts at consolidation, although it would stretch the evidence to argue for consolidated holdings as the norm. *Stol'nik* Nikita Ivanovich Akinfov purchased as much land as he could between 1666 and 1701, all within Vladimir Province, in Bogoiavlenskii and Bogoliubskii *stany*. By 1673 he had accumulated only 255 *cheti* of his 830 *cheti* allotment, all of which was located in Vladimir. Over the next 30 years he made at least four more bids to buy *votchina* land specifically in Vladimir or to receive it in state grants.[91] Bogdan Evtifeev Rokotov, a provincial servitor from Pskov, for some reason developed an interest in building his real estate holdings in Vladimir Province, and so over the course of 26 years, from 1668 to 1694, he traded off bits of his service lands elsewhere in the country in exchange for land in Vladimir.[92] Andrei Ivanov Khonenev, too, consolidated his holdings in Vladimir. He traded his service estate in Nizhnii Novgorod for a large piece of land in Vladimir at the same time that he purchased some *votchina* land in Vladimir.[93] Petr Kochiukov worked toward centering his landholdings not only within Vladimir Province but within a single corner of it, Krisinskaia *volost'*. In 1662/63 he exchanged his *pomest'e* in another part of Vladimir with his cousins for their *pomest'e* in Krisinskaia *volost'*. As he still lacked 114 *cheti* of his 250 *cheti* entitlement, he simultaneously requested specifically that any unclaimed land within Krisinskaia *volost'* be registered to him.[94]

Land consolidation can be discerned as a possible underlying motivation for several of the marriages in the areas under investigation.

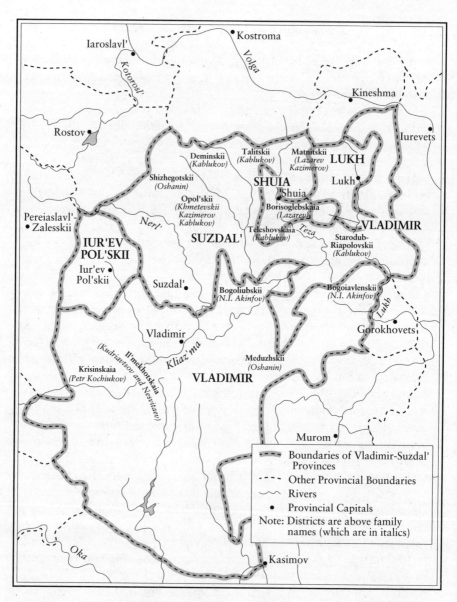

MAP 3. Consolidation of Family Holdings in Shuia, Suzdal', and Vladimir Provinces. Adapted from E. Ia. Vodarskii, *Naselenie Rossii v kontse XVII-nachale XVIII veka* (Moscow, 1977), pp. 248–49, by permission of the author, with additional information from M. K. Liubavskii, *Obrazovanie osnovnoi gosudarstvennoi territorii Velikorusskoi narodnosti* (Leningrad, 1929; reprint Gulf Breeze, Fl, 1969), map enclosure. Information on Kablukov landholding is found in Chapter 2, footnote 88. Information on Akinfov is found

The chain of liaisons between the Mishukov and Kablukov families, described above, served not only to cement a bond of peace between two potentially rival clans, but also to prevent the alienation of property beyond the limits of the two groups.[95] Marriage sealed a triple alliance between the Miachins, Orlovs, and Nemtsovs in Suzdal': Boris Orlov's widow married Zakharii Miachin, bestowing on him half of her late husband's estate. The other half of Orlov's land went to Miachin's close relative, Maksim Nemtsov, to support his service expenses.[96] A woman named Ustina brought five *cheti* in the village of Kocheneva to her husband as dowry, which complemented the fifteen *cheti* that he had purchased in the same village.[97] Marriage was not only a political act but also a wise investment.

Provincial gentrymen of the Vladimir-Suzdal' region may have lacked some of the emotional ties to a given piece of land that characterized Western gentries and harbored few sentimental illusions about particular plots of land, but their bond to their native region proved no less enduring. Their enthusiasm for the provincial life and for the acquisition and consolidation of properties within their home communities meshed with the government's scheme in the second half of the seventeenth century to resettle extraneous gentry militiamen into their native provinces. With the blessings of the state and the active participation of the gentry, provincial gentry communities developed, by the mid–seventeenth century at the latest, from home bases for the families of itinerant warriors into the parochial centers of a landed, gentry class.

Community and Family: The "Life of Iuliania Lazarevskaia"

One of the mechanisms involved in perpetuating stable communities is found in the role of women in the community. Proponents of the idea that Muscovite gentrymen wandered from assignment to

---

in *RGADA*, f. 1112/1, nos. 69, 72; on Kazimerovs in *SPbFIRI*, f. 21, Borisov Collection, no. 496; on Khmetevskiis m *ibid*, no. 516; on Kochiukov in *RGADA*, f. 1112, *opis'*1, nos. 47, 139, 166; on Kudriavtsovs in *RGADA*, f. 1112, *opis'* 1, nos. 12, 15, 63B, 128, *ll*. 1–7; on Lazarevs in *SPbFIRI*, f. 21, Borisov Collection, nos. 530, 626; on Nesvitaevs in *RGADA*, f. 1112, *opis'* 1, nos. 15, 63A and B.

assignment and had no home base have ignored the implications of the fact that over half of the gentry—i.e., gentry women and children—was completely uninvolved in service. Even if their husbands and fathers were as itinerant as historians would like to believe, women and children had to live somewhere. Documents from the Vladimir-Suzdal' region show very clearly that women tended to live in their native provinces throughout their lives. Men requested leaves from service to return to their homes to see their wives and children or to attend their wives' funerals.[98] While their husbands were away, whether on service assignments or as prisoners of war, wives managed estates and instigated judicial proceedings.[99] Wives stayed at home when their husbands went off on business or into hiding, as evident in the number of cases in which wives greeted officials sent out to provincial estates looking for men wanted by the law.[100] As represented in the documents, all of these women lived on their provincial estates, whether their husbands were present or not.

The "Life of Iuliania Lazarevskaia," an unusual hagiographic tale of a pious gentrywoman from Murom, serves as a particularly neat example of the role of women in gentry communities in the ancient towns of central Zamoskov'e. The tale was written by her devoted son, Kalistrat Druzhina Osorin, in the early seventeenth century. Osorin developed the notion of woman as keeper of the home and portrayed a separate world where women fostered among themselves and their daughters a sense of security and continuity, of home. Iuliania's parents were a Moscow-rank servitor and a gentrywoman from Murom. After her mother's death, she was taken from Moscow back to Murom, her parents' home town, "by her grandmother, who raised her in piety for six years. When the grandmother died, Iuliania's aunt, Natalia, wife of Putila Arapov, took, at the grandmother's behest, the young girl to her house. [There,] she respected and honored her aunt and her aunt's daughters."[101] In this enclosed, female world, Iuliania and her kinswomen sustained a lasting bond with the Murom community and fostered a sense of home that endured over many generations.

All of the marriages mentioned in the tale linked members of the Murom gentry community. Iuliania's father, like the Vladimir-Suzdal' men of Moscow rank, married the daughter of a man from his native region. Iuliania's husband came from the small town of Lazarev, also in Murom province. So, although she moved into her in-laws' home upon getting married at age sixteen, Iuliania lived most of her life within the confines of her home province. While her husband spent long stints in distant places on assignment, Iuliania stayed at home. She lived her private life of charity and good deeds, bore thirteen children, raised those who survived infancy, and kept a home, farm, and estate together. In advanced age, the saintly widow was forced to move by the exigencies of the famine of 1601. She lived out the last few years of her life in Nizhnii Novgorod, but the transportation of her corpse back to Murom in 1604 indicates that her bond with her original home never weakened.

Iuliania lived in Murom, not in the Vladimir-Suzdal' area, but her case can readily be accepted as a representative of provincial gentry of an old central Russian town. The story is revealing in several ways. It focuses attention on the question of where the women and children lived while the men spent their lives serving in distant places. It underscores the perhaps commonsensical, but easily ignored, continuity of home, family, and estate in the absence of men and under the supervision of a tight-knit community of local women. It provides emblematic representation of the role of women and marriage in solidifying provincial communities of gentry, despite the better documented scattering effects of mobile service and upward aspirations toward Moscow.

Assumptions about the deleterious effects of scattered landholding and about the rootlessness of the Muscovite service gentry have created an impression of a roving group of transients, spiraling around the magnetic center of Moscow, with no eye to the provinces they wandered through and with no sense of themselves or their potential power outside the context of Moscow's favor and approval. Including individuals documented only once in the available sources, figures on stability and duration of settlement and on concentration of landholding within a given province indicate that overall a significant proportion of gentrymen, particularly those of high Moscow rank or the poor, marginal ones at the other extreme, followed the transitory patterns that the historiography assumes was dominant. The majority of gentry servitors of provincial rank or with historic provincial connections, however, pursued an entirely different pattern of residence and landholding, settling early in the Vladimir-Suzdal' region, establishing extended families or clans within their provincial locale, and concentrating their landholding within their own provincial borders. Those who concentrated their real estate holdings and those who concentrated their family members within the region overlap to a very high degree, indicating that this is indeed a distinct group of people following a characteristic set of priorities and family strategies. For some, economic conditions or the demands of Moscow may have dictated the course they took. Some men did not have the land or wealth to support themselves or to launch their sons in the local provincial milieu. Others rose to high Moscow rank and perforce spent most of their time in the capital or on distant assignments. For others, however, the difference appears to have had a volitional aspect to it; individual families appear to have made choices about their focus and interests. Families such as the Kablukovs manifested little interest in rising in the hierarchy of titles, showing much more discernable enthusiasm for wheeling and dealing, trading, lending, and marrying within the confines of their own home province.

CHAPTER 3

Partible Inheritance and Local Marriage: Gentry Families and the State

In the eighteenth century, as Western political thinkers turned their attention to the pursuit of democracy and political equality, one of the central matters of interest to them was replacing the antiquated rules of primogeniture, which were seen to perpetuate a privileged aristocracy, with the more just and democratic practice of equal partition. When Virginia abolished entails and primogeniture, Thomas Jefferson praised the move for ending a system that served the "perpetuation of wealth in select families" and for instituting equal partition, "a system by which every fibre would be eradicated of antient or future aristocracy and a foundation laid for a government truly republican," effecting an "aristocracy of virtue and talent."[1] Jefferson, if he had wished to add Muscovite history to his already impressive font of knowledge, might have been surprised to discover that the Muscovite nobility, notorious for its subservience to an all-powerful tsar, had anticipated American innovation and had practiced partible inheritance since the dawn of written history. The results in Muscovy, however, were far removed from the happy republican egalitarianism envisioned by Jefferson. Instead of encouraging democracy, partible inheritance coexisted easily with autocracy. Indeed, in the somewhat alarmist view presented by traditional historiography, the very absence of primogeniture undermined the economic viability of the nobility and condemned it to a servile status before the tsar.

While the logical link between partible inheritance and republican democracy is distinctly inappropriate in the context of Muscovy, the hostile view—that the Muscovite nobility willfully destroyed itself by fragmenting its estates among its heirs—also misses the mark. Muscovite provincial landholders valued their conjugal families, their sisters, wives, and daughters as well as their brothers, husbands, and sons, and practiced a form of inheritance that fit well with their family ambitions as well as with the economic realities of their time.[2] Gentry inheritance practices, which guaranteed support for daughters and widows as well as for sons, sometimes in accordance with formal law and sometimes in systematic violation of the law, reveal the quiet power of the gentry to insist on its preferences, even against the written law of the tsar. Gentry practices of marriage and inheritance reveal some of the deepest values of the gentry community and show at a very crucial level how the gentry and the state worked out a tacit understanding and tolerance of each other's needs and demands. The very distinctive marriage and inheritance practices of the Muscovite gentry go a long way toward explaining Muscovite political relations and the differences between the Muscovite gentry and many of its Western European contemporaries.

The interpretive paradigms of Muscovite court politics proposed by Edward Keenan and Nancy Kollmann have already underscored the centrality of kinship relations at court. Marriage into the grand princely family was the ultimate marker of political success, and the leading boyar clans ran the state with their networks of affines, clients, and dependents.[3] Among the provincial gentry too, kinship played a very important organizing role, but the gentry worked out its own concepts and uses of kinship, which were quite different from the patterns of clan identification found at court. Boyar clans maintained lengthy genealogical records, all traced through the male line. Individuals calculated their standing within their own clans and negotiated the status of their clans relative to others through a complicated formula of genealogical seniority, in order of descent in the male line from a real or imaginary male progenitor. The men of a clan had to function together for the common good, and individuals could not advance alone but only in conjunction with the rise of their entire stock. *Mestnichestvo*, a precedence system based on generational ranking of individuals within patriarchal clans, worked together with marriage and kinship politics to determine advancement at court, distributions of offices, rank, and power.[4]

In this clan-based system, women were important in binding clans together through marriages but had little relevance to either their natal or marital genealogical lines. Many genealogies omitted daughters altogether, labeling a man *bezdeten* (childless) if he produced only daughters. Wives often appeared in family trees without their own names, merely as daughters of a certain father or girls from a particular clan. The symbolic relegation of women to the status of nonentity or conferring on them existence only as extensions of their fathers suggests that the Muscovite aristocracy treated its distaff side as items of barter and exchange among males, as has been noted in anthropological studies of many other societies.

Among provincial gentry servitors, by contrast, clan played a rather insignificant role, although it was not an alien or unknown concept. Different contexts called forth different concepts of kinship, and provincial Muscovite families used their broader clan affiliations flexibly, but only when the circumstances warranted it.[5] When called upon to submit extensive genealogical charts of their lineages, provincial clans did so without difficulty, showing that they were fully aware of their extended kin and of the official uses of membership in a patriarchal clan.[6] Otherwise the far more intimate ties of immediate family, relationships of the first or second degree, were primary. These paramount relationships extended to grandparents and grandchildren, uncles and aunts, nephews and nieces, but rarely beyond.

Concepts of lineage and clan were not limited to the paper on which genealogies were inscribed, however. Provincial landholders were quick to protest, for instance, any threat of dishonor to the good name of their extended clan. A scandalous case in Iaroslavl' in 1678 illustrates the ways in which provincial gentry used the concept of extended clan. Eleven members of the Volkov family with their children, all Iaroslavl' servitors, petitioned against Vaska, the illegitimate son of their deceased relative, Ivan Alekseev Volkov. Vaska, masquerading as his father's legitimate heir, had claimed his father's *pomest'ia* and *votchiny* and had enrolled in cavalry service in the Iaroslavl' service register. The relatives claimed that the *vybliadok* (bastard) was actually one of two children Ivan had conceived out of wedlock with a slave woman before his legitimate marriage to his wife, who had died childless. The Volkovs begged that the authorities have "that bastard Vaska, who styles himself 'Volkov,' imprisoned and questioned in the Chancellery of Military Affairs as to why he, a bastard, calls himself Ivan Volkov's son and why he dishonors us, your slaves, . . . so that we, your slaves, will not be dishonored by that bastard, together with our entire clan." Appealing to clan solidarity, the chief plaintiff wrote, "And the entire Volkov clan knows about those bastards, and honorable people of many towns, *stol'niki* and *striapchie* and Moscow gentrymen and provincial gentrymen and priests and various people [know] that they are bastards and not legitimate children of my brother." The litigants supplied a list of 30 Volkovs who could testify, as well as a detailed genealogy of the closest kin, "brothers and sisters and brothers-in-law and nephews and nieces" of the deceased.[7] The anxiety of the Volkovs about their collective honor and their ability to summon up support from distant Volkov relatives in Moscow and other towns demonstrate that the concept of extended clan was as much alive among the lesser gentry of the provinces as among the Muscovite boyar aristocracy.

When pragmatic interest pushed provincial landholders, they remembered their clan links, as is demonstrated by a petition from a pair of distant cousins requesting title to the land of their tragically deceased relative, who perished along with his entire family in a fire. The petitioners called their distant kinsman "brother," a term which could refer to any kind of cousin but which appears in documents primarily in reference to close kin or in situations like this one, where petitioners wanted the Moscow officials to recognize their clan identity.[8] Another potential manifestation of clan affiliation, *rodovoi vykup*, or kindred right to repurchase *votchina* land that had been alienated by any of a clan's members, scarcely affected provincial gentry families. People of provincial rank held relatively little *votchina* land and so rarely acted upon their right to retain it in the family line.

These instances all demonstrate that gentry servitors understood and utilized clan connections under appropriate circumstances, but *dvoriane* and *deti boiarskie* trotted out their genealogies and clan memberships only in very official representations of themselves to state authorities, within a context where clan was the dominant idiom. Pierre Bourdieu makes a useful distinction between formal, or representational, and informal, or practical, kinship. Bourdieu emphasizes the need to consider kin relations not as inherently significant but as relations constructed to serve certain functions. He could be describing Muscovite rather than Algerian kinship practices and uses of official genealogy when he writes that "*representational kinship* is nothing other than the group's self-representation and the almost theatrical presentation it gives of itself when acting in accordance with that self-image. By contrast, practical groups exist only through and for the particular functions in pursuance of which they have been *effectively mobilized*."[9]

Within the local community, clan was a largely inactive concept. The much more closely knit nuclear family, including female as well as male relatives, provides a far more relevant category of analysis, one that played a far more significant role in the lives of the individuals concerned. An analysis of the activities and values of the bilateral nuclear family, as seen in landholding and inheritance practices, provides a far more important key to understanding the interactions of the autocratic state and its lesser provincial servitors than does the lofty agnatic clan. Members of the gentry individually displayed far more concern about their immediate family than about their clan. They were more interested in the welfare of their children, female and male, of their mothers, siblings, and widows, than about their male cousins. In only one case, that of Anna Izmailov, in all the documents I have examined for the region did second-degree kinsmen in the male line supplant a widow's claim to her late husband's property.[10] In no case did relatives interest themselves positively in the concerns of a relative more distant than the second degree. Uncles arranged marriages for nieces and endowed them with movable or immovable property as dowries. Aunts ceded property to nephews, and nieces to uncles, in return for lifelong care and sustenance. But never did a cousin shoulder responsibility for a cousin. When estates were divided, only in the absence of first- or second-degree relatives of either sex would that amorphous category of "cousins" surface to claim the inheritance. As evident in gentry practice, family bonds were close and limited in scope.

Inheritance practices illustrate the close family focus in very concrete terms. Gentry testators consistently left their goods and property to their immediate family.[11] With the significant exception of the two ruling dynasties, the Daniloviches and then the Romanovs, members of the Russian landholding elite practiced partible inheritance, dividing their lands more or less equally among all their sons, and sometimes among their daughters as well. Muscovite law recommended partition as the generally accepted practice. The 1649 *Ulozhenie* stipulated:

> Concerning *dvoriane* and *deti boiarskie* who have two or three sons, . . .
> order that the service landholding of their father's be given to all of them,

that the inhabited land and the waste land be divided by acres. . . . Divide up for such petitioners their father's service landholding, plus their new grant, equally among all the brothers [after] having measured out the inhabited and the waste land in portions by acres so that none of them will be wronged by another.[12]

In practice as well as in law, partition held sway. When Vasilii Ivanov Oshanin was killed in 1688/89 while serving in the Crimea, he left his extensive *pomest'ia* to be divided among nine heirs: his widow and four young children (one son and three daughters), his widowed mother, and his three brothers.[13] Three young Terent'ev brothers, Fedka, Kirichko, and Vaska, still calling themselves by their childish diminutives, reported during a land dispute in 1671 that they had jointly been granted the *pomest'e* that had belonged to their grandfather and then to their father, and that they currently lived there and held the paternal *pomest'e*.[14] When they reached adulthood, according to common practice, they would divide the property evenly among themselves. In these cases and hundreds of others, the paternal legacy neither focused on a single heir nor privileged onc over any others.

If all sons received equal shares of the paternal inheritance, what was the role of daughters? In Muscovy, both the law and the practices of provincial testators were mixed on this score.[15] As Daniel Kaiser has demonstrated, the law changed repeatedly across the centuries, generally favoring male offspring over female, particularly within the same generation, but varying in its weighing of the rival claims of direct female descendents as opposed to collateral male kin. Finally in 1676 the law settled on a formulation by which "females of the first degree of blood relation were the equal to males of the second degree."[16] As Ann Kleimola discusses, a series of decrees through the seventeenth century progressively restricted women's rights to inherit property, putting increasing limits on the kinds of land that women could receive.[17] In spite of the creeping legal limits on female inheritance in Muscovy, the mixed sympathies of the law and of the administrators who administered it surfaced in individual decisions, where the female line of inheritance frequently received consideration and protection in contested cases. In the absence of sons, daughters were often favored over their uncles, who should have had a strong claim as the closest surviving male relatives of the deceased. Marfa Vasil'evna Simanov's uncle and cousin sued to gain control of her father's *votchina* on the grounds that they had raised the orphaned girl for nine years and had arranged her marriage. The court rejected their suit and granted the land to the daughter and her husband.[18] Another case in which the courts favored the daughter over immediate male relatives in the paternal line involved Anna Drutskaia and her paternal uncle, Semen. Both claimed a *votchina* plot of her late father's, but in its judgment the court again favored the daughter and her husband over the brother of the deceased.[19] Direct rather than agnatic descent rated top marks from the courts.

Most testators favored male over female heirs but provided quite generously, in land as well as in movable goods, for their daughters. When Aleksei Fedorovich Kablukov arranged a marriage for his daughter Maria in 1671, he furnished her and her new husband with a *votchina* estate of 42 *cheti*, approximately one-sixth of his 240-*cheti* holding. As father of six children, Kablukov apparently was planning on an equal six-way division.[20] Vasilii Nikitin Kozynskii bestowed a dowry *pomest'e* of 20 *cheti* on his daughter Fekla and his son-in-law Nikita Kablukov when they married in 1667.[21] When Kozynskii died in 1694, his three sons inherited only 23 *cheti* each, just a trace more per person than their sister had received earlier.[22] When Avdotia Il'in married Tito Khrushchev in 1694, her brother Iakov turned over the land left to her by their father for her support, her *prozhitochnoe* or maintenance portion. In accordance with their father's distribution, Iakov split the estate with her so she and her husband received 44 *cheti* (42 percent) and he retained 61 *cheti* (58 percent) for himself.[23] Konstantin Likhachev provided his daughter and son-in-law with 100 *cheti* in Vladimir on their marriage in 1649/50, keeping 130 (56.5 percent) in another province for himself.[24] Petr Telesnin conferred 37 of his 127 *cheti* on his daughter when she married Petr Lodygin in 1626, keeping 90 *cheti* (71 percent) for himself and his small son, Pronka. If Telesnin intended to keep a share for himself and a share for his son, then the distribution works out to almost even thirds for each family member.[25] A female testator, Agrafenia, the widow of Aleksandr Roganovskii, divided her portion of her late husband's estate in Vladimir and Suzdal' between her husband's nephew, Nikita Ivanovich Roganovskii, and her daughter and new son-in-law, Grigorii Prokof'ev Vladykin. The lands were divided equally, but the household plot specifically went to the daughter.[26]

Many women received shares of their fathers' estates more commensurate with that inherited by Agaf'ia Bitiagovskaia in 1684 than with the generous portions described above. Agaf'ia inherited only six *cheti* of *pomest'e* while her paternal uncles each acquired three times that amount.[27] According to the 1649 law code, daughters stood to inherit a maximum of 10 percent of their fathers' estates: 10 percent if the father was killed in action; 7.5 percent if he died while in regimental service; and 5 percent if he died peacefully at home.[28] Agaf'ia's share, 14 percent, like those of all of the women in this sample, significantly exceeded the amount prescribed by law, even though it was still ludicrously small and inferior to the shares received by her male relatives. In a similar manner, Ivan Nesvitaev's widow and two daughters by his previous marriage had to share a maintenance portion of 12 *cheti* while his two brothers were jointly granted the remaining 46 *cheti* of his *pomest'e*. The widow petitioned to transfer her allotment to a new husband and was granted half of the 12 *cheti*, leaving the orphaned girls with only 6 *cheti* between them.[29]

It is difficult to establish a general rule with the small sample of cases that I have of gentrywomen in the Vladimir-Suzdal' region. I have evidence concerning 142 female landholders, of whom I can trace divisions among male and female heirs in 44 cases. Of these women, the majority received shares roughly equal to those of their brothers. Lands were divided most commonly in a ratio of roughly 40 percent to the women and 60 percent to the men, although the numbers vary widely. Girls often received their share of the father's wealth as dowry during the father's lifetime. All but 2 brides of the 46 in the region on whom I have dowry information received some land as part of the arrangement, although it should be noted that my sample of documents contains a bias toward dowries containing land. Much of the evidence I have on dowries comes from land documents rather than directly from marriage agreements, and hence I tend to find those marriages in which land was exchanged.[30] If a father died before his daughters were married, he generally either left them some land to support them and serve as dowries or entrusted his sons with the obligation to support their sisters and provide them with dowries. Konstantin Ivanovich Kablukov, for instance, split his estate with his sister when he contracted her marriage in 1683/84, giving her and her husband 40 percent of his real estate.[31] In some cases, particularly when widowed female relatives bequeathed land, female legatees fared better than men, perhaps compensating for previously unequal distributions carried out by male legators.[32]

The division of estates among a number of heirs inevitably resulted in fragmented holdings. Each heir received only a sliver of the paternal estate. When the wealthy and distinguished Nikita Alekseevich Kablukov died, his three sons divided his sizable estate among themselves, each ultimately receiving only a relatively small legacy. Each son inherited between five and nine adult male peasants, plus their families, to work their lands. From their father's riches, each son received just about the average number of peasants held by provincial gentrymen.[33] Antrop Sarychev left a smallish *pomest'e* of 38 *cheti* in Vladimir at his death in 1686, but when it was divided among his *six* sons, each received just over six *cheti*, not nearly enough to support a man in full service regalia, much less his family. Fortunately for them, each already held seventeen *cheti* from some other source, but even so, after inheriting their father's legacy, their grand totals reached only 23 *cheti*, well below the 100 *cheti* minimum required in principle to support a man in service.[34]

Because of the resultant splintering of holdings, the custom of partible inheritance has drawn the gentry nothing but censure from Western observers and later critics alike. Giles Fletcher commented on the impoverishment of the nobility, who passed on noble titles to all sons, not just to the eldest, and thereby made a mockery of those titles:

> The fourth and lowest degree of nobility with them is of such as bear the name of kniaz'ia or dukes but come of the younger brothers of those chief houses through many descents and have no inheritance of their own, save the bare name or title of duke only. For their order is to deliver their names and titles of their dignities over to all their children alike, whatsoever else they leave them, so that the sons . . . of a kniaz' or duke are called kniaz'ia though they have not one groat of inheritance or livelihood to maintain themselves withal. Of this sort there are so many that the plenty maketh them cheap, so that you shall see dukes glad to serve a mean man for five or six rubles or marks a year, and yet they will stand highly upon their beschest'e or reputation of their honors.[35]

At the most basic level, critics of partible inheritance perceived a threat to the viability of gentry estates in the practice of subdivision, a perception which had some truth to it, as seen in the decline in estate sizes over the course of the seventeenth century.[36] In 1714, Peter the Great voiced disgust with the practice: "We, Peter I, Tsar and Autocrat of All Russia, etc., issue this *ukaz* for the knowledge of all subjects of Our state, regardless of their social status. The division of estates upon the death of the father causes great harm to Our state and state interests and brings ruin to subjects and the families concerned."[37] But the criticism from the West went deeper than the financial level and took on invidious, moralistic overtones. Samuel Collins, an Englishman who published his colorful account of Muscovy in 1671, included Muscovite inheritance practices in his list of ways in which Muscovites "differ in their actions from all other Nations." He concluded his discussion saying, "These are their odd customs, which we may justly censure."[38]

Partible inheritance came to represent a sure path to social disorder and systemic collapse. By the late sixteenth century, primogeniture had caught on among elites throughout Western Europe. In England, by the early seventeenth century, the gentry and even the upper levels of the merchant class had adopted this aristocratic practice. The French nobility was constrained to practice primogeniture, while commoners aspiring to win their way into the hereditary nobility attempted to bypass requirements for the equal partition of estates demanded by customary law in order to concentrate wealth and preserve estates in the hands of the eldest son. Most of the Italian nobilities practiced functional unigeniture, either leaving estates intact to a single heir or leaving them undivided to a collective of brothers, only one of whom would marry. The bachelor brothers would, in time, return their portions to the heirs of their married brother. Each of these systems worked out some way to support younger sons and daughters, whether through annuities, usufructuary tenures, or dowries, but by the seventeenth century the privileging of a single heir and the effort to avoid dividing property holdings had caught on throughout these elites, among both aristocracies and lesser nobilities or gentries.[39]

Among Western writers, primogeniture was widely considered one of the fundamental preconditions for preserving a strong, independent nobility and one of the distinguishing features of the West. As Bishop Aylmer wrote, "For nothing soner destroieth greate houses, than the devision of thinheritance, as it appeareth in Germany."[40] An Englishman, Thomas Starkey, wrote a dialogue in the mid–sixteenth century in which his characters took both sides on issue of primogeniture. One objected to the cruelty of excluding younger brothers from the patrimony, while the other defended the current usage, saying that

if the lands in every great family were distributed equally betwixt the brethren, in a small process of years the head families would decay and by little and little utterly vanish away. And so the people should be without rulers and heads the which by their rudeness and folly would shortly disturb this quiet life and good policy which by many ages they have laid here in our country . . . wherefore . . . you shall take away the foundation and ground of all our civility, . . . for if you . . . take their great possessions, . . . you shall in process of years confound the nobles and the commons together after such manner that there shall be no difference betwixt the one and the other.[41]

This confounding of nobles and commons, of course, seemed a terrible thing.

Following this early-modern lead, many historians of Russia blame the stubborn persistence of partible inheritance for creating an enfeebled nobility, dependent on the state for infusions of land and thereby rendered incapable of independent organization or action. Gustave Alef, for instance, discusses "the immemorial system of partible inheritances, practiced with monotonous regularity by the Eastern Slavs," which explains the Russian nobility's precarious economic position and "its almost abject dependence upon the state for sustenance." Partible inheritance, in large part, "allowed for the creation of a monarchy with virtually unlimited powers."[42] Partible inheritance, the theory goes, creates an impoverished, dependent, and enslaved nobility.

Yet partible inheritance did not leave the provincial gentry without resources or place it in an abject relation of dependency on the state. On the contrary, the system of land ownership and acquisition had developed in order to accommodate such splintering and had cultivated means to compensate for it. Throughout the century gentrymen managed to augment their small inheritances by a variety of means. The most significant of these was that young men who reached maturity during their fathers' lifetimes were entitled to receive their own, separate *pomest'e* estates to support their military service, so state service remained an important source of land grants, even after the traditional sources of state grants (state and court lands) had been exhausted. Many young servitors successfully availed themselves of this entitlement. Mikhail Cheliustkin's two sons provide a typical example of the successful route. The young men inherited their father's 73 *cheti* in Iur'ev Pol'skii, gaining a mere 32.5 *cheti* each, but they already possessed 318 *cheti* granted to them to support their military service, so their paternal legacy served merely as icing on the cake.[43]

Gentrymen and -women managed to find and acquire abandoned, unclaimed lands (*porozzhie*) in their own immediate neighborhoods with great regularity. In many cases, the petitions or official inquiries into the current status of the plots explain the history of past ownership and how that land came to lie unclaimed. Occasionally people requested properties that the state had confiscated from previous owners for various misdeeds. In other cases, owners of *pomest'ia* had died without any heirs. In a case exemplifying both of these possible routes by which land fell vacant, Grigorii Buganovskoi, a foreigner enrolled in the tsar's service, requested the former *pomest'e* of a fellow foreigner, Matvei Svetitskoi. The land had been granted to Svetitskoi by the cadaster books of 1629/30 but had been taken from him the following year and granted to native Vladimir servitor Aleksei Bologovskoi. "Aleksei died without wife or children, and those unclaimed, deserted lands were not given to anyone as *pomest'e* or *votchina*." In response to Buganovskoi's petition, the Chancellery of Service Lands ordered the governor of Vladimir to dispatch a retired servitor to investigate and, if the land was unclaimed, to register it as requested.[44] In many other cases, official inquiries report the previous landlords of pieces of property without stating the reason for the lapse of ownership. Nikita Kablukov, for instance, profited by a grant of six *cheti* from the pool of "unclaimed land" in 1673. The village in question, Fediunkino in Shuia, had been granted to State Secretary (*d'iak*) Ivan Bolotnikov by an award of 1608/09 and in the interim had belonged to Semen Chemodanov and then Elizarei Redrikov. When and how these three previous owners vanished remains unstated.[45]

A petition of 1641 from the poor servitors of Arzamas, Suzdal', and Vladimir illustrates clearly that the Muscovite system of gentry landholding was constructed with the expectation that young men would accrue land independently over time, not relying entirely on inheritance alone. The poor young men of Arzamas appear to have taken the initiative in this matter, and then the Suzdalians and Vladimirites hopped on the bandwagon, appending their own lists of names and descriptions of their poverty to the Arzamas petition, which ran as follows:

> We, your slaves, poor Arzamas servitors with small and poor *pomest'e* estates, without slaves and without peasants, petition you. It has been ordered, Sovereign, that we, your slaves, should be in your Sovereign service in Moscow, and at this time we, your slaves, are wandering about in Moscow without anywhere to stay. We, your slaves, have nothing to eat, while in Arzamas, by the will of God, pestilence devastates us, and the spring grain came up withered with the drought. Merciful Sovereign . . .

have mercy upon us, your slaves. Order us, O Sovereign, to be released to Arzamas so that in the future we will not have to miss your Sovereign service.[46]

The names and assets of 30 indigent Suzdalians and 18 straitened Vladimirites appeared on sworn statements, which were signed by local *okladchiki* and glued to the Arzamas petition. Prominent among the names of the "destitute" were all of the local power brokers of the next few decades. Aleksei Fedorovich Kablukov, still young in 1641, had a generous theoretical entitlement to 400 *cheti* but had yet to accumulate laborers to work his land. He testified that his "*pomest'e* is empty—no peasants." Similarly, other future leaders of Suzdal', including four young Tregubov brothers, two Kazimerov cousins, and a collection of other familiar names, appeared on the list of those requesting service exemptions due to poverty.[47] All of these young men came from relatively high-ranking local families. Their fathers occupied the rank of *dvorovoi syn boiarskii* or selectman, ranks which the sons were likely to achieve or surpass by birthright alone. Youthful poverty, thus, signified a stage of life for this group of upwardly mobile young men in a system in which gentrymen were expected to acquire property in as many ways as possible during their lifetimes.

Members of the service gentry, then, did not rely solely on their fragmented inheritances for their economic support. Instead or in addition, they built their own fortunes, which might be enhanced by their fraction of their parental inheritance. Nor did they rely solely on the beneficence of the state. Provincial gentrymen and -women did not wait passively for the state to grant them pieces of land; as opportunities arose and properties became available, land-hungry provincials would submit requests to have those properties registered in their names. The records of an active market in land shows that property changed hands frequently as men sold, gave away, and traded bits of real estate. At least for the success stories, those families and individuals who survived to leave their marks as members of the gentry, the splintering process was apparently to a large extent counterbalanced by the accumulation of wealth and property during the lifetime of each generation, thus building the family fortune anew with each fresh start.

Not all gentry families, however, managed to counteract the deleterious effects of partible inheritance and the disintegration of estates. Already disadvantaged by the smaller estates with which they began, poorer members of the community could not benefit equally well from these tactics. Families could be torn apart by the need to find available lands to support numerous sons. Registration on the muster rolls of other towns, separate from their kinsmen (registration *v otvode*), frequently took elder sons out of the district and sentenced them to service with unfamiliar communities. When supplemental land grants did not come through or did not suffice, partible inheritance could destroy descendants of *gorodovye deti boiarskie* who inherited minuscule slivers of their fathers' subdivided estates. These unfortunates had to farm their own land for lack of serfs and thus eventually forfeited their prerogatives as military servitors. These were the kinds of marginal gentry who slipped out of the privileged category of hereditary servitors during the seventeenth century and disappeared into the lower service classes, banditry, or slavery.[48]

How destructive partible inheritance was to the economic well-being of the gentry is not altogether clear. Average landholdings, calculating *pomest'e* and *votchina* properties combined, do diminish by over 30 percent across the century in the limited sample of 718 cases for which I have fairly complete property figures. They decline from a mean of 120 *cheti* per individual in the beginning of the century (1600–20) to 80 *cheti* at the end (1681–1700). An even steeper decline is evident if landholders of Moscow rank are excluded, with the average holdings of people of provincial rank sinking from 114 *cheti* at the beginning of the century to 63 at the end.[49] Yet the causal link to partible inheritance is equivocal. Not only actual real estate holdings but also *oklady* (theoretical land entitlements) decline across the century, and the two follow parallel curves. Adjusting for the amount of land that the state allowed to each servitor, I find no discernable decrease in property totals. If theoretical entitlements dwindled through the century as average service rank increased, this suggests either that the state valued gentry service less as the century wore on, which would accord with Richard Hellie's theory of gentry servitors' midcentury crisis of impending military obsolescence, or that the state had to curtail grants of land because it had exhausted its land fund. Both of these factors appear to have contributed to the diminishing size of gentry landholding.[50]

In a system such as the one in Muscovy, where land remained available from a variety of sources, the effects of partible inheritance cannot be assessed in isolation. Division and subdivision of properties undoubtedly fractured traditional family holdings, with particularly harmful effects on the ancient *votchina* estates, which were expected to pass from generation to generation within a single family. For the average service gentryman, however, inherited clan *votchina* held little relevance. His lands consisted primarily of service land, *pomest'e*, with a small admixture of earned *votchina* (land converted from *pomest'e* to *votchina* by favor of the tsar, usually for extraordinary military service) and some purchased land. Throughout the seventeenth century, all three of these varieties of land remained available to supplement estates pared away by partible inheritance.

For the gentry class, partible inheritance was a way of life, and one with some negative effects on the financial stability of the landowners as a whole, but the practice reflected a deeply ingrained cultural expectation that all offspring should receive approximately equivalent shares of their patrimonial inheritance and should build up their estates independently from that base.

Moreover, Muscovites evidently held less fervent attachments to particular plots of land than those so romanticized among Western nobilities, so the dissolution of family estates had little emotional impact or relevance to status and standing. Although it is risky to venture into speculation about emotional attachments, provincial landholders displayed none of the multigenerational attachment to a single plot of land or an ancestral manor house that their Western, particularly English, counterparts displayed. They conformed to their general image in the historical literature in that they sold, traded, gave away, and exchanged land with one another at a rapid pace. Their lasting attachment was rather to the region at large. This difference in attitude appears to explain a good deal about gentry land practices. If the particular plot of land held no ritualized, sentimental significance, then parting with that land through sale or trade, or making the parental estate nonviable by subdivision, carried no onus. Heirs easily dissolved patrimonial holdings, dividing them or selling them as proved convenient, in order to sustain all of the claimants. If each heir received a mere sliver of land, in the context of a fluid land market, he or she could convert that sliver into cash and buy a more profitable bit elsewhere in the region, and shed no tears in the process.

It strikes me as very curious that we so often find the Muscovite system of partible inheritance to be peculiar relative to the primogeniture of aristocratic early-modern Europe. After all, the Muscovite version of the self-made man, the gentry servitor who accumulated his own wealth and property through labor and service, should resonate far more with current standards than the preservation and channeling of wealth inherent in the primogeniture system. Furthermore, in the modern West, most parents see it as their duty to provide for all of their children as well as possible, not to privilege one to the exclusion of the rest. Even in their treatment of female offspring, the Muscovites, with their insistence on nearly equal division of wealth among daughters as well as among sons, resemble the society we live in far more closely than do the seventeenth-century aristocrats of the West.

Clan Against Family: Widows and Female Ownership of Property

In the vast emerging literature on inheritance and the family in early-modern Europe, historians have identified two principles that consistently battled for dominance in regional norms and individual practice: those of the agnatic clan and the nuclear family. In Muscovy as elsewhere, the state faced the question of whether to preserve the holdings of extended clans in the male line in order to guarantee the viability of its noble warrior elite or to provide support for widows and children at the expense of clan holdings. Individual testators faced the same dilemma. Muscovite laws vascillated over the centuries, at times offering powerful protection to clan rights and at other times favoring widows.[51] A 1627 law that Ann Kleimola and others have pointed to as marking the sharp decline of women's legal rights to inherit property placed severe restrictions on the kinds of land that could be left to widows, and the 1649 Law Code elaborated on that law's prohibitions. According to these codes, widows could inherit a set, small percentage of their husband's *pomest'e* lands. Widows could also receive bequests of purchased *votchina* land (that is, lands bought by their husbands). But they were categorically denied rights to the two other varieties of *votchina* property: hereditary clan *votchina* and earned *votchina* (granted for meritorious service).

In practice, these constraints had little impact on the widows of the petty gentry of the Vladimir-Suzdal' region. The restrictions on the more prestigious forms of *votchina* were largely irrelevant, as petty gentrymen held little land in those categories anyway. When these gentrymen did have earned *votchina* land, they occasionally

TABLE 3.1

Women's Property in Vladimir-Suzdal', 1600–1702

Kind of property	No. of cases	Pct.	Kind of property	No. of cases	Pct.
Pomest'e	82	64%	Hereditary *votchina*	0	0%
Unspecified "*votchina*"	29	22	Unspecified "land"	6	5
Purchased *votchina*	6	5	TOTAL	128	100%
Earned *votchina*	5	4			

SOURCES: *RNB, Ermitazhnoe sobranie*, no. 343/2, *ll.* 21, 25 ob-26, 29–31; *Muzeinoe sobranie*, *f.* 178, no. 1393, *ll.* 7 ob, 8, 10, 13-13 ob; *f.* 532, nos. 368, 668, 826, 829, 985, 1046, 1061, 1062, 1103, 1717. *SPbFIRI, f.* 62, *Koll. Kablukova*, nos. 62, 63, 113, 128, 152, 157, 170, 181, 225; 261; *f.* 21, *Koll. Borisova*, nos. 169, 185, 320, 370, 459, 477, 494, 495, 496, 607, 626; *f.* 252, *Suzdal'skie akty*, no. 20. Khilkov, *Sbornik kniazia Khilkova*, no. 55, pp. 146–48. *RGADA, f.* 1112, *opis'* 1, nos. 5, 10, 12, 15, 17, 44, 47, 55–57, 62, 63A–B, 67, 70, 81, 83, 92, 99, 103, 106, 108, 111, 114, 116, 130, 131, 133, 138, 139, 141, 142, 164–166; *f.* 210, *opis'* 4, *Dela desiaten'*, bk. 302, *l.* 79; *f.* 210, *Prikaznyi stol*, no. 819, *ll.* 125-128, no. 863, *ll.* 118-138; *f.* 210, *Vlad. stol, stlb.* 63, *ll.* 55, 56, 67, 72; *stlb.* 73, *l.* 388, *stlb.* 132, *l.* 86; *stlb.* 159, *l.* 6. *AAE*, vol. 3, no. 174. *AIuB*, vol. 3, no. 334, pt. ix-x, cols. 300–303. *ChOIDR*, 1847, no. 5, *Smes'*, pp. 21–24. *Sbornik starinnkh bumag, khraniashchikhsia v muzee P. I. Shchukina*, 2: 157–59, 269–70. Stashevskii, *Zemlevladenie. VGV*, 1856, no. 29, 1857, nos. 7, 11, 1858, no. 3. *Vremennik OIDR*, 1852, bk. 15, *Smes'* 23–30, pp. 24–25.

left it to their widows or daughters in spite of the law.[52] In the Kablukov family, for instance, Aleksei Fedorovich included in his daughter Maria's dowry one of the forms of real estate expressly forbidden to female heirs: an earned *votchina* and manor house in Suzdal' Province, in the traditional family stronghold in Deminskii District. In addition, the young couple received icons, clothing, jeweled belts and buttons, bowls, crosses, furs, and serving women.[53] In his sample of testaments, Kaiser finds that women rarely controlled the forbidden categories of property. Of his sample, only two female testators (5 percent) bequeathed earned *votchina* estates to their heirs, and only a single woman had a hereditary *votchina* in her possession to bequeath.[54] Very similar results emerge from my sample of 128 property-owning women in Vladimir-Suzdal' (see Table 3.1).

The great majority of women who held property held *pomest'e* land, the kind of property that the state favored as the means for providing widows' and daughters' maintenance allotments. This was not a difficult role for the provincial gentry to follow, as its holdings consisted primarily of service land (*pomest'e*), not *votchina*. Legal limits on the percentage of *pomest'e* that a widow could inherit were also irrelevant because they were flagrantly ignored by testators and claimants, and the oversized claims of widows were routinely confirmed by state authorities. In only two cases in my sample group was a widow denied any part of her husband's estate because it exceeded her legal quota. In one of these cases, the widow proved to be exorbitantly wealthy by local standards, holding 240 *cheti* scattered in a number of provinces, so she would scarcely have missed the meager 19 *cheti* that she was forced to cede to one of her late husband's impoverished relatives.[55]

In principle, childless widows fared worst of all in the Muscovite pecking order. The church frowned upon remarriage, and property laws discouraged removing land from one male lineage to another through a widow's remarriage. Several articles of the 1649 Law Code insisted that a widow's land return to her first husband's line if she remarried.[56] According to most writings on the subject, brides remained outsiders, grudgingly tolerated in their husbands' and in-laws' households until they produced heirs to the family line. If still childless on the death of her husband, a widow was entitled to receive only her dowry or its equivalent, with some annual increment, and was unceremoniously returned to her own kin.

In fact, however, childless gentry widows frequently fared quite nicely in the central provinces. Young widows easily converted their substantial widow's portions into attractive dowries for second marriages. Boris Orlov's widow took nearly half of his Suzdal' estate with her when she married another Suzdalian servitor in 1633/34.[57] Stepan Kurov's daughter Fedora proceded along a similarly lucrative marriage path. She married Dmitrii Sychov in 1663/64 with a dowry of 55 *cheti* granted by her father. When Sychov died seven years later, she almost doubled her investment. She received her original dowry back, along with an additional 50 *cheti* bequeathed to her by her late husband. With this new affluence, she married a second time.[58] Vasilii Voeikov's widow evidently did not anticipate that she would remarry, because she ceded her maintenance allotment to her nephew Fedor Oshcherin after Voeikov's death. When she then became engaged to marry *striapchii* Ivan Rzhevskoi, she changed her mind and retrieved her land in order to turn it over to her new spouse.[59] Neither the nephew nor the courts complained about the breach of contract involved. The woman in my sample who profited most by the remarriage racket, Ogafia Soboleva, married three times, each time augmenting her holdings and her standing. She came from a family with holdings and long-time affiliations in the Suzdal' region. Her first husband, also a Suzdalian, left her 67 *cheti* in *votchiny* scattered through three provinces. Her second, not a local man, topped up her real estate portfolio with a hefty addition of 133 *cheti*, which allowed her to attract a rich and prestigious Moscow-rank man for her third and final husband.[60] These childless widows took land from the male line without encountering any opposition either from kinsmen or from the state.[61]

The generous endowment of widows bespeaks both a pervasive cultural expectation that they should be well supported and a strong element of choice on the part of their husbands and families. Studies of Western European aristocracies have established that families often provided large dowries to their daughters reluctantly, yielding to the unpleasant necessity of purchasing suitable mates for daughters in a highly inflated dowry market. High dowry figures, therefore, often made daughters objects of male relatives' fear and resentment and cannot necessarily serve as indicators of a family's emotional attachment to its daughters or of parental generosity. Magnanimous provisions for widows, on the other hand, particularly when those widows were free to use their holdings as second dowries, resulted more from choice than from necessity and indicate that Muscovite landholders placed high value on maintaining members of the immediate family.

Not all widows managed to play the system with equal success. As discussed above, some widows forfeited title to whatever land their husbands might have left in excess of the appropriate widow's portion. Others lost in struggles with surviving male relatives on the husband's side. Anna, widow of Prokofii Izmailov, emerged from her marriage with nothing at all. Two of her husband's relatives, some sort of cousins, divided the 440 *cheti* of earned *votchina* he left behind, allocating nothing to her.[62]

While the allocation of property to female heirs among the Vladimir-Suzdal' gentry ranged widely—from 100 percent of the paternal estate going to the daughter or widow in some instances when there were no sons to nothing at all in a number of cases in which sons or nephews inherited—the overall means for the 98 women and 620 men for whom I have quantifiable landholding figures (as opposed to the figures on division of estates discussed above) suggest that women held between one-third and one-half as much land as their male counterparts in the seventeenth century.[63] Female landholders averaged 77 *cheti* in combined *pomest'e* and *votchina* properties, while males averaged 237 *cheti*, a ratio of one to three. If the landholdings of men and women of Moscow-rank families are excluded, the ratios are closer: 85 women whose husbands were of provincial rank averaged half as much land as their 445 male coun-

terparts (67 to 134 *cheti*). Much of the women's property may have
been held in usufruct during the women's lifetimes, reverting to their
sons or brothers-in-law on their deaths, but much male property
ownership was similarly restricted. The evidence of remarriage further suggests that life-tenure restrictions must have been easily
waived if they had been imposed in the first place, because widows
were able to transfer permanent rights to their new husbands and any
future children. Considering that women were categorically excluded from service, the primary means of obtaining land in their
service-based society, the significant proportion of land under their
control indicates that their families went to considerable effort to
secure property for them by private means.

Most Vladimir-Suzdal' gentrywomen appear to have held at least
some land. Of the 210 women who appear in seventeenth-century
documents from the region, 69 percent (146) are explicitly listed as
landholders of one sort or another, whether as inheritors, recipi-
ents of dowries, purchasers, or holders of *prozhitochyne* (dowagers'
portions). These figures are much higher than those found in other
studies of Muscovite property holding by gender. Daniel Kaiser's preliminary study of women's property in Muscovite families from 1500
to 1725 shows that few women controlled property.[64] Unlike the
women in Kaiser's sample, many Vladimir-area gentrywomen were
landholders, and their shares in their parents' and husbands' estates
seem to have been significantly higher than Kaiser's figures would
suggest. With such divergent figures available, assessing the status of
women as property holders becomes difficult. The statistical profile
presented here may represent a peculiar regional variant on a very
different national pattern, or the sources may somehow skew the
study. Some of the disparity may result from differences in source
bases and populations studied. (Kaiser's sample includes nongentry
and sixteenth-century cases.) Whatever the differences in figures signify, the number of cases in which daughters and sons shared their
inheritance indicates that the tradition of partible inheritance for all
heirs, female as well as male, held sway in Vladimir-Suzdal' throughout the seventeenth century. The high rate of female landholding
suggests that inheritance practice favored surviving widows and
daughters over close kin in the male line, uncles and cousins, whose
claims should have been at least equivalent to the women's by law.
What is more striking, the custom of bestowing large amounts of
real estate on women persisted in defiance of increasingly restric-

tive laws, which set limits on the amount and kinds of land that women could own. A handful of women received the forbidden earned *votchina* land in their dowries or by inheritance.[65] Every one of the female landholders in the admittedly small sample of women whose property can be traced back to a paternal or fraternal estate received a bequest far exceeding the percentage advised by the 1649 Law Code. Moreover, the courts of the state chancelleries persisted in confirming the transfer of large quantities of land of all varieties to women, in spite of the state's ostensible effort to curb the drain of property from the service pool.

Local Marriage and the Ramifications of Female Inheritance

Early-modern Western commentators worried a good deal about the dangers of frittering away gentry estates by dispersing them through the female line. Christiane Klapisch-Zuber documents how jealously Renaissance Florentine families monitored the dowries that they gave out to their daughters and how ferociously they repossessed their wealth if a daughter was widowed. "In Florence, men *were* and *made* the 'houses.' . . . Kinship was determined by men, and the male branching of genealogies drawn up by contemporaries shows how little importance was given, after one or two generations, to kinship through women."[66] Kenneth Lockridge, in discussing what he calls "the sources of patriarchal rage" in eighteenth-century America, points to male anxieties about "leakage" of property and wealth from the agnatic clan to outsiders through exorbitant marriage portions.[67] Historians of Muscovy picked up on this anxiety about female inheritance expressed in European literatures and legislation, adding it to their existing dismay at the fracturing effects of partible inheritance.

The only people who seem not to have worried in the slightest about the risks involved in leaving land in the hands of women were the Muscovite landholders themselves. What allowed them to persevere in their habit so serenely, when other contemporary elites fretted and devised complicated customs of entail limiting female rights to land and property? Pleasant as it would be to conclude that Muscovites had a more egalitarian view of women than did their Western counterparts, passing acquaintance with Russian folklore and the tenets of Orthodoxy preclude such a notion. Vituperative misogyny was very much a part of Muscovite church teachings, literature, and popular culture.[68] One must look elsewhere to explain the Muscovites' relative indifference to female inheritance, and marriage practices offer an important key for solving the puzzle.

Marriage practices contributed greatly to solidifying and reinforcing local communities, as statistical analysis reveals in a dramatic way. Marriage within a single province overwhelmingly predominated among those that I have been able to trace in my region. In 78 percent of traceable marriages, both partners came from families that were well established in the area prior to the match.[69] The numbers involved here are admittedly small: a total of 76 cases can be tallied to discover marriage patterns as practiced by the provincial gentry and to determine whether its members married within their local communities or sought spouses from the outside.[70] Although the sample is limited, the figures are unequivocal. Of the 76 marriages, 59 (78 percent) joined two families previously established in at least one of the five provinces of the region. Further, of those 59 marriages, all but 5 conjoined residents of a single province; that is, Suzdalians married Suzdalians and Vladimirites married Vladimirites (see Table 3.2).

In general, families of equal wealth and position intermarried. Thus, those owning land in multiple provinces tended to marry into families with equivalent landholdings, and those of Moscow rank for the most part chose others of Moscow rank or women of high local standing. Poorer, rank-and-file provincial gentry families married among themselves, with both partners usually owning land in only one (and the same) province. Using Moscow rank as an identifier of social groupings, the sample group displays 76 percent of marriages occurring between families of equal stature and only 24 percent crossing that barrier of rank (see Table 3.3).

TABLE 3.2

*Families Established in the Vladimir-Suzdal'
Region Prior to Marriage*

Family	No.	Pct.
Man's only	4	5%
Woman's only	13	17
Both	59	78
TOTAL	76	100%

SOURCES: Author's compilation.
NOTES: See note 69. Where regional origins were unclear, families were classed as nonlocal.

TABLE 3.3
Marriages Between Moscow-Rank and Non-Moscow-Rank Families

Type of marriage	No.	Pct.
Between different social categories	18	24%
Husband (or his immediate family) of Moscow rank only	15	20
Wife's immediate family of Moscow rank only	3	4
Within same social category	56	76%
Both families of Moscow rank	14	19
Neither family of Moscow rank	42	57
TOTAL	74	100%

SOURCES: *RGADA, f.* 1112, *opis'* 1, nos. 10, 17, 44, 51, 55, 57, 63 (A), 63 (B), 67, 69, 77, 81, 103, 106, 107, 108, 111, 114, 131, 139, 142, 165, 166; *RGADA, f.* 210, *Prikaznyi stol,* no. 273, fols. 972–89 v; *SPbFIRI, f.* 62, *Koll. Kablukova,* nos. 51, 52–56, 63, 100, 117, 127, 138, 181, 191, 200, 225, 261; *SPbFIRI, f.* 21, *Koll. Borisova,* nos. 496, 553, 626; *RNB, f.* 532, nos. 447, 668, 829, 1717, 3055; *RNB, Ermitazhnoe sobranie,* no. 343/2, *l.* 29; *AIuB,* vol. 3, no. 334, pt. ix–x; Ikonnikov, *Noblesse de la Russe,* vol. Y, pp. 227–35; "Riadnaia rospis' "; *VGV,* 1856, no. 29.

The numbers bear out the pattern seen in the tale of Iuliania Lazarevskaia, discussed in Chapter 2: provincial gentrymen routinely married within their immediate local community. Even on rising to Moscow rank, the men within this sample usually returned to their roots when seeking a bride. Families could use their daughters as stepladders to higher circles and occasionally negotiated marriages between their daughters and well-placed men from other towns. Even in these cases, however, the women's offspring might retain an interest in their mother's native town through her dowry lands. The norm for marriages remained intensely local, contributing to the strength of localism and regional loyalty among the provincial gentry.

At times the practice of local marriage was followed so rigidly that the situation became untenable. In 1639, for instance, an official decree banned exchanges of land between local landowners and men of Moscow rank, which made it impossible to transfer dowry property to high-ranking men from other provinces. Provincial families complained that without the incentive of dowries, Moscow-rank men refused to marry provincial women. They wrote that "in the towns there is no one to marry to the widows and girls, because in their own towns widows and girls are closely related to many people, but it is forbidden to give *pomest'ia* in the towns to men of Moscow rank, and so it is impossible to betroth widows and girls to them, . . . [Reverse this decree] so that the widows and girls will not remain unmarried."[71] That particular decree was soon overturned. The practice of local marriage, which had created a situation in which many residents of a province were related by blood, marriage, or godparentage, both predated and outlasted the decree of 1639.

Muscovite parents and legators evidently did not suffer from the kind of anxiety about parting with their patrimonies that many Western European societies displayed in the early-modern period. Local marriage, in conjunction with the nature of gentry landholding, provided a safeguard against dissipation of landed property in a society in which custom and expectation demanded relatively equal partition of estates among all immediate family members. Partible inheritance and female landholdings were not problematic issues, situated as they were in a specific cultural and economic context in Muscovy. The distinguishing characteristics of that cultural context become clear if we recall the prevalence of local rather than scattered landholding and the absence of sentimental attachment to particular manorial estates, and then add these factors to the practice of local, class-confined marriage and remarriage. While other cultures fretted about loss of property through the female line, Muscovite gentry families had little cause for concern. In the short term a family might lose by giving out sizable dowries, but in the long run, in such a closed system, "what goes around, comes around." If a sister married and took local properties out of the family, a brother would soon marry and bring other local properties back into the family. No emotional charge was spent if particular pieces of real estate left the family's possession, and the properties could be replaced with others. The combination of marriage exclusively within the ranks of landholders and the high likelihood of local marriage meant that specific pieces of real estate might change hands, but, overall, local landholders would remain local landholders. The costs and dangers posed by female inheritance were thus radically reduced.

Other practices also facilitated female property holding without undue costs to patriarchal society. Local marriage, remarriage, *inter vivos* transfer of property, bequests to offspring and relatives, and taxation and conscription all kept women's lands in circulation and actively supporting military and administrative servitors of the tsarist state. All of these practices contributed to the continued support and well-being of the service gentry as a class and as a local community. Women may have given land to monasteries at a somewhat higher rate than men, but still most of their land stayed very much in circulation.[72] Even when a widow insisted on holding onto her real estate until her death, the land did not escape entirely from the state's service requirements. Whatever his or her service capabilities, every landholder had an obligation either to provide a mounted warrior to perform military service or to contribute toward hiring an alternate. Town governors carefully surveyed the holdings of widows and young children in order to assess them for the number of conscripts they owed or the amount they should pay in service equivalency. For instance, a survey carried out in Lukh in 1626 found that Agafia, Ivan Alferev's widow, had a maintenance *pomest'e* of eighteen *cheti* with ten peasants and five cottars. From her land, together with that of an orphaned neighbor boy and two other widows, "two conscripts [*datochnye*] were taken on horses with bows and arrows and swords." Domna, Ivan Oshanin's wife, "has a one and a half year old son. Her maintenance *pomest'e* is 130 *cheti*, unpopulated. No conscripts were taken from her because her land is empty and the sovereign so ordered."[73] This latter case has particular poignancy because in that same year, Ivan Oshanin had been murdered by his brother-in-law, who had then disappeared, abandoning his sister and her small son.[74]

For individual families, especially ones rich in daughters and poor in sons, marriage and widows' portions could still pose a threat, seriously depleting the family's holdings and alienating important resources from the family coffers. Calculated marriage policies, strategic supervision of family properties, and foreclosure on loans could, at times, counteract those processes. The rapacious Kablukovs never willingly parted with property. At the very end of the century, in 1699, Petr Nikitich Kablukov recited the history of previous ownership of his peasants for officials who were investigating his property rights. He declared that some of his peasants in Shuia Province, Deminskii district, had formerly belonged to his grandfather Aleksei Fedorovich. Others in the same district had been given to Gavrilo Semenovich Dolgovo-Saburov as part of the dowry portion he received when he married Luker'ia Alekseevna Kablukova. After Dolgovo-Saburov's death in 1689/90, his widow sold her dowry lands and peasants back to her brother Nikita, who then left it to his eldest son. Thus, the land given out as dowry returned to the family within a single generation.[75]

Another instance involved Maria Nikiforovna Kablukova and her daughter Praskov'ia Pimenovna, whose precise relationship to the Kablukov family is unclear. (Praskov'ia must have been Maria's daughter by an earlier marriage, because no Pimen Kablukov appears in the family genealogy.) A 1683 marriage agreement records Maria's contract to give her daughter, and a dowry consisting of a share of the village Babkino, to Iur'i Akinf'evich Vysotskii. Three years later, the same Vysotskii ceded a peasant family in Babkino to Nikita Kablukov, some kind of step-cousin by marriage. According to the document, Vystotskii acted voluntarily, and no recompense is mentioned. The Kablukovs may well have applied pressure to return one of their peasant households.[76] Generous in the dowries they bestowed on their daughters, the Kablukovs pounced on any opportunity to regain title to lands when they became available. Aided by natural attrition and perhaps by the ferocity of their women, the family was fortunate in the fact that most of the men who married into the family died young and without heirs. This allowed dowry properties to return to the fold undisputed.

Muscovite gentry landholders remained fundamentally uninterested in any potential problems posed by female inheritance of land. Embedded in a culture in which partible inheritance was the norm and nuclear families were highly valued, in a landed economy in which plots of land circulated rapidly within a largely closed circle of local landowning families, and in a landscape devoid of the mossy stone castles of ancient family seats, the gentry had no particular reason to view female landholding as a threat. The issue was not strongly differentiated in Muscovite custom from partible inheritance among male heirs, and neither assumed much significance as a problem of any urgency until Peter the Great attempted, unsuccessfully, to force the nobility to adopt the alien notion of unigeniture.

In all of these regards, the Vladimir-Suzdal' gentrymen and -women assume a very different cast from that generally attributed to them in the literature. The fluid land market suggests a vibrant economy quite independent from the state and its service-related land grants. The evidence of exchange and inheritance of *pomest'e* estates shows that although still officially recognized as conditional service grants, *pomest'e* lands had passed almost fully into the hands of the gentry, taking on the coloration of family rather than state property. Official acceptance of provincial inheritance practices indicates that interactions between state officials and local society were elastic, and adaptable to community pressures and requirements. Autocratic control enters very little into the picture, while community norms and individual decisions exercise far greater force. In the early-modern equivalent of a "civil society," evolving within the particular constraints of autocratic rule and in the absence of institutionalized civil associations or print culture, the provincial gentry conducted its local and familial business in a distinctly social sphere.

What do all of these insights into Muscovite inheritance practices show about the function of autocracy in the provinces? They illustrate three significant and unexplored aspects of the relationship between autocrat and servitors. First, they show that the pattern of clan politics of the boyars and princes in the Kremlin had little bearing on the petty landholders of the provinces. The nuclear family, something far more similar to what we know today than to the great boyar houses of Moscow, was the relevant unit, and the Muscovite notion of family included both sexes. It did not at all replicate the agnatic network of males that comprised the great patriarchal lineages in the capital.

Second, this evidence of the centrality of family demonstrates that, when an issue mattered deeply, the "spineless" gentry was ready to resist, and the state to capitulate, without any hesitation. What truly mattered to members of the Vladimir-Suzdal' gentry, evidently, was family, defined as male and female relatives in the first degree, and spouses, but not extended male kin. When laws constricted parents' rights to secure good marriages and stable futures for their daughters or to set up their widows comfortably, gentry fathers and husbands simply ignored the law. Seemingly acknowledging the state's inefficacy or irrelevance in this sphere of life, local governors and chancellery staff of the central bureaus routinely approved and registered transactions that violated both the spirit and the letter of the law.

Third, this insight into what truly mattered to members of the provincial gentry sheds new light on the traditional question posed by Western observers concerning the Muscovite gentry's seeming lack of interest in political participation. The focus on the immediate family and its preservation may confirm as well as help to explain this lack of interest in the politics of the center. Domestic security and prosperity for offspring mattered far more than Moscow politics or clan status. The preservation of family comprised the central goal of political life, involving marriage politics, land politics, and local maneuvering. It mattered so much that gentry families were willing to face down the tsarist state, its functionaries, and its legal system. In this quiet confrontation, the autocratic state was the one to blink.

Autocracy functioned marvelously well in the Muscovite provinces, in large measure because of its ability to accommodate a sphere of autonomous action for the locally based elite. This area of early-modern life, for which we lack appropriate terminology, served many of the same functions as the public sphere of the eighteenth-century West, allowing society to express and enact its views in contradistinction to those of the state and to negotiate satisfactory solutions to problems that it considered important without resorting to those more modern and Western implements provided by print culture and openly critical discussion.

In comparison with Western gentries, the Muscovite gentry's focus on the material standing of the nuclear family and its interactions with the state over this issue set the outlines for its very different political development. Muscovite concepts of "gentlemanly" conduct did not revolve around responsible civic virtue or political participation. Nor did concern over local standing produce interest in solidifying local institutions. Instead, members of the Muscovite gentry concentrated their efforts to gain local power on acquiring land and consolidating status for their families. Their interactions with the state were functional, goal-oriented, and short term. When no particular issue provoked their interest, members of the gentry were content to stay at home. The responsiveness of the state, and the mediation of relations with the state through personal relations with particular officials, allowed the gentry to achieve its goals without articulating them in political or institutional terms. Yet the gentry's actions resulted in de facto if not de jure policy changes. Thus, for example, state legislation against female ownership of land accumulated on the books at the same time that land of all kinds accumulated in female hands.

CHAPTER 4

Intersecting Authorities: State and Community Officials in Their Local Context

Between the local community with its inward-looking concerns and the tsarist government with its claims to universal control stood an array of officials, bureaucrats, clerks, and agents. Although in principle representing the power of the tsar in the local environment, these officials frequently acted on their own authority or that of segments of the community in varying measure according to the circumstances. Situated at the crossroads between state and local power structures, local officials personified the tension and overlap between local and central interests. Delegated by an increasingly regularized chancellery system, entrusted with enforcing the tsar's law to the letter, officials instead made themselves comfortable in the communities that they administered, functioning by various combinations of accommodation, co-optation, intimidation, exploitation, flexibility, and personal ties.

On first examination, Moscow seemed to exercise phenomenal control over even the minutia of provincial life. Yet, at every level, the state and its control mechanisms proved incapable of regulating people's actions. Unable to command all aspects of local life, the state tolerated some manipulation of positions of power on the part of its provincial representatives, so long as taxes were collected, service obligations performed, and the important items on the governmental agenda satisfied. Moscow left regional officers to work out the details of distribution and collection of fees and duties on the local level. The center apparently shrugged its shoulders and turned away, conceding the particulars of micromanagement to the local community.

In light of this complex and contradictory assessment of Muscovite state power, the strategic position of tsarist officials at the intersection of state and society offers a useful way of untangling the seeming contradictions. The concurrent power and impotence of the state, the simultaneous tight control and chronic anarchy in the provinces, all flowed from the kinds of indeterminate and multi-faceted affiliations characteristic of provincial officials. In the fusion of their official and personal identities, chancellery officials, governors, and local authorities embodied the eliding of social and administrative spheres, the multiplicity of tracks, loyalties, interests and structures that composed the far-from-unified entity that we label "the state." The multiple roles of intermediary officials underscore the extent to which the categorical divisions between "state" and "society" serve as useful constructs but have never held rigid, clearly divisible content. The two categories permeated each other and the margins between them blurred. The interpenetration of state and society suggests a way to rephrase the question of Muscovite state power, to view its ability to govern the provinces through a hybrid, early-modern form of effectivity.

Indeed, recent work on early-modern Western European monarchies has shown similarly that the clear boundaries previously assumed to have been established in this period between center and periphery or between state and society often dissolve on closer inspection. In the context of early-modern England, Michael Braddick critiques the "tendency to reify the state or to consider it as a purely institutional phenomenon. This obscures the function of the state as one of a range of social institutions through which people try to pursue their interests."[1] By accommodating the interests of local notables, new monarchies, with "a degree of normative consensus and organizational co-ordination," arose across Europe. The nature of the consensus varied among countries. In England, the voluntary cooperation of provincial elites in a participatory, self-regulating, diffuse system built a strong and effective central state. In France, consensus derived more from the distribution of office, wealth, and privilege than from the integrating effects of self-rule. Both arrangements allowed for the growth of a reciprocal relationship between provincial elites and the crown and their joint participation in building a powerful state.[2]

This broader view of what constituted "the state" in early-modern monarchies also demands a fresh look at the nature of "society." Although Muscovy lacked a term to designate "society" until the late seventeenth century, provincial communities had an important voice in shaping events and relationships on the local scene, whether by bribing or co-opting officials sent by the state, uniting in opposition to particularly indigestible officials and decrees, or simply ignoring the mandates of the center. Thus society assumed an active role in interactions with the state, all of which were mediated by individuals, officials situated both within the local community and between that community and the state. The ubiquitous background presence of state regulations, demands and claims indisputably set Muscovite provincial society apart from the Habermasian concept of a civil society, defined as an arena of civil transaction autonomous from the control of the state.[3] Nonetheless, local voices joined in active dialogue with the state and its representatives. Such voices did not always ring out in harmony, and the power of local notables to alter the score might redound to the detriment of opposing factions or classes in the provinces, but the presence of those voices as an integral, active, and accepted part of the Muscovite administrative system cuts significantly against views of Muscovite society as either passive and powerless or blindly anarchic. By problematizing certain aspects of the work of the state, and by setting aside the binary oppositions that normally structure the debate on the nature of state power, we can approach these questions from a different angle, measuring the efficacy of central control not *against* but rather *with* a component of local control, assessing autocracy as a system inclusive rather than exclusive of pockets of local autonomy and community participation.

Administrative Structure

Notorious for its irrationality, duplication, and jurisdictional confusion, the Muscovite administrative system would be impossible to contain on a flow chart. Various chancelleries combined judicial, administrative, and financial functions, and their jurisdictions were allotted on a variety of bases, some territorial, some functional, some according to the social or service standing of a population group. Despite the dizzying array and mind-boggling divisions and overlaps of jurisdictions, the administrative system served state ends quite

well, according to some evaluations. Moreover, the high level of redundancy built in an important element of malleability in the judicial and administrative systems, providing another dimension to the
provincial gentry's ability to manipulate the centralized tsarist bureaucracy to local ends. Litigants navigated their way through the
complex court system, choosing judges who were most favorably
disposed toward them and venues most likely to produce the desired
results. Duplication of jurisdictions offered gentrymen valuable
flexibility in prosecuting their cases.

The law code of 1550 assigned provincial servitors to the jurisdiction of provincial governors, but jurisdictional lines were rarely
clear-cut in Muscovy.[4] Major officials in provincial towns, most notably the *voevoda* (governor), were appointed by the central chancelleries in Moscow and were dispatched to the locales to carry out the
orders of the center in the peripheries. Governors and *chetverti* (territorial administrative units or chancelleries) shared their hazily divided authority over provincial territories.[5] Even if a case clearly
belonged to the jurisdiction of a governor, sometimes it was unclear
which one. In administrative terms, Shuia fell almost entirely under
the jurisdiction of Suzdal' but still had its own local bureaucratic
machine and governor. Similarly, Lukh and Iur'ev Pol'skii were subordinated in some respects to the governors of their larger neighboring towns, Suzdal' and Vladimir.

As provincial residents, members of the gentry were subordinated
to the local governor in minor local affairs, but as members of the
hereditary service class they fell under the jurisdiction of a number of
central Moscow chancelleries, depending on which facet of life and
service was involved. The gentry could turn to the courts of the
Chancellery of Service Lands with disputes or questions concerning
property rights. The Chancellery of Military Affairs was in charge of
the gentry's military service obligations and adjudicated any cases
remotely connected with service performance or capability. The
spheres of influence of these various authorities coincided in many
areas, particularly concerning the financial status of the gentry,
whose landed wealth was the concern of the Chancellery of Service
Lands but whose economic viability was the concern of the Chancellery of Military Affairs. The local governor's court often served as the
court of first instance for the Chancellery of Military Affairs, while
the Service Land Chancellery occasionally sent out special agents to
resolve land disputes in the peripheries. The next stage of the judicial

process, appeals or official summonses to higher courts for review, brought litigants and witnesses to the capital for trial in one of the chancellery headquarters. These second-stage proceedings could be conducted either by the Military or Service Land Chancelleries or at one of two special courts of appeal for military servitors, the Vladimir Judicial Chancellery or the Moscow Judicial Chancellery.[6] The welter of agencies competing for control over the Vladimir-Suzdal' area and the local service population, instead of crushing regional particularism or local variation under a surfeit of bureaucratic centralism, gave provincials a wide choice of authorities among whom to maneuver and negotiate for the most favorable terms.

Jurisdictions duplicated each other and overlapped, leaving officials themselves baffled as to which chancellery should adjudicate which disputes and which official should shoulder which responsibilities. Such traits, however, were shared by all early-modern states and were crucial aspects of successful administration at the time. Confusing and shifting jurisdictional boundaries were the product of a political culture based on personal bonds of kinship and favoritism, mediated by state and local officials who operated as representatives of both state and local interests, with strong ties in each world.

State Officials in Their Community Context: The Town Governors

Historians have conventionally viewed local administration as the site of a power struggle between the center, with its regulations and mandates, and various disruptive forces in the provinces. In some accounts, the central state attempts to assert order and control over outlying regions that are characterized by corrupt particularism and arbitrariness. Other accounts reverse the roles and portray the center as the bearer of arbitrary oppression and provincial communities as forces of democratic representation. At the center of any discussion of provincial administration in seventeenth-century Muscovy is the figure of the *voevoda*, the town governor. This position and its corresponding clerical staff filled an ambiguous and multifaceted slot in Muscovite perceptions of the nature of provincial governance. At the first level of generalization, the town governor represented the power of the central state on the local scene. In principle, he was an outsider with no ties to the community, serving the interests of the tsar and his chancelleries. In this capacity the governor was endowed with tremendous power on the local scene as the envoy of the tsar himself and of the central chancellery system, but the governor's ability to abuse that power posed a threat to central control. Fearing the governors' tendency to turn the provinces into their own feeding troughs, the state simultaneously conferred great authority on them and hobbled them with requirements to refer all decision making to the center.

Other contradictions and ambiguities complicated the position of town governor. Although as an agent of the state the governor was legally required to be an outsider to the community, many governors participated in the internal structure of local power and patronage.[7] Thus, the role of the town governor itself embodied the kinds of tensions inherent in relations between central and provincial administration: the governor both represented and undermined state power in the provinces; he represented state interests, local interests and his own personal interests; he was both an insider and an outsider to the community he governed; his authority in the province was absolute, but shared in indefinite ways by many other agencies and hampered by state regulation.

The office of *voevoda* was created to fill the vacuum in local administration left after the abolition of *namestniki* or vicegerents in the mid–sixteenth century. In the early centuries of Muscovite rule, leading boyars and princes had been granted vicegerencies in provincial localities on a *kormlenie* or "feeding" basis; that is, they were to provide minimal governance to their appointed regions and in return were authorized to support, or "feed," themselves fully by exacting food and revenues from the local population. Partially to curb these exactions and partially in response to the inefficacy of *namestnik* control, Ivan the Terrible's regime phased out the vicegerents and established systems of local tax-collection, the *zemskii* system, and local policing and justice, the *guba* system described below. These specialized units, however, did not fill all of the coordinating administrative and military functions required for local governance, and so gradually during the tumultuous years of the Time of Troubles, *voevody* were appointed to head critical provincial regions. The *voevoda* served as an all-in-one military-administrative official who combined the functions of local governor and regimental commander and served under more restricted mandates than the *namestniki*, with more regularized methods of remuneration. By the

1620s, the institution had spread throughout the tsardom and *voevody* headed not only key militarized areas but all of the Muscovite provinces.

From the very beginning of the seventeenth century, the five provinces of this study each fell under the jurisdiction of the governor of the major town in the area. All five of the towns fit the pattern of administration for towns of the Muscovite heartland as opposed to that of militarized border areas, where the strategic importance of the fortress towns endowed governors with significantly more autonomy and responsibility than in the placid central provinces. Town governors were appointed by the Chancellery of Military Affairs or the territorial chancelleries. Once in office, they provided administrative leadership in their assigned districts and served nominally as regional military commanders, although in the sheltered, interior provinces of the Vladimir-Suzdal' area invasion was not a problem after the Time of Troubles. Governors received their assignments in the same way that they might receive other military commissions. Chancelleries granted town governorships to members of the upper- or middle-service-class ranks of the service elite exclusively. Governorship of a town counted in the complex honorific hierarchy at the same level as court service and so was usually allotted to men of Moscow rank.[8]

Because they were safe, comfortable, and at least relatively prestigious and lucrative, town governorships were considered desirable posts. Because the state could not spare able-bodied men for administrative positions, however, governorships in nonmilitarized towns, such as the ones in the Vladimir-Suzdal' region, were reserved for long-term veterans and the disabled.[9] A decree in 1661 declared that henceforth only men wounded in service, former captives of war, or meritorious retirees would be rewarded with peaceful administrative posts instead of active military duty.[10] This regulation seems to have been obeyed, or at least such men were favored when competition arose for a certain position. An instance in Shuia in 1662 illustrates this preferential principle at work:

> In Shuia: Ivan Iakovlevich Tregubov was sent out [to be governor] in 1660, in March, and in 1662, on the 27th day of September, . . . Grigorii Borisov Koisarov was sent out to take Ivan Tregubov's place, since Ivan had spent two years there. On March 7, . . . for enduring imprisonment and for wounds, Suzdalian Ivan Karpovich Kazimerov was sent [to Shuia to be governor] in Ivan Tregubov's place, . . . and Grigorii Koisarov was ordered

not to go, because in the memorandum from the Chancellery of Petitions it was ordered to send men wounded in service [to be governors], but Grigorii is not wounded and he is too healthy to serve as a governor.[11]

Eligible servitors petitioned the Chancellery of Military Affairs or the tsar for a governorship. Terms were usually set at two years but actual stays varied greatly. Applicants had to present a good and moving case to secure an appointment. Arguments put forward to justify appointments used formulaic phrases to stress the petitioner's poverty, age, wounds, or meritorious past service. Semen Il'ich Zmeev, for instance, appealed to the tsar for an appointment as governor of Shuia in 1647. He wrote that he had been in the tsar's service for twelve and a half years, and he listed the numerous places and campaigns at which he had served: at Vitebsk he had been wounded by an harquebus; while he was fighting against the Crimean Tatars his horse had been killed beneath him; at Karpov he had served as a captain and built earthen ramparts and walls. "But I have not been released [from military service] to your sovereign's administrative service." Dripping with formulaic modesty, his memorandum begged the tsar to grant him the post "for my meager service [*sluzhbishka*] and for my blood." The tsar responded favorably, saying that when the incumbent governor completed his term, Zmeev should take office.[12]

Having secured a suitable governorship, a serviceman found himself with what might be called "supervised plenipotentiary" power in his district. His authority extended into virtually all areas of local affairs and over the course of the seventeenth century grew to engulf the few remaining enclaves of separate jurisdictions, and yet his every action or decision, no matter how trivial, had to be cleared with Moscow, especially if it involved distributing precious resources, land, or money.

Town governors were entrusted with widely varied powers for maintaining a functioning regional unit. In 1631 the new governor of Shuia, Ivan Gur'ev, repeated his working orders to signify that he understood his role: "I was ordered to serve in Shuia, replacing Petr Veliaminov, and to supervise and protect and judge the city and service people and townspeople and various [other] people in Shuia in the town and the countryside and to seek out any thievery and [illegal] sales of alcohol and prostitution."[13] In the military sphere, governors oversaw the muster, service rate assignment, and land allotment of the men serving from their towns' lists when these events took place locally rather than in the capital.[14] Town governors rarely had sufficient authority to conduct any of these exercises alone. Special emissaries were dispatched from the central chancelleries to perform specific tasks involved in registering provincial servicemen. These men were assisted by the *okladchiki* or locally selected informants, who provided information about the district population. Moscow demanded detailed reports chronicling each land transaction and prohibited governors from authorizing promotions in rank, which would necessarily entail additional expenses to the state treasury.[15]

Governors of central Russian towns often commanded pathetically meager forces. Sad and desperate petitions bear witness to the fact that they lacked sufficient troops to track criminals or even carry messages, much less to wage war. Vasilii Mikhailovich Kozlov, sent to Shuia to replace town governor Ivan Borkov, sent this mournful missive to Moscow in 1673:

> I was ordered to . . . send Ivan Borkov to Moscow, and I sent clerks to Ivan Borkov repeatedly to tell him that he should draw up a surety document for himself and go to Moscow, but he, Ivan Borkov, did not turn in a surety document, so I sent chancellery guards from Shuia . . . to him and he kept those bailiffs by force in his inn, and he beat and maimed them until they were barely alive, and, having beaten and maimed them, he ordered them put in jail, for unknown reasons and with unclear designs. And they were my only two men at the bureau office for sending on tasks, and they are now in jail, and of your troops no one remains to send out, Great Sovereign, in your service.

Kozlov ended his report with a plea that the tsar not cast him out in disgrace or fine him for failing to carry out state business as ordered.[16] Similarly shorthanded, the new town governor of Suzdal', Fedor Ivanovich Lovchikov, lamented in 1631 that after sending off all of the town's *deti boiarskie*, presumably to serve in the Smolensk War, "no one remains for me, your slave, to send out on your business."[17]

More than a lack of resources and staff undercut the governors' efficacy. Suspicion on the part of the government, as exemplified by its extensive surveillance and restrictive regulations, characterized interactions between it and its regional representatives. The range of independent action that the town governor and his staff might take was tightly circumscribed by ministerial decree and inspection. In S. M. Solov'ev's words, the government sent governors out to the provinces having "swaddled them hand and foot with long directives and orders."[18] A multitude of entertaining petitions confirms that town governors were supervised at an extraordinarily minute level. They did not have the authority to carry out the most obviously necessary fundamentals of law and order without central approval. A petition by Shuia's governor S. S. Ushakov, for instance, informs the tsar that the town hall had burned down, by the will of God, during the tenure of the previous governor. Without a town hall, Ushakov could not conduct daily business, but "without your approval, Great Sovereign, I dare not rebuild the town hall."[19] On a similar level, Governor B. V. Iakovlev did not "dare" punish a local landlord, even after the man had violently assaulted the town clerks and had tried to force them to make unauthorized copies of legal documents.[20] Other governors complained about the lack of even bare essentials for administrative business: candles, paper, ink, and literate clerks.[21]

The government's mistrust of corrupt and unprofessional governors was well founded. Untrained in administrative practices, retired cavalry officers rarely made the transition to gubernatorial office with great skill or commitment to any noticeable principles other than self-enrichment.[22] The latter principle they pursued vigorously. In spite of the level of central supervision and suspicion, governors frequently managed to do whatever they wished during their tenure. In historical retrospect, the administration of town governors has come to be considered synonymous with corruption and arbitrary, tyrannical rule.[23] According to A. A. Kizevetter, governors turned their districts into veritable satrapies with no checks on their arbitrary decisions.[24] A horrifying example of a governor's capricious cruelty comes from a complaint lodged by the townspeople of Shuia in 1665 against their governor, Ivan Borkov (who was mentioned earlier as having beaten and imprisoned the clerks of his replacement):

> And while he was governor he began to oppress us, your orphans, the townspeople, and to impose big fees and fines for no reason and to cause us losses. He beats us, your orphans the townspeople, without investigation and without guilt, and he puts [us] in jail for his greed; and taking us out of the jail, he beats us half to death with cudgels without charges and without guilt. And in the past year 172 [1663/64] he, the governor, beat the customs officer, Volod'ka Selivanov, half to death after having locked him up in his house, and he caused great disruption to the collection of customs duties.

The complainants continued, saying that the governor had overcharged and ruined craftsmen and merchants. Others he had chased away or put in jail. He had beaten the chief of a state posting station half to death in the preceding year, "and now that chief is maimed from that governor's assault."[25]

The state lacked the resources and personnel to control its local representatives and had to resort to stopgap measures to prevent the devastation of the population and the bankruptcy of the treasury at the hands of irresponsible governors. Central chancellery administrators ordered clerks in provincial governors' offices to report on their chiefs' activities. The entire staff of a provincial office was bound by mutual suretyship to inform on each other. If the provincial clerks failed to report on the governor, they and their fellow clerks could be subjected to heavy fines, imprisonment, or torture. More immediately, however, they would have to face the wrath of their direct superior, the governor himself, if they did inform on him. This informal threat appears to have kept most provincial clerks silent. Other measures used by the center to keep town governors in check included brief terms for and frequent replacement of governors, end-of-term audits, and a constant flow of reports, accounts, and orders between Moscow and the provincial towns. Town governors were obligated to send constant records of income and expenditures, and each departing governor signed over every document, all munitions and food supplies, and lists of servicemen to his successor. The measures apparently met with limited success, as incoming governors frequently reported empty archives and storehouses, missing munitions, and nonexistent troops.[26] When the outgoing governor G. B. Koisarov signed over the inventory of Lukh to his successor in 1658, the new governor reported to Moscow that "the town has been empty for many years. The walls and towers have crumbled, and there is no fortress at all. There are no keys to the city, no supplies, no money." Stockpiles of gunpowder, lead, and food were likewise exhausted.[27] Hampered in everyday affairs by Moscow's stultifying control, town governors still managed to enrich themselves and to ally with some of their subjects while alienating others in the course of a brief tenure in office. A telling example recounted by Solov'ev shows the extent of corruption practiced by town governors. The expense register of one tax collection office testifies that the local tax collection official brought "gifts" to the town governor every day without fail between the first and twentieth of September 1669—one day a pie, the next day fish, then candles, beef, and money.[28]

With a virtual monopoly on information flow between the provinces and the capital, town governors had tremendous obstructive power at their disposal, power which they could use either against or in collusion with the gentry communities they governed. Local people of all social groups could appeal to the tsar through the governor, filing petitions in the local bureau office and relying on the local administration to forward their requests to Moscow. Members of the gentry class had the right to appeal to the tsar directly, and in fact the formulaic salutation of the typical serviceman's petition addressed the tsar personally: "Sovereign, Tsar and Grand Prince Mikhail Feodorovich! Your slave humbly beseeches you." Despite the formulaic salutation, however, nearly all servicemen's petitions passed first through the hands of the local governor. All transactions had to be finalized in Moscow, but unless the parties involved could afford to send a man or go themselves to Moscow to register the arrangement, they had to rely on the governor to forward their petitions to the appropriate office in Moscow.

When acting as intermediaries between gentrymen and Moscow, town governors were ostensibly subject to the same close scrutiny that encumbered them in all of their actions. Governors were required to send every petition and every local decision to Moscow for registration and confirmation, but central chancelleries could control only those transactions about which they knew. In practical terms, the mediation of the town governor could have serious consequences for the supplicants. A common complaint in the gentry's petitions was a town governor's failure to register an action taken or a decision rendered, or to pass on petitions to the appropriate chancelleries. Prince I. B. Repnin, for instance, petitioned repeatedly before the paperwork for a land deal worked its way through the local governor's office and finally reached the central Chancellery of Service Lands in Moscow.[29] In a case in Vladimir in 1679, a number of members of the Kuroedov family protested that they had been trying to register a land transaction in the official record books for seven years, but the previous governor had never sent their petitions to Moscow.[30] In Shuia in 1681, a petitioner denounced the governor for refusing to accept a petition about a runaway peasant and for failing to inform the Chancellery in Moscow of his complaint.[31]

In an ongoing effort to keep governors from favoring their friends and relatives, the state attempted to appoint outsiders to the position. Foreign visitors asserted authoritatively that town governors had no local loyalties or connections and that they were sent out

from the capital to an intentionally alien environment and were ro-
tated to new posts before they could establish themselves as part of
the local gentry communities.[32] At the end of the sixteenth century,
Giles Fletcher had pronounced already that governors had no roots in
the districts where they ruled: "They are men of themselves of no
credit nor favor with the people where they govern, being neither
born nor brought up among them nor yet having inheritance of their
own, there or elsewhere."[33] In the middle of the seventeenth century,
Adam Olearius reported similarly that "in the administration of the
provinces and towns the Tsar . . . does not leave a voevoda or chief
official in one place for more than two or three years unless there is a
compelling reason. This practice is followed, on the one hand, so that
a locality may not be subjected too long to an unjust administration,
and, on the other, so that the namestnik may not become too friendly
with the inhabitants."[34]

Interactions with locals were limited legally by a series of decrees.
An edict of 1620 prohibited town governors and chancellery personnel from purchasing horses, clothing, or other merchandise except
for food supplies in local markets, presumably to prevent them from
extorting goods at low prices from powerless merchants. Another
series of injunctions barred town governors from entering into contracts, lending money or supplies, or accepting indentured servitude
within their districts. Such prohibitions applied equally to kinsmen
of town governors.[35] A decree issued in 1672 stated that governors
should not own land in the districts in which they served "so that
the inhabitants will not be oppressed through enmity nor indulged
through friendship."[36] In light of the number of violations of these
decrees that appear in the sources, the constant reiteration suggests
how difficult it was for the state to prevent governors from forming
friendships and alliances within the communities they governed.

Contrary to explicit state policy, governors often participated in
local affairs not as impartial envoys of the tsar but as native members
of the community. At the most basic level, their personal involvement in local affairs can be seen in the significant number of men
with local origins and family heritage in the area who served as governors in their own provinces, all legal regulations and historical
assumptions to the contrary notwithstanding. Over one-fourth (27
percent, or 47 out of 172) of all governors serving in the five towns
between 1609 and 1700 had close, identifiable kinsmen within the
greater five-province area, and 24 percent (41 out of 172) had blood

relatives who served or held land within the very province where they held office. Regardless of how the data are examined, between one-quarter and one-third of the 172 governors in the region appear to have had long-term, multigenerational ties to the towns they governed, and the numbers increase if one includes the four neighboring towns in the calculation.[37]

Karp Neronovich Volkov, who served as governor of Vladimir from 1626 to 1627, is a good example of a man administering his own home province. His family connections to Vladimir and Suzdal' dated back to at least the mid–sixteenth century. Recorded already, with his brother Stepan, as a rank-and-file gentry calvalry man in 1609, Karp Neronovich had been promoted to selectman from the Vladimir muster roll in 1611/12. Having served from Vladimir before, Karp Neronovich continued a family heritage of service in the area during his tenure as governor. Throughout the century, the Volkov family maintained its notable position in local society, as testified to by the marriage of a Volkov man to Avdot'ia Ivanovna Kablukova, Aleksei Fedorovich's granddaughter, almost 60 years after Karp Neronovich's term in office.[38]

The state had genuine grounds for concern over appointing local men as governors. Numerous court cases record the problems that could arise when governors exerted their authority in pursuit of "old friendships" or "previous animosity." In 1690/91 a group of landholders in Shuia complained that Nikita Kablukov had abducted their peasants and engaged in other illegal activities with the complicity of Governor Petr Grigor'evich Kashintsov, a Suzdalian himself.[39] Governor Lavrentei Ovdeevich Obukhov came from an established Iur'ev Pol'skii family, and was appointed governor in his home town in February 1658. The following year he found himself embroiled in a suit initiated against him by the local *guba* elder, a petty gentryman of the town named Aleksei Kuroedov, who charged that the governor had been extorting bribes from lesser town officials. In response, Obukhov asserted that Kuroedov was slandering him in order to avenge a long-standing grudge.[40] Both of these examples demonstrate that a governor with native roots in no way guaranteed harmony within the community. Communities produced their own internal dynamics and hostilities, and local governors played right into the factional divisions, friendships, and feuds that characterized community relations. Rancor between neighbors complicated the business of administering the town. In this context, intensive state surveillance of governors' relations with their constituents testifies to the tenacity of localism and personal relations in shaping Muscovite politics.

Not only locally born governors involved themselves in the partisan issues of community politics. For instance, in 1672 a Shuia gentryman, Semen Vasil'ev Kozynskii, accused Governor Buinov, not a local man, of blatantly favoring his brother in a court case. Semen insisted on transferring the case to the Moscow Judicial Chancellery because in Shuia the governor would harass him with bureaucratic delays and expenses.[41] Ten years later in Shuia, a petitioner complained that another governor was linked "in friendship and through favoritism" with a certain widow, Anna Poroshin, and that he obstructed due process to her advantage. "And he allows her, the widow Anna's, peasants to go free while my masters' . . . peasants sit in prison and are dying of starvation."[42] Whether or not the charges of collusion and favoritism were justified, it is clear from these cases that governors were not perceived as impartial outsiders but rather were recognized as partisan participants in local affairs.

Guba Elders: Community Officials in Their Local Context

The haziness of lines of authority and allegiance that characterized the position of town governors, who in principle functioned as representatives of central authority, is all the more noticeable in the case of locally selected officials, who served simultaneously as arms of the central state and as representatives of local communities. Some of the same issues surface in the historiographic assessment of local institutions that we saw in the discussion of the town governors, but with higher ideological stakes. In the practice of local election and administration, historians have detected possible roots or traces of representative democratic institutions and elements of popular control under the carapace of autocracy. Thus, the century-and-a-half-long power struggle between the envoys of the central state chancelleries (the town governor and his clerical/bureaucratic staff) and local administrative organs (the *guba* and *zemskii* offices) is read as a battle between centralized control and regional autonomy, with virtue on the side of the latter. Closer observation shows, however, that the solidarity of community itself was often undermined when particular local factions or classes seized control of local organs and used them not to promote harmony but rather for self-interested purposes, with devisive, conflictual results.[43]

Locally chosen officials included *okladchiki*, representatives to the Assemblies of the Land, selectmen, and sometimes the town clerks in the governor's office, but most significant of the local officials were the *guba* elders, provincial brigandage-control officers. Established in the early sixteenth century, the *guba* system allowed some local participation in crime control and justice. According to the original charter of 1539, a group of landholders and other residents of the Beloozero Province petitioned Ivan the Terrible's regime for permission to police their district themselves, through elected officials, rather than relying on the corrupt and ineffectual state officials then in charge of brigandage control. The grand prince (then only a child) reiterated their charges in his reply:

> You have petitioned us, saying that in your cantons bandits are plundering many villages and hamlets and stealing your property and burning villages and hamlets, and that they are robbing and beating many persons on the roads, and are killing many people. . . . And we have [earlier] dispatched [sent] our investigators [*obyshchikov*] to you in Beloozero, and you allege that great losses are caused you by our investigators. And you [further] allege that with our investigators you are not apprehending the evildoer-brigands because you are greatly delayed and hampered by red tape.[44]

The state responded favorably to the request, allowing first Beloozero and then other regions to choose their own brigandage-control officials. Evidently pleased with the results, the state later extended the *guba* system throughout the realm. The state clearly had nothing to lose and much to gain in brigandage control when it substituted unpaid, locally selected agents, who had a genuine stake in preserving the peace and safety of their region, for corrupt and ineffectual state investigators. Furthermore, the compliance of the elected officials was guaranteed by the stern loyalty oath exacted from them on taking office, according to which the grand prince placed responsibility for full and fair justice "on their souls" and, if they did not prevent banditry in the area, threatened to levy "from you the sum of damages suffered by those persons who are plundered in your canton, and double the amount without trial; and you yourselves shall [in addition] be punished and fined by me."[45] Community elders thus became a cost-free extension of the state's limited supply of police officers and administrators. This observation has led historians to debate whether the "popular" element of *guba* administration had any

representative, democratic content at all or whether it was merely a
sham, masking expanded state control in the guise of broad "elec-
toral" participation.[46]

Popular response to the reforms was mixed. While some local residents requested to return to a system of governors' courts, others
sought to protect the new institutions from the gradual encroachment of the town governors, who increasingly trespassed into the
guba sphere of authority in the course of the seventeenth century.[47]
On one hand, selection of police officials from within the community
meant the possibility of eliminating a layer of extortion by appointed
officials and of placing responsibility for law and order in the hands of
a local resident with a vested interest in keeping the peace. On the
other hand, it meant entrusting tremendous power over life and death
to a fallible individual with his own local history of patronage and clientage and with his own particular antagonisms to pursue.

Guba "elections" appear to have closely resembled the selections
of representatives to Parliament that Mark Kishlansky describes in
England prior to its civil war. Kishlansky employs the terms *selection* or the more contemporary *giving voice to* in preference to *election*, because selection was not resolved by open choice but rather by
informal caucusing prior to the nomination of the single candidate.
Selection was made without contest, unanimously, by a public that
gave assent to rather than chose a winner. Majority rule had no
meaning in this system. Contested selections did occur, but in both
England and Muscovy they were considered unfortunate malfunc-
tions of a consensual process. In the colorful phrase used by the English in the early seventeenth century, contested elections were "ad-
dled" ones and signified a serious breakdown of accepted hierarchies
of honor and social harmony.[48]

All estates of local society, with the exception of slaves, participated in *guba* elections, making them unique among Muscovite
estate-specific institutions. While all estates voted, however, not all
could hold office. Retired or impoverished members of the local gentry generally held the post of elder.[49] The law specified that "worthy
and prosperous gentrymen, who have been discharged from service
because of superannuation or because of wounds, or whose children
and kinsmen are serving for them, and who are literate, shall serve as
elders. . . . Those who are illiterate shall not be elected as elders."[50]
Most elders in the Vladimir-Suzdal' region signed documents themselves, so the literacy rule apparently was observed.[51]

The *guba* office was run by an elected *guba* elder, his sworn assistants, and several clerks and guards. The post of *guba* elder demanded significant physical exertion, time, and labor in seeking out criminals, keeping track of servicemen, and resolving disputes in the town. Perhaps more discouraging than the work itself, the job also carried tremendous risk because the state held the elders personally accountable for any failures in maintaining law and order. This accountability could be exacted in monetary fines, prison terms, or ordeals by righter, a torture involving the daily pain and humiliation of public beating on the shins. Upon assuming office, *guba* officials had to sign oaths of mutual responsibility, thereby shouldering responsibility for their fellow officials and for the population at large as well as for themselves.[52]

By the mid–seventeenth century communal administrative organs had passed their prime. According to some historians, shortly after the Time of Troubles they were subsumed into the newly established town governors' apparatus. Others place their effective demise in the second half of the century.[53] Communications to and from *guba* officials in the Vladimir-Suzdal' region demonstrate that these officials continued to function actively until they were temporarily abolished in 1679 and again when they were revived sporadically in the 1680s and 1690s. The idea of locally selected police officials retained popularity until the end of the century. In 1691/92, during a period of temporary abolition, the Metropolitan of Sarai and the Don region begged the tsar to allow *guba* officials once again to oversee justice, "now and henceforth, . . . so that [the peasants] will not be utterly destroyed and scattered by the governor of Suzdal' and the chancellery people and bailiffs."[54] The *guba* system was not finally abandoned until 1702.[55]

As long as the office existed, local elders executed their functions, albeit increasingly under the town governors' command. The legal powers of *guba* organs were extended and their jurisdiction formally differentiated from that of the town governors' in 1649, when the new law code clarified their subordination to the Chancellery of Brigandage Control and removed them from gubernatorial control. The law code provided them with no new means to exercise their legal independence from the governors, however, and in practice they rarely could assert their authority.[56]

Although in principle they were chosen by the people they served, *guba* elders had a reputation, apparently deserved, for exploiting

their position and extorting money and favors from the townspeople
and peasants in their district. The townspeople of Shuia, for instance,
protested in a petition to the tsar that the *guba* elders of Suzdal' and
Shuia had come to their town ostensibly in search of brigands, but in
the process

> the *guba* elders of Suzdal', Matvei Krotkoi and Miriai Kazimerov, and
> Shuia *guba* elders, Posnik Kolachov and Petr Kriukov, with their brothers
> and nephews and lesser *guba* officials and criminal investigators come to
> Shuia and feed themselves and their horses and drink in the taverns and
> use our carts and conscript our guards and collect fees everyday from some
> of us, and they arrest many people . . . and torture them and house them in
> our homes instead of putting them in prison under guard, and we, your
> orphans, Sovereign, are unable to live with their violence and fees. Many
> townspeople have fled, and those who remain want to flee.[57]

According to a second petition of protest, one of these same elders,
Posnik Kolachov, threatened the townspeople with "evil threats and
ordered them to bring him food all the time, bread and meat and fish
and drink and honey and wine."[58]

One of Kolachov's successors, Frol Fedorovich Kishkin, held office
from 1622 until 1634/35, in spite of numerous complaints throughout the entire period against his cruel exploitation of his position. In
1622 one of his subordinates reported that Kishkin and his cronies
had a habit of taking him by the throat and threatening to kill him
"on the road or in his house or anywhere." They terrorized him, saying, "[We] won't leave you alive, because you aren't in league with us
and you don't do things our way." "But I, your orphan, act in truth according to [my] cross-kissed oath to you, Sovereign." Their schemes
involved collecting bribes from villagers when they were supposed to
be out searching for criminals.[59] In response to this and other denunciations, Kishkin received a stern warning from the tsar, chiding him
and his fellow elder for overstepping the limits of their jurisdiction
and usurping the governor's authority. Kishkin was reprimanded for
imposing fines on the town population inappropriately whenever
someone was found "suffocated or knifed or having drunk himself to
death or burned or drowned or having died by whatever other means,
or if dead bodies float by the town in the river, or whoever fights
while intoxicated." All of these matters belonged by law to the governor's court, not the *guba* court. "And if in the future you charge the
townspeople fines, you will be assessed double those fines and will
be in great disgrace."[60]

Guba elders could derive great personal profit from their positions even when the townspeople complained and the Moscow chancelleries attempted to curtail their arbitrary power. Frol Kishkin, for instance, kept his post for another twelve years after his run-in with the central authorities, conducting regular business but habitually exploiting the townspeople on the side. The townspeople submitted another complaint against him in 1634/35, accusing him of locking honest folk in jail on the basis of the slanderous stories of notorious brigands.[61] Particular families tended to keep the post of *guba* elder for themselves generation after generation, thus continuing to gain at the expense of the local population. Kishkin's utterly corrupt family, for instance, occupied the position of *guba* elder in Shuia and Suzdal' for many generations.[62] Once in office, elders were very hard to oust.

The position of *guba* elder, although potentially powerful and attractive to petty landlords such as the Kishkins, was not one much sought after by the real notables of local society. Among provincial servitors the epithet "*guba* elder" could be hurled at an enemy as a stinging insult. In 1664, for instance, a selectman complained of the dishonor of being posted at an equal level with a man whose uncles had served as lowly *guba* elders, captains of the musketeers, soldiers, and bondsmen.[63] Important local families very rarely served as *guba* elders. The typical *guba* elder came from an undistinguished local family of rank-and-file gentrymen, with perhaps one or two members of the extended clan who advanced as far as *dvorovoi* or even selectman. Such were the Belenikhins of Lukh, the Chertovs of Vladimir, the Kishkins of Shuia and Suzdal', and the Kuroedovs of Iur'ev Pol'skii, all of whom included one or more *guba* elders in their ranks.[64] The one major exception to the norm of *guba* elders coming from undistinguished families, Abram Makar'evich Mishukov, assumed the office very reluctantly. When he was initially selected as *guba* elder in 1640 he refused to accept the responsibility. His predecessor, Semen Frolov Kishkin, had to call on the tsar to force him to take over:

> By your sovereign order, Abram Mishukov was ordered to be in Shuia in my place as *guba* elder and to sign everything over from me, but he, Abram, has not come to me at this time, Sovereign. When I [had to] leave Shuia on my own unavoidable business, not knowing [whether] I would soon be replaced, I, your slave, went to that Abram three times, and that Abram Mishukov, Sovereign, refused to sign over with me.[65]

After this inauspicious start, Mishukov, who married Aleksei Ka-blukov's widowed mother and founded a successful and important line of Suzdalian servitors, managed to turn his humble *guba* office into a bulwark of local authority. He may have actually used the *guba* post as a springboard to advance formally to the post of town governor, but some ambiguity remains on this point. Some documents refer to him as *"voevoda"* in the later years while others continue to designate him by his former title, *guba* elder.[66] This profile, however, did not typify the career pattern of the usual petty gentry-men who served as local elders. This is understandable, because for a community leader the rewards of the job could not often compensate for the work and high risks involved. For a lesser gentryman, how-ever, for a Kishkin, Kuroedov, or Chertov, the post offered countless paths to enrichment and probably a way to ingratiate himself with the gentry leaders of the province by performing favors or overlook-ing debts.

The existence of locally selected officials in Muscovy has been used to argue for the roots of a democratic tradition in Russia and with equal vehemence to show that autocratic interference always reduced democratic forms to a sham, turning them into yet another powerless branch of tsarist absolutism. The democratic view was particularly popular in the mid–nineteenth century, when the Great Reforms encouraged Russian historians to look for earlier demo-cratic experiences in the Russian past.[67] N. E. Nosov, typifying the Soviet view, claimed that the reforms heralded an epoch of "estate-representative monarchy" from the mid–sixteenth to the mid–seventeenth centuries, during which time autocracy was tempered by the voice of the social estates. With the eclipse of the *guba* system in the mid–seventeenth century, the contest between two governing "principles," the "communal" or "estate-representative" principle and the "centralizing" or "autocratic" principle, was definitively de-cided in favor of autocracy.[68] Some Western historians see in the *guba* institutions a tinge of "popular flavor," which crept in despite the state's efforts to harness locally selected officials to serve its needs. Hans-Joachim Torke, for instance, sees a "state-controlled so-ciety," but one in which the weakness of the center allowed for some local control.[69] Horace Dewey develops the notion that the local *guba* and *zemskii* offices served local and central interests simulta-neously, giving the state greater purchase on the slippery, unmanage-able provinces and allowing local communities some autonomy in allotting tasks and burdens.[70] One aspect of the historical discussion thus focuses on the perceived tension between central and local, autocratic and democratic, state and society. However, for the *guba* elders and their constituents, as for the governors, these categories would have made little sense. *Guba* elders, like everyone else around them, served the central state in local society, but also participated in, aligned with, served, exploited, and abused that society and that state. The *guba* system provided a valuable participatory aspect to autocratic rule, valuable both in its practical addition to the numbers of state servitors and the scope of their actions as well as in its validation of the ideology of participation and consultation that underlay Muscovite autocratic political culture.

Although the tsarist state responded to popular requests and allowed local selection of *guba* officials, in the Muscovite context this participation signified something very different from the Western, humanist imperative, described by J. G. A. Pocock, which "held that there was in the human animal something planted there by God, which required fulfillment in the practice of active self-rule."[71] The concept that virtuous men should take an active part in the governance of their land had some counterpart in Muscovy, where wise and righteous people (usually meaning highly placed and well born) were obligated to provide sage counsel to the tsar when and if he needed it. For the most part, however, the population had nothing to do with the business of governing the tsardom.[72] As exemplified in the *guba* system, popular participation was understood in a broader sense not as active, responsible citizenship (an unthinkable concept in an autocratic state) but rather as license to develop the local autonomies and particularized interests that made up the actual politics of the countryside.

The most successful historical analyses of the *guba* system, like Dewey's, consider what it offered state and society, not what it failed to offer. The provincial gentry of the Vladimir-Suzdal' region showed no sign whatsoever of using local institutions to solidify a corporate identity, to articulate defiance or to defend estate autonomy and prerogatives against the state. Yet, through the *guba* system, local inhabitants gained some discretionary authority in precisely *how* orders from the sovereign tsar were carried out. Furthermore, *guba* elders accrued a large degree of personal power and authority. The office of the elder did not alter the balance of power between state and community institutions, which was clearly weighted toward the center throughout. Rather, it provided for flexible, negotiated interaction. It mediated among multiple realms of power. Within the provincial community, it added another facet to the internal politics of patronage and power.

Muscovy and the West: Some Comparative Notes

Overlap, redundancy, particularism, and personalism were integral elements of Muscovite political culture. They were the rules by which Muscovite society and politics ran. Historians of early modern Europe have shown analogous interpenetration, overlap, and mutual reliance of state officials and local communities. Of Tudor-Stuart England, for instance, Braddick writes, "The state was not bureaucratized. Central government depended on the co-operation of unpaid local officials, and these local brokers of central authority acted as mediators between central government and the locality."[73] In his study of more highly institutionalized French absolutism, William Beik writes that *intendants*, those quintessential agents of central government, similarly worked together with other central and local agents. "They worked through and not against the local system of authority, for without a network of local contacts they were helpless, and this network could only be developed by sensitivity to local interests. Intendants should be thought of as intermediaries who linked a congeries of local ties to a variety of national ties."[74]

The implicit comparative framework that has shaped Muscovite historiography since the early-modern era itself has set a defensive course for Muscovite historians, who have demonstrated an urge to prove, explain, or deplore Russia's backwardness in comparison to those paragons of development, England and France. More recently, Muscovite historians have evinced some unease at the conventional comparisons and have searched for more fitting standards for comparison. Some look to the Ottoman Empire, others to the early Middle Ages for more appropriate comparative models. Yet, when one takes into account the productive revisions of the Whiggish histories of England and France that Western European historians have produced over the last few decades, England and France come to look a good deal more like Muscovy and a good deal less like their own eighteenth- and nineteenth-century images than has been commonly assumed. England and France in particular always present certain problems for comparative history, since their respective paths

were so unique—England with its democratic, participatory government and France with its institutionalization and centralization of
bureaucratic control—and yet even these two extreme cases of Western development manifest deep structural similarities with Muscovy. Muscovy was not an archaic holdover from an earlier age but a
thoroughly early-modern phenomenon.

Muscovy could not, of course, be mistaken for France or England.
The self-governing, self-taxing, participatory elite of England has no
echo in Muscovy, although the boyar elite *were* the government in
Muscovy. Seventeenth-century France shared many characteristics
with Muscovy—focus on the crown as the source of all privilege,
emphasis on marriage politics, merging of local and central interests
and personnel—but Muscovite elites did not form national corporate
groups or institutions; they chose to play national policies out on the
local scene instead. In Muscovy the connections of provincial gentrymen to the center did not produce broader networks, either in support or defiance of the tsar. Instead, they remained limited, indi-
vidualized, and fragmentary. The kind of autonomy preserved by the
Muscovite provinces involved the freedom to engage in highly particularistic, local competitions. Nor did Muscovite provincial institutions develop a sense of rights as the French *parlements* and other
regional institutions and corporations did. Holding positions created
by the crown, *guba* officers and other local officials used their posts
as profitable local seats of power but never acted as heads of corporate
bodies with independent rights and inviolable privileges to defend.

On the other hand, provincial communities expressed a strong
sense of what they expected as their due, an understanding of their
"rights" that was couched in the language of right and wrong rather
than that of corporate charters or laws. When a state official abused
his position of trust and imposed exorbitant fees, or snubbed the
usual gifts and bribes offered by hopeful litigants, or threw people
into jail and beat them without cause, provincial communities recognized that the unspoken moral contract had been violated. They
knew that they had grounds for complaint and could feel fairly con-
fident that the state officials would respond to their denunciations by
condemning the improprieties. State and society worked together in
this regard in an effort to supervise the workings of officialdom and
to clean up corruption, at least after the fact. Despite laws on the
books, neither side showed much interest in preventing altogether
the local officials from using their posts to serve their friends and

themselves or in severing personal ties between state officials and local communities. Such ties allowed the system to function. For the state, these ties ensured that the few isolated officials dispatched from Moscow to administer the vast provinces would be guaranteed the support and cooperation of at least a fraction of provincial society. Without such local support, central officials and laws would have been rendered completely ineffectual. For members of the gentry community, personal ties to their administrators gave them a foothold on an otherwise smooth and slippery surface of impersonal regulation, and the wide variety of chancelleries, offices, and individuals available for administering and judging the gentry's matters allowed a crucial degree of flexibility and play in the system. In and around those multiple sites of autocratic authority, the gentry of the provinces constructed an active and interactive "civil society."

CHAPTER 5

Kinship and Patronage in Provincial Politics

Early modern states functioned to a significant degree on the basis of patronage and clientage. Historians of France and England describe a shift over the centuries from the feudalism of the Middle Ages to what is known as new feudalism or bastard feudalism in the late fifteenth and early sixteenth centuries. This shift replaced relations of vassalage and fealty based on the exchange of land and services with an equally personalized relationship based on the exchange of favors and connections. In the seventeenth and early eighteenth centuries, with the rise of more powerful, centralized, bureaucratized states, the nature of patronage again altered. In France especially patronage tied provincial elites increasingly to the crown, which deliberately bestowed formal privileges on a wide variety of corporate bodies, institutions, and venal offices. During all these phases of development, kinship networks, patronage, and clientage served to link various levels of society, as well as the center to the periphery. In addition, clientage alternately contributed to and undermined the centralizing, state-building project of the monarchies.[1]

In the historiography of state building in the "new monarchies" of Western Europe, the traditional view, which assumes conflict between centralization and localism as seen in the previous chapter, similarly describes a struggle between the rising centralizing states and the entrenched nobilities and their patronage systems, a struggle in which the success of the crown was determined by its ability to crush the nobles and their clienteles. As we have seen with localism and centralization, so too regarding patronage and centralization; more recent works generally assert that the two were more easily reconciled than had been previously believed and that privilege and patronage grew alongside, in harmony with, and in support of the centralized monarchies. Michael Mann asserts that what he calls the "spoils system" originated in the early-modern period as a crucial aspect of state building. The increased central distribution of favor and privilege of early-modern courts played a key role in extending monarchical rule.[2] Sharon Kettering argues that "brokers mediated between the provincial power structure and the national government in Paris, performing the critical function of linkage in a state with a weak central government. . . . Broker-clients were recruited and used by the Paris royal ministers to integrate the peripheral provinces of France and to create a strong central government." Reliance on "interstitial, supplementary, and parallel structures," such as patron-broker-client ties, was characteristic of incompletely centralized states in which official institutions alone did not suffice to govern the provinces because of the weak hold of royal authority.[3]

The Muscovite picture looks very much like that described by scholars of the early-modern West. Muscovite administration was no more efficient and was certainly understaffed when compared to the Western monarchies, but the state developed efficient compensatory mechanisms to counteract those shortages. In particular, kinship ties and clientage were integral to the functioning of the emerging bureaucratic state system, as they were to the informal politics of provincial communities. Patronage mediated not only between center and periphery but also between the bureaucratic system and the personalized practices and expectations of Muscovite tradition. "Interstitial, supplementary, and parallel" to the state structure in Muscovy as they were in France or England, personal bonds of reciprocal obligation contributed as much to the successful functioning of the tsarist apparatus as did the rules and procedures of the chancellery offices. By personalizing relationships within an increasingly regulated and routinizing administrative system, patronage and preferment gave the provincial gentry a way of navigating in and comprehending a new and fundamentally alien approach to governance. In fact, the inextricable intersection of public and private spheres worked to the advantage of centralizing states by obscuring and offsetting the potential conflicts between new, routinizing, bureaucratic norms and traditional "ascriptive hierarchies" in which value had derived from birth and custom, not from merit or regulation.[4] Even Max Weber, although he defined bureaucracy as the form of organization best suited to rational and efficient governance, acknowledged that rigid formality and departmental rivalries might rob a bureaucratic system of flexibility and hinder the administration of justice in individual instances.[5] John Armstrong, in an article comparing the French *intendant* system of the seventeenth century with the Russian gubernatorial system of the eighteenth century, goes even farther, postulating that premature bureaucratization in a premodern society may prove dysfunctional.[6]

Seventeenth-century Muscovy managed to circumvent most such problems of rigid bureaucratization by relying on patronage networks to bridge the foggy boundaries between public and private, state and society. Hostile to impersonal regulation and administration by undistinguished, non-noble secretaries and clerks, the provincial elite managed to make the new system more palatable by forming personal connections with officials and to soften the hard edges of impersonal procedure with a gift here and a bribe there. The gentle subversion or co-optation of the official system allowed the Muscovite state to grow and prosper. Rather than reflecting the inadequacies of an imperfectly centralized state, the prevalence of patronage within the Muscovite system indicates a successful adaptation of state and society to a new phenomenon—the rise of bureaucratic administration—which itself grew in the interstices of a patrimonial regime.

Formal and Informal Ties with the Capital

In the corridors and waiting rooms of the chancelleries in Moscow, one's connections and pull mattered a great deal in determining who gained access to the chief officials and whose cases would be expedited. Gentrymen in the provinces could present their cases to the local governor, and if he was well disposed toward them, they could rely on him to advance their causes in Moscow. Alternatively, they could go to Moscow themselves and hope for a generous reception in one of the chancelleries. If they followed this more direct route, it was critical for provincial servitors to find shelter under the protective wing of a Moscow servitor or a friendly bureaucrat.[7]

With governors and administrative personnel cycling rapidly through the provincial towns, and with provincial and Moscow-rank servitors living in close proximity in the provinces and sharing local concerns, ordinary provincial gentrymen did not lack connections in the capital. Although their concerns were by and large local, limited to worries about property holding, local prestige, and local administration, they had to pursue many of their goals in the courts and chancelleries of the capital. When they arrived in Moscow, they immediately sought out their compatriots from the provinces and worked the central governmental offices in the same informal, personal, particularist way in which they conducted their political lives at home.

The need and utility of such a connection emerges in the remarkable correspondence, undated but probably from the early 1670s, among members of the Belin family of Suzdal'. The Belins were a provincial gentry family in the service of the Suzdal' Convent of the Intercession.[8] Ivan Vasil'evich Belin was sent as a young man to represent the convent in Moscow and to transact all of the convent's business there. His father Vasilii sent him frequent, sometimes daily, instructions about what he should do and how he should do it. In one urgent set of letters, the father reminded his son to submit his petitions specifically to the Chancellery of Service Lands, and only to the secretary of the chancellery, Konstantin Kurbatov. A Suzdalian himself, Kurbatov had worked his way up from service in the Suzdal' governor's office to a lofty post in the chancellery in Moscow.[9] Kurbatov, the father wrote, would protect their concerns, while another group of officials, all interlinked by marriage and kinship, had antagonistic interests in the Belin family's own village, Dubenki, and should be avoided:

> And about what has been written to you about clerk Dmitrii Fedorov who handled the case of the village Dubenki and who released the charter according to State Secretary Ivan Evstaf'ev's petition: clerk Dmitrii Fedorov, they say, is related by marriage to Luk'ian Novokshchenov and to State Secretary Ivan Evstaf'ev. They say that Luk'ian Novokshchenov's sister is married to Dmitrii Fedorov. If Dmitrii is indeed related by marriage to Luk'ian and to State Secretary Ivan, petition that the matter be transferred from him and given to another clerk.[10]

In another letter, Vasilii instructed his son that he should go with Mikhail Rodionov, another servitor from the same convent, to appeal to the clerk Emel'ian Telitsyn, a Suzdalian and a family friend, so that Telitsyn would allow them to see the head of the Printing Office, Maksim Fefanov, so that he, in turn, would let them appeal to Pavel Ostaf'ev, who had previously supported Mikhail in court cases. Maksim Fefanov was useful as a conduit because, according to Vasilii's inside knowledge, Fefanov's sister had married Ostaf'ev. Maksim Fefanov also had close ties to Mikhail Rodionov.[11]

These recitations of liaisons, sounding like the tangled plots of daytime soap operas, reflect the serious alliances and rivalries of which power and politics in Muscovy were made. More than idle interest motivated the politically astute to keep an eye on the marriages, friendships, debts, and loyalties of state officials. In another letter, the father advised the son that two friendly personages had left Suzdal' for Moscow. Ivan should petition them, his father wrote, "so that they will favor you and not abandon you, and they will . . . grant that you be protected by their mercy." Backstage networks and interlinkages based on kinship, marriage, or patronage provided the key to success in the central administration. The stakes were high, so the game had to be played well. Vasilii Belin warned his son that he should be careful in a suit he was fighting against a Moscow man: "It is dangerous. He is a Moscow man while you are a young man and have been little on business, and you understand little about the court system. . . . [It] is dangerous; guard yourself, for God's sake."[12]

Prudent people fostered their useful contacts in Moscow with great care. Vasilii Belin evidently had cause for anxiety about his son's conduct in Moscow. A letter from Vasilii's other son, Fedor, to his brother Ivan, shows how seriously these personal resources were regarded. Fedor reported that when the clerk Emel'ian Telitsyn had visited Suzdal' he had complained about Ivan Belin. Telitsyn had said that Ivan was *nedobr* (rude) to him and did not behave "like *striapchie* in the old days." Fedor cautioned Ivan, "It would be good, brother not to abandon good people, and to use good words, and not such as he said you used previously. And our elders were also *striapchie* and they followed after him and didn't distress him. Our lord and father told me to write this to you, for he is upset with you, and he said that we don't obey good people and we don't conduct ourselves properly."[13] Fedor conveyed to his brother their father's suggestion for a way to gain access to useful officials. Ivan and the other convent servitors should petition to the *wives* of the various officials in order to engage their sympathy and to induce them to appeal to their husbands for clemency: "Petition . . . to his [Pavel Mikhailov Ostaf'ev's] wife Theodosia Ivanovna. [Ask] her to grant [us] her favor and talk with Pavel Mikhailov so that for her sake he would agree not to abandon [us] and not sue or harm [us] financially."

The Muscovite administrative system with its flexible and overlapping jurisdictions left room for strategic maneuvering by clever or well-connected litigants. Vasilii Belin advised his son at one point that their opponents wanted to have a case heard in the Patriarchal Court but that he should try instead to transfer it to the Monastic Chancellery, where "our brothers" would hear it.[14] In this way provincial servitors could try to bring their cases to whichever chancellery offered them the brightest hopes, wherever they had friends, relatives, or patrons. Their opponents presumably pressed equally hard to have their cases heard where their own connections predominated.

It was imperative that a litigant have a personal agent in Moscow to push his case through the chancelleries. Letters indicate that during sojourns in Moscow gentrymen took the cases of relatives, friends, and neighbors to the various chancelleries, often in return for favors carried out at home in their absence. When Nikita Kablukov took a trip to Moscow, Lev Zvorykin and Konstantin Kablukov wrote asking him to attend to their affairs along with his own in the Chancellery of Service Lands and in the Chancellery of Military Affairs.[15] A letter from Konstantin Ivanovich Kablukov to his grandfather Aleksei Fedorovich reveals that the Kablukov patriarch dispatched his grandson to Moscow to transact the family's business in person. In his letter, Konstantin assured the old man that "I will soon run to Moscow on your business." In the capital he promised to straighten out some confusion over title to a particular plot of land. "And please, if you will, lord, write to me in Moscow without delay about the uninhabited field at Novinki, in what year it was given to you. If there is a deed for it, I can't find it. I searched for a long time and didn't find it." The relationship worked both ways; in return for his help in Moscow, Konstantin requested that his grandfather take care of his affairs at home.[16]

Contacts in Moscow were useful for a wide array of purposes. A friend or neighbor with a house in Moscow could provide welcome hospitality and spare a provincial gentryman the burdensome expense of finding lodgings in the capital, an expense about which gentrymen complained in petitions throughout the century. Nikita Kablukov stayed at the house of his fellow Suzdalian, Ivan Obukhov, when he went to Moscow, as is evident from the address of a letter sent to him by his nephew: "Give this letter in Moscow . . . on Stolovaia Street, in the house of Ivan Obukhov, to my lord uncle,

Nikita Alekseevich Kablukov."[17] A number of other members of the provincial communities also kept houses in Moscow.[18] On a more prosaic level, a trip to Moscow might evoke a rash of shopping requests: "Please, my lord brother, buy me some German stockings, and for sister Polageia Iur'evna, also German stockings, white."[19]

Even the most powerful people in Muscovy sought out highly placed acquaintances and begged them for protection. "I petition your mother, Princess Tatiana Ivanovna, for her kindness, that she not abandon my mother-in-law and little children in our troubles," wrote Ivan Kurakin, a man of high rank and court connections, to his powerful protector of the moment, Prince Vasilii Golitsyn.[20] Lavish gifts and appeals for protection passed frequently between members of the boyar elite, although according to Robert Crummey, such exchanges rarely show up as lasting patron-client relations.[21] If they are difficult to trace at the highest levels of society, such relationships are even harder to document for the provincial gentry. Some may have entered into clientage relations with very highly placed aristocrats, but evidence of such relations is very rare.[22] Far more common and effective among provincial gentry were appeals directed to each other or to low- or midlevel officials in local and central chancelleries. These pragmatic, horizontal links at the functional level of the bureaucracy facilitated the transaction of business with the state. Handy though connections to high boyars might have been, personal ties to clerks in the chancelleries and personal agents on the scene in Moscow provided provincial gentrymen with the best available resources for pursuing their goals. They could not rely on the law or standard procedure to work properly without a bit of extra help.

When direct connections failed to produce the desired results, or when a petitioner simply did not know anyone in the right places, gifts and bribes might do the trick. Vasilii Belin admonished his son Ivan: "Be ready to spend 30 or 40 rubles to avoid bureaucratic delays and abandonment [by patrons]."[23] Hans-Joachim Torke, in an article on the Muscovite bureaucratic system, writes that "bribery is the point where the bureaucracy, the society and, moreover, the entire population were closely interrelated."[24] Bribery did play a central role in linking state officials in Muscovy with those whose fates they controlled. Probably the most common accusation lodged against officials throughout the century was corruption and bribe taking.[25] The law codes and intermittent decrees reiterated the unconditional prohibition of accepting bribes. Muscovite society clearly recognized bribery as derailing of the justice system. It is also clear, however, that a certain degree of favoritism, personal pull, and reciprocity of favors and loans was necessary to the system. Members of the Kozlov service community actually lodged a protest against their town governor because of his incorruptability. Brian Davies describes how the upright governor had to use cudgels to drive off insistent representatives of the community when they tried to deposit gifts on his porch and how, as a reward for his probity, the service population of Kozlov drove him out of town. They felt that his refusal to accept their bribes placed him out of reach of their influence and deprived them of any intimate purchase on the workings of state power.[26]

Protection or intercession was highly valued in Muscovite culture. The Mother of God held a particularly revered place in the Orthodox pantheon precisely because of her role as intercessor between Christ and the Orthodox people.[27] Churches dedicated to *Pokrov*, the Intercession of the Virgin, abounded, and a very popular scene in holy icons depicted the symbolic protection of the Orthodox flock by the Mother of God, who held her sheltering veil over otherwise defenseless Christians. Believers followed the same course in their appeals to divine authorities that they utilized in interactions with secular authorities: they turned to their best, most favorably disposed connection and appealed for mercy and patronage.

A Scandal in Shuia

On the eighteenth of April, 1677, Ivan Ivanovich Borkov and Petr Grigor'evich Kashintsov left the home of Gavrilo and Grigorii Koisarov, where they and their men had enjoyed an evening of drunken revelry. The festivities had involved a distinguished company of local notables. Borkov was the town governor of Shuia, Kashintsov a Moscow-rank *striapchii* who lived in Shuia, and their hosts, the Koisarovs, were important local figures on the rise, both Moscow-rank gentry at the time of the incident.[28] Grigorii had served formerly as governor of Lukh and then of Shuia. After leaving the Koisarov house in the village of Lukhushino, two versts from town, the groups of visitors parted ways, each heading home with his entourage. Instead of going peacefully home, however, the two factions turned against each other in a vicious fight. According to Kashintsov's deposition, Borkov and the townspeople of Shuia were conspiring against him because he had earlier filed a petition against them. In

Kashintsov's words, on that fateful night, Borkov, "having drunk himself drunk, . . . plotted with his people and began to beat and maim [Kashintsov] and his men." Borkov himself pulled the rings from Kashintsov's fingers and grabbed the necklace from his neck, and tore his robe and gown from him. Borkov sent some of his men to town for reinforcements. The new arrivals ran out to the field, eager to "avenge old hostilities." The townspeople, who were "in league with" Governor Borkov, threw Kashintsov and two of his men onto a sled and took them to town, beating them almost to death on the way. Arriving in town, they cast Kashintsov and his men in prison, "without your sovereign order." Kashintsov's "spiritual father" (his priest-confessor) came to visit him in jail and saw "wounds on his face and hands and how they tortured him with chains."

That same day, Kashintsov's mother, brothers, and wife heard rumors that he had been killed, and they set out to retrieve his body. When the mourning party arrived in Shuia, Borkov's people, joined by a crowd of townspeople, beat the Kashintsov's men and imprisoned them, and they beat and maimed two household serving girls and pulled their braids. "They swore at his mother and wife with various bad words." Kashintsov's brother, Petr the Younger, rode into town on horseback, "and many townspeople chased after him and hacked the horse out from under him and wanted to beat him to death."

At last, Governor Borkov visited his victim in jail and found him half dead, "sick from wounds and from being tortured with chains," and ordered him released. After lying near death at home for six weeks, Kashintsov petitioned the tsar that his foe be punished "for assault and mutilation and foul language and beatings and for putting him in jail without the tsar's mandate, and for chaining him to the wall with chains on his legs and for the dishonor of his mother and wife and the dishonor and beating of his people." He further implored the tsar to order the release of his men, who still remained in jail for no fault of their own. Responding to this denunciation, the tsar, or his delegates in the Chancellery of Military Affairs, ordered that the two culprits face each other in an "eye-to-eye confrontation" and that special agents from Moscow conduct a thorough investigation.

The first investigator sent from Moscow received a chilly welcome from the plaintiff. According to a new complaint filed by Kashintsov, the agent was unsuitable as an impartial observer because he was a friend of Ivan Borkov's relative, Fedor Borkov, and by extension was a friend of Ivan's. Moreover, Kashintsov claimed, the investigator harbored a private grudge against Kashintsov's brother-in-law and hence by extension against Kashintsov himself.

In mid-June, the Chancellery of Military Affairs responded affirmatively, removing the case from the special agent's jurisdiction and ordering all of the concerned parties to appear for questioning at the ministerial offices in Moscow. Kashintsov and his people promptly produced a signed surety bond guaranteeing that they would appear as ordered. A collection of gentrymen signed the surety bond, promising to pay fines or go to prison themselves if Kashintsov and his men did not fulfill their obligations. The men who signed the guarantee, mostly *striapchie* and *zhil'tsy*, had only marginal affiliations with the Shuia region.[29] It is not surprising that Kashintsov had to look outside of the circle of local magnates to find sponsors: his family was widely disliked in the province because of a long record of criminal misconduct. For almost 50 years the townspeople of Shuia had been complaining about "various losses" inflicted on them by Petr Grigor'evich, his grandfather, father, and brothers (see Fig. 2.2, the Kashintsov family genealogy). In 1630 a priest in Shuia accused the grandfather, Aleksei Moiseev Kashintsov, of beating him. In 1643 the tsar had been moved to issue a special edict protecting the townspeople of Shuia from the extortion, assaults, and insults of the father, Grigorii Alekseevich, and some of his henchmen.[30] Petr Grigor'evich followed closely in his father's unattractive footsteps: in 1682 the entire town of Shuia petitioned against him for initiating groundless lawsuits against them, slandering them, and charging them falsely with unpaid debts to him: "Living in close proximity to us, your orphans, he, Petr, causes us, your orphans, many offences and gouges us and harrasses us with groundlessly fabricated and false petitions."[31]

Petr was in the habit of falsely accusing the inhabitants of Shuia of stealing his livestock, but meanwhile he was busy driving the townspeople's animals onto his fields, where he starved them and slaughtered them. He forced townspeople to pay off contracts that they had already settled, and if they did not, then he had them beaten about the shins. "Because of him, many people wander homeless around the world." "He comes to townspeople's homes and dishonors them and their wives and children and destroys them."[32] Many of the "losses" inflicted by the Kashintsovs over the years took feathered form: some years after the clash with Borkov, the townspeople charged Petr Grigor'evich with stealing over 100 ducks and geese from various owners.[33] Petr was probably right when he claimed that the townspeople wanted to "avenge old hostilities." His local reputation forced him to look out of town for sureties.[34] He found them by looking primarily up and outward, to his Moscow acquaintances, where, as we shall see, he had distinguished connections.

After Kashintsov's second petition, the Chancellery of Military Affairs ordered Governor Borkov removed from office and replaced by a man named Vasilii Kozlov. Borkov proved less compliant with governmental orders than his opponent. Kozlov repeatedly ordered him to collect sureties to guarantee his appearance at the Chancellery, but Borkov refused. The new governor dispatched two guards to escort him to Moscow, but Borkov beat them and had them locked up in jail, although he no longer had the authority to do so. This act rendered the new governor powerless, since the two guards formed his entire staff. Borkov then disappeared. When questioned, his wife claimed that he had left for Moscow on September 25, but on October 3 he still had not materialized at the Chancellery. Ministerial agents arrested two of Borkov's men and transported them to Moscow at his expense in order to hold them hostage.

At last, on October 6, Borkov submitted a surety document guaranteeing that he would appear at the Chancellery and remain there until released. His sponsors, similar in caliber to Kashintsov's, were mostly relatives or other men of low Moscow rank from his native Iaroslavl'.[35] Along with the guarantee document, Borkov filed his very different version of the story, which cast Kashintsov as the aggressor. According to Borkov's testimony, as he and his men were heading home from the Koisarovs' house, Kashintsov and his people chased him, beat him and his men, robbed him and pulled his beard out by the roots, leaving his denuded face blue and swollen. A few townspeople of Shuia saw what was happening and rang the town bells to alert the population. Kashintsov and his men ran off, but the townspeople caught them and fought with them and ultimately imprisoned them.

Eyewitness accounts supported Borkov's version. The sympathies of the townspeople and the local bureaucratic officers clearly lay with their former governor. Clerks from the *guba* office and the governor's office testified in favor of their former chief.[36] Not only his office staff but also the townspeople of Shuia sided with the governor in the dispute. In lively testimony, townspeople described how at the

time of the incident some were at the customs house counting re-
ceipts and others were drinking at the tavern. As soon as they had
seen the conflict they had run out to help Borkov, but the two had
continued to fight for a while, "and tore their clothes and dirtied
them." Borkov's men had declared their loyalty unambigously, saying, "Go away, Petr Grigor'evich. . . . We will defend our master ourselves." Finally someone sounded an alarm on the church bells, and
Kashintsov's people ran away. The townspeople "lifted the governor
from the ground, scarcely alive." The testimony concludes simply
that "after their fight, we all separated to our homes."

Sad to say, no resolution to the case survives. In early November,
Borkov received permission to leave the Chancellery confines for one
month in order to track down fugitive peasants in Kazan'. After that,
the documents fall silent, but it is clear that neither man was punished very harshly, if at all. Kashintsov served as governor of Shuia in
1690/91 and held the rather prestigious rank of *stol'nik* in Moscow
until at least 1691.[37] Borkov's service record ends at approximately
the time of the scandal, but no particular penalty is recorded for him.

Whatever the resolution, the story serves as a splendid catalogue of
the rich variety of ruses, ploys, and other methods exploited by leading members of local society. The opening scene, the alcoholic revelry at which four pillars of local society imbibed liquor together
with "their people" and clerical personnel, displays the vertical social networks into which Muscovite provincials clustered. The hosts
and patrons of the groups all boasted important titles and leadership
roles in the community, but they did not socialize with only their
equals. They shared their celebrations with the clients and dependents whose loyalties they hoped to keep. Brawls and social occasions alike bound groups together with their leaders. Patrons had to
distribute rewards—liquor or the jewelry torn off of an opponent's
fingers—among their clients to assure their loyalty. Clients, in return, had to earn their keep by carrying out their patrons' requests—
pummelling members of a rival faction or testifying favorably in
court.

The court proceedings from the case highlight the importance
bonds of family as well as patronage. Petr Kashintsov might have lan-
guished in prison, at the mercy of his tormentor, had not his mother,
wife, and brother arrived on the scene with their people. Energetic
women such as Kashintsov's mother and her maidservants took
an active role in protecting the integrity of the family. Friendship

and hostility were assumed to follow family lines almost automatically, as seen in the assumption that a friend of Borkov's relatives was necessarily Borkov's friend and that an enemy of Kashintsov's brother-in-law would transfer his animosity to Kashintsov himself. Kinsmen stood by each other in the face of outside attack: Borkov's kin rallied round to sign his guarantee of appearance even after he had proven himself to be less than reliable on that score.

The help and protection of a powerful patron was a valuable asset in the rough world of the Muscovite provinces. The extraordinarily unpleasant Kashintsov evidently profited from the help of an unusually prominent patron, which helps to explain the impunity with which he acted in Shuia and Suzdal', not only against the defenseless "orphans" of the town, but also against the tsar's appointed governor, Ivan Borkov. The key to this protective relationship appears in one of the complaints against him, filed by the Shuia townspeople in 1682. The townspeople's petition explains that Petr Kashintsov "at that time called Artamon Matveev his nephew, through his, Petr's wife."[38] Artamon Matveev was none less than the favorite of Tsar Aleksei Mikhailovich toward the end of his reign and the sponsor of the Tsar's second wife, Natalia Naryshkina. When Matveev had visited nearby Lukh, Kashintsov had forced the townspeople of Shuia to provide transportation, 15 horses and 35 foot soldiers, to accompany the visiting dignitary back to Moscow, and had threatened anyone who did not comply with "destruction." The horses (needless to say, given Kashintsov's affection for livestock) had "disappeared without a trace."[39] Matveev's star fell after Tsar Aleksei's death in 1676, when the children of Aleksei's first wife, Mariia Miloslavskaia, claimed the throne. Finally, in May of 1682, precisely the time when the town filed this petition, Matveev suffered a terrible death, being ripped apart by an angry crowd during the Musketeers' Rebellion of that year. Kashintsov had enjoyed some immunity from attack as long as his "nephew" and patron was alive and in favor. With Matveev's gruesome demise, the people of Shuia realized that their local oppressor might finally be vulnerable to the tsar's justice, and so they submitted their petition. Few other provincial gentry families could claim such lofty connections, but the principle of patronage functioned in the same way for all.

The Kashintsov-Borkov feud serves as an overview of the range and manifestations of local political behavior. It shows the leaders of two rival gangs that infiltrated official ranks, abused state institutions, and bribed and intimidated bureaucrats and townspeople alike. The leaders competed for the dividends of local politics: power, prestige, wealth, and support. Their clashes assumed a wide range of forms, from pathetic pleas to the capital, to reliance on pull within the local administration, to the ever-popular form of recreation in Russia, the all-out brawl. The particular issues at stake in this and other local conflicts had little to do with Moscow and its elaborate hierarchy and ritual but rather everything to do with family, wealth, and local standing.[40]

Social Relations Among the Gentry of Suzdal'

Relations among the landholders of the provinces cannot be easily categorized or formulated. Like people anywhere, they had their personal likes and dislikes, incidents of friction, and periods of cooperation. In general, however, some patterns of interaction emerge from the accumulation of evidence from the hundreds of petitions, agreements, and lawsuits that have survived from the most well documented of the five provinces, Suzdal' and Shuia. At the first level of generalization, standards of conduct varied according to the rank and social standing of the parties involved. Although the brutal gang fighting between Kashintsov and Borkov gives quite a different impression, the top families of Suzdal' and Shuia very often displayed a restraint and mutual respect in dealings with each other that was unusual in a violent society.[41] Perhaps one of the reasons for this restraint was that most of the leading figures in local society were related to each other either by birth or by marriage (while Borkov had been an outsider). Distinguished provincial families tended to marry into as many equally distinguished families of the region as they could. Whether this inbreeding followed from conscious design, with self-defense or financial and political strategies in mind, or instead from convenience and familiarity with the local supply of eligible mates, the result produced a closely interlinked local elite.

When conflict did erupt within the highest circles in Suzdal', it tended to revolve around financial dealings, and the opponents usually fought their battles in court. Often the leading families of Suzdal' actually managed to cooperate. For instance, between the Tepritskiis and the Kablukovs existed a bond of respect, and probably friendship, that lasted for many years. The two families repeatedly relied on each other's wisdom and fairness in settling disputes. In

1647, for instance, the brothers Aleksandr and Nikifor Osipovich Tepritskii turned to Aleksei Fedorovich Kablukov as a third-party arbitrator in their disagreement over dividing their father's estate between them. The single available record of discord between the two families describes a suit filed in 1660 by Aleksei Kablukov against Ignatii Fedorovich Tepritskii for wrecking his fields. The incident clearly did not poison relations between the two families: Kablukov trusted another Tepritskii to arbitrate the dispute even though it involved that Tepritskii's own cousin.[42] Over the years, the two families peaceably traded plots of land, signed petitions together concerning local issues, and testified for each other before official investigators.[43] In 1660, two Tepritskii brothers signed as guarantors on the marriage contract of one of the Kablukov women.[44]

Relations between the Tepritskiis and Kablukovs were unusually harmonious, but similar restraint, if not respect, characterized interactions among other important clans. The Koisarovs and the Kablukovs conducted numerous trades of land and issued each other loans over a 50-year period without much friction. Consolidating their long-term rapport, in 1660 Nikita Semenovich Koisarov married Evdokia Alekseevna Kablukova. The magic of marital ties, however, did not secure smooth relations forever. In 1683/84 Nikita Kablukov complained about dishonor inflicted on him by Mikhail Fedorovich Koisarov, who had lodged false accusations against him. Kablukov sued repeatedly, but Koisarov refused to appear before the judges, thereby causing Kablukov to suffer "losses by judicial red tape." Finally, in 1685, Koisarov retracted his accusations and the matter was dropped.[45]

In relations with their social inferiors, the leading families conducted themselves with significantly less compunction. The lesser gentrymen returned the favor, displaying no scruples about physically abusing their superiors or the dependents and possessions of their superiors. Interactions between the social strata and among members of the lesser gentry were strikingly brutal. Lesser gentrymen continually complained about attacks, assaults, threats, and robberies inflicted on them by their neighbors. Charges of *boi i uvech'e* (beating and maiming) appear in hundreds of petitions. Toward the end of the century an infantryman filed a dishonor complaint against Moscow gentryman Petr Nikitich Kablukov in which he claimed that Kablukov had beaten and maimed him. Cavalry officer Ivan Volzhinskii charged Ivan and Vasilii Bludov (members of the criminally inclined Bludov family) with coming to his village in Shuia where "they wanted to kill him." A monk of the Suzdal' Savior-Evfimii Monastery complained that three *deti boiarskie* with a troop of their slaves and peasants had beaten and robbed him.[46] Occasional documents provide graphic descriptions of violence among lesser gentrymen and their peasants. A slave belonging to Suzdal' landholder Z. V. Kishkin petitioned in his master's name against his neighbor *syn boiarskii* in 1630, accusing the latter of "ruining his fields with his horses, beating his animals and beating his shepherd to the verge of death."[47]

Proximity frequently served as a catalyst for conflict. In the Kashintsov-Borkov feud, Petr Kashintsov described the Shuia townspeople's grudge against him using the wonderfully evocative phrase *sosedskaia nedruzhba*, "neighborly enmity." He wrote that the special investigator from Moscow had been ordered to find the people "who carried out such outrages against me, your slave, . . . and with whom as neighbors I have hostile relations."[48]

Similarly, Kashintsov rejected the investigator sent from Moscow to conduct the case on the grounds of neighborly acrimony. He complained specifically that the investigator was ill-disposed toward him "because previous to this he [the investigator], as a neighbor, had hostile relations ceaselessly with my brother-in-law Ivan Nekliudov."[49] In many cases, proprietors of adjacent estates found themselves in conflict over boundary settlements, communal pasture and forest rights, or peasant altercations and depredations across private borders. Neighborly relations were, almost by definition, hostile. One man even argued in court that he should receive the properties of his late neighbor on the grounds that while the latter was alive they had fought incessantly and he now deserved the lands "for being a neighbor" (*iz-za sosedstva*).[50]

Belying the overwhelming brutality of their image in court records, provincial landlords were not beyond resorting to cooperation. The nature of judicial sources darkens the picture of the local scene by emphasizing the negative, the conflictual, and the illegal. Occasional personal letters survive to provide some suggestion of how *dvoriane* and *deti boiarskie* interacted when they were not beating and maiming one another. In their more amicable interactions they demonstrate a horizontal exchange of assistance rather than the hierarchical relations usually implied by patronage. The surviving private letters requesting help suggest that people developed their own small circles of mutual assistance and consistently relied on the same few individuals. The Kablukov family assisted and relied on the help of Lev Zvorykin, the brothers Lev and Vasilii Kruglikov, and members of the Volokhov family during the last quarter of the seventeenth century.[51] Appeals for help were couched in the subservient, flowery language of clientage, but it should be stressed that the letters do not establish the existence of formal patronage networks. Instead, the reciprocal patterns of assistance reveal informal clusters of friends and allies.

A letter from Lev Kruglikov, a man of Moscow rank in his own right, to Nikita Kablukov illustrates the kind of favors that one provincial landlord could do for another as well as the ingratiating, almost abject language that equals within the local community employed when addressing requests to one another. The letter opens with the formulaic salutation of good wishes and mutual health bulletins: "To [my] lord, my brother Nikita Alekseevich, Lev Kruglikov petitions! I wish you, lord my brother, and your entire household, long life. Please, lord-brother, write to me about your robust health, for I wish to hear about your health. And about me, if you are pleased to know, I am in Moscow and, as of April 2, by the grace of God I am alive." After the formal salutation, the letter broaches the core of the matter:

> And I ask, lord-brother, that you grant me your favor with regard to the oats that I borrowed from you, and give me a new deadline [for repaying you] and please, lord my brother Nikita Alekseevich, order that I be given 20 *cheti* more of seed oats, so that I can plant the land in my villages. Right now I have nothing to plant, and I personally petition for your favor, and for this purpose I have specifically sent my man Liubimka to you. Please, lord my brother, show me your kindness. Promise me some oats, so that I can seed the earth in my villages in Shuia and Lukh. Please, lord my brother, show your kindness to me, lend me some oats, and I am relying on your kindness in everything. Please, lord my brother, do not despise my request to you in which I beg your kindness. I beg you very much.[52]

As this letter illustrates, Lev assumed the role of supplicant and dependent when he implored his "lord-brother" for a loan of oats. The Kruglikovs wrote to Nikita Kablukov on several other occasions asking him to look after their villages and mill while they were out of town, and Kablukov arranged to rent half of Vasilii's lucrative water mill.[53] An ongoing relation of indebtedness and loyalty bound the two families in mutually beneficial dependency.

The same kind of exchange of favors could take place within a family, expressed in the same language of petition and deference. In a letter Konstantin Kablukov addressed his "lord uncle," Nikita Kablukov. In another letter Konstantin highlighted the literal meaning of the term *bit' chelom*, which means "to beat one's forehead" but which meant in normal usage merely "to petition." In an extra show of deference, he closed his letter with the sentence, "On this matter we write to you little, lord, but we strike our foreheads and our faces down to the earth."[54] All of these letters begin with the requisite baroque salutations but eventually discuss business matters in straightforward terms. In a letter to his grandfather, Konstantin reported on the business he was carrying out for his grandfather in Moscow and what he needed to pursue the matters. In return, Konstantin asked his grandfather to do him some favors back at home.

> And please, if you will, write to me and I ask you lord my grandfather Aleksei Fedorovich a favor. I ordered [my village] elder to go to Nizhnei for salt, and told him to take money from the [sale of] the uninhabited field for the salt, and if they don't give him money for the uninhabited field now, then you, my lord, lend [it] to me please, lend my elder money for salt, and he, when he gets the money for the uninhabited field, will repay you. Please, lord, if he doesn't get the money, please Grandfather, lend [it], and I am relying on your kindness.[55]

These letters and the ongoing relations among allied gentry families in the Vladimir-Suzdal' region illustrate the loose but indispensible linkages of dependency and mutual assistance that allowed provincial landholders and servitors to pursue their affairs in Moscow chancelleries and courts and to maintain their villages at home.

The sources provide no positive term to describe these personalized reciprocal relations. When seventeenth-century documents refer to patronage relations explicitly, it is almost always in a negative sense. The individuals and the relationships involved prove difficult to identify. When gentry leaders acted in tandem with allies, dependents, or clients, the formulaic language of the time described these people by type rather than by name. Terms of clientage included *roditeli* (relatives), *druz'ia* (friends), *sovetniki* (counselors), *khleboiazhtsy* (clients), *zakhrebetniki* (dependents), *dolzhniki* (debtors), *zakupaiachie* (bought-off people), *liudi* (bondsmen or slaves—literally, people), *krest'iane* (peasants), and *bobyli* (cottars).[56]

Most of the terms have straightforward meanings. At the highest level, the concept of kin is clear, although how far it extended varied according to the context. In the provinces, kin generally encom-

passed relations only to first or second cousins, although Aleksei
Kablukov called a third cousin once removed his "uncle" and a third
cousin his "brother" (meaning cousin).[57] At the other extreme, peasants and cottars were legally defined categories of rural, agricultural
laborers. *Liudi* (people) apparently referred loosely to overseers, estate supervisers, military personnel and other kinds of nonagricul-
tural bonded personnel and household slaves.[58] *Zakhrebetniki* were
homeless people who lived in other people's houses, or "behind their
backs," as the etymology of the word implies. They were frequently
craftsmen who peddled their skills or wares in town market stalls.[59]
The term carried some degree of opprobrium: in 1665 G. M. Chirikov, a Vladimir landholder, accused a lower-level servitor of having
beaten and robbed him. In order to strengthen his case, Chirikov
painted his assailant in dark terms, claiming that he had participated
in the 1662 uprising against the tsar at Kolomenskoe and had been
exiled to the provinces but escaped back to Moscow. Throughout the
petition Chirikov employed the phrase "criminal *zakhrebetnik*" to
describe his opponent.[60]

Gentrymen probably reserved the epithet "friend" to describe people of a social stature equivalent to their own. Debtors, however,
could come from any social caste. Documents from the Vladimir-
Suzdal' region indicate that leading families lent money to each
other, to members of their own immediate and extended families, to
their own and each other's peasants and "people," and to townspeople. Who *sovetniki* (counselors) were is anyone's guess, but the in-
ference of respect implies that they came from among the circle of
friends and relatives. The term *khleboiazhtsy* appears frequently in
documents from the Vladimir-Suzdal' region. Its precise connotations are unclear, although the word certainly denotes some kind of
obligation or subordination. The label was derogatory, accusatory.
Litigants employed the term to discredit their opponents. Reliance
on *khleboiazhtsy* implied abuse of the system. Most analysts have
assumed that *khleboiazhtsy*, like *zakhrebetniki*, were dependent
peasants or townspeople, but the term could also refer to petty gentrymen who were somehow committed to a powerful patron.

Patronage and mutual aid functioned as a particular form of *ge-
meinschaftlich* ties, horizontal and vertical, within provincial communities. Recognition of such ties in the eyes of the community
signified a great deal in the politics of local power. The strength and
breadth of a man's connections served as a public measure and ac-

knowledgement of his prestige within the community. Among the provincial gentry, as Robert Crummey notes of the boyar elite, "patronage ties often had a primarily defensive purpose. In the confusion of seventeenth-century court politics, individuals and families strove to avoid isolation and to maintain working relationships with as many of their fellows as possible."[61] A broad collection of friends, benefactors, and followers could translate directly into political gains, whether by pulling strings in the central chancelleries or the provincial governor's office, by tilting an investigation in someone's favor, or directly challenging opposition with pure brawn. Patronage did not take on formalized structure and did not harden into lasting, distinguishable factions or organizations. This was not the "new feudalism" of early-modern France, not a society of liveried supporters of Capulets and Montagues.[62] A Muscovite patron did not expect his followers to show up in livery or wearing his device, nor was there any formal oath or indenture involved in Muscovite provincial clientelism. Rather, provincial landlords rounded up temporary support however they could when an issue was pressing and allowed their supporters to disperse when the matter was resolved. The most effective webs encompassed allies from all walks of life: peasants for strong-arm assaults, lesser gentrymen for signing petitions and gaining weight in local gentry elections, officials for subverting the system. Each level of clients rendered its own variety of indispensible services to their patrons, masters, or friends.

Force and Followers

In an endemically violent society, where people might be openly assaulted by neighbors in broad daylight or in the evening by people with whom they had just been socializing, and where anyone on the streets was at risk for "beating and maiming," a strong following of hefty supporters had definite advantages. Not only Petr Kashintsov and Ivan Borkov relied on the brute strength of their men to achieve their ends in local politics. Surviving documents show that gentrymen of all stripes appeared and acted in the company of their "people and peasants" in addition to their more highly placed "kin, friends, and clients."

In hostilities among landlords, peasants were often the ones to suffer most directly. Gentrymen and their people were often accused of beating other people's peasants and destroying their homes and livelihoods. One Shuia landowner complained that his cousins had forcibly appropriated his peasants' households and grain stores. In the process the cousins had seized the peasants and "beat them almost to death and broke their arms and legs."[63] Peasants and bondsmen were also legal substitutes for their masters in run-ins with state authorities. By law, authorities could arrest peasants and slaves and hold them as surety bonds for their masters.[64] Thus Ivan Borkov's peasants were imprisoned when their master resisted arrest and refused to appear for trial in Moscow, and Kashintsov's men were locked up and continued to languish in jail long after Borkov had released their bruised and broken master.[65]

Peasant proxies were not only victimized for their masters' sake; they also took a more active role in perpetuating feuds between estates. They sometimes did their masters' dirty work, attacking neighboring peasant villages and preying on neighboring estates. In a series of suits brought against the Koisarov family in the 1630s, Ivan Shalimov, an undistinguished Suzdalian servitor, accused his grander neighbors of inciting their peasants to attack his peasants and threaten them. In one petition Shalimov stated that the peasant in question had attacked "at Koisarov's bidding."[66] The Koisarovs had been at the receiving end of just such a scheme a few decades earlier, according to a complaint filed by Dmitrii Koisarov. He claimed that another petty servitor, Vasilii Kopnin, had "sent his people, with many other people and peasants" to his estate, where they had beaten and tortured a family of slaves and had stolen livestock, grain, and clothing from the peasants. Kopnin's men then had proceded to Koisarov's house and stable, where they had stolen valuable weapons, clothing, and tack and induced one of Koisarov's household slaves to run away with them.[67]

Since peasant voices generally remain silent on the subject, one can only speculate on their feelings about being used as public intermediaries. Landlord-peasant relations could never have been entirely rosy, particularly in the seventeenth century with its sequence of famines, wars, and peasant uprisings. Nonetheless, relations of reciprocal dependency were structurally inherent in the landlord-peasant relationship, just as they were in relations among the gentry. The essence of the relationship between a peasant or slave and a master was reciprocal assistance, although the terms of the relationship were heavily weighted in the landlord's favor. The peasant or slave was bound to toil for the master, to turn over rather arbitrary amounts of produce and money to the master, and to obey the master's authority and judgment. In return, the master had to give his dependents at a minimum enough land to farm and some degree of protection from the aggression of other peasants, gentrymen, brigands, and state officials. The relationship was absolutely personalized, since the state had little leverage in the world of lords and peasants. For a peasant to survive, he or she had to appeal to the mercy and patronage of the master or to the protection and intercession of an intermediary bailiff or overseer. The use of dependent laborers as surrogates in battle and in court, then, was systemically of a piece with the use of personal connections, patronage, and pull at higher levels of society. Intercession, favor, and mercy formed the stable tripod on which Muscovite informal politics rested. Whether asking for an aristocratic patron's favor, the tsar's mercy, a master's protection, or intercession of the Mother of God, the patterns of Muscovite understanding of how business should and could be done were the same. Doors would not open without grease on the hinges, and judges—whether on the landlord's estate, in the chancellery offices in Moscow, or at the Last Judgment—would not render favorable verdicts without a personal appeal for mercy from the litigant and his or her well-connected sponsor. The dividing line between informal and formal politics, then, was a very blurry one. For all the rigidity of laws in the statute books and for all the insistence on impartial justice in Muscovite rhetoric, the practical language of politics was that of personal relationships and private appeal.

Favoritism, Equity, and the Dual Nature of Muscovite Political Culture

Patronage and favoritism were integral parts of the Muscovite system and were indispensable to the conduct of administrative affairs in the provinces. Both in Moscow and in the provinces, Muscovites relied on family groupings and patronage networks to keep the system functioning, yet that same system roundly condemned any use of family or cliental connections and "pull." The law code of 1649 specified that "no one on his own initiative shall out of friendship or out of enmity add anything to or remove anything from judicial records. No one shall favor a friend nor wreak vengeance on an enemy in any matter. No one shall favor anyone in any matter for any reason."[68]

In spite of the law, friends in strategic places were not only helpful but essential to success in dealings with tsarist or provincial administration. In general, the state turned a blind eye to favoritism and nepotism, but when such manipulation was brought to the attention of the courts, it was inevitably presented as a transgression of the law, an unjust and intolerable utilization of connections. Charges of *druzhba* (friendship) or *nedruzhba* (enmity) were leveled with great frequency against successful manipulators. Plaintiffs expressed indignation and outrage at their opponents' reliance on cronyism, yet the cases make clear that the real offense was that the plaintiffs' own patronage network proved unequal to the greater strength and cohesion of their rivals'. Just such a double standard underlay Petr Kashintsov's condemnation of Ivan Borkov. Kashintsov complained that Borkov "plotted with his people" against him and that the special investigator was "friendly" with Borkov's clan and unfriendly with his. Whenever possible, however, Kashintsov, too, conspired with "his people" and operated with the assistance of his family.

Everyone valued and relied on ties of friendship and kinship, for without them nothing could be accomplished. Yet litigants could reverse these traditional values of loyalty and obligation and accuse governors and chancellery personnel of administering biased justice. Kondratii and Vasilii Kudriavtsev and their widowed mother complained that their inheritance was being claimed by Boris Serbin, who had filed a "fanciful" (*zateinyi*) petition in which he had applied for ownership of their villages but had deviously made up different names for them so that no record of ownership could be found. The Kudriavtsevs asserted that Serbin had contrived to have the court send out a clerk who was a "known criminal and swindler" to investigate the case. To tip the scales in Serbin's favor, the clerk had questioned only a very few people about the land, among whom were Serbin's "clients, people he had bought off, and friends," who had all given false testimony.[69] On this subject, the *Ulozhenie* of 1649 stated, "Instruct the investigators sternly about this, and write to them in their working orders with great emphasis that they must conduct the investigation justly, under the sovereign's oath, not favoring a friend and not wreaking vengeance on an enemy. They must see to it and take utmost care that the people being interrogated do not collude in family groups [and] lie in the investigation."[70] If the Kudriavtsevs' charges were accurate, witnesses and investigator alike had violated the law of the land, the former by manufacturing, the latter by recording deliberate lies.

In another instance, retired captain Zakharii Ivanovich Miachin combined force with clever manipulation of the legal system, all realized through the assistance of clients and collaborators. In 1652 Zakharii Miachin faced legal charges lodged against him in Shuia by his cousin Bogdan, but the resourceful Zakharii journeyed from Moscow back to Shuia in the company of the special investigators sent from the Office of Brigandage Control to resolve the dispute. He "rode around with the investigators to the people being questioned [about the case] in monasteries and villages and hamlets distributing drink, and he bought and cajoled his friends and counselors and clients and carried out a selective rather than universal search so that the witnesses' testimony would malign [his opponents]."[71] The examples show the efficacy of one of the crudest approaches to winning clients—bribery. Boris Serbin relied on his "bought-off ones" to provide false testimony. Zakharii Miachin counted on the magic of liquor to charm supporters. In a system where gift giving was not only a necessary but also an expected and desirable component of the relationship between the population and its administrators, criminal charges of bribery demonstrate a value system riddled with contradictions.

A bizarre case from Suzdal' underscores the inherent inconsistency of the government's stance on family networks within official institutions. The case pitted Seresha Pigasov, the tax-elder of the town, against all of the clerical personnel of the town governor's office. He charged that the Kurbatov clan had monopolized all of the positions as town clerks, in a reprehensible display of nepotism. The clerks, incidently, were indeed all directly related to each other by blood or marriage, as depicted in a tidy genealogical description drawn up by the ministerial investigators who were sent to look into the case. The investigators called their report "a list of the clerks of the governor's office who are related in kinship among themselves." The Kurbatov faction countercharged that Pigasov had trumped up the accusation with the aid of his own band of family and supporters. Kosta Kurbatov wrote that he had been summoned to the court of the Chancellery of Military Affairs by petition of Pigasov and his "brothers and brothers-in-law, and friends and *khleboiazhtsy*."[72]

Nepotism seems a curious charge to level at chancellery clerks, whose recruitment, training, and advancement routinely depended on family connections. As a matter of course most young men started their bureaucratic careers in the same offices where their fathers and kinsmen served, and that was how beginners obtained their specialized education and training in a society without schools. The historian S. B. Veselovskii, in his work on chancellery personnel, noted that provincial branch offices and central ministries were staffed with "whole nests of kinsmen."[73] Entrance into bureaucratic ranks, one must recall, was closed to the general public. In principle the only people eligible for bureaucratic positions were the sons of clerks. In practice, literate townspeople, soldiers, and petty gentrymen sometimes crossed over into bureaucratic ranks, but ministries and local offices looked especially kindly upon applications from the children of their clerks.

The Suzdal' nepotism case reflects the deep ambivalence toward patronage and kinship politics that pervaded the state and society. Any significant action or accomplishment required the cooperation and assistance of a broad-based support structure. Everyone understood that he or she could not stand alone in Muscovy. But in spite of its common acceptance and constant practice, patronage, like nepotism, could leave an unpleasant odor. Muscovites resented successful use of pull by their rivals, and the state condemned it. The mechanisms that greased the system, indeed that *were* the system, also threatened the system.

In regard to the use of personal connections in Muscovy, one might ask, first, whether it was a distinctive trait unique to Russia and, second, whether it was in some significant way structural or systemic.[74] The answers to these questions would be no to the first, but yes to the second. Reliance on family and faction to was not at all unique to Russia; in fact it characterizes most societies at most times. Yet it assumed a particular form in Muscovy, where personal and family connections were explicitly acknowledged as the key to political, social, or economic status. Within the boyar aristocracy and the Moscow elite, *mestnichestvo*, the elaborate system of genealogical seniority, determined all military, administrative, and ceremonial assignments and hence status and career advancement, until its abolition in 1682.[75] Under the rules of *mestnichestvo* an individual could go only as far as his (or her) clan status and birth order dictated. People were *supposed* to follow their parents' course, to inherit their status, and derive social standing from their relatives' birth and service records. It would have violated the social order if they did otherwise. The double standard in Muscovy did not reflect abuse of the system. Rather, it emerged from contradictions deeply rooted in the political culture. Favoring friends and relatives was roundly condemned as corrupt in both law and litigation, but at the same time equally official practices within the tsarist state relied entirely on patronage and kinship as the clear and acknowledged operating principle. Inherited status and wealth were not merely useful benefits but actually endowed a man with his central and defining status in the society.[76]

The incongruity of a state system overtly built with kinship as its core element yet simultaneously condemning use of family pull reflects the confusion of a system in the process of change. The sixteenth and seventeenth centuries witnessed Muscovy's metamorphosis from a small, traditional princely court into a vast, bureaucratically administered imperial state. Reliance on personal ties no longer fit with the depersonalized, universalizing regulations of state institutions, but kinship and patronage connections retained both their immediate utility and their cultural legitimacy.

In his stimulating work on the Muscovite historian Andrei Lyzlov, David Das has recently suggested that the late seventeenth century witnessed a transition in high Muscovite culture from an emphasis on *chest'* (honor), which derived from clan status and birth, to a striving for fame or *slava* (glory), which denoted personal accomplishment and heroism. "Honor had depended on place and rank within a system of families; at birth one acquired the honor that would continue throughout life. . . . Fame was completely the opposite. . . . Honor was inherited, fame was sought."[77] This transition, Das argues, was reflected in the cultural artifacts of the period—the histories, portraits, and panegyrics—which for the first time in Muscovy celebrated individual actors. It was also embodied in the political reforms of the 1680s: the eclipse of the old Boyar duma as the supreme ruling body, the establishment of alternate governing chambers, the creation of new and more glorious titles for provincial governors. The change was most dramatically evident in the abolition of *mestnichestvo* in 1682 and the public burning of the genealogical books by which *mestnichestvo* rank had been calculated. With the fiery end of the old clan-based system, Muscovites had to develop a new set of values and a new yardstick for measuring worthiness. Das argues that at the highest levels of Muscovite society, merit and ability emerged as the new keystones. Fame replaced honor as the goal of tsarist courtiers.[78]

This transformation in high culture helps to explain Muscovy's late–seventeenth- and early–eighteenth-century transition from a political culture explicitly based on family connections and patronage to one based, in principle, on individual merit and unbiased judgment. But the ancient and enduring presence of both currents in traditional Muscovite political culture indicates that the transformation was not the product of high culture (and emulation of the West) alone. The cultural material for such a transformation had long been present outside of the Moscow elite as well. The clash of opposing principles was inherent in the Russian political tradition from as early as 1397, when the Pskov Judicial Charter decreed that an official "will conduct trials justly . . . will not avenge through his court decisions, and will not favor his relatives; and will ruin no innocent."[79] The principle of equal and unbiased justice antedated the late–seventeenth-century transformation by hundreds of years and provided fertile cultural ground for the reforms of the late Muscovite and the Petrine eras.

The standard of dispassionate justice to which judges and officials were held, however, was not the same as the principles by which society itself was organized. As is clear from the emphasis on kinship at all levels of society, Muscovites imagined their community as one built upon bloodlines and family identification and solidarity, not as one constructed upon individuals and merit. Under Peter the Great high culture and legislation increasingly emphasized individual achievement and justice on the basis of merit, while provincials kept on doing what they had always done, assisting their relatives and friends whenever possible and relying on a helping hand from a well-placed contract whenever necessary.

1a

1. Various ranks of Muscovite men in appropriate attire, from Augustin Meyerberg, *Albom Meierberga*, St. Petersburg, 1903. 1a: an archpriest; 1b: merchant, gentryman (rear view), and boyar's servitor (side and rear views); 1c: boyar, prince (rear view), *sotnik*, and high merchant (*gost'*); 1d: musketeer, Kalmyk (tribesman), Astrakhan' Kalmyk. Other than the Kalmyk tribesman, costumes are only subtly differentiated. All wear loose, long, form-concealing coats and have their heads covered, but the details carry tremendous weight in indicating social status. Notice the traditional tall hats of the prestigious boyar and prince. The inclusion of the wild tribesmen completes Meyerberg's display of Russian "exotica." Courtesy of the James Ford Bell Library, University of Minnesota.

1b

1c

1d

2a

2. Various ranks of Muscovite women in appropriate attire, from Augustin Meyerberg, *Albom Meierberga*, St. Petersburg, 1903. 2a: a boyar's wife, a townswoman, a "simple urban girl," a gentryman's daughter in winter attire, a Moscow girl, a Moscow maiden, 2b: a resident of Moscow wearing rain-gear (an inside-out sheepskin coat), a boyar's wife greeting guests, and a Russian gentrywoman; a Russian maiden of simple estate, a Tatar woman from Viatka, a Cheremis woman. Women are shown with slightly more differentiation, but share with the men the form-concealing, loose overgarments and indispensable head covering. The boyar wife displays her finery on her sleeves. Only unmarried maidens and girls allow their braided hair to show. Married women modestly hide their hair under more or less elaborate headdresses. Courtesy of the James Ford Bell Library, University of Minnesota.

3. Erik Palmquist's engravings of a Muscovite cavalry soldier in action (3a) and of a Muscovite gentryman confidently surveying the landscape (3b). Notice the curved Turkish-style sword. *Någre vich sidste Kongl: Ambassaden till Tzaren i Müskou giorde Observationer öfver Rysslandh,* 1674; facsimile ed., Stockholm, 1898. Courtesy of the James Ford Bell Library, University of Minnesota.

3b

4

4-6. Seventeenth-century sketches of gentry houses and household compounds taken from illustrated maps drawn up by scribes dispatched from the Chancellery of Service Lands in Moscow. Maps augmented the written descriptions of landholdings, boundaries, and peasant households contained in the cadaster books of the period. These three are the house of G. M. Skvortsov in Toropets Province, a gentry house in the village of Krasnoe in Pereslavl'-Zalesskii Province, and the house of I. Chertkov, also in Pereslavl'-Zalesskii Province. These three sketches show a range of gentry wealth and ostentation, from a simple, two-story log cabin, poorly differentiated from a substantial peasant house, to the fenced compound containing several houses, storehouses, and outbuildings, to the rather grand, palatial manor house, part of another, extensive fenced compound. The decorative woodwork in the final sketch was (and is) typical of Russian wooden architecture, including peasant houses. The smoking chimney in Figure 6 connotes unusual luxury. Most Russian homes at the time, even among the gentry, were "black" or without chimneys to let out the smoke. Courtesy of *RGADA*, *f.* 1209, Toropets, *st.* 22652, *ch.* 2, *l.* 148, and *RGADA*, *f.* 1209, Pereslavl'-Zalesskii, *ed. khr.* 485/21993, *ch.* 1, *l.* 253.

5

6

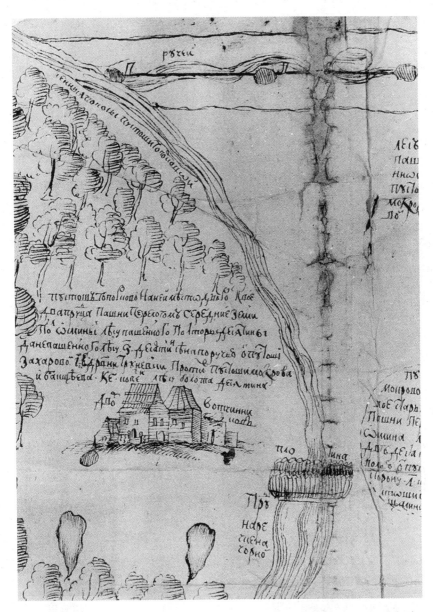

7. A detail from a surveyor's map, showing the household compound of a *votchinnik* in Moscow Province. The caption above the house lists all of the arable fields, deserted fields, hay fields, swamps, and woods belonging to the householder. The text precisely duplicates the formal chancellery language used in cadasters and official deeds to lands. To the right of the *votchinnik*'s house and slightly below it, a dam blocks the river. Courtesy of *RGADA*, *f.* 1209, *op. Moskva, ed. khr.* 33020, *ch.* 2, *l.* 230.

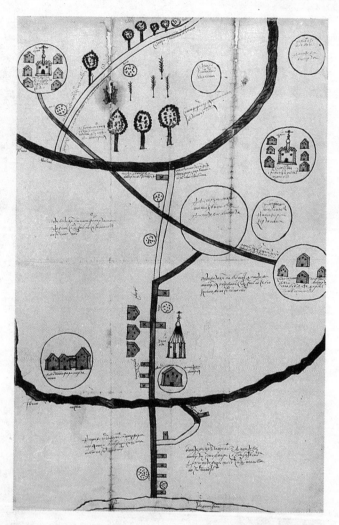

8. A schematic map of a section of Iur'ev Pol'skii Province, showing, in the circle at the lower left, the household compound of Nikifor Koriakin, a member of a large Iur'ev Pol'skii and Vladimir gentry family. Nikifor Volodimerov syn Koriakin was listed as a *zhilets* and owner of an estate in 1676. Koriakin's estate, located on the banks of the River Kist', abutted the lands and churches of the Danilov Monastery (shown in circle to the immediate right, directly under the church bell tower). Above Nikifor's house lay his arable fields and half a settled village belonging to him. Below and across the river lay more of his lands and another half a settled village. The small houses along the main road are labeled "peasant houses," while the small rectangles marked with x's and the circles filled with small dots indicate surveyors' posts and pits, which were carefully placed and maintained as boundary markers. Courtesy of *RGADA, f. 1209, op. Iur'ev-Pol'skii, ed. khr. 34226, ch. 2, l. 214.*

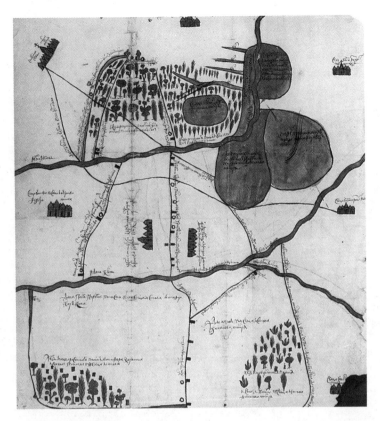

9. Map of part of Iur'ev Pol'skii. At the top left, this fragment shows a village and church belonging to the powerful Trinity-St. Sergei Monastery, which had properties throughout the tsardom. At the top right, is the household compound of *stol'nik* Ivan Alekseev Golovin. The darker areas marked to the right, along the River Liuban', indicate meadows and abandoned fields belonging to various monasteries. The boundary lines to the south of the river indicate official divisions, established by cadastral survey, between the properties of Nikifor Koriakin and Prince Grigorii Shekhovskoi. Dark rectangles and circles lining the boundaries are posts and pits erected and dug to indicate the property line. The houses at the middle left, between the rivers, are labeled "village which was the abandoned field Chiuriakovo, belonging to Fedor Miachkov." The Miachkovs were a large, not particularly distinguished family of servitors from Iur'ev and Vladimir, who produced the scandal involving the kidnapped aunt discussed in Chapter 6. Courtesy of *RGADA, f.* 1209, *op. Iur'ev-Pol'skii, ed. khr.* 34226, *ch.* 3, *l.* 429.

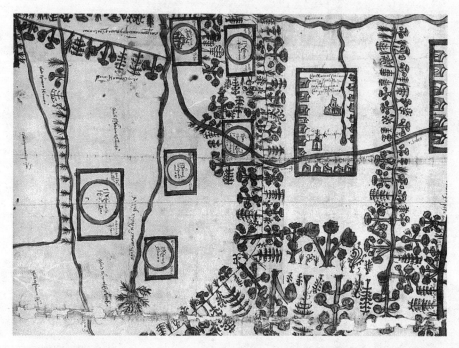

10. This beautiful, tapestry-like rendition of a map of part of Iur'ev Pol'skii Province indicates that the surveyors of the Chancellery of Service Lands took some artistic pride in their work. The large, fenced estate to the right, nestled among the flowery shrubbery, belonged to *stol'nik* Prince Grigorii Fedorov Dolgorukii. His household complex stands in the middle, surrounded by peasant houses. The compound also contains the prince's own church, dedicated to the Nativity of Christ. To the left, the rectangles inscribed with circles represent unpopulated fields. Courtesy of *RGADA*, *f.* 1209, *op. Iur'ev-Pol'skii, ed. khr.* 34235, *ch.* 2, *l.* 180.

11. Petitioning ritual, as recorded by Augustin Meyerberg. Caption reads: "Petition or supplication, which is given by beating one's forehead or bowing to the ground to the Tsar or to his father-in-law, Il'ia Danilovich Miloslavskii, or to Chamberlain Grigorii Ivanovich Romadanovskii, or to State Secretary Almaz Ivanovich." The picture shows supplicants lined up to submit their written petitions to the presiding boyar (identifiable by his lofty hat and brocaded gown). By the seventeenth century, "beating one's forehead to the ground" seems to have given way to a slightly less profound obeisance, as shown in this engraving. A foreigner, dressed in gaudy Western show, waits his turn with the others. Courtesy of the James Ford Bell Library, University of Minnesota.

12. Swearing an oath with a kiss. The "cross-kissed oaths" discussed in Muscovite criminal procedure usually involved kissing the document itself in the presence of a cross, rather than kissing an actual cross. In Adam Olearius's rendition, the oath is ritually sealed in the local administrative office, before an array of officials and witnesses. As when submitting a petition, the oath-taker bows low, while the presiding official sits behind his table and cross, officiating. Notice the bare walls, unadorned costumes and general simplicity of the office. The tablecloth, invariably red, would have provided the only visible grandeur for the occasion. Engraving from Adam Olearius, *Voyages très-curieux & très-renommez, faits en Moscovie, Tatarie, et Perse, par le Sr. Adam Olearius*, ... 2 vols. in 1. Trans. Sr. de Wicquefort (Amsterdam: M.C. Le Cène, 1727), by permission of *RGADA*.

13. Execution and punishment in Moscow, in Red Square, with the Kremlin in the background. In the months following the Moscow Uprising of June 1648, Red Square was the site of numerous executions. Olearius himself did not witness these events, but evidently drew upon his knowledge of Muscovite practices to draw this horrific vision. Scenes of Russian barbarism presumably helped to sell Olearius's book in the West. Convicts are beaten with heavy sticks, broken by hanging from their wrists, and subjected to other indescribable tortures, more suggested than shown, while elegantly dressed foreigners watch from the foreground, perhaps supplying the Western perspective desired by Olearius's readers. Engraving from Adam Olearius, *Voyages très-curieux & très-renommez, faits en Moscovie, Tatarie, et Perse; par le Sr. Adam Olearius*, ... 2 vols. in 1. Trans. Sr. de Wicquefort (Amsterdam: M.C. Le Cène, 1727), by permission of *RGADA*.

14. *Novissima Russiae Tabula*: Map of Muscovy attributed to the Dutchman Isaac Massa. Ostensibly based on a map drawn by Boris Godunov's son Fedor around 1604. First printed by Hessel Gerritz in 1611; then reprinted in England as part of an ambitious plan by Johannes Janssonius Van Waesbergen and Moses Pitt to publish in an English edition a large, high-quality, multivolume atlas of the world. The ambitious scheme was cut short by Jansson's death and by Pitt's incarceration in debtors' prison. Massa's map appeared in the second of the four volumes that were eventually published, 1680–83. "Moscua" is indicated by a tiny cross-topped church right in the middle of the map. The "Wolodimera" region is marked in large letters just north-east of Moscow, and the towns of "Wlodimer" and Suzdal' are labeled in tiny letters along the "Clazma reca," or the Kliaz'ma River. The cartouche in the lower left corner is draped in furs, suggesting the nature of Western merchants' interest in the riches of Muscovy.

In the Interstices of the Autocratic State: Informal Community Politics and Central Control

The tsar and his state apparatus were very far removed from the provinces, and his few agents in the countryside were as much a part of the local communities as they were officials of the state. Like any early-modern monarchy, the Muscovite tsardom exerted very limited control over society. Even at the points of direct contact between the servitor and the state, such as military service and land-holding rights, local communities exercised considerable discretion in shaping the interaction. In less well-regulated aspects of provincial life, informal networks and influence escaped entirely from the state's supervision and assumed primary significance. The gentry managed to create a lively and often brutal localized world of informal politics within and beneath the strictures of patrimonial absolutism.

The primary problem in considering the question of the relation between informal and official spheres of politics arises from the unavoidable skew of the sources. The overwhelming majority of sources produced in the Muscovite provinces emerged from official milieux and reflect institutional concerns. Relatively few private letters from the region have survived, and they generally speak of business matters in formulae rather than discuss personal issues in spontaneous language.[1] How, then, can we hope to discuss a layer of unofficial politics, outside of and beneath the purview of state institutions?[2] Much local business that was initially transacted beyond the bounds of official institutions eventually made its way into court proceedings or other official documentation. For instance, *poliu-*

bovno contracts, drawn up informally by voluntary agreement, ultimately had to be registered with the appropriate chancellery if they involved land. Privately contracted loans and obligations were reviewed in court if their terms were disputed. Court cases occasionally record ingenious ways in which locals bypassed or abused the system in the early phases of a private dispute, because eventually the culprits found themselves before a court of law. Some cases make it clear that people attempted to use the legal system to achieve their own goals, which were completely unrelated to the goals of the state or the interests that they claimed to voice in their petitions. Records of abuses of the legal system and of administrative procedure reveal the kinds of behavior that went on outside the bounds of official control, hence counteracting the centrist, legalistic bent of the surviving documents.

Another difficulty arises in interpreting court documents. The resolutions of most cases have not survived, and even where they do survive, it is never clear who was telling the truth, whether true guilt or innocence was actually established, and whether the events discussed actually occurred. Rather than assuming the role of judge in these matters, I have tried to accept all of the testimony as representing constructions or perceptions about behavior that drew on a set of experiences or expectations. I assume that litigants and witnesses reported either what they believed to have happened or what they felt would make a plausible story in court. The 1550 *Sudebnik* Law Code specified that if a complainant lied he should be "publicly flogged and cast into prison."[3] Even witnesses were at risk if they were caught in a lie or an inconsistency. They not only stood to lose money, but they could find themselves forced to participate in a judicial duel, an armed battle fought to establish guilt or innocence, to defend their testimony.[4] Given the extremely harsh penalties for bearing false witness, people presumably would not have testified to a story that would not be likely to be believed. Court testimony thus provides a plausible picture of provincial conduct, even if some of the details may have been fabricated or misreported.

Tacit Armistice: Interacting Spheres of Official and Unofficial Politics

The next problem in studying Muscovite informal political life is to define precisely which areas escaped central governmental control in order to establish the limits of tsarist rule. In the seventeenth century, the Muscovite state involved itself in the affairs of its people to a remarkably intrusive degree. Muscovy had always displayed a fondness for bureaucratic paperwork: even the dead had to be buried with passports allowing them to enter the Pearly Gates. The 1649 *Ulozhenie* Law Code marked a new high in Muscovite regulation. The English merchant Giles Fletcher observed in the 1590s that "they have no written law, save only a small book that containeth the time and manner of their sitting, order in proceeding, and such other judicial forms and circumstances, but nothing to direct them to give sentence upon right or wrong."[5] By the middle of the seventeenth century, the situation had changed substantially. Adam Olearius, ambassador from Holstein, wrote in his 1656 account:

> Formerly there were very few written laws and customs, . . . and these dealt only with traitors to the country, criminals who offended His Majesty, thieves, murderers, and debtors. . . . A few years ago, however, in 1647 to be exact [actually 1648], upon His Tsarist Majesty's order the wisest heads of all stations were gathered together to compose and set down certain laws and statutes, which His Majesty and the boyars then confirmed, and these were subsequently published. This book, in folio, is a good two fingers thick and is called the *Sobornoe Ulozhenie.* . . . Now they render judgments, or at any rate are supposed to, in accordance with this law.[6]

The hefty tome of the *Ulozhenie* signaled the state's inclination toward militantly interventionist surveillance of Muscovite life. The *Ulozhenie* regulated behavior down to an incredible level of minutia: "If someone spoils . . . a bird blind belonging to another [person], smears it with tar, or garlic, or anything else, and thereby drives away the birds from that blind; or someone steals a cone-shaped net for black grouse or a partridge net . . . beat him mercilessly with bastinadoes."[7] It legislated with equal attention the particulars of behavior, personal honor, and family inheritance patterns.

In sharp contrast to the interventionist agenda presented in the *Ulozhenie* and other Romanov legislation, however, there were many matters beneath the concern of the apparently ubiquitous state system. If governmental revenues and service requirements were unaffected, the state took no initiative in bringing such petty cases to court. Bird blinds, fish weirs, beehives, and beaver dams could be raided, destroyed, stolen, or smeared with any foul substance without fear of state intervention, unless the injured parties' ability to serve or pay taxes suffered because of the damage or if they brought suit themselves. From a practical perspective, the state remained indifferent to local squabbles until the participants deliberately involved the authorities.

For their part, members of provincial society familiarized themselves with the procedures and priorities of the autocratic system, and then they applied their knowledge to exploiting the system to suit their own interests. Provincial leaders built their own local empires but did not frame them in opposition to the state. Rather, with the assistance of governmental regulations, they built their power bases in the interstices left between and below those regulations.

"Not Under Any Rules, But by Their Own Will": The Impunity of the Provinces

Members of provincial society attacked and robbed each other and each other's peasants with extraordinary impunity. They displayed complete lack of concern about maintaining anonymity. Cases such as that of Vasilii Tret'iakov underscore how thoroughly provincial people disregarded the threat of the state system and how they acted as they pleased. Tret'iakov sued the peasants of his neighbor, Timofei Klokachev of the village of Martimanova in Shuia, who had caused him losses and threatened him with murder and arson. According to Tret'iakov's accusation, as he was leaving Shuia on the main road, passing through Martimanova, Klokachev's peasants attacked him to avenge an old grudge. The peasants claimed that Tret'iakov had started the fight by beating them and chasing them with a sabre. "But I didn't have a sabre with me at the time," Tret'iakov explained. These same peasants had routinely chopped wood on Tret'iakov's land, carted off his berries, and hunted his game. Furthermore, while poaching on his land they had destroyed both his milled and growing grain. "They threaten me and my people and peasants . . . with various schemes and with slander and unfounded libelous charges and murder and arson, and they have incorporated my uninhabited plots into their village." He implored, "Save me from being utterly ruined by these peasants and their schemes!"[8] In Muscovy, as in most places, theft and assault were prohibited by law and subject to severe penalties. Undeterred by severe legal penalties, however, neighbor attacked neighbor in broad daylight, without any attempt to assume disguises or otherwise hide their identities. As a desperate governor of Suzdal' reported in 1666 about some insubordinate townspeople, "[They] don't want to live under any rules, sovereign, but want to live by their own will."[9]

To a large extent, this kind of audacity reflected the critical shortage of routine administration in the provinces. While the Muscovite state had developed a powerful apparatus for targeted, disciplinary response in particular cases, it had yet to build the staff and structure necessary for routine management. As a consequence, provincial residents worked out their own solutions to many local problems, sparing the state apparatus the bother and leaving local matters in local hands. The first moves in settling local disputes often entirely bypassed or ignored official procedure or offices. Extrainstitutional confrontations usually involved a combination of moral and physical support from a coterie of allies.

The dramatic tale of the kidnapping of Mar'ia Nemtsova illustrates this phenomenon.[10] In May 1651, Mar'ia Zabelina, a widow of a Suzdalian landholder, filed a petition complaining that her mother, Mar'ia Nemtsova, a poor, helpless widow, had been forcibly abducted by a man who was holding her hostage until she ceded her estate to him. The alleged abductor, Bogdan Miachin, a Suzdalian landholder in his own right, turned away the first few agents sent out to bring the widow Nemtsova and her captor to Suzdal' for questioning. He proffered the excuse that "she lies sick, and it is impossible to bring her to Suzdal'."[11] The tsar, or whoever was writing in his name, instructed the local governor (the same Ivan Borkov of the Kashintsov brawl; see Chapter 5) to send investigators, gunners, and guards to bring the widow in for questioning and, if Miachin resisted arrest, to seize some of his people and peasants and hold them hostage. The governor responded pathetically that he had dispatched two agents to Miachin's estate, but "Bogdan Miachin's wife, Fedora, began forcibly resisting your sovereign order and would not give up the widow Mar'ia or her people or peasants, and I have no one else to send. There are no musketeers in Suzdal', and of gunners and guards there are only eight men in Suzdal', and they are distributed around Suzdal' according to your sovereign orders on errands and on your sovereign business and preparing saltpeter." For lack of available staff, the governor had to send his report to Moscow with the Suzdal' gentryman Fedor Zabelin, a relative of the plaintiff.[12] Interrogation of nearby peasants confirmed that Fedora had indeed defied the governor's agents. They testified that she had declared, "My husband, Bogdan

Mikhailovich, is on the sovereign's service and I won't give up the widow Mar'ia without my husband, and I won't give up my people or peasants either. And if [you] try to take [them], I will order them to fight."[13] True to her word, she had encouraged her peasants to fight off the sovereign's officials.

The original plaintiff, the widow Zabelina, evidently grew impatient with this display of inefficacy on the part of the local authorities. In August she filed another petition, complaining that nothing had been done, the scoundrels had yet to be brought in for questioning, and added with appropriate pathos that "Bogdan keeps her by force on account of her estate and wants her to die of hunger. And my mother is in great ancient age, misery and infirmity and without kin, and except for me the poor thing has no other relatives."[14] Bogdan, by this time, had shown up in Moscow but still had not brought his captive with him. Shortly thereafter he promised to bring her to the Chancellery of Military Affairs in Moscow for questioning, and six Suzdalian gentrymen signed a surety guaranteeing that he would keep his word.[15] On October 10, 1651, after five months of legal wrangling, Mar'ia Zabelina's mother finally appeared before the highest officials of the Chancellery. The case ended with a surprising twist when the missing mother was questioned about "whether she wants to live on her widow's estate with her daughter and her children or with her *nephew*, the Suzdalian gentryman, Bogdan Miachin." Nemtsova replied in court that she was living with her nephew, the so-called abductor, by choice:

> And the widow Mar'ia Nemtsova under questioning said that she wants to live on her dowager's estate in Suzdal' . . . and she will not leave her home to go to live with her daughter and her children and her grandchildren. And she will not give them her estate. She wants to live on her estate until her death, and she has given her estate prior to this to her nephew, Suzdalian servitor Bogdan Miachin, of her own free will.[16]

After Nemtsova's definitive testimony, the case was thrown out of court.

This emotional family saga illuminates the difficulties that the tsarist government had in translating paper regulations into actual compliance. Also, more significantly, it shows how the state took advantage of the local community structures and social organization to push its agenda through when pure official or coercive power was inadequate to the job. Using the diffuse power of peer pressure within provincial society, the limited state apparatus elicited compliance.

When orders from the governor failed to awe, and threats to take peasant hostages failed to coerce, the state relied on the powerful custom of collective responsibility and mutual suretyship. When Miachin's neighbors and peers signed the surety document guaranteeing that he would bring his aunt to speak to the authorities, he had little choice but to capitulate. On their surety document his guarantors agreed to pay any fine the sovereign chose to exact from them if their man failed to live up to his promise. In their words, they would proffer their heads "in place of his, Bogdan's, head, head for head."[17] They clearly had a great deal riding on his good behavior. Bogdan did too. He would have to go on living in Suzdal', where his fate would depend on the good will of his neighbors in countless ways. His service capability and reimbursement rate would be assessed by members of his community at the annual muster. His ability to find third parties to arbitrate disputes or to underwrite any loans, trades, or sales he would negotiate would depend on his reputation for reliability within the Suzdalian community. Most directly, his personal safety and his ability to mobilize a security force when necessary might depend on his local standing. Thus the state ultimately benefitted from its toleration of zones of autonomous local social organization.

As it turned out, within the year Bogdan did find himself in need of ready fists to back him up in another family confrontation for custody of the same trouble-prone widowed aunt, Mar'ia Nemtsova. This time, another nephew, Zakharii Miachin, who appears to have held the prestigious rank of selectman of Suzdal' and to have enjoyed the protection of influential officials, managed to lure Nemtsova to his estate with a dinner invitation. There he kept her locked up, fulfilling her daughter's paranoid fear that she would be forced to turn over her widow's estate against her will. Not waiting for the legal process to work its course, Bogdan organized an expedition of his bondsmen and dependents to liberate Nemtsova themselves.[18] In both scrapes with his cousins, Bogdan Miachin's solid network of boosters buttressed his position through brute force. Alone, he would have been helpless before the superior status and convenient connections of his cousin Zakharii or against the official authority of the governor's bailiffs. Bolstered by his supporters, the lowly *gorodovoi syn boiarskii* and his wife could stand their ground.[19] Mutual suretyship served as a powerful tool through which the state assured compliance, but it derived its force in society from the structures of power that evolved within local society and from individuals' desire to maintain their local reputations. These reputations were critical to provincial servitors in their daily interactions with their neighbors and peers and in local matters quite divorced from the concerns of the central state apparatus.

The reciprocity and mutual support in state-society relations, of course, had their limits and should not be overstated. Not all manifestations of provincial autonomy could be utilized by the state. Bogdan Miachin's initial disappearance and failure to appear at court, his wife's decision to oppose official orders by force, Zakharii Miachin's kidnapping of his aunt and his subsequent bribing of witnesses in the case, all signaled a breakdown of state control. These actions did not in any way contribute to successful, mutually advantageous relations between central state and local society. Yet the state was able ultimately to win the cooperation of enough elements of Suzdalian gentry society to pressure the Miachins to resolve their difficulties and submit to state arbitration. By acknowledging the superiority of state courts, even such disorderly families as the Miachins heightened tsarist legitimacy and extended central control.

Bureaucratic Obstructionism and Resistance Through Compliance

Even as they promoted tsarist authority by turning to state authorities as arbitrators in their disputes, members of the provincial gentry also twisted official rules and regulations to their own advantage. In a society as reliant on subjective relations of power as Muscovy, bureaucratic tools proved malleable in the hands of local agents and could undermine rather than uphold the interests of abstract regulation and impersonal justice. A number of cases from the Vladimir-Suzdal' region illustrate that bureaucratic formalism not only resulted in tremendous inefficiencies but also placed formidable obstructive power in the hands of local participants. For instance, in a typical bureaucratic conflict over jurisdictional divisions, the *guba* elder of Iur'ev Pol'skii refused to allow the town governor to place tax evaders in the *guba* jail. Governor Obukhov wrote in his petition to the tsar that previous governors had routinely sent criminals convicted in their courts over to the *guba* prison until guarantors for their good behavior were found and the prisoners could be released. "But *guba* elder Aleksei Kuroedov will not let me put people in jail pending a guarantor, whether for disobedience or for guilt, or for fighting with someone while drunk."[20] By insisting on his state-granted authority to determine who sat in his jail, the elder safeguarded his sphere of influence from the governor's encroachment. Kuroedov appears to have had the law on his side; when Governor Obukhov's replacement reported on the state of the town after Obukhov's departure a year later, he noted with particular dismay that "the jails for criminals and political prisoners are together."[21]

The broader context of the case suggests that more than personal concerns over relative position was at stake. The particular provocation for the elder's insistence on rigid jurisdictional boundaries was a decree sent from Moscow ordering town and provincial residents "to select sworn trustees to collect musketeers' and postal fees [the two most onerous taxes] and to put anyone who fails to pay in jail." By blocking access to the jail, Kuroedov, a member of a large and established gentry family of Iur'ev, protected his own and his neighbors' peasants, as well as townspeople, from exploitative taxation or imprisonment. Since Governor Obukhov complained further that the troublesome *guba* elder had also accused him of exacting large bribes from lower *guba* officers and prison guards, the facts and motives of this case become extremely muddled. It is nonetheless clear that, for whatever reasons, in his capacity as a local official, Kuroedov was able to use the regulations of the law against the intent of the law itself and of high officials of the state.

In a number of other cases, control of town record books and other sources of information allowed local petty officials to sabotage the conduct of state business without ever reaching the point of confrontation with the governor or higher authorities. In 1647 Karp Kazimerov, governor of Iur'ev Pol'skii, received an order to notify all Moscow-rank servitors residing in Iur'ev, Suzdal', and Shuia to report to the capital for ceremonial duties or else face heavy fines and punishments. His orders instructed him to dispatch retired *deti boiarskie* and musketeers and gunners to spread the word. "But in Iur'ev Pol'skii, there are no musketeers or gunners or artillerymen, only one messenger, and I have no retired *deti boiarskie* to send out, [because] I have no reliable list [of them] and the *dvoriane* and *deti boiarskie* of Iur'ev will not tell me about them." Whether this information blackout stemmed from a deliberate policy of local resistance or from some other combination of incompetence, inaction, or indifference, the result was a decisive blockage of state activity. Whether their behavior was deliberate or not, by controlling access to information, the petty gentry of Iur'ev effectively protected their members from obligations of local service. Although confounded by the silence in Iur'ev, Kazimerov accomplished his assignment without a hitch in the other two towns. In his report, he attributed his successes to the availability of personnel in Suzdal' and Shuia, where he counted 30 available messengers. His task may have been lightened in those communities by the fact that he was a Suzdalian himself and knew the roster of local residents.[22]

Officers of the tsar also faced defiance masked as rigorous legalism or devoted loyalty. Sergei Afonas'evich Bykov, duly instated governor of Lukh, suffered a nightmarish experience in which the population of Iur'ev turned the authority structure on its head and created its own version of legally sanctioned order. Bykov dispatched a bailiff, V. G. Shigalev, to search the province for *netchiki*, unauthorized absentees from service assignments. Shigalev failed to discover any truant servitors, but he did find a pair of undocumented vagrants, a Novgorodian petty servitor named Ivan Matveev Maslov and his man, a runaway soldier from the Don Cossacks, named Ivan Fedorov Aksaev. Maslov, wasting no time, beat the bailiff, tore out his beard, and brandishing a knife, threatened to "slice him up." The Novgorodian Maslov then rode into town, where he hurled insults and "unbecoming curses" at the governor. "And when they brought that Ivashko [Aksaev] to the city hall, he called me, your slave [the town governor], a thief."

In an impressive display of chutzpah, Maslov then claimed that he had been sent to Lukh by the tsar to replace Governor Bykov. Many provincial people stopped complying with the real governor's orders, choosing to believe the impostor's claim. The townspeople's disobedience led to delays in transacting the tsar's business and in collecting taxes, for which the helpless governor begged forgiveness. Authorities in Moscow responded sternly. In a follow-up communiqué to a document that has been lost, the tsar demanded that Governor Bykov immediately send the two charlatans to Moscow under heavy guard, as he had been commanded to do previously. The missive accused Bykov of defying orders and refusing to send the men "because of his limitless greed." Bykov's humble reply explained that he had already dispatched Ivashko Aksaev to Moscow, escorted by the bailiff Shigalev, who evidently survived the original assault, but Ivan Maslov had disappeared, "we know not whither."[23]

In this riotous episode, the people of Lukh inverted the social order and took tangible power into their own hands while ostensibly paying homage to the established political order. Although they refused to obey their appointed governor, their refusal was on the most patriotic grounds: they purported to credit another man with governing according to the tsar's imprimature. A petty servitor drifter and a shady runaway soldier presented an unlikely pair to administer a town, but the people presented a united front in accepting the story. All ranks of the provincial population had good reason to play along: the resident gentry servitors because they wished to evade service obligations, the townspeople and peasants because they saw a way to avoid taxes and town service jobs. Since their defiance touched the two areas of most crucial concern to the state, taxes and service, the Lukh townspeople and servitors needed a plausible, "official" justification for their evasion. How conscious their decision was to believe (or pretend to believe) the impostors is an open question, one familiar to those who study the recurrent and ever-popular appearances of pretenders to the throne in more or less implausible guises. Maslov and Aksaev embody in humble form the same phenomenon as the array of False Dmitriis, rag-tag pretenders to the throne, that colors the early years of the seventeenth century. Maslov's effortless escape from jail suggests at least some degree of deliberate collusion by local officials: the prison wardens must have looked the other way as their charge rode off toward the horizon.[24]

Specious legality thus provided members of the Muscovite gentry with a means of resisting unwanted demands on their time, money, or local autonomy without requiring them to risk acting as rebels either in their own minds or in the eyes of the law. Manifested as loyal obedience to a presumed letter of the law, legal obstructionism gave provincial officials and residents momentary leverage against the petty tyrannies of corrupt officials and even provided a safe base of resistance to particular mandates of the central government.

In a nation that moved from apparently unshakable and unquestioned autocracy to terrorism and revolution over the course of several centuries, the question of political movements of opposition and participation looms large over the historical profession. The subject of conflict and resistance in Muscovy has produced a large number of widely diverse theories over the past century and a half. Fitting the gentry into such theories turns out to be quite difficult. Its interests were fundamentally aligned with those of the state, the guaran-

tor of its social status, financial well-being, and hold over the peasantry. The gentry demonstrated its commitment to maintaining the
tsarist state intact by its voluntary participation in the "militia of national salvation" during the Time of Troubles, its recreation of a
tsarist dynasty with the election of Mikhail Romanov in 1613, and
its staunch loyalty in crushing Cossack and urban uprisings in the
second half of the century. By all practical measures, the gentry had
little cause to rebel against the state, and it did not do so to any
significant degree.

Yet a picture of gentry-state relations in which all is rosy skims
over a good deal of tension and even veiled conflict between the two.
For all that Muscovites highly valued harmony and consensus in
their political and social relations, conflicting interests and severely
limited resources made that ideal state at times unachievable. Acceptance of the framework of tsarism did not necessarily guarantee
practical compliance in all details. Muscovites dragged their feet in
fulfilling obligations, they refused to pay fines as they were ordered,
they beat state officials, and, on occasion, they made use of a convenient hyperlegalism to justify inaction or opposition to official orders. With a wide variety of small acts of noncompliance, largely of
the kind made famous by James Scott under the label "the weapons
of the weak," the service gentry of the Vladimir-Suzdal' region demonstrated an undercurrent of muted defiance, but, I would add, without any overarching political content or agenda.[25] Landholders who
beat state officials and disobey orders issued in the name of the tsar
cannot be said to be cooperative and obedient, but neither can they be
counted as political dissidents.

Military Absenteeism: A Site of Resistance?

By the second half of the seventeenth century, the gentry militia
had achieved notoriety for its level of absenteeism. Evasion of service, known as *netstvo*, became a standard variant of military performance, and the phenomenon has given the gentry a reputation as
either shirkers or as passive resisters. However, for all that has been
written about the brazen absenteeism of gentry cavalrymen during
this time, evidence from the Vladimir-Suzdal' region suggests that
the dimensions of the problem have been exaggerated. Of the 3,890
local men about whom I have gathered information, only 189 appear
in any documents as *netchiki* (absentees).[26] This represents about a

5-percent absentee rate. Of these 189, 79 had convincing excuses for their failure to serve: 9 were dead (a good excuse), 6 lay sick in bed, 15 were unknown to the *okladchiki* and had never held land or served in the province, 10 were in service already and had been listed as absentees by mistake, and 39 were too poor to serve. Thus only 110, or 3 percent, of all the known servitors in the Vladimir-Suzdal' region were appropriately listed as absentees. Even if the sources are incomplete and the rate was somewhat higher, these data suggest very good compliance overall with the state's service demands.

Records of town governors' efforts to track down shirkers confirm the low rate of genuine truancy. Combing their provinces for gentry truants, town governors consistently reported that they could find none except those with legitimate excuses. Officers of the muster in Iur'ev Pol'skii in 1636/37 displayed a curious sequence of logic when they described Voinko Makar'evich Voronov with the following words: "Serving as an infantryman. No trace of him. Truant. Died in the year 7138 (1629/30)."[27] A 7-year-old boy begged to have his registration deferred until he came of age: "I, your slave, am little, only seven years old, and I will not be in your service."[28] Of 29 men investigated for truancy in Suzdal' in 1629, Governor A. F. Naumov found that 4 were dutifully serving from other lists, 1 was sick, and 14 were desperately poor and unable to serve.[29] In 1668, when Governor S. M. Bykov tried to find the eight *netchiki* recorded in Lukh, he discovered that one was ready and willing to serve, two were unknown in the province and had never held land there, one was serving from the *zhiletskii* list and another from the *reitarskii* list, and one was "old and wounded and has lain in bed for many years." Only two remained under suspicion, but their estate elders testified that they were away in service. The governor threw the missing servitors' estate elders and peasants in jail while he investigated the cases.[30] Thus even state officials preoccupied with catching and punishing truants found that few of them turned out to be the villains they expected.

Of 110 unexcused *netchiki* that I have found, almost one-third (34) held the rank of *zhilets* or higher Moscow rank and so may well have missed their local musters because they were actually serving from Moscow lists. Ivan Tikhmenov of Lukh, for instance, was recorded as a *netchik* until his estate superviser proved that his master served from the *zhiletskii* list rather than the regular town list and so was not obligated to appear at the regular muster. Ivan Bezobrazov of Vladimir was initially listed as a *netchik* and denied his fourteen-ruble grant until local witnesses certified that he was serving in the border-lands as town governor.[31] Recidivism was negligible among absen-tees. Instead of displaying patterns of chronic absenteeism, the ser-vice vitae of one-time *netchiki* exhibit regular and gradually rising rank titles over time. Fedor Nekhoroshevo Markov, for instance, was listed as a truant in 1640/41, but in 1648 he was recorded serving at the frontier.[32] Two members of the Kablukov family, Gavrilo Ivanov and Afanasii Il'in, appeared among the *netchiki* in 1645 but other-wise in no way disgraced their family name. Gavrilo appeared as ordered at the muster Suzdal' three years later and received his fourteen-rubles pay. In 1648 Afanasii again failed to come to the Suz-dal' muster, but for good reason: he had given all of his land away to his daughter and could no longer afford to serve.[33] Including Afanasii Kablukov, only five men with continuing records appeared more than once "among the truants." Of these, Afanasii and three others were judged genuinely too poor to serve by local witnesses, and one had an exemplary service record up to that time but had fallen sick "on the road."[34] Only one of the repeat offenders was described as a real shirker, with a record of running from service. Even this bad egg, the 17-year-old Vasilii Alekseev Lazarev, came to understand his re-sponsibilities better with age: by the time he was 27 he had achieved the rank of Moscow gentryman, which he held for another 20 years.[35] Thus, except for those who retired, died, or fell from gentry ranks (presumably the fate of the numerous absentees reported living as wandering beggars), truants tended to miss just one round of service and then return to the front.

Many cases of absenteeism were due to the harsh conditions of life for the petty gentrymen in the provinces, and their absences were eventually formally excused by the government. In Suzdal' in 1629, neighbors and relatives testified to the profound poverty of some of the absentees: "He drifts among houses of good people"; "He lives off of relatives"; "He leads a wandering life and there is nowhere to look for him"; "He has no *pomest'e* and no people or peasants. He has nothing from which to serve." One man was so poor that a kinsman had to care for his mother, and the father of another reported, "My son doesn't live with me. He is a yurtless person [*chelovek beziurtnyi*]. He drags himself from house to house."[36] In 1659 Aleksei Kablukov requested and received a year's exemption on the grounds that his estate had burned down, which witnesses and investigators verified. *Zhilets* I. F. Shafrov obtained permission to skip service for a year after bandits attacked his home, tortured and burned his wife, and destroyed his estate.[37] In 1649 the governor of Suzdal' discovered that presumed *netchik* I. G. Miakishev had been "beaten and hacked up" on the road while en route to his service assignment five years earlier.[38] The phenomenon of intermittent *netstvo* thus in large part reflected the economic tenuousness of the Muscovite provincial gentry and the violence and precariousness of life.

At least in the central provinces, *netstvo* appears to have posed less of a threat to Muscovite military efficiency than has been generally assumed, and the gentry appears to have quite reliably fulfilled at least its minimal service obligations.[39] Gentry families needed the cash income, the land allotments, and the social status that they derived from service in the tsar's armies and could not afford the legal, economic, or social costs of chronic evasion.

There was, however, a perception in the seventeenth century that high rates of military absenteeism posed a danger. The Chancellery of Military Affairs consequently instituted a program of substantial rewards for militiamen who fulfilled even the minimum requirements of mandatory service. In large measure because of the monetary and land incentives for service, most provincial gentrymen actively sought service assignments. In the first half of the century, some submitted desperate pleas requesting that they receive service postings. Many young novices were registered in service ranks and allotted their service land rates "by petition," indicating that they had initiated the process themselves.[40] In 1648 a servitor from Lukh, Ivan Ivanovich Iarygin, entreated the Chancellery of Military Affairs to let him join his older brother in active service, "so that we do not altogether perish on one service [income]." In the same year, a pair of servitors from Lukh petitioned to switch their assignment from one regimental "half" to the other so that they could serve in the regiment due for active posting. That way they would get full pay and would not "lose time from service."[41] Fewer of these requests survive from the second half of the century, when the state was gradually phasing out gentry cavalry regiments, but a good service record retained its practical utility until the end of the century. In addition to the basic benefits of land allotments and monetary payments that came with service assignments, men could also use the excuse of active-duty assignments to win extensions in repaying loans.[42] Satisfactory performance of service could bring more direct returns. For instance, the tsar frequently favored gentrymen with good records of service with grants converting landholding title from conditional (*pomest'e*) to outright (*votchina*).[43]

In order to make a living, most gentrymen had to serve their time in the tsar's army. While the rewards for long-term service and hardship could be generous, the penalties for avoiding service could be harsh, in ways calculated to motivate materially minded gentrymen. In 1625 Governor Meshkov-Pleshcheev of Vladimir received orders to announce to the *dvoriane* and *deti boiarskie* residing on their estates in his province that they should prepare for service and collect fodder for their horses and supplies for themselves and report immediately to Moscow, "to the very last man." "And if they don't make it on time, We order their *pomest'ia* and *votchiny* taken away, irrevocably, and distributed to those who do come on time." This was certainly a threat with teeth, a good way to mobilize troops whose primary interest in military service was its tangible, material rewards. If any Vladimirites failed to appear for service, "or being in service, ran away," "or instead try to stay at home," the governor was instructed to

> order those *netchiki* rounded up right away, according to Our previous orders, and having punished them, send them immediately to our service once and for all with signed sureties and under guard. . . . Any *netchiki* who try to run away and hide, catch their slaves and peasants and put them in jail while you hunt for them themselves. When you catch them, punish them and send them to service with signed sureties and under guard, and then release their slaves and peasants from prison.[44]

These orders were often enforced. A number of men from the Vladimir-Suzdal' region forfeited portions of their landholdings and of their cash payments for evading service. Grigorii Aleksandrov Telesnin, for instance, had a rocky career in part because of choosing the wrong side during the Time of Troubles. At the military muster in Lukh in 1636, the *okladchiki* reported that he was healthy, held *pomest'e* lands amounting to 435 *cheti* populated by thirteen peasants and thirteen cottars, and had previously been eligible for eight rubles cash payment for service. However,

> During the King's son's campaign [the fight against the Poles, whose prince claimed the Muscovite throne in 1618] he deserted from Moscow, and for this 50 *cheti* and 5 rubles were deducted from his service compensation rate, and now he is granted 3 rubles. . . . According to a memo from

the Military Service Chancellery . . . in 1622/23 Grigorii was given an additional 100 *cheti* to add to his 400 *cheti* and 14 rubles from the Regional Chancellery for service in Novgorod in 1613, but in 1618/19 for truancy and desertion from the King's son's campaign, 50 *cheti* and 5 rubles were taken away from him and now he has a service compensation rate of 450 *cheti* and 3 rubles.[45]

The rises and falls in Telesnin's fortunes, like the less erratic fortunes of other servitors, derived directly from his service record.

Absenteeism, thus, serves as a poor indicator of gentry resistance to state policies or demands. The gentry servitors of the Vladimir-Suzdal' region by and large fulfilled their mandatory turns of duty. Their poverty and reliance on the income derived from military service forced them to do at least the required minimum so that they could receive cash payments and land grants. The same poverty, when it reached extreme proportions, at times drove them to evade service. If truancy represented a political statement or a principled oppositional stance, its meaning was utterly obscured by the servitors' precarious economic condition, their reliance on service income, and their consistent return to service after a single episode of *netstvo*.

Local Politics and Provincial Leadership

Local politics is a slippery term when applied to the endeavors of the seventeenth-century Muscovite gentry, covering a broad spectrum of interests and activities ranging from municipal elections to neighbors' disputes over raspberry bushes. All gentry landholders and servitors participated to some extent in the politics of the locality, but certain individuals and families involved themselves with particular assiduousness in local affairs, emerging as influential leaders on the local scene. In discussing local politics it is essential to determine specifically whose interests dominated in local affairs and what were the core issues of concern. Certainly the various local officials—the governors sent from Moscow and the *guba* elders, selectmen, and *okladchiki* elected by the province—officially directed local business, but members of the community without any formal position in local administration also wielded significant authority. Prominence on the local scene generally correlated with rank in the service hierarchy but was not limited to those who held official titles in local administration.

The titles that scholars have associated with leadership within the gentry community were *vybornyi dvorianin* (selectman) and *okladchik*. Selectmen occupied the highest rung of the provincial service hierarchy, received the highest service compensation rates, and performed the most arduous service as captains of cavalry hundreds in distant, front-line campaigns. *Okladchiki* functioned as local investigators and expert witnesses for the officers of the state who came to register men in the appropriate service category, allot land and monetary stipends, and assign duties. The state granted *okladchiki* elevated status; while most servicemen needed an *okladchik* to verify that they had reported their physical and economic status honestly at the annual military muster, the *okladchiki* themselves were trusted enough to be exempt from this requirement. The muster roll of 1648, for instance, reports that "Bogdan Andreev syn Kalitin was given his wage payment at the category indicated, and no one signed for him because he is an *okladchik*."[46] By and large, *okladchiki* came from the wealthiest, largest, and most powerful families in a province and passed the title down within dynasties (see Appendix Table A.1).[47] Once ensconced in their positions, these families could take advantage of their powerful situation to assign friends and kinsmen to high ranks and high compensation rates while dispatching their enemies on all the most difficult and dangerous assignments. Thus, in 1652/53 the Suzdalian gentry servitors begged the tsar to remove one of their *okladchiki* who was favoring his friends and penalizing his enemies in assignments to service duties.[48]

Another distinguished group that clearly occupied a prominent position within the provincial community was the set of men selected to represent the gentry at the Assemblies of the Land, consultative bodies summoned to Moscow occasionally to discuss and approve important policies. The lists of representatives to the Assemblies of the Land of 1642, 1648, 1651, and 1653 confirm that gentry communities followed the government's instructions and selected the "best" people, sometimes defined as prosperous, wise, reasonable, and literate, to attend the assembly.[49] Almost all of the Vladimir-Suzdal' delegates held high rank in the provincial service hierarchy. Of 32 delegates from the five provinces, 18 were selectmen, 10 were *dvorovye deti boiarskie*, and one was a *zhilets* (see Appendix Table A.2).[50] Gentry communities conferred these important jobs—selectman, *okladchik*, and delegate to Assemblies of the Land—on men of substance whom they knew well, men from distinguished local families with long ties to the region. Once in office, these men commanded positions of leadership and some discretionary power within the community.

Selectmen and *okladchiki* were community leaders entrusted with formal office, but they were not the only local notables who took active part in provincial affairs. Members of the gentry of the Vladimir-Suzdal' provinces who were actively involved in local controversies and decision making voiced their common concerns in a number of collective petitions addressing particular local problems.

The issues raised in local collective petitions varied and included a wide array of local matters, but the majority concerned the crucial issue of the selection of clerical staff to work in the governor's office. Local residents always had strong feelings about the choice of clerks, because the success or failure of any legal matter depended on the favor of the local administrative personnel. In 1630/31, for instance, the Vladimir *dvoriane* and *deti boiarskie* submitted a collective petition complaining about the governor's clerks and requesting that their own candidates be instated instead. In this particular case, the *dvoriane* and *deti boiarskie* not only signed a petition but also falsely asserted that their petition had the backing of the townspeople, a claim the townspeople angrily denied. The gentry further demonstrated their commitment to the cause by physically barring the unwanted clerks from entering the governor's office.[51] In a similar case in 1635, the *dvoriane* and *deti boiarskie* of Suzdal' as a collective unit (*vsem gorodom*) petitioned to have their town clerk removed.[52]

The social profile of those who submitted local petitions told as much as the nature of their complaints. Early petitions, from the 1630s, were composed in the name of the gentry living in the province and serving exclusively from the provincial lists. By 1663, however, the social composition of petitioners in local provincial matters looked quite different. In that year a petition requesting an official inquiry into the corrupt administration of Iur'ev Pol'skii governor A. F. Novokshchenov was drawn up in the name of the "*stol'niki* and *striapchie* and Moscow gentry and *zhil'tsy* and Iur'ev *dvoriane* and *deti boiarskie* and widows and children" of the province and their slaves and peasants.[53] Already by this date, individuals of relatively lofty Moscow rank (*stol'niki, striapchie,* Moscow gentry) and of the transitional *zhiletskii* list were expressing their active concern with provincial affairs. This upward trend among the inner circle of people who dominated local politics continued through the last quarter of the century. A cluster of collective petitions from Suzdal' in the

1670s and early 80s, also dealing with the governor's clerical staff, illustrate the shift. The first two petitions, dated 1678 and 1679, requested that the authorities in Moscow instate a certain Grigorii Manat'in as the town clerk in the Suzdal' governor's office. Four years later, in 1682, a third petition implored the chancellery agents in Moscow to remove that same Manat'in from office and never to allow him to serve in any governmental capacity again. In his term in office, Manat'in had proven himself corrupt and cruel and had exploited his position by taking advantage of taxpaying peasants and townspeople.[54] Again, the identity of the petitioners rather than the content of the petition is of central concern here. Most of the signatories on these petitions held Moscow rank, even though the issue was a purely local one (see Table 6.1).

A petition submitted in 1688 in Shuia about an altogether unrelated issue, the right to run a mill on the River Teza, shows substantial overlap with the list of names on the earlier petitions, indicating that these individuals and families were those who consistently interested themselves in local politics.[55] They were not single-issue participants. These rosters reveal the names of people who actually took the time and made the effort to participate in the business of local politics in the latter part of the century. The lists of signatures establish that toward the end of the century the leaders in community affairs were not the *okladchiki* and selectmen who headed provincial service lists but were men of Moscow rank who chose to participate in provincial instead of or in addition to central politics. Prominent among these men of Moscow rank who signed the various petitions were members of leading local families: Kablukovs, Koisarovs, Kozynskiis, Kruglikovs, Lazarevs, Mishukovs, Stromilovs, Tregubovs.

The active participation of Moscow-rank servitors in local politics is surprising in light of the common perception that provincial servitors aspired to climb out of their local backwaters by achieving Moscow rank and that once they had done so they never looked back.[56] Indeed, some of the people of Moscow rank who acquired land in the Vladimir-Suzdal' region in the last quarter of the century behaved as expected, demonstrating little interest in and even less connection with the scattered provinces in which their estates lay. These were the Moscow-rank landlords whose real estate portfolios included scattered bits in far-flung regions of the realm and who displayed such different patterns of landholding from those of the core Vladi-

TABLE 6.1

*Ranks of Signers of Suzdal' Petitions
of 1678 and 1679, 1682, and 1688*

Rank	1678 & 1679 petitions	1682 petition	1688 petition
Stol'nik[a]	2	4	8
Striapchii	3	6	16
Moscow gentry	8	1	13
Zhilets	2	1	2
Selectman	0	1[b]	0
Dvorovoi	0	0	1
Gorodovoi	2[c]	0	0
Other	0	1[d]	1
Unknown	6	6	21
TOTAL	23	20	61

SOURCES: *RGADA, f.* 210, *Prikaznyi stol,* no. 784, *ll.* 91–97, no. 819, *ll.* 125–28; *RNB, Sobranie Zinchenko, f.* 299, no. 1017.

NOTE: The 1678 and 1679 petition was submitted by "Shuia *pomeshchiki* and *votchinniki* of Moscow and provincial rank." The 1682 petition was submitted by "Shuia *pomeshchiki* and *votchinniki* and townspeople and estate overseers and elders and peasants." The 1688 petition was submitted by "*stol'niki* and *striapchie* and Moscow gentry and *zhil'tsy* and all ranks of service people and *pomeshchiki* and *votchinniki* of Suzdal' and Shuia provinces."

[a]For most of the *stol'niki*, their men (slaves, bailiffs) sign.
[b]Widow of selectman.
[c]*Gorodovoi* designation uncertain for these men.
[d]Chancellery translator.

mirites and Suzdalians. Basing his assumptions on this stereotype of Moscow-rank behavior, Novosel'skii even described what he felt was the "collapse" of provincial gentry communities in the 1670s and 1680s, when the capital city could no longer accommodate the growing numbers of Moscow gentry and a wave of Moscow-rank servitors flooded out of the capital and settled in the provinces. He assumed that the well-documented diaspora of men of Moscow-rank diluted and quickly destroyed existing provincial "corporations."[57]

However, the effects of Moscow-rank settlement in the provinces were not at all destructive. Moscow-rank men did not make merely nominal homes in the countryside or destroy the integrity of provincial communities with their focus on the court and capital. Instead, as illustrated by their signatures on the local petitions discussed above, they participated fully in provincial affairs. Furthermore, most of the new men of Moscow rank who appeared in the Vladimir-Suzdal' region fit a profile very much akin to that of the rest of their provincial neighbors. These new Muscovites swarming into the provinces effected not an alien appropriation of local land but rather a return of native sons, basking in new glories. Of the Vladimir-Suzdal' men who achieved Moscow rank for the first time after 1665, 83 percent had kinsmen in the area before midcentury and half had roots in the area dating as far back as 1625.[58] The "vast influx" of Moscow-rank outsiders turns out to have comprised primarily men such as Aleksei Kablukov and his sons and grandsons, who managed to attain Moscow rank in the wave of promotions of the 1670s and 1680s but whose connections with their local provinces endured untouched by the alteration of rank.[59] Genealogical records illustrate that families with established links to the Vladimir-Suzdal' region did not abandon the area after achieving Moscow rank. Instead, they maintained those affiliations for generations.

For men recently raised to Moscow rank, the continuing association with their ancestral provinces was dictated in part by the state. A register from 1685/86 documents the dismissal of Moscow-rank servitors from the capital and orders their relocation in their home provinces.[60] Each man appears on the list with a brief history of his own and his father's service record that establishes his town of origin. "Vasilii Andreevich Kuzminskii: Vasilii was raised from 'adolescent' to *podkliuchnik* in 1676/77 and to *striapchii* in 1681/82. He has seven peasant households. His father served from the Vladimir lists in town regiments [*z gorodom*]."[61] Although bearing Moscow rank and inscribed on Moscow service lists, Kuzminskii, along with the other men on the list, returned to his father's home province to live and serve. In Kuzminskii's case, this was where his forefathers had served since the sixteenth century. The same register explains that upon retirement "Moscow-rank people who were inscribed as *zhil'tsy* and whose fathers served with a provincial town are ordered to be inscribed in regimental service *with the same towns where their fathers served*." The enumeration includes 47 men who retired from Moscow-rank service to one of the five Vladimir-Suzdal' provinces.[62] All of these men returned to their native provinces and took up active roles in the local gentry communities. Their high Moscow titles in no way hindered their involvement in provincial affairs. The same family names that had dominated local petitions earlier in the century continued to appear prominently, but in the latter part of the century they sported fancy Moscow titles.

The who's who of local politics thus can be established by examining provincial court records and interactions within the community. The men who dominated community affairs did not necessarily derive their status from official positions in local administration, nor were they always men of provincial rank. Rather, in the latter part of the century, at the heart of the community were the very Moscow-rank men who have been assumed to have caused the decay of provincial gentry solidarity. The leaders of the provincial communities tended to come from old, rooted local families and to gain authority back at home after rising into the Moscow ranks on the national scene.

Wealth, Rank, Honor: The Stakes of Local Politics

Local politics revolved around three related sets of issues: wealth in its various forms, service with its accompanying titles and perquisites, and individual and family prestige. Provincial families devoted their most conspicuous efforts to increasing and solidifying their wealth. Land and peasants ranked first among their economic interests. They tried incessantly to obtain more land, by either legitimate or unscrupulous means. Having acquired plots of land, they sometimes attempted to consolidate their holdings into unified blocs.[63] Another aim was to convert *pomest'e* land, held by conditional tenure and encumbered with various limitations on sale and bequest, into *votchina*, which was owned outright.[64] Russian and Soviet studies on feudal landholding in sixteenth- and seventeenth-century Muscovy have established that landowners preferred *votchina* tenure and that lands owned outright proved far more profitable. Expenditure for capital improvement on *votchina* properties far exceeded that on *pomest'ia*. This differential continued until the late seventeenth century, even though the legal differences between *pomest'ia* and *votchiny* were gradually eroded by both common-law practice and legislative reform. Owners tended to transfer peasant laborers from their conditional properties to their *votchiny*, making the latter viable if not lucrative for agricultural production but meanwhile turning the *pomest'ia* into depopulated wastelands.

The frequency with which the term *pustosh'*, depopulated land, crops up in land records provides a clear explanation for the Vladimir-area landlords' preoccupation with another problem: securing peasant labor. Landholders expressed sharp concern in their petitions about obtaining workers and about preventing the ones they had from running off to the borderlands or to larger estates where the peasants hoped to find more tolerable conditions. The challenge of guaranteeing peasant labor to landlords in a poor and underpopulated land, particularly during the tremendous territorial expansion of the sixteenth and seventeenth centuries, was the central and defining problem of the Muscovite state during this period, and the gentry as a powerful interest group played an important role in its resolution.[65]

Other forms of income also contributed to cumulative wealth and so entered prominently into local interactions and contestations. Rental properties generated income both for the owners and for the renters, who could exploit the land however they saw fit. Loans brought in money through interest charges and penalties for late payment. Foreclosure, the frequent consequence of indebtedness in this impoverished society, expanded the real estate holdings of those fortunate enough to be in the position of power. Operating mills on rivers must have been extremely lucrative, judging by the number of suits arising around their construction, operation, fees, and sale.[66] Land, labor, and loans were the three primary sources of wealth in the Vladimir-Suzdal' area.

A far more complex set of issues relating to individual and family prestige formed a second focus of local politics. Authority and social standing derived from a combination of birth, honor, and the strength and breadth of one's social support network. Preservation of their honorable status, consequently, was exceedingly important to Muscovite servitors.[67] Petty gentrymen in Muscovy were noted by foreign observers for their prickliness on points of honor. Giles Fletcher reported that the top three degrees of nobility "have the addition of 'vich' put unto their surname [actually, on their patronymic], as Boris Fedorovich, etc., which is a note of honor that the rest may not usurp. And in case it be not added in the naming of them, they may sue the *beschest'e*, or penalty of dishonor upon them that otherwise shall term them."[68] Adam Olearius, in the next century, found that a poor prince took grave offense when the traveler's party failed to recognize his princely status: "The prince gave him to understand that he did not take this error kindly, [and] the translator had to apologize for having mistaken the prince for a peasant."[69]

Members of provincial communities paid tribute to individuals' honor and vested them with local authority when they asked them to serve as third-party arbitrators in disputes. Since arbitration took place outside the tsar's courts, only the personal status of the arbitrator guaranteed compliance. Aleksei Fedorovich Kablukov arbitrated disputes among his neighbors at least three times between 1646 and

1653/4 while serving from the Suzdalian lists as *dvorovoi syn boiarskii* or perhaps as a selectman.[70] The Kablukovs themselves had to turn to neighbors for third-party arbitration as well, once to Nikifor Osipov Tepritskii and once to Gerasim Pimenovich Poroshin, who came from another distinguished Suzdal' family.[71] The intangible element of personal or family honor is clearly implied in arbitration agreements, which included clauses concerning preventing or recompensing dishonor to any of the involved parties. One third-party arbitration agreement stipulated that if either litigant defaulted on his end of the bargain, or if either failed to accept the arbitrators' judgment, then the defaulting litigant would forfeit 100 rubles to the arbitrator as dishonor compensation.[72] Arbitrators risked damage to their personal stature if their ruling was ignored, and hence were protected by this indemnity clause. The same kind of default penalty protected women and their kinsmen from breach of promise of marriage. N. S. Koisarov promised Evdokia Kablukova an impressive 500 rubles if he failed to marry her by Thursday of the week of the meat-fast.[73] This enormous penalty clause safeguarded her reputation, which would have been besmirched and her chances of contracting an advantageous match ruined if her fiancé were to cast her aside.[74]

In a society where physical strength and the size of the gang of supporters at a man's disposal contributed greatly to his social standing, physical assault on that man or his subordinates threatened his position in the community. If physically disabled, a man lost his ability to serve in the army and consequently both his title and his income diminished. Further, if he or his men suffered physical injuries, he lost the strength to engage in brawls and raids on neighboring estates, which played such an important part in social intercourse. Yet violation of a person's body undoubtedly carried complex connotations beyond the purely physical, functional effects. Litigants in dishonor suits complained as bitterly about the indignity and insult of a physical blow as about the actual pain or damage.[75]

The dishonor suits involving the Vladimir-Suzdal' gentry reflect a predictably down-to-earth concept of honor. They complained of dishonor involving a combination brutal physical assault, verbal abuse, and a peculiarly Muscovite touchiness about administrative procedure. One Shuia landlord accused his own brother and the brothers' men of "assault and mutilation and dishonor" of him and his people.[76] An indignant Egor Ianov complained that the *guba* elder of Shuia, Karp Sekerin, had done him a terrible wrong: "In this year 1679/80, he, Karp, wrote my, your slave's, [name] as Segor, and thereby dishonored me, for I, your slave, am not Segor, but Egorko. Merciful Sovereign, Tsar and Grand Prince Fedor Alekseevich! . . . Order this my dishonor [suit] against him, Karp, to be given your tsarist trial."[77]

Landlords often sued for dishonor compensation on behalf of their wives, daughters, peasants, and other dependents. The humiliation or denigration of a peasant or female dependent, if unchallenged, reflected poorly on the honor of the master, father, or husband.[78] Ivan Semenovich Volkov summoned his brother, Nikita Semenovich, to court in 1652, charging him with dishonoring their mother, along with his wife and daughter, and for kidnapping two young female relatives.[79] In 1683/84, T. O. Voronin sued Nikita Kablukov for dishonoring his peasants and their wives and children with assault and battery.[80] Ten years later, Nikita Oshanin agreed to drop charges against Nikita Kablukov for dishonoring him and "devastating his peasants."[81] Maintaining one's own honor meant constantly patrolling one's circle of dependents to assure that no insult to them went unchecked. Questions of honor heightened the stakes of violence and petty quarrels; dishonor compensation fees awarded by the courts could vastly increase the penalty payments for ordinary violence.[82]

Service and service assignments also reflected on the honor of gentrymen and their families. The *dvoriane* and *deti boiarskie* of Suzdal' expressed concern about maintaining appropriate status in 1652/53 when they jointly requested that the tsar remove as *okladchik* Semen Ivanovich Shishelov, whom they had selected themselves three or four years earlier. They charged that he insulted them and their families by assigning them ranks below their station.[83] The particulars of service assignments and titles needed to be carefully monitored if gentrymen wanted to protect their status among their provincial neighbors as well as in the state hierarchy. Service assignment not only bestowed but also reflected standing in the local community. An unsatisfactory service record might earn a man a poor reputation among his peers, and that could translate into practical problems. Mikhail Kapustin, for instance, an impoverished Suzdalian with no land and one solitary cottar to his name, could find no one in Suzdal' to vouch for his trustworthiness at the annual muster in 1648. The *okladchiki* said, "He runs from service and doesn't serve out his term, and they will not sign guarantees for him for cash payments." In other words, his service record was so suspect that the *okladchiki* could not recommend that he receive his service stipend.[84] On the other hand, men with solid reputations could glide by without serving for awhile on the basis of accumulated service and good standing in the eyes of their neighbors. At the same muster, *okladchiki* defended the reputation of Semen Pavlov, who failed to appear at the muster due to illness, but "the *okladchiki* said that he serves out his time in service. He doesn't run away." They explained that he was a good man, deserving of his cash payment.[85] To what extent Pavlov merited this reputation for steadfast service is not entirely clear: in 1643/44 he had served locally chasing down bandits, but the following year he had failed to come to the muster.[86] So 1648 was not the first time his name had appeared among the truants. Whether he was indeed chronically ill, or whether he simply carried enough weight among the local leaders to get away with recurrent absenteeism, he relied on his neighbors the *okladchiki* to uphold his honor and on his reputation to uphold his service obligations.

Personal and family honor were inextricably intertwined with service. Pavlov's honor, as well as his salary, was at stake when the *okladchiki* certified that he was reliable and "did not run" from duty. Although Muscovites had a wide and colorful vocabulary of insults to sling at each other, one of the most piercing barbs, one that sent them scurrying to court to lodge dishonor suits, was the accusation of not serving. The Suzdalian Ivan Ianov submitted a petition in 1679/80 complaining that Karp Sekerin

> abused me, your slave, with various words without cause and accused me of not serving, alleging that I didn't serve, . . . and with this dishonored [me]. But I, your slave, served your sovereign grandfather of blessed memory, great Sovereign tsar and Grand Prince Mikhail Fedorovich of all Russia, and your sovereign father of blessed memory, great Sovereign tsar and Grand Prince Aleksei Mikhailovich of all Great, Small and White Russia, autocrat, and you, great sovereign, with many years of service. And I served according to your sovereign order and according to assignment, and I served . . . those assignments from summons to dismissal without treachery, and I have [committed] no treason. And he, Karp, called me, your slave, a nonserver, alleging without any basis that I didn't serve and dishonored me thereby.[87]

Karp's libelous aspersions threatened Ianov's standing in the community as well as endangering his income, so Ianov vigorously protested the dishonor.

Power in the Vladimir-Suzdal' provinces derived from a complex nexus of physical, material, and cultural components. Some level of violence, if organized along lines of local clientage, was an integral part of the social structure and was accepted as functionally legitimate in the locality. Brute force exerted a compelling logic of its own, but without the seal of community respect, physical force could not convert to honorable authority. Members of local gentry communities conferred leadership status on certain of their peers. Such status could not derive solely from Moscow, nor could it be appropriated without reference to the judgment of the community.

Wealth, honor, rank, and local influence, the prizes over which provincial families competed, were inextricably intermeshed and could not be acquired separately. Wealth required service, and profitable service required advanced rank, which in turn depended on the testimony of members of the community, particularly of *okladchiki*. Influence and status within the community were associated with rank and wealth but were expressed through patronage, clientage, and connections. All of these demanded support from allies, whether clerks and *okladchiki* in administrative and command posts, lesser gentry servitors as signatories and sureties, or peasants and dependents as enforcers. Without the respect of the local community, none of these were possible. Social validation confirmed or rejected individuals' claims to authority and mediated between rival claimants.

In her work on violence, Hannah Arendt distinguishes force, which relies on coercion to ensure compliance, from power, which rests on social acknowledgment and is at least one step removed from physical force.[88] Michael Mann, in his study of the sources of social power, responds to this taxonomy by saying the distinction is largely irrelevant: "It is rare to find power that is either largely legitimate or largely illegitimate because its exercise is normally so double edged."[89] As Mann suggests, legitimate and illegitimate manifestations of power were not clearly demarcated in the Muscovite countryside.

Provincial Politics and State Interests

At the peripheries of autocratic control, provincial communities pursued their own local interests without encountering much resistance from the central authorities. For their part, provincial gentrymen did not build local power bases in opposition to Moscow, for they had no interest, or at least never evinced a shred of interest, in shaping policy at the level of high politics. Instead, they turned their dealings with the state system to their own advantage on the local scene. Because the state offered some rewards it did not need to fear disloyalty or rebellion among its servitors, but because the rewards were so paltry, the gentry constructed its own local political arenas, separate from the concerns of the state. Muscovite gentry by and large operated in conformity with implicit rules, conducting their private affairs in the lacunae that everyone knew but no one acknowledged to exist in the state's regulation of its people.

As in all early-modern monarchies, the Muscovite state built and enhanced its authority by its collaboration with the privileged elite, and each side of the partnership benefited by the growth of the other. Everywhere, privilege and the state arose together, neither predating the other. At the heart of the unspoken compact between members of the elite and the centralizing monarchies of Europe was the issue of the peasantry. As Perry Anderson writes in *Lineages of the Absolutist State*, "The nobility could deposit power with the monarchy: . . . the masses were still at its mercy."[90] In this respect, Muscovy followed the pack. The Muscovite state could not have grown without the cooperation and support of the gentry in supervising, policing, and taxing the peasantry, and the gentry could not have maintained its dependent labor force without the privileges and coercive might of the state to back it. Fear of peasant flight and rebellion solidified the symbiotic relation between state and gentry.[91]

Both sides in the tacit alliance had reason to court the good will of the other. The interests of the two parties intersected and reinforced each other but remained to a significant degree separate. The increasingly restrictive bonds of serfdom welded gentry more tightly to the state as the seventeenth century progressed and firmly cemented gentry and state interests together after midcentury, but this union of interests in no way undermined the gentry's localism. Instead, the growing emphasis on the gentry as a landholding and serf-owning estate intensified the activity and autonomy of provincial gentry communities.

CHAPTER 7

Muscovite Political Culture in Principle and Practice, 1600–1648

By and large, the provincial gentry of the Vladimir-Suzdal' region lived, served, and quarreled in a world far removed from the elite thinkers, writers, artists, and policy makers who surrounded the tsar in the Moscow Kremlin.[1] The gentry's connections with abstractions such as "the state" took very concrete, specific, and personal forms: an exchange of bribes and favors with a local town governor; a marriage into the family of a central chancellery clerk; a brawl with a recruiting officer or a tax collector. On occasion, however, events drew the gentrymen into the lofty air of Kremlin politics and forced them to think, act, and express themselves within a broadly political framework. In these moments of interaction with the center, with the tsar himself or with his august council, the gentry expressed ideas about proper political conduct and social order that expose a good deal about the expectations and assumptions inherent in Muscovite political culture. These interactions illustrate the power of the unifying myth of the tsarist Orthodox community and the ways in which that myth was utilized, as well as the vibrancy of localism and particularism beneath that uncontested ideological framework.

Most of what we know about the ways in which Muscovites conceptualized politics derives from sources produced at or near the tsar's court, which delineate an official point of view. Official representations or, more bluntly stated, tsarist propaganda illustrates the concepts of legitimacy and political authority that state ideologists hoped to inculcate into the population at large. Popular reception of the various instruments of state propaganda is, of course, much more difficult to establish. As a group, the gentry left few tracts chronicling its attitude toward politics, its conception of the state, or its understanding of the basis of tsarist legitimacy. The gentry did, however, register its opinions and visions of matters of broad, national concern in a series of collective petitions filed throughout the seventeenth century. By examining gentry interactions with state authorities through the evidence of the collective petitions, we can begin to appreciate the degree to which the gentry's conceptions about political life and legitimacy corresponded with official notions and where the two diverged.

The shift of focus to the national level necessarily leaves behind the particularities of the Vladimir-Suzdal' region, but Vladimirites and Suzdalians were well represented among the *"dvoriane* and *deti boiarskie* of all the towns of Zamoskov'e" who submitted the collective petitions and whose interests those documents expressed. On occasion these gentrymen even submitted their own separate petitions, repeating the moral tone and endorsing the concrete goals of the national campaigns. One document in particular, a draft of the instructions drawn up in June 1648 by the gentry of Vladimir to guide the soon-to-be-selected delegate to the Assembly of the Land, establishes the direct participation of the Vladimirites in national politics.[2] Produced by and for the Vladimir gentry community, the draft instructions contain all of the central points raised by the national gentry during the broad petition campaigns of the 1630s and 1640s and illustrate the relevance of Moscow politics to the landholders of the provincial region.

Moreover, although the rhetoric employed in the collective petitions differed somewhat from that used on documents involving local affairs, the underlying assumptions about the principles and workings of political life were the same. The national petition campaigns refined and generalized many of the themes expressed in local complaints over issues of corruption, bureaucratism, patronage and favoritism, banditry and violence, paternalism and protectionism. Even when gentry petitioners represented themselves as part of an integrated national whole, their experiences with local officials and patronage connections molded their conception of how justice, administration, and commerce should work.

Muscovite Political Ideology and Official Representations of Legitimacy

Images of tsarist power, of the state, and of the bases of tsarist legitimacy abound in the surviving sources from seventeenth-century Muscovy. From the late fifteenth century on, state ideologists consciously developed and publicized a ritualized image of the tsar as the leader chosen by God, piously ruling a flock of Orthodox sheep. The sources on official imagery are varied and include court and religious writings and ceremonies, fresco cycles, and architectural ensembles. The most salient feature of all this imagery is the unlimited nature of the tsar's autocratic power. This is the image that foreign visitors took home with them, the image of tsarist despotism that has had such a hold on the historical imagination. The kowtowing of the country's highest nobles, the claims of sanctity for previous tsars, the absence of any legal or constitutional limits on the tsar, all fostered the image of the tsar-autocrat, an image confirmed in the tsar's official title: Sovereign, Tsar, and Grand Prince, Autocrat of All Russia.[3]

Yet it is important to note that this was not the only image advanced in official representations.[4] The image of absolute autocrat was diluted by imagery promoting several other equally significant and equally official facets of the tsar's political legitimacy. First, the tsar was often represented as functioning in conjunction with his boyars and kinsmen. The standard formulation with which important decrees were issued read, "The Tsar decreed and the boyars affirmed. . . ." Much controversy has raged over whether or not this affirmation by the boyars constituted a mandatory step and a real limit on the tsar's legislative capabilities. Whatever the resolution of what debate, the *image* advanced in the official formula suggests collective decision making, not autocratic whim.[5] The impression of collective rule is reinforced by the stress in official sources on the importance of kinship relations and marriage, a web of relations in which the tsar was as intimately involved as any of his boyars. Court ceremonials, processions, and graphic imagery displayed the tsar in the company of his leading courtiers, who sat in state just a bit below the level of the tsar's throne. Robert Crummey observes, "The Tsar, then, appears as superior to the boyars but close to them, more than a first among equals but far less than a terrifying autocrat."[6] The carefully choreographed and deliberately publicized official representations of power thus interspersed symbols of unlimited autocracy with indications of collective rule.

Another important theme advanced in official representations of tsarist power, that of religious obligation, also served to mitigate the image of unlimited autocracy. More than anyone else, Daniel Rowland has explained the ways in which literary-religious ideology placed limits on the acceptable behavior of the tsar. The theory of state expressed in literary works of the Muscovite period "is God-dependent rather than independent. Without God, it makes no sense. It is religious and prophetic rather than secular and constitutional."[7] The literary and iconographic production of the Moscow court and high church institutions conveys a coherent philosophy of legitimate sovereignty built on religious and moral principles. As Rowland observes, "Matters that we would call political—for our purposes, the nature, derivation, and limits of royal authority—were almost always discussed in a religious context."[8] As represented in literary and artistic works, the tsar, the keystone of the Muscovite political and moral ideological framework, derived his legitimacy first and foremost from God, who selected him from all other men to rule wisely, justly, and piously. Divine selection, however, entailed weighty responsibilities; tsars had to conduct themselves with a degree of piety and righteousness worthy of their sponsor. If the tsar acted impiously, if he failed to chastise wrongdoers or to show his mercy to his humble subjects, Muscovite literary sources raise the possibility that he might, in fact, not be the true, legitimate tsar, chosen by God. The frightening alternative suggested instead that an impious tsar, behaving in defiance of God's instructions, must be the Antichrist.

All these threads of political understanding were woven together by the theme of advice in Muscovite culture. The tsar, legitimized both by his dynastic descent from ancestors "of blessed memory" and by his selection by God on high, was to rule as patriarchal autocrat but in moments of doubt was obligated to confer in righteous brotherhood with his boyars and other worthy advisers.[9] State propagandists and ideologists praised the idea of the tsar's consultation not only with the inner circle of boyars and royal kinsmen but also with "the land" meaning the Russian people as a whole. Ritualized deference to public opinion is evident in the importance of the ceremony of popular acclamation at the accession of new tsars, who had to be presented to an assembly of people of many different ranks for their approval before their coronation. Dark rumors plagued the reign of Aleksei Mikhailovich (1645–76) because he had forgone that crucial step in his haste to solemnize the coronation.[10] The ritual acclamation was often pro forma or even completely orchestrated, as in the case of Boris Godunov, who drummed up a claque of supporters to back his unconventional candidacy in 1598. Godunov grabbed the throne after the death of his brother-in-law, the pathetic last member of the dynasty that had ruled Moscow since its inception. Having no blood claim to the throne, Godunov needed to deploy whatever mechanisms he could find to legitimize his seizure of power. The fact that he bothered with staging this particular ritual demonstrates that popular acclaim, not just birth and divine selection, held weight as a plausible basis of legitimacy.

The tsarist administration found many ways to display its respect for and responsiveness to popular opinion. In the wording of its decrees, the administration stressed that it was responding to complaints and suggestions raised by "all the land." Numerous edicts opened with references to the collective petitions that had spurred the tsar to adopt particular measures. For instance, a decree in 1614/15 stated that provincial landlords of various towns had complained to the sovereign about the disorderly registration of their properties, and consequently the boyars had ordered an investigation "according to their petition."[11] A 1619 decree enacting major reforms explained the measures not only as a response to petitions from many people (primarily gentry) but also as the result of extensive consultation. The decree described how the tsar had taken counsel with his "spiritual father, the most reverend Patriarch Filaret Mikitich of Moscow and all Rus', and with the entire holy council and with boyars and with *okol'nichie* and with all the people of the Muscovite state." With the advice of these varied counselors he had resolved to send out surveyors to all towns to conduct a general survey and to set up a special commission that would investigate charges of offenses and violence committed by powerful people against the weak. The tsar went still further in proving his commitment to involving his subjects in administering and even shaping the realm. He called a new, broader council together to advise him:

> And from the towns, from all of them, for information and for establishing [practices], should be brought to Moscow, chosen from each city: from

ecclesiastical people one man per town, from *dvoriane* and *deti boiarskie* two solid and reasonable men per town, and two men per town from the townspeople, who would be able to tell about offenses and violence and destruction, and how to replenish the Muscovite state and [how to] reward the soldiers and structure the Muscovite state so that all may live according to their status.[12]

This passage describes the summoning of an Assembly of the Land, one of the consultative gatherings that met sporadically from the mid–sixteenth through mid–seventeenth century and with particular frequency during the early years of Romanov rule. The Assemblies of the Land were the most pronounced manifestation of this tradition of official salutes to the importance of popular opinion. In a particularly well-publicized instance, in 1648 Tsar Aleksei Mikhailovich and "his spiritual father and intercessor, the most holy Iosif, Patriarch of Moscow and all Russia, decreed and the boyars affirmed" that an assembly of men of all ranks from all over the land should convene in Moscow to hear the terms of the newly compiled *Ulozhenie* law code. Those sent "were to be worthy and prudent men so that his sovereign tsarist and civilian business might be affirmed and put into effect with [the participation of] all the delegates so that all these great decisions, [promulgated] by his present royal edict and the Law Code of the Assembly of the Land, henceforth would in no way be violated."

The preface to the Law Code also stated that the completed *Ulozhenie* was to be read to "the delegates who had been chosen in Moscow and from the provincial towns for the common counsel so that in the future the entire *Ulozhenie* would be solidly based and unshakable."[13] The public introduction of the law code thus stressed the importance of popular participation and affirmation through the delegates to the Assembly of the Land and implied that their participation in some way guaranteed the efficacy of the new legislation, which it otherwise would lack.

Whether these obeisances were mere formalities or whether the popular input was actually seriously taken into account in formulating policy, the publicity granted to public involvement shows that the individuals who formulated official ideology placed great value on maintaining at least the appearance of a responsive, interactive relationship between tsar and people. Thus, in formulating its public facade, the self-proclaimed *samoderzhavie* (autocracy) in its Muscovite variation chose to include many varied elements that contributed to legitimizing and solidifying the rule of the God-chosen, dynastically descended, paternal, responsive, publicly acclaimed autocrat.

The National Petition Campaigns and the Moscow Uprising of 1648

The cultural significance ostentatiously attributed to public opinion in official sources reverberated in the broader political culture. The gentry's conception of proper political interactions responded to the possibilities available in the cultural repertoire. In broadcasting its respect for suggestions from the population, the state encouraged the people of "all the land," particularly the gentry, merchants, and townspeople, to formulate opinions on issues of broad concern. It also gave these groups a sense of their entitlement to express such ideas and their grievances and inspired the empowering notion that consultation and advice formed an indispensable aspect of the political order. That sense surfaces distinctly in the tales of the Time of Troubles (1605–13), when the gentry and townspeople banded together to reconstruct a state from a war-torn shambles and to select a tsar in the absence of any obvious contenders. During the second quarter of the seventeenth century, the gentry and merchants evolved an even clearer sense of themselves as distinct entities with particular interests and grievances. In the 1630s and 1640s the gentry and merchants mobilized to write series of petitions in which they expressed an increasing awareness of their own estate interests.[14]

In its collective petitions, the gentry articulated its conception of how the ideal political system should work and how relations among tsar, state, and subjects should be structured. The early collective petitions give a relatively clear indication of the gentry's political expectations, assumptions, and ideals at those moments when individuals' interests left the level of the local and the particular and intersected with matters of national import. Political discussion at the level of tsarist authority differed significantly from the discourse of local politics, largely in its strong infusion of religious and moral categories and language. This elevation of tone resulted in part from the petitioners' sense of what was proper in dealing with the tsar and boyar elite and of what tack would be effective and produce results. But in part the difference in tone derived from a real disjuncture between the rough, hands-on experience of daily struggle in the provinces and perceptions of the exalted, distant, and powerful tsar, surrounded by religious symbols and beliefs. Spirituality had little role to play in a brawl or nasty lawsuit against a provincial rival, but it had a great deal to do with an individual's broader conceptions of state and society. A look at the gentry's more abstract understanding of the tsarist state, then, adds a useful complement to the local study of the gentry at home, in its own element. It also allows us to discover to what extent the ideas expressed in literary works and artistic compositions by court ideologists and church dignitaries affected or were reflected in popular political conduct.

The collective petition was the primary mechanism for voicing systemic or abstract concerns within the Muscovite political tradition. The convention of direct access to the tsar through petition functioned as a cornerstone of the Muscovite political structure, allowing all levels of society, from peasant to boyar, an avenue of communication to the autocrat. The government encouraged the tradition of direct petition to the center by accepting and responding to petitions from all ranks of society. The customary form of a petition, with its self-denigrating, slavish manner of styling the petitioner and its panegyrical form of address to the tsar, furnished symbolic affirmation of the ethos of devout servants and autocratic rulers. At the same time, its appeal for clemency played into the image of the tsar as father of dependent children, and its function furthered the myth of direct communication between tsar and people. Although certainly formulaic, the phraseology of Muscovite petitions communicated and affirmed the dual nature of the relationship between tsar and subjects. It demonstrated the petitioners' insignificance before the all-powerful tsar, but it also signified the subjects' right to call attention to their woes and the tsar's paternal obligation to respond to them.[15]

Dozens of collective gentry petitions submitted in the name of particular groups of gentry or of "*dvoriane* and *deti boiarskie* of all towns" survive to document the collective grievances and political vision of the Muscovite gentry in the seventeenth century. The first references to collective petitions from the service gentry and other groups appear in scattered chronicle entries during the years of the Time of Troubles and immediately afterwards, in 1608, 1610, 1611, 1614, and 1619.[16] These petitions do not survive, but chronicles and decrees note their existence. For instance, in 1611 the *New Chronicler* reports that "the regimental soldiers . . . and the gentry and all service people, having taken council with the Cossacks," submitted a petition about the urgent problems of securing land for landless servitors and food and support for the rank-and-file troops. Their solution, appropriating and redistributing the lands of the boyars, did not win support from high circles.[17] Gentrymen from many regions again banded together to submit petitions on issues of general concern in 1637, 1641, 1645, 1648, 1657, 1676, 1677, 1682, 1684, 1685, 1686, 1694, and probably most years in between.[18] From 1648 until the end of the century, enough evidence survives to document the active participation of Vladimir-Suzdal' gentry in the petition campaigns. Although no specific evidence of Vladimir-Suzdalian participation survives for the earlier petition campaigns, the concerns expressed by members of the gentry from the region in 1648 strongly suggest that their interest had been engaged all along.[19] Some of the collective petitions survive in the original form, while others can be reconstructed from responses in official decrees or, in the case of the 1648 petitions, from foreign accounts. After midcentury their contents changed quite markedly, and so the later petitions will be discussed separately.

The gentry formulated these petitions at times when the state was hard-pressed by military difficulties and civil unrest and therefore was most likely to respond favorably to the demands of its fully mobilized, heavily armed, and clearly disgruntled cavalry officers. The petition of February 1637, the first surviving national gentry petition, came from *dvoriane* and *deti boiarskie* of Zamoskov'e and borderland towns who were serving at the time in the tsar's army in the borderlands.[20] They drew up the petition during the military muster of all gentry cavalrymen at a time when the Tatars threatened the realm and the cavalry's services were in great demand. The 1641 petition from "*dvoriane* and *deti boiarskie* of all towns [together] with all the land" has not been preserved, but a careful summary survives in an internal administrative document that records each item of the petition and the official response to it.[21] The military situation in the south was tense, and the gentry militia had been assembled en masse in Tula and other southern muster points, where the petitions were drafted. I. L. Andreev stresses that the gentry displayed anything but the traditional humility of supplicants in 1641 when it submitted its petitions to the tsar. "Without doubt in 1641 the government clashed with an imposing opposition movement of *pomeshchiki*. . . . The petitioners at that time were extraordinarily many."[22] According to some contemporary sources, the service people who handed in the petitions did so "with noise," that is, loudly and angrily. One redaction of the *New Chronicler* reports that in the capital gathered a multitude of servicemen, who "roamed around Moscow in groups and petitioned against the boyars concerning peasants and their other offenses."[23] Prokhor Kolbetskoi, a petty gentryman from Nizhnii Novgorod, described in a letter to his father how "in Moscow the confusion [*smetenie*] became great." Kolbetskoi predicted that the "strong people" would have to be put in their places or else the land would rise up.[24]

The government responded to each of these petitions by calling an Assembly of the Land with which the leading boyars discussed major issues of the day. It also enacted decrees that partially resolved the problems laid out in the petitions, while it avoided facing many of the problems directly. The primary issue raised in 1637 and 1641 had to do with securing the small landholders' grip over the peasantry and protecting their labor force against the depredations of the "strong people." In the early collective petitions, the gentry asked that the statute of limitations on the recovery of fugitive peasants be extended from the customary five years or eliminated altogether.[25] A short statute of limitations worked to the advantage of the very rich, who could afford to hide stolen peasants or transfer them to distant estates, thus foiling the attempts of petty landholders to recover their workers. Furthermore, poor servicemen could not afford the time or money to search for runaways immediately and needed a longer interval between their peasants' disappearance and the expiration of their seignorial rights.

The animus of the petitions of the 1630s and 1640s was directed against "church authorities, monasteries and metropolitans and archbishops and strong people of Moscow of various ranks," who

> carry off [our] fugitive peasants to their distant *pomest'ia* and *votchiny*, relying on the five-year statute of limitations set by you, Sovereign. And when the set number of years passes, they bring our runaway peasants and people back to their nearby *pomest'ia* and *votchiny*, which estates are contiguous with ours, your slaves', and . . . they lure away from our *pomest'ia* and *votchiny* the rest of our peasants, whom we hold according to your grants.[26]

Complaints about violent and illegal depredations by "strong people," formed a recurring theme of gentry petitions, one that was linked to the problem of the flight and kidnapping of peasants. Such complaints appeared in collective petitions as early as 1619 and continued throughout the century. "Strong people," *sil'nye liudi*, became an established legal term in the early seventeenth century, referring to boyars and high ecclesiastical and administrative authorities. The term gained such currency that an official chancellery, the Chancellery in Which People Petition Against Strong People, was established in the early part of the century. The gentry of Vladimir echoed the general concern with the conduct of the "strong people" when, in 1648, it expressed the hope that "the strong and rich" would "set aside all kinds of untruth and offences and soul-destroying greed" and renounce their current practices of bribery and deception.[27] Andreev, in his extensive work on *sil'nye liudi*, defines them as people who had the power to inflict violence, arbitrariness, and lawlessness and who wielded that power based on wealth, birth, social position, and wide-ranging connections with various elites and within the chancellery apparatus.[28] Muscovite "strong people" raided the estates of weaker neighbors with impunity, knowing that they would never be convicted by the corrupt legal system.

The petitions of 1637 and 1641 called for abolition of the statute of limitations, but the state responded by merely extending the time period for recovery of runaway peasants. Although it did make minor concessions on the length of the statute of limitations, the government ignored the call for its abolition and disregarded the equally critical sections of the gentry petitions dealing with judicial reform.[29] Still, true to its custom of advertising its responsiveness to public opinion, the state played up the petitions and its responses to them in its evasive answering decrees.

Discontent about both the statute of limitations and the corrupt judicial system smoldered until it burst out in a new round of petitions in 1645. In that year, in response to yet another gentry petition from "*dvoriane* and *deti boiarskie* of all towns," the state finally promised to carry out a new general census and, after the census was completed, to bind "peasants and landless peasants and their children and brothers and nephews" to their landlords according to the new census books forever, without a statute of limitations.[30] This decree, rather than the more famous *Ulozhenie* Law Code of 1649, marks the state's commitment to bind the Russian peasantry inescapably and permanently to serfdom, although some scholars doubt the seriousness of the state's intention to fulfill its promise at that time.[31] A national census was initiated, but the statute of limitations endured, presumably pending the completion of the census, which would officially establish peasants' perpetual legal residence. The 1645 decree had so little practical effect that the gentry still included the abolition of the statute of limitations on runaway peasants among its primary demands in late June of 1648. The Vladimir gentry's delegate to the 1648 Assembly of the Land went to Moscow with a directive "to speak about the peasant years [statute of limitations] and to demand firmly that the sovereign order census books without statute of limitations."[32]

The high point of the national gentry petition campaign was reached in the rebellious year 1648. As had been the case for earlier petitions, the gentry took advantage of a time of national unrest, when violent rebellion had swept through the capital and many other towns of the realm. As a group the gentry did not participate in the widespread uprisings of 1648, but it did not actively side with tsar and state either. Rather it maintained what Andreev calls "hostile neutrality," neither joining the rebels in armed insurgency nor lending armed support to the crown.[33] A brief description of the events of the 1648 Moscow riot is useful as a context for understanding the conduct of the gentry at that tumultuous time.

Beginning in the late spring and early summer of 1648, mutinies gripped towns all over the country, sparked by harsh taxation policies, tardy payments of state cash and grain stipends to gentry and musketeers, corruption, depopulation, and famine. An anonymous Dutch eyewitness to the rebellion reported that the townspeople complained about oppressive tax burdens foisted upon them by the boyar oligarchy and chancellery staffs, such that "they were not able to hold out any longer: yea they desired rather with their wives and children to undergoe a present death, then to suffer any longer in such a transcendent oppression."[34] In this general background of discontent, trouble began when a crowd of loyal subjects greeted the young tsar, Aleksei Mikhailovich, as he returned from a pilgrimage outside the city. The crowd offered the tsar traditional welcoming gifts of bread and salt and also attempted to hand him petitions complaining of the excesses of Levontii Pleshcheev, the head of local courts and tax collection in Moscow. Pleshcheev had a well-earned reputation for being particularly corrupt and exploitive, even by the standards of the day. He also happened to be a protégé of Boris Morozov, the tsar's brother-in-law and mentor. Contrary to all custom and expectation, the tsar refused to accept the petitions, and when the would-be petitioners pursued him and then his tsaritsa, whose cortege followed some distance behind, Morozov ordered the musketeer guards to shoot at the crowd to disperse it. A fracas ensued in which a number of people on both sides were injured and sixteen prisoners were taken. In the following days, the crowd of petitioners grew into a mob of rioters who stormed through the streets of the finest neighborhoods, looting and destroying the homes of boyars, merchants, and officials and, when they found them, mutilating the owners. Adam Olearius recounted what he had heard about the death of Nazarii Chistyi, a much hated merchant-official. Hearing of the riot, Chistyi cowered in his house under a pile of twigs, but "the maddened people threw themselves upon the house, dragged Nazarii out from under the twigs and then, by his feet, down the stairway and into the courtyard, where they beat him to death with cudgels. His head was so battered that he could no longer be recognized. Then he was cast into a manure pit, and boxes and trunks were thrown on top of him."[35]

A turning point in the uprising came when the musketeer units guarding the Kremlin defected to the side of the rebels and allowed them through the gates. The protesters burst into the Kremlin and insisted on speaking directly with the tsar, accepting no intermediaries. They demanded the release of the sixteen prisoners, as well as the execution or banishment of some of the most hated noble officials, including both Pleshcheev and Morozov. When fires mysteriously broke out throughout Moscow, killing thousands and destroying half the city, the outrage of the crowd grew even more intense, and the tsar had to concede first Petr Trakhaniotov, another highly placed associate of Morozov, then Pleshcheev, for execution. Trakhaniotov was torn apart by the crowd before the executioner had a chance to dispatch him. Pleshcheev was lucky enough to be beheaded in more dignified fashion. On June 12, Aleksei Mikhailovich finally had to agree to exile his beloved Morozov from Moscow and from public affairs. After ten days of violence, the uprising subsided.

In the aftermath of the uprising, the state made a number of concessions to the demands of the rebels, reducing a few taxes, replacing unpopular (and now dead) officials, and scrupulously paying the musketeers all their back pay as well as wooing them with generous gifts of money, food, and liquor.[36] The gentry, too, received the cash grants it had been owed for years. Huge tracts of land were simultaneously distributed to "landless and sparsely landed" gentrymen, with the properties deriving in large part from the confiscated estates of Morozov and his cronies.[37] The tsar's public relations campaign was so effective in regaining the musketeers' loyalty that a few months after Morozov's "perpetual" exile he was quietly brought back to the capital and reinstated as the tsar's right-hand man. The state also conducted an undercover campaign of retribution, arresting rebels on trumped up, gratuitous charges and sentencing them to harsh penalties.[38]

The victors of the June uprising were the provincial gentry and respectable town population. These groups had stood aloof from the violence but had submitted petitions on issues close to their hearts at the moment when the state was weakest and consequently most likely to concede much in order to secure their loyalty. Two petitions survive from June 1648, one submitted in the name of "the Christian people, children of the Church of Christ," the other "from the simple Moscow gentry, the provincial service people, merchants and trading people of greater and lesser ranks, and from all the simple people."[39] These petitions speak in the name of "all the people," but most scholars agree that the gentry must have composed the petitions on the basis of its decades of experience in collective petitioning.[40] As sources, the petitions are far from ideal because of their dubious provenance. One survives in an encoded Swedish translation, put into code by Karl Pommerening, a Swedish resident in Moscow, who had to smuggle it out of the country past Muscovite censors at the time of the 1648 riot. It is available in a Swedish reconstruction, poorly decoded by Swedish clerks in the seventeenth century, and in a Russian translation of the Swedish decoded version.[41] Without the benefit of proficiency in Swedish, to discuss it in English one must use it at five steps removed from the original: an English translation of a Russian translation of a Swedish decoding of a Swedish encoding of a Swedish translation of a Russian original! Fortunately, Heinz Eberhard Ellersieck's doctoral dissertation devotes some space to cracking the original code of Pommerening's missives and revising the Russian version.[42] Furthermore, the general accuracy (in spite of many layers of translation) of the Pommerening version of the June petition is confirmed by the indisputably authentic instructions to the Vladimir gentry's delegate to the 1648 Assembly of the Land. The instructions repeat the primary issues raised so sharply in the Pommerening petition and even quote the same supporting passages from the Psalms. In content and in form, the Vladimir instructions so closely parallel the Pommerening version that they must have been inspired by the same original Russian source that Pommerening encoded.[43] The second version of the June petition survives in a Russian text discovered by M. V. Shakhmatov in the Tartu archives. Some scholars question the identification of this petition as distinct from the Pommerening petition. Linguistic evidence suggests that it may even have passed through the same convoluted Russian-Swedish-Russian translation process as Pommerening's.[44] The two do display striking similarities (as do all Muscovite petitions) but differ in significant passages. In either case, they illuminate much about the political vision of the Muscovite gentry. To keep the sources straight, I will refer to them as two separate documents.

Publicly announcing its action as a response to the petitions, the state summoned two Assemblies of the Land, a preliminary one in July, immediately after the uprising subsided, and another, better organized one in September of 1648. That second assembly produced the Assembly of the Land Law Code, or *Ulozhenie*, of 1649, which enshrined a number of the most pressing and most controversial of the demands put forward by gentry, merchants, and townspeople over the years. The gentry finally gained the long-desired abolition of the statute of limitation on recovering runaway peasants, which had been promised in 1645 but had not yet been enacted. The townspeople gained equally dearly held goals: the abolition of tax-exempt "white places," where tax-free bondsmen of great monasteries had enjoyed an advantage over taxed merchants and ordinary artisans, and the legal binding of townspeople to their taxpaying communes.

These were the concrete measures that came out of the riots, but the most interesting and unique passages of the 1648 petitions, and indeed of all of the collective petitions of the first half of the seventeenth century, do not focus on the concrete. Instead, they discuss political morality at a high level of abstraction, and hence provide valuable insights into the political culture that informed the behavior and expectations of the Muscovite gentry.

The Meaning of Justice in Collective Petitions

The topic of justice figures conspicuously in the gentry petitions of the 1630s and 1640s. The same collective petitions that addressed the problem of the statute of limitations also confronted the failings of the existing legal system. For instance, three particular dates in the year—Trinity Day in the spring, St. Semen's Day in the fall, and Christmas Day in the winter—were set for trials involving servitors. "But at those times," the provincial servitors pointed out in their 1637 petition, "at Trinity Day and St. Semen's Day, we, your slaves, . . . are in your Sovereign service, and at Christmas, because of our poverty and the length of the journey, and because of devastation by strong people, we, your slaves, cannot manage to arrive in time. And in many years, Sovereign, at Christmas the road is not passable."[45]

All litigants had to travel to the capital and stay there until their cases were heard. The costs of the journey and the stay strained the purses of poor provincial gentrymen, particularly if they had no friends or neighbors who could put them up in the capital. Provincial servitors complained that wealthy troublemakers harassed them with the expenses of groundless lawsuits in order to force them to accept unfavorable terms. The petition of 1637 declared, "And they cause us, your slaves, great injury and losses with their slanderous suits and they collect your sovereign summonses against us and our people and our peasants, relying on their privilege, that your sovereign legal fees do not apply to them."[46]

In their petitions, the gentry of all Muscovy formulated a remarkably radical solution to the problem. The proposal not only addressed the immediate practical problems of inconvenient timing and expensive procedure, but also raised fundamental questions about the most appropriate and justifiable basis for meting out justice. In 1637 the provincial gentry recommended a complete overhaul and decentralization of the judicial system:

> Order, Sovereign, that we be given trials *in provincial towns* against church authorities and monasteries and people of all Moscow ranks about our runaway peasants and people and [other] offenses, and against their estate overseers and peasants, at those times when, Sovereign, we are able to petition you, Sovereign, against them, when we are not in your sovereign service. And order, Sovereign, that [judges] *be chosen in the towns, from among the gentry and the taxpaying people,* and order [them] to judge us, your slaves, in the towns according to your sovereign orders and according to your sovereign law code.[47]

This suggestion for a decentralized justice system paralleled the servitors' experience with the *guba* and *zemskii* systems of local administration, which made use of the services of locally selected officials from all free ranks. The key difference was that in the proposed plan, true judicial authority would devolve on community leaders.

The proposal, so antithetical to the Muscovite trend toward centralization of authority, reflects a good deal about the gentry's understanding of what constituted true justice. The petitioners advocated the establishment of local courts, staffed by familiar, local judges, who would know their constituencies and administer justice accordingly. The 1641 petition, although less explicit about the solution, also complained that trials were not held in the provincial towns and requested that "the Sovereign order that their [cases against] all [ranks of] people should be tried in Moscow *and in the provincial towns* without time limit."[48] In the 1648 Shakhmatov petition, "people of all ranks" repeated this suggestion and requested that the tsar "root out unjust judges and remove incapable ones, and he should choose righteous [people] as judges, whomever God informs him, or else the sovereign should entrust it to all ranks of the people, *and the people would choose judges among themselves*—righteous, reasonable, great people."[49] With this recurrent demand, the gentry advocated a return to what was perceived as godly justice, administered by judges designated by God through the agency of the tsar or selected by the people, the other receptacle of Orthodox tradition and piety.

An integral part of these proposals was a wish for more intimate local justice, in which judges would come from the local community and hence would be able to mete out traditional, highly personalized justice. Judges would know the community and the character of its members and would be able to take into account the reputation, social standing, and family status of litigants. The principle of judgment on the basis of "reputation" was integral to the Muscovite concept of justice. "Known bandits" suffered far harsher penalties than "known good men," and character witnesses played a critical role in trials. The gentry's plan to choose "righteous, reasonable" judges from the community indicates that personal character, honor, and local standing were seen as equally essential characteristics for judges as for defendants and witnesses. The petitioners insisted that judges and chancellery clerks should be held responsible for their actions: "You [Sovereign] should . . . order all dishonest judges to be rooted out, the ignorant to be replaced, and in their place to be chosen just people, who would be able to answer for their judgments and for their service before God and before your tsarist majesty."[50] The unfamiliar outsiders who judged cases in the central chancellery courts, distinguished only by their proclivity toward corruption, bribe taking, and inefficiency, epitomized what the gentry hoped to abolish.

In 1637, in response to the gentry's complaint that service obligations made it impossible to come to Moscow for trials at the three set times of year, Tsar Mikhail Fedorovich decreed that military service should henceforth be reduced by half, from year-round to half a year, except in times of war.[51] After each round of petitions, decrees poured forth duly affirming that bribe taking and perversion of the legal process were heinous offenses. However, the state assiduously ignored the radical proposal for establishing local courts with locally selected judges, the essence of the gentry's proposal on legal reform. The state had to avoid implementing these particular proposals, because they grew from a conception of the nature of justice consistent with traditional Muscovite political culture but fundamentally at odds with the increasingly regularized, impersonal bureaucratic administration of the centralizing state.

"And Moscow Is the Root of All of This Terrible Graft": Mercy Encounters Bureaucracy

On the face of it, the gentry's collective petitions of the first half of the century complain about straightforward issues: magnates' assaults on their possessions and livelihood, the hassles and expenses of red tape, and, above all, corruption. However, none of these issues was as uncomplicated as it might first appear. These three evils—"strong people," red tape, and corruption—were integrally interconnected and represented a peculiarly charged set of signifiers at a moment when the gentry reluctantly encountered profound systemic change.

In each of the collective petitions, corruption of the legal system emerges as the core of the problem, especially corruption of the chancellery courts by avaricious chancellery officials and arrogant magnates. In 1648, the initial irritant that eventually triggered popular rebellion was the excessive malfeasance of Levontii Pleshcheev, the administrator in charge of the city's affairs. As one chronicle explains, "All the land petitioned the sovereign about Moscow City Chief [*zemskii sud'ia*] Levontii Stepanovich Pleshcheev, that from him the taxpaying community suffered heavy fees and they were groundlessly charged with all sorts of robberies and thefts at his,

Levontii's, instruction."[52] In other words, at one level corruption and abuses of power precipitated the 1648 revolt. S. V. Bakhrushin accurately noted that Nazarii Chistyi died "for salt," for introducing the salt tax, and Trakhaniotov for not paying the musketeers and other servitors the cash grants they were owed.[53] Corruption, in its many ingenious forms, appears over and over again among the people's complaints. In their petitions they describe bribes, forced gifts, excessive fees, slander, violence, graft, and injustice: "Chancellery officials of duma and nonduma ranks have strayed into bribery and craftiness. No one is allowed anywhere in the chancelleries without paying a fee, and no one anywhere is given the sovereign's service payment without their taking a cut. They sell everything for high prices, and in the towns, because of these chancellery people, the taxpaying community has perished and is currently perishing."[54] The people themselves, from gentry and merchantry to common taxpayers, identified corruption as the most immediate cause of their discontent.

However profound, corruption was not new in the 1630s and 1640s. The two major landmarks of Muscovite legislation prior to the *Ulozhenie*, the law codes of 1497 and 1550, both devoted most of their limited number of articles to reining in and punishing judicial and administrative corruption of various forms. Although a chronic problem, corruption assumed new and more central importance in Muscovite perceptions in the early seventeenth century. Particular issues provoke paramount concern at particular times, depending on the broader anxieties of a given culture. What turned the chronic corruption of Muscovite administration into such a highly charged issue was the pace of growth and bureaucratization, which provoked a perception of a decline in overall moral standards and deviation from the Orthodox past. Nostalgia for a purer Orthodox past resounds throughout the petitions. The petitioners situated the current "radiant sovereign tsar" in his rightful place in the procession of "Orthodox tsars and grand princes in the memory of eternal generations." They reminded him that his father "of blessed memory" and he himself in the past had devoted their attention to helping the people with their "stern but merciful hands." They complained of arrogance and presumption, "which of old, under previous sovereigns," did not occur.[55] In their protest the petitioners denounced changes taking place at a deep and sweeping level: the rise of the bureaucratic state and the concurrent depersonalization of relations with the rules and representatives of state power.

Until the beginning of the seventeenth century, ordinary Muscovites probably had little contact with the state, aside from taxation or required service duties. In the seventeenth century, the state enlarged its aspirations and attempted to control the lives of its subjects to an unprecedented degree, as manifested in the far-ranging legislation of the 1649 *Ulozhenie*. At the same time that the state attempted to crush the varied population into fixed strata, new categories of people cropped up, undermining traditional notions about the correlation between birthright, occupation, and power. In the past, military service had been exclusively the prerogative and obligation of the elite. In the early decades of the seventeenth century, however, when Muscovite horsemen encountered Western infantrymen, the state introduced conscription from among the peasantry and established New Formation Regiments following Western models. Military service now became increasingly the domain of the common taxpayers. Provincial gentry, whose general poverty left them little enough to distinguish themselves from their own peasants, must have felt this blow to their prestige sharply.[56] Lines of birth and authority grew confused in administrative spheres as well. In the late sixteenth and seventeenth centuries, a professional bureaucracy arose alongside the traditional small ruling clique of boyars and princes. The presence of new clerks and state secretaries, people without noble blood to legitimize them and yet vested with tremendous authority as agents of the tsar, threw off all previous calculations about power and upset the assumptions of the reigning political-ideological paradigm. The ostentation of such non-noble upstarts aroused indignation, as seen in the ire of the gentry petitions. In 1642, at an Assembly of the Land, the gentry complained, "Your Sovereign's state secretaries and clerks . . . bought many *pomest'e* and *votchina* estates and built themselves many houses, stone palaces and such, which are beyond description. In the times of previous sovereigns, of blessed memory, even the great and well-born, who were worthy of living in such homes, did not have such homes."[57] In 1648 they repeated the charge that state secretaries and clerks were building large stone houses "not appropriate to their rank."[58] Low-born merchants and administrators, such as the unfortunate Nazarii Chistyi and his fellow merchant-official Vasilii Shorin, suffered the consequences of popular resentment of the disrupted social order. Leading merchants and chancellery staff were among the victims of uprisings all over the country, in 1648 and later.

Along with the new, unfamiliar bureaucrats arose a new, unfamiliar system of laws and impersonal, bureaucratic regulation. In earlier centuries the Muscovite state apparatus had been negligible, but it developed recognizable institutional structures in the sixteenth century and its staff grew tenfold, from hundreds to thousands, in the seventeenth.[59] To facilitate standardization of procedure and centralization of control, the state sponsored the first official printing press in Muscovy, under the auspices of the Patriarchal Court. Although the amount of material printed remained small until the time of Peter the Great, the seventeenth century saw the first relatively large-scale printing and dissemination of laws and decrees. The *Ulozhenie* reached all provincial governors' offices, and Muscovites of all ranks, with the assistance of the local town-square clerk or scribe, were able to refer to its statutes when writing petitions. Print runs of the law code sold out quickly, as not only officials but also individual buyers in the capital and in the provinces purchased their own copies.[60]

In addition to the intensification of state intrusion into people's lives came a concomitant depersonalization of relations with authorities. The gentry petitioners articulated their unhappiness about this bureaucratization. In 1648 the petitioners complained not only about particular incidents, manifestations, or perpetrators of corruption; they complained in general about *volokita*, variously translated as red tape, delays, bureaucratism. They depicted the miserable straits to which corrupt chancellery staff had reduced the population: "All ranks of your sovereign chancellery people strayed into bribery and craftiness and from this in the community [*mir*] the lowborn and defenseless perished, and now too are perishing from their destroyers and only in death they received a place to live." They continued, "At this point they still endure delays through red tape. They serve among the last ones, the most wretched, [who] in the last stage of destitution have nowhere to rest their heads, and with their wives and children feed every day on the bread of tears."[61] The chancelleries and the people who staffed them consistently appeared as the villains and most resented aspects of the increasingly regulated judicial system. The petitions condemned "all chancellery officials," not just particularly notorious ones. "And *Moscow* is the root of all of this terrible graft. In Moscow they sell power, but to ordinary people the chancellery personnel cause misfortune," says the Shakhmatov petition, condemning the bureaucratic system itself.[62]

The petitioners suggested dismissing not only the chancellery courts and their corrupt lowborn officials but also the entire boyar bureaucracy. The 1641 petition had requested specifically that trials be held "not in the judicial chancelleries," where administrative staff would judge cases, but had asked instead for judgment by the boyars sitting collectively in a judicial chamber.[63] By 1648 the petitioners preferred to do away with both chancellery trial and the boyar court. A long tradition stood behind the seventeenth-century tendency to label boyars as villains. In folklore, the tsar was usually good, the friend of the little man. It was the evil boyars and advisers who caused all the trouble, blocking communication between tsar and people, whispering untruths and deceptions into the ear of the unsuspecting tsar. Legend had it that the tsar would act mercifully and kindly if only he knew the plight of his people, but the advisers and bureaucrats cunningly erected an impenetrable barrier by insinuating themselves between tsar and people.[64] Precisely this image shaped the 1648 petitioners' perception of the boyars' role in perverting the tsars' attempts at justice. They explained how the current tsar and his father both had wished to help their subjects and, after hearing the people's lamentations, had set up special high-level commissions headed by the leading boyars to investigate the abuses committed by the "strong people." However, the commission itself became part of the problem:

> By this time these officials, with the help of this investigation, [should] have investigated everything about the common people truthfully, and in accordance with your tsarist highness's order should have presented everything before your tsarist highness; but the whole thing was covered up and whitewashed, and thus much was not implemented, because they, no less than others, were participants in this outrageous business, concealing one evil after another, until it seemed as if this were all being done for the tsarist majesty's profit and benefit. . . .
>
> And also because we brought to your tsarist majesty such a lawful complaint, those above-mentioned judges and strong people and chancellery people, with the greatest slyness and craftiness, are trying to oppress, crush and destroy us, so that before this reaches the ears of your tsarist majesty as is seemly, it will be forgotten.[65]

The interference of boyar judges and chancellery clerks, who interposed a layer of bureaucracy between tsar and people, offended Muscovite sensibilities. The solution, as perceived by provincials, involved eliminating the corrupt, alien element and returning jurisdiction to the chosen leaders of local communities or to the tsar himself. Both of the petitions from June 1648 made a particular point of requesting that boyars no longer judge appeal cases, which they had previously.[66] The Pommerening petition explained with only slightly specious logic that if the tsar would order corrupt and ignorant judges removed and allow the people to choose their own judges, boyars would no longer have to bother with the onerous affairs of state:

> By this means the tsarist majesty would be so much relieved from all sorts of superfluous labor that your tsarist majesty with complete calm could attend to your tsarist affairs, and not as it was before, when your tsarist majesty was so overburdened. And also the boyars in like manner would be able to manage and direct their household affairs with much greater ease, after they give up and relinquish your tsarist majesty's judicial [affairs] and all military affairs and orders, so that they wouldn't have to burden themselves with such public matters, but, however, without it happening that in their place your tsarist majesty should be burdened by all these petty matters.[67]

This proposal for doing away with boyar judicial oversight came too late, however. The new legal codex of 1649 fixed the boyar *Palata* (judicial chamber) in law: "Disputed cases which for any reason cannot be resolved in the chancelleries shall be transferred from the chancelleries in a report to the Sovereign, Tsar, and Grand Prince of all Russia Aleksei Mikhailovich and to his royal boyars, and *okol'nichie*, and counselors. The boyars, and *okol'nichie*, and counselors shall sit in the Palace [of Facets], and by the sovereign's decree shall handle the sovereign's various cases all together."[68] The boyars, not the tsar, thus became the judges for appeals.

The gentry's collective petitions set forth many suggestions for overhauling the system of justice, all of which reflected the general assumption of Muscovite provincial society that justice should be merciful, tailored to particular circumstances, and in keeping with Orthodox moral order. Beneath this national, Orthodox firmament, the political habits developed within local communities contributed to shaping gentry political values and demands. Informal local practices of maintaining and utilizing personal connections, of mitigating the severity of the tsarist system through rituals of mercy and protection, of utilizing the intimate relations of family, neighborhood, clientage, and patronage, of turning the system to best advantage through gifts, bribes, or threats—all appear dressed in grander, religiously informed language in the national gentry petitions.

Rational Law and Merciful Justice

Although the fundamental principles of gentry political life rested on personalized relations, informality, and flexibility geared to each individual situation, the gentry also appreciated the benefits of equity and rule by law. Since the fifteenth century Muscovites had had an opportunity to grow accustomed to the concept of a regularized legislative order, mandated from above and implemented by deputized officials of the grand prince, or later, of the tsar. The long historical experience had demonstrably affected gentry attitudes toward the administration of justice by the seventeenth century.[69] Gentry petitioners expressed deep hostility to the increasingly depersonalized regulation of justice and administration, but they also wove into their petitions appeals for equal justice for great and small alike, all in accordance with the sovereign's written law. The petitioners even manifested great respect for official documents, the end products of the bureaucratic red tape that they so detested. Their petitions invoked the authority of paperwork as the supreme standard of authenticity. The 1641 petition affirmed nostalgically that "in previous years and under previous sovereigns there was no statute of limitations about their runaway peasants; peasants were bound to [gentrymen] on the basis of their *pomest'e* grants, land cadasters, and extracts from official documents. [Peasants were bound] to whoever had the oldest documents."[70]

By the early seventeenth century, the concept of the law as an abstract body of rules was familiar in Muscovy and commanded great respect. In the 1637 collective petition the gentry requested, "Decree, Sovereign, that we, your slaves, be tried in the provincial towns on the basis of your sovereign decree and *according to your sovereign legal statute book*."[71] The 1641 supplication likewise appealed specifically for trial "in all of their cases according to the law code of Tsar and Grand Prince of blessed memory Ivan Vasil'evich of all Rus'."[72] The Vladimir gentry similarly expressed its understanding that true and fair justice should issue from a centralized judicial system established through the sovereign's courts: "And among us would be no injustice or offences at all, and the Sovereign would establish among us his righteous sovereign trials, and trials would be given to all people equally whether they were great or insignificant."[73] These requests called unambiguously for trial according to standard, written laws and show that the legislative process had already acquired strong acceptance.

Yet, in the years prior to 1649, the phrase "trial according to law" had a very different connotation from what it would afterwards. The laws of Ivan Vasil'evich regulated courtroom procedure and threatened harsh penalties for judges who favored friends, who prevented access to trial, who lied or covered up testimony. Throughout the law code of 1550 the presence of the tsar was immediately felt, as both the highest judge in cases of appeal and the determiner of final sentencing, as seen in the vague warning that a penalty shall be "whatsoever the tsar decrees." What trial according to law signified, above all, was fairness and honesty in judicial procedure and freedom from corruption or bias on the part of the judges. When the rioters and petitioners in June 1648 turned their attention to the problems of the justice system, they framed their criticisms and proposals in traditional terms of morality and virtue and expressed dismay at the increasing bureaucratism of the courts. What they ultimately received in answer to their complaints was the *Ulozhenie*, the great codification of all the preexisting statutes and law codes plus significant additions that extended the scope of the law beyond its former bounds.

The new *Ulozhenie*, that quintessentially bureaucratic document, was produced after the June uprising by the tsarist chancellery administration. Although popular delegates to an Assembly of the Land cooperated in its formulation and ultimately endorsed it with their signatures, the *Ulozhenie* was not a response to any public call for a new law code.[74] Neither the rebels nor the petitioners mentioned a law code at all during the uprising itself. They concentrated instead on the need to revise the way in which justice was administered, first, by removing judicial affairs from the jurisdiction of the irredeemably corrupt and culturally alien chancelleries and, second, by replacing avaricious and dishonest judges with upright and honest men. They viewed justice as the purview of individuals, not institutions, and they understood it to depend on the character and worthiness of the individuals entrusted with administering it.

The June petitions referred to codes of law only indirectly, in an analogy drawn between the present reign of Aleksei Mikhailovich and the reign of the Byzantine Emperor Justinian, known to history as the force behind the influential Code of Justinian and other legal compilations:

Remember, your Tsarist Majesty, also the tale that is in your tsarist palace, which describes the Greek Emperor Justinian in Tsargrad [Constantinople], how in his time the punishment of God's wrath threatened the Greek land, but because of the just verdict and decree that he ordered to be issued, to wit, that in all of his land all injustice and oppression of the poor should be stopped, God took away that punishment and transformed his wrath into mercy.[75]

The analogy is made explicit in the following lines, which state, "Now your tsarist majesty can do the same thing, if you wish to avoid God's punishment, which now similarly threatens your tsardom." But the lesson that the gentry petitioners extracted from the Justinian example is not the expected one about the need to compile a law code. Instead, their reading of Byzantine history underscores precisely the issues of individual worthiness or unreliability as the essence of the problem. Rather than suggest he draft a new law code, the petitioners advise the tsar, "[You must] order unjust judges rooted out, ignorant ones removed, so that bribe taking and lawlessness and red tape and evildoing would be punished, the flowing tears of the many innocent would be dried and averted, the humble and the poor would be protected from violence and offence."[76]

The petitions similarly emphasized the divine source of the ruler's personal righteousness and justice with a passage from Psalm 72, containing King David's prayers for the reign of his son Solomon, which was quoted in both versions of the June petition:

> Give the king Your judgments, O God,
> And Your righteousness to the king's Son.
> He will judge Your people with righteousness,
> And Your poor with justice.
>
> . . . .
> He will bring justice to the poor of the people;
> He will save the children of the needy,
> And will break in pieces the oppressor.
>
> . . . .
> For He will deliver the needy from the powerful,
> The poor also, and him who has no helper.[77]

Like the Justinian parable, this passage was used by the petitioners to stress traditional Muscovite notions of the personal obligations and responsibilities of the ruler to mete out justice according to God-given wisdom. David's hope for his son is that he should use that God-given sword of justice to defend the poor and needy and to punish the wicked, not particularly that he should develop or abide by a set of laws.[78]

The Muscovite rebels and gentry petitioners called insistently for a meeting with the tsar himself, pleading for a chance to see the tsar's "shining eyes" in person. In this request, they expressed the same desire for personal, protective justice from the ruler. They hoped for an opportunity to express their woes directly to their tsar-protector. The actual issues they wished to discuss remain vague in the petitions, but their desire to speak directly with the sovereign is perfectly clear:

> If you, Sovereign, would hear the weeping of all the people, you would summon to yourself, Sovereign, Moscow-rank gentry and provincial gentry and petty gentry, and Moscow merchants . . . [of various degrees] and all kinds of people . . . to read out this humble little petition [expressing] the weeping of all the people [*mir*], . . . and having read it out to them [you], the sovereign, would question all the people about what graft and violence causes them to groan and weep, and they themselves will tell the Sovereign all about this.[79]

As this passage illustrates, the petitioners called for personal access to their tsar, relying on his pious mercy and righteous wrath to right the country's wrongs.

The draft of the instructions to the gentry's delegate to the 1648 Assembly of the Land from Vladimir province illustrates the faith that the gentry had in the fruits of dialogue with the sovereign. Since the document is a rough draft, it contains errors and omissions and addresses its message to "who[mever] and what[ever] his name is, whom the town selected," but it nonetheless shows that the Vladimir gentry took seriously the process of selecting and instructing a delegate. The text repeats the official order that the man chosen should be an "upstanding gentryman," deserving of the privilege of "seeing the sovereign's eyes."[80] In the draft, the community entrusted the as-yet-unnamed delegate with a carefully compiled set of instructions, emphasizing primarily his obligation to communicate directly and honestly with the sovereign and great nobles at the council and to report back fully to the community about what transpired, whether it concerned issues raised in their instructions or other matters.

> And with our brethren, the chosen people, [he is] to speak about various matters and grievances in all [matters] without reticence and without fear. And [he is] to meet the Patriarch and church hierarchs and boyars and

duma-rank people and our brethren the strong and rich in truth, without reticence, and to speak without deception, so that they set aside all kinds of untruth and offences and soul-destroying greed and love the truth. And among us would be no injustice or offences at all.

Like their "brethren" who framed the nationwide collective petitions, the gentrymen of Vladimir said nothing in their instructions about forming a new law code but rather spoke about righteousness, fairness ("trials would be given to all people equally whether they were great or insignificant"), truth, friendship, and love. Above all, they emphasized the salutary effects of forthright communication "without reticence and without fear." The Vladimir gentry placed high hopes in unmediated discussion with their sovereign and his boyars but also stressed that the delegate must report back to the community fully and honestly: "And whatever they start to say, oppose, or argue about [concerning] articles in addition to [those included in our instructions] or included in our instructions, and whatever [the delegate] decides upon, he and all elected gentrymen are to inform us about such articles and discuss [them] with us, so that [omission in text] would be firm and constant, unshakable, on which the truth would stand forever unmovably."[81] They rather grandly anticipated that if forthright communication occurred then "the truth would stand forever unmovably" on that basis. "And the sovereign's name would become acclaimed in all surrounding countries and kingdoms because the truth would be established by him after many years. And through his Sovereign favor, among us, slaves, would be friendship and love, and no weepers and importunate petitioners and extortionists at all would exist." As the assemblies met, however, the gathered delegates found themselves interacting far more with a committee of boyars and bureaucrats who had drafted the new law code than with their revered sovereign.

In concrete terms, the Vladimir delegate was instructed to advance only the standard gentry proposals: abolition of the statute of limitations, the completion of a new census, the creation of a high boyar court of appeals outside of the chancellery courts. In addition to these traditional gentry demands, the delegate was to ask for the abolition of *zakladchiki*, bondsmen with tax-free status who did great harm to taxpaying merchants and artisans in towns by selling similar items at lower prices.

Public interest in a law code arose not during the rebellion but rather in the course of the first Assembly of the Land, which gathered in a great hall in the Kremlin. Attending the assembly were "the holy Iosif, Patriarch of Moscow and all Russia, and the church hierarchs and boyars and *okol'nichie* and chancellery people, and also at the Assembly were *stol'niki* and Moscow servitors," as well as an assortment of lesser provincial servitors, merchants, foreigners, "and the best people of the urban tax-paying communes."[82] A memorandum dated July 16, 1648, from the office of Prince N. I. Odoevskii, the boyar in charge of drafting the new law code, reports that at that assembly, delegates of middle ranks of the service and urban population suggested "that the sovereign [should] order to be written up on all sorts of judicial matters a law code [*sudebnik*] and statute book [*ulozhennaia kniga*], so that henceforth all matters would be done and decided according to that statute book."[83]

When Vladimir's delegate (Samoilo Vasil'ev Berechinskii) and the other representatives to the first Assembly of the Land of 1648 requested a new code of laws, what they envisioned and what they ultimately received were worlds apart. Before 1649, the primary models of formal law with which the mass of Muscovites was familiar were the particularistic edicts issued in response to individual cases and the earlier law codes, the *Sudebniki* of 1497 and 1550, which scantily outlined fees, trial procedures, and penalties for abuse of the legal system. Both previous codes had concentrated on regulating officials and official procedure, stipulating harsh penalties for corrupt judges and other agents of the law. With this circumscribed experience with law, the petitioners could not have expected that the new statute book, which they hoped would merely straighten out contradictions in precedent and force judges and chancellery people into line, would differ so fundamentally from the previous slim volumes on courtroom conduct. They could not have anticipated the massive, aggressively controlling *Ulozhenie*, a legal code strikingly innovative in its effort to regulate not only judicial procedure but also the conduct of society at large. Regulation of life did not, of course, begin abruptly in 1649, and a huge number of decrees regulating various aspects of life had already accumulated prior to 1649, but these had not constituted either a *sudebnik* or an *ulozhennaia kniga*, the terms used by the petitioners and assembly delegates. The *Ulozhenie* responded to popular calls for judicial reform, but the end product must have differed radically from the initial expectation.

The intrusive, interventionist *Ulozhenie* contradicted and undermined many of the principles that the petitioners held dear. It most directly negated the petitioners' aspirations by including no provision for the tsar to act as the final arbiter in disputes. The law specified that the boyars and counselors would "handle the sovereign's various cases." Furthermore, where previously cases that the boyars could not resolve had been "referred to him, the sovereign," giving the gentry some means of direct access to the tsar, the *Ulozhenie* resolutely closed that avenue of approach with its routinizing procedural norms.[84] To a group of petitioners who had consistently imagined the tsar as the ultimate source of mercy in an increasingly merciless administrative network and who dreamed of an idyllic state of direct, open contact between tsar and people, the *Ulozhenie* must have been a travesty of all they valued.

The delegates' requests for code-based justice and a new statute book take on a new light if situated within the context of the foregoing examination of Muscovite political culture, particularly within the context of the petitioners' desire for personal, local justice. For a decade, petitioners had begged for a reform of the judicial system based on principles of mercy, derived from piety and familiarity. It was not the idea of a legislated legal order or even of a standard application of law that they had opposed, for they had already accumulated almost two centuries' experience with a such system. As seen in their demands for statute books and equal justice, they understood and valued laws as guidelines by which administrators and officials should operate to guarantee fairness to all, according to each person's status. What the petitioners objected to was, instead, the heartless, unjust, and corrupt application of laws by unfamiliar administrators with neither social status nor personal mercy to lend legitimacy to their judicial rulings. The petitioners protested against a legal process without a human face.

As evident from the various options suggested over the decades by exasperated petitioners, they learned through experience and failure. Over time they had formulated three possible models of reform for the corrupt legal system. Ideally, the tsar would allow local selection of upstanding men from the communities to judge according to personalized standards of mercy and righteousness. When for ten years that proposal garnered no response at all from the Kremlin, the gentry suggested that the tsar appoint godly men, who would judge in virtue and piety. When that route so patently failed, as seen in the appointment of scoundrels such as Pleshcheev and Trakhaniotov, the petitioners fell back on the third option, the one already em-

ployed in earlier codes on judicial procedure and the only one appear-
ing to hold out any hope for reform: legal regulation of the tsar's
officials. The petitioners' requests for justice by code drew on Muscovite tradition, dating back at least to Ivan III's 1497 Law Code, but
fit with an increasingly pressing need to rein in the tsar's oppressive,
irresponsible deputies in a polity bent on centralization. The administrators of the central chancellery system were evidently there to
stay. As the Muscovite state administration gradually developed in
the direction of bureaucratization and impersonal routinization in a
slow, ongoing process of change, the gentry's attitudes toward the
evolving state structure went through their own gradual phases. Neither the concept of justice as a personal relationship based on stern-
ness and mercy nor the concept of a centralized, legislative judicial
order was new in 1648, but the tensions between the two had grown
more acute. As lowborn administrators and unknown officials from
the central chancelleries replaced familiar governors in the provinces
and as regulation of judicial and administrative procedure intruded
into all aspects of life, the acceptable and even desirable effects of
justice by legal code came to be viewed as destructive and offensive.
The events of 1648 thus marked a watershed in legal and political
perceptions. The petitioners, like the state authorities, found themselves at a juncture between two political cultural systems, torn between the two.

CHAPTER 8

The Year 1648 and Beyond: The Transformation of Muscovite Political Culture

Although it is difficult to locate major historical changes precisely in particular dramatic incidents, it is safe to say that the year 1648 represents an important transitional moment in Muscovite political culture. Specific events that occurred before and during the uprising, as well as the unprecedented scale of the law code that came out of it, demonstrate that by midcentury new currents of possibility had entered the Muscovite political mainstream and were mingling uneasily with traditional practices and expectations.

When the occasion arose to address issues of concern to the realm as a whole or the gentry as a collective entity, or even to assess the performance of the tsar and his advisers, the provincial gentry demonstrated a striking degree of understanding of the religious cosmology propounded by the state and the Orthodox church and also showed its ability to make use of that ideology, at times opportunistically, at times deeply critically. This censorious deployment of official ideology surfaces most clearly in the petitions of the watershed year, 1648. As the century progressed, Muscovites became increasingly adept at using the bureaucratic and legal system to serve their interests. After 1649 petitioners began to beg for more enforceable regulations and increased state intervention, but in June of 1648 the (old) traditional and (new) rationalizing conceptions of law and justice still had little in common. Gentry, merchants, musketeers, and townspeople turned to the latter mode only when their more familiar conception of merciful, personal justice proved untenable.

Moral Cosmology and the Limits of Tsarist Legitimacy

When Tsar Aleksei Mikhailovich refused to accept the petitions offered to him by his subjects on June 2, 1648, they responded with ten days of bloodshed and destruction. The violence of their reaction corresponded to the egregiousness of the tsar's violation of his appointed role. Fully in keeping with the ideas expressed in gentry petitions of the previous decades, the petitioners had hoped that the tsar would take them, his "loyal slaves and poor orphans," under his protective wing and shield them from bureaucratic red tape and corruption. Steeped in a tradition in which the tsar played a fatherly role, protecting the poor and defenseless and chastising the wicked, the petitioners felt abandoned when the tsar would not even listen to their cries. Both the surviving collective petitions refer to the tsar's rejection of the initial supplication with a sharp sense of betrayal. They remind the tsar that in the past, both he and his father before him "with *your awesome hand* [*strashnoiu svoieiu rukoiu*] took care of us with gracious charity. . . . You *personally* [*sami*] took our bloody-teared petitions from us" and listened to them and acted on them.[1] The tsar had failed to uphold even the appearance of serving as the refuge of last resort, as intercessor on behalf of the "poor, lowly and defenseless" of his realm. Evidently in an attempt to prevent a repetition of the events of June 2, the new law code of 1649 formalized this radical revision of traditional norms: Chapter 10, article 20, states that people must submit their petitions to the appropriate official in whichever chancellery holds jurisdiction in the case, not to the tsar. If someone attempted to bypass this new classically bureaucratic procedure and handed a petition to the sovereign himself without first petitioning in the chancellery, the code stipulated, "Punish such petitioners for that; beat [them] with bastinadoes. If [the petitioner] is too high-ranking [to be bastinadoed], imprison that person for a week so that others looking on will learn not to do that."[2] Chapter 1, articles 8 and 9, similarly forbade the handing of petitions to the tsar or patriarch during church services. "If someone, forgetting the fear of God and disdaining the Tsar's order, proceeds to petition the sovereign, or patriarch, or any other high church officials about his personal affairs in God's church during the church services: cast that petitioner in prison for as long as the sovereign decrees."[3] The *Ulozhenie* makes not the slightest nod toward preserving the traditional role of the sovereign as the guardian of the people and highest court of appeals.

The new prohibitions did not succeed in terminating the practice of direct petition to the tsar, however, for it was too integral to the political culture to be stopped by fiat. More than a century later Catherine the Great still found herself overwhelmed by petitioners and issued another series of prohibitions. Yet Tsar Aleksei's refusal of the June 2 petition and the subsequent attempts to insulate the sovereign from contact with his subjects signaled a great sea change in official attitudes toward the business of ruling the tsardom. By spurning the proffered appeals, the tsar demonstrated that he had little interest in preserving the traditional image of a merciful tsar extending personal protection to his people. Most historians attribute the nineteen-year-old tsar's refusal of the petitions to youthful panic. Accustomed to seclusion in the Kremlin, interrupted only by ceremonial, highly choreographed public appearances, the teenage sovereign was terrified when he found himself surrounded by an unruly, unregulated crowd, and fled.[4] He certainly had good reason to be afraid, yet the very possibility of such a breach of tradition occurring suggests that Tsar Aleksei viewed himself in quite a different light from that of his predecessors and had distanced himself from his people through an expanding administrative organization. However rarely the image of tsar-as-"little father"—the protective, caring, approachable tsar—had resulted in actual benefits for the people, Aleksei Mikhailovich's act reverberated with significance: the age of personal intercession had given way to the age of the law code and the civil servant. The Muscovite populace was right in suspecting that people at the top were betraying their traditional ways. A new form of authority had entered the corridors of the Kremlin while the public still responded to authority as it had been traditionally conceived, as the earthly incarnation of a moral, divine cosmology.[5]

In expressing their discontent with a changing political system, Muscovite petitioners represented their political world in terms consistent with the traditionally dominant theocentric, patrimonial construction of their culture, in which religious devotion and piety intermeshed inseparably with political loyalty and obedience. Yet acceptance of the official discourse did not engender political passivity or "naive monarchism," in which the tsar was assumed to be infallible. On the contrary, the discourse of tsar as divine representative and protector of the Orthodox flock generated a highly subversive counterdiscourse, one which enabled the tsar's subjects to turn the essence of the official language of politics against the tsar himself.[6]

The petitioners accepted that the tsar had been chosen and exalted by God himself, but they reminded their ruler that in accepting such great honor he accepted the responsibility to rule the Orthodox flock with piety, humility, and justice. The 1648 petitions are full of examples of this conception of authority. The Shakhmatov petition states, "God chose your Sovereign father of blessed memory and you, Great Sovereign, above your peers and entrusted to you, Sovereigns, the tsarist sword for the quelling of evildoers and the praise of the virtuous."[7] The Pommerening petition adds that not only God but also the people of Muscovy at the Assembly of the Land in 1613 had participated in the selection of Tsar Mikhail: "Your royal majesty, like your majesty's deceased father the Sovereign who, after the total and complete destruction of the Muscovite state by the evil people, was raised up and chosen as Sovereign and Great Prince by God and the entire people, so the sword was entrusted to you for the punishment of evil and to show mercy upon the good—and thus was then all kind of injustice punished."[8] Nothing in these lines in any way contradicts the official rhetoric of tsarist legitimacy. Aleksei Mikhailovich himself described his intention to rule "with threats and mercy." He wrote in a letter just a few years after the riot, "We, the great Tsar, daily pray to the Lord God and His Most Pure Mother and all the saints that the Creator should accord it to us, the great Tsar, and you, the boyars, to be of one mind and rule the people in fairness and justice to everyone."[9]

Commonality of language and understanding did not, however, guarantee harmony or submissiveness. Even within this Orthodox, paternalist political culture, the tsar was not immune to criticism. The petitioners' language in June 1648 expressed an ambiguous message of loyalty and menace, for the same ideological vocabulary that fostered harmony and social integration could also serve as a destabilizing force, turning the most loyal subjects against the tsar himself. The petitioners who took advantage of the regime's moment of weakness to press their demands used the power of the dominant moral discourse to advance their own interests, even going so far as to turn that discourse against the tsar himself. The petitions called for punishment of corrupt officials and "strong people" by invoking the tsar's accountability to God. "Remember that you, Sovereign, were called to the tsardom by God himself, not by your own wish."[10] They drew a direct connection between the tsar's failure to punish the wicked and the uprisings. They stated that God had bestowed on the tsar the sword of justice with which to root out evil, "But today, as a consequence of the fact that your tsarist highness is so patient, evil people . . . accrue all sorts of advantages and riches from serving on state business, regardless of the fact that through them destruction overtakes the entire people."[11] They hinted at the possibility that the bond between tsar and people might be irrevocably severed by the tsar's toleration of evil-doers, who "by their destructiveness and greed . . . are fomenting trouble between you, the sovereign, and the whole land, and they have almost accomplished this."[12]

The petitions state that great prosperity and blessings lie within reach, but the tsar must take drastic action to attain them. If he fails in this, "God's punishment" awaits him and his land: "Now, your tsarist highness, . . . if you wish to avoid God's punishment which now threatens your tsardom, . . . you will order unjust judges extirpated, the ignorant driven away, so that bribe taking and illegality and red tape and malfeasance will be punished, the flowing tears of many innocent people will be dried and averted, the humble and the poor will be protected from violence and offence."[13]

The tsar's failings emerge again in direct reference to the gentry's long-term petition campaign, which the tsars had treated with indifference: "Many times we petitioned your deceased father to punish the above-mentioned destroyers of us and of the people after a council and investigation of the above-mentioned officials, and still we await and desire the same thing from you, but instead of this they treat us worse than the worst people under the sun and do not want to listen. . . . And we do not know what answer you wish to give us about these, our destroyers and violators."[14]

The petitioners upbraided the tsar in harsh terms for causing the ongoing rebellion by his lax attention to justice:

And thus the entire people in the whole Muscovite state and its borderlands are being aroused to rebellion because of such injustice. As a consequence of this a great storm is rising in your tsarist capital city of Moscow and in many other places, in towns and provinces. If your tsarist highness, [ignoring] the extreme oppression of the poor people, allows such a gang of scoundrels to remain unpunished, they will feel themselves all the more secure in taking bribes and judgment payments and in their injustices. Even now for the most part, the whole people has been deprived of its possessions and ruined, so that instead of prosperity and security, they have reached a state of most extreme poverty and mortal danger and they no longer value nor take care of their own lives and property.[15]

The petitions thus portray a people so abused and impoverished that it has nothing left to fear and nothing to gain by remaining loyal and peaceable. The petitioners here counterpose corrupt with just judgment rather than explicitly contrasting bureaucratic with personal justice, but it is the tsar whom they find to be ultimately responsible for the corruption of his own judicial system.[16]

Having drawn a dire picture of the state of the land, the petitions proceed to threaten the tsar with worse to come:

> You, Sovereign and Grand Prince, should heed the bitter, tearful supplication of your slaves and orphans and all Orthodox Christians who are devoted to you with all their soul, but without any aid and intercession are standing [alone] because your royal majesty is not receiving them in his heart. [We] have . . . reminded you that the punishment of God's wrath, which in former times broke out over the Muscovite state for such lawlessness, now again must strike us.[17]

This passage admonishes the tsar for failing to live up to the protective role to which God appointed him and goads him with only loosely veiled threats of a renewed Time of Troubles, for which he will be directly to blame.

The petitioners reminded the tsar in no uncertain terms of his "cross-kissed oath," sworn at his coronation, to protect the poor and weak, and added that his standing in public opinion was suffering:

> We hear among all the people moaning and wailing because of the injustices of the strong people, and of the town governors in the provincial towns and of chancellery secretaries in Moscow and because of the great corruption of all chancellery people. And everyone is crying out against the sovereign, saying that the sovereign does not stand up for us poor people, for the lowborn and the defenseless, having handed over his realm to thievery.[18]

With this catalog of faults, the petitioners demonstrated that they found the tsar's performance reprehensible, and they condemned it on precisely the same moral, theological grounds that official ideologists employed in defending the legitimacy of tsarist autocracy.

Long before 1648 Muscovite literary ideology had developed a culturally acceptable, theologically sound basis for opposition to the tsar. In general, Muscovite philosophy advocated patient endurance and humility in the face of adversity. Whether it came in the form of foreign invasion, natural disaster, or tsarist tyranny, adversity was usually interpreted as the wrath of God, punishment inflicted for sinful behavior. However, Muscovite thinkers also acknowledged that when the image of the tsar as divinely ordained protector departed too obviously from perceived reality, a second image of the tsar, as tsar-tormentor or tyrant, was available in biblical and patristic texts. By the middle of the seventeenth century, sermons, frescoes, and historical tales had utilized and developed these dread alternate images of the evil ruler. If he patently failed to rule as the most holy representative of God on earth, this literary ideology suggested, the sovereign had to be judged a traitor to God and people.[19]

By and large, this powerfully seditious counterimage of the unholy tsar emerges only in the writings of elite court and church thinkers. However, in 1648 the petitioners showed that they understood this concept and used it to justify their outrage. In their petitions, the gentry and urban petitioners implied that the Orthodox community was obliged to correct or even depose the tsar if necessary in order to restore the divine order as they conceived it. Against the blazing background of the urban riots, the implications would have been quite clear.

The gentry petitions of the 1630s and 1640s, especially those "of all the land" in 1648, demonstrate that the political theology or moral cosmology articulated in literature, art, and ritual at the highest levels of church and state held deep resonance in the minds and political conceptions of ordinary Muscovites. As far as the sources indicate, no rival set of values competed with the official ones to set up alternative notions of political legitimacy. The same complex, multitiered cultural imagery of political legitimacy shaped the political universe in both the Kremlin and the provinces. This imagery, which combined divine selection and direction of the tsar with election and advice "from all the land" and united autocracy in its highest form with responsiveness to popular appeals, provided a basis for both loyalty and resistance. The official rhetoric and imagery at court drew on a political culture powerfully based on shared values of personalism, mercy, and piety. The common moral language of politics opened up spaces for contestation and autonomy at the same time that it precluded other forms of resistance and condemnation.

The various configurations of accommodation, appropriation, and contestation worked out by the Muscovite gentry testify to the complexity inherent in all relations of power and domination. As far as can be determined, the gentry never questioned the principle of autocratic tsarist rule. The gentry had good reason to stand staunchly by the autocratic system. As the historian I. A. Iakovlev writes, the gentry was characterized by the fact that it collected service grants from the state, a consequence of which was that "a service person

naturally became the faithful bearer of Muscovite centralization."[20]
Perry Anderson, writing about Eastern absolutist states in general,
comments on the "umbilical cord" of serfdom that bound noble landholders' interests to those of the state.[21] Outright resistance remained the territory of the lower strata and the peripheral elements
of Muscovite society: poor townspeople, Cossacks, non-Russian peoples of the borderlands, and peasants.[22] Yet between the extremes of
submission and resistance lie many various courses by which relations of power may be mediated and negotiated.[23] In 1648 the gentry
made telling and creative use of the culture of its subordination to
negotiate its position within society. In formulating its criticisms
and demands, the gentry and "all the people" leveled a critique based
on official and cultural tradition against corruption and exploitation
on one level but against the unwelcome advent of innovative, depersonalizing, secular practices on the other. In retrospect, 1648 can
be seen as a turning point because after the events of that year the
gentry and the Muscovite population found themselves interacting
with quite a different state, under quite novel circumstances. Aleksei Mikhailovich's refusal of the petition on June 2, 1648, a precedent codified into law in the 1649 *Ulozhenie*, signaled the consolidation of the new political order based on impersonal, systematic
procedure administered by chancellery personnel. The process of re-
versing the cultural value placed on informal, personal intercession
and mercy with that placed on impersonal, abstract procedure had
gained momentum.

Transformations of Political Culture in the Second Half of the Seventeenth Century

In the Muscovite case, in the first half of the seventeenth century what might be loosely labeled "enfranchised groups" played the
game of politics according to a uniform set of rules, whether they
lived in the provinces or in the capital. By midcentury, as the events
of 1649 demonstrate, a single set of practices and expectations no
longer lent coherence to Muscovite political interactions. Traditional political culture collided sharply with creeping routinization,
and local autonomies encountered redefined boundaries as the self-
aggrandizing state extended its ambitions and its control into previously untouched reaches. After its trenchant critique of the corrupt, merciless, and increasingly depersonalized state apparatus in

1648, the gentry won some policy concessions but in turn made concessions to the now firmly entrenched reality of bureaucratism as a governmental form.

In the second half of the century, new Western ideas of government and state slowly percolated into the highest educated Moscow circles, gradually but significantly changing the appearance, language, and ideological rhetoric of Muscovite political life. For the first time tsars, boyars, and solid citizens commissioned portraits of themselves, flaunting their individuality and their worldly status, defying a culture that had traditionally honored the religious icon to the exclusion of all other pictorial forms. A transitional figure in his own right, the often staunchly traditionalist Tsar Aleksei Mikhailovich established the first Western-style theater in the Kremlin, and his daughter Sophia translated a piece by Molière in which her favorite, Prince V. V. Golitsyn, acted.[24] In a startling flurry of reform activity in 1682 the boyars and high noble advisers of Tsar Fedor Alekseevich agreed to demote the role of birth in determining precedence. They oversaw the dramatic public burning of the *mestnichestvo* books, which had determined birth and precedence, and attempted to draw up a new scheme whereby merit and service, not birth, figured at the heart of a novel hierarchy of ranks.[25] Although most of these elaborate schemes never reached fruition, they foreshadowed Peter the Great's Table of Ranks and ultimately might have transformed marriage from the most crucial public and political act to a manifestation of a newly invented private life.

Little of this cultural Westernization touched the broader Muscovite society. Judging from the concerns raised in legal cases and petitions and the goods listed in wills and marriage agreements, the provincial gentry showed little interest in the German-style clothing or richly adorned palaces of the tiny Moscow avant guard.[26] What touched the gentry far more directly were the homegrown changes in the ambition, scope, and outreach of the state. The state launched a far more activist, interventionist agenda in the second half of the century. For the first time the state began to interfere actively in what had previously been considered purely ecclesiastical matters, such as church attendance and proper conduct during mass. The *Ulozhenie* created an Monasterial Chancellery. It prohibited working on Sundays or holidays as well as riding or walking at night during lent.[27] In 1669 the state asserted its right to intervene forcefully in landlords' relations with their peasants to enforce the ban on Sunday labor, mandating imprisonment for a landlord whose peasants violated the ban.[28] The state increased its interest in the secular sphere as well. Its legislation aimed at maintaining public order and regulating conduct in all of its smallest manifestations. The *Ulozhenie* included four articles dictating how people should leash and fence their pet dogs.[29] A long series of decrees regulated tobacco smoking, card playing, and alcohol manufacture and consumption. In 1686 an official edict prohibited littering on public streets.[30] The growing regularization and institutionalization that the gentry had already detected with alarm in 1648 assumed increasingly concrete form. Rather than reducing the number of chancelleries and chancellery personnel in response to the proliferation of complaints in the 1630s and 1640s, the state added more chancelleries and chancellery officials until the end of the century.[31] Procedures within the chancelleries and in all branches of government assumed ever more concrete, institutional form.[32]

In interactions within their local communities, members of the provincial gentry remained remarkably consistent throughout the century. Nothing in particular distinguishes the local maneuverings of the Vladimir-Suzdal' gentry in the first half of the century from those of the second. But in addressing itself collectively to the tsar and the central administration, the gentry demonstrated its ability to adapt itself creatively and productively to the changing practices of the state and to its own changing circumstances. For the provincial servitor-landholders, the goals of political agitation evolved over the course of the century as service requirements were reduced and ownership of serfs came to occupy a more central role in their lives. At the same time, they accommodated themselves to the more interventionist state and the ever more institutionalized forms and mechanisms of politics.

Many collective gentry petitions survive from the second half of the century, between 1653 and 1694. The first and most pressing issue that confronted the gentry after the successful resolution of the campaign to abolish the statute of limitations on the recovery of runaway peasants was the problem of enforcement. The law now supported the absolute right of the petty landholder to keep his or her serfs, but as long as the law remained only on paper, it would have no more effect on the "strong people" than had any previous legislation. Powerful magnates still had the ability to abscond with peasants and hide them on their scattered estates beyond the reach of the impoverished gentry. Moreover, several categories of dependent people fell outside of the purview of the 1649 code and thus could be legally abducted. Furthermore, the court system was still utterly corrupt, and between searching for peasants and fighting with hassles and delays in court, the time and money involved in the process of recovering a runaway could still far exceed the resources available to a small landholder.

The problem of controlling the serf population appears to have grown even more difficult in the second half of the century, after the enserfment legislation. This most likely resulted from the opening of vast new unsettled territories in the south and east and the government's need to populate and defend those lands. The army's need for ablebodied men in the borderlands created an opportunity for runaways to claim with some plausibility "that according to your Great Sovereign decree they have been granted departure to the border towns."[33] A 1653 decree exempted runaways from extradition back to their masters if they had settled in border towns before the *Ulozhenie* law code, "so that the abatis line would not be depopulated." A 1675 ruling stated even more explicitly that no one should be returned from the frontier without a special order, "because those regimental people have been trained as lancers and horse guards and dragoons and infantrymen and they are needed for current service and for campaigns."[34] This deliberate practice of sheltering runaways in frontier regiments naturally upset the gentry, which petitioned in 1682 that town governors should "not receive our runaway people and peasants in the future and not register them in . . . any kind of [military] service." Out of its own pressing need for troops, however, the state continued to vacillate.[35]

D. A. Vysotskii writes of the shifting content of the gentry petitions: "If in the petitions of the 1630s and 1640s corruption by strong people is the first order of business and peasants are more a passive subject of struggle among the seigneurs, then in petitions of the second half of the century the peasants themselves emerge as the first order of business, constantly threatening the peace and quiet of the landlords."[36] The later petitions did, indeed, present the peasants in very dark and dangerous hues:

And those, our runaway people and peasants and cottars, . . . flee from those lower and borderland towns and run to Ufa and to Siberian towns and to the Khoper [River]. And returning from flight, those, our runaway people and peasants and cottars, destroy us, your slaves, steal horses and burn our houses and villages. And on the road they rob [people] and they have killed many of our brothers, and they inflict cruel abuse, and they convince our remaining people and peasants and cottars to [join] them.[37]

Runaway peasants, according to the petitions, gathered on the roads in groups of a hundred or more, with guns, bows, lances, rifles, poleaxes, and other implements of destruction. "And our runaway people and peasants, having gathered in those border towns, rob us, your slaves, on the road, and beat our little people to death, so that we, your slaves, are fearful and won't go after them in the future."[38]

In February 1658 the state issued a decree addressing the rash of antilandlord violence. Like others in his situation, Lavrentii Obukhov, the town governor of Iur'ev Pol'skii, was ordered to conduct a thorough inquiry into the problem and return the peasants to their former masters. The order required that he have both the runaways and those who had harbored them beaten, and peasants found guilty of beating their masters or their families or burning their houses were to be executed.[39] Nationwide, tens of thousands of peasants were found and returned to their former owners after being impounded from the great magnates and ecclesiastical estates that had harbored them illegally. Studying *otdatochnye knigi,* books that recorded the return of runaways, Novosel'skii discovered that a single investigator found and returned more than 1,200 runaways in Arzamas in the course of four and a half months in 1658. In 1667, 1,203 runaway peasants and slaves were found in Riazan'. In Nizhegorod province in 1658, in less than two months, 1,532 runaways were returned to their owners.[40]

If the peasants appear as the most obvious villains of these pieces, however, the same themes of "Moscow legal harassment," corruption and injustice still sound in petitions of the second half of the century. Just as the petitions from the beginning of the century had complained that it was impossible to convince provincial and chancellery officials to give fair trials against "strong people," so in the second half of the century petitioners continued to complain that "in the towns governors and chancellery people, forgetting your Sovereign's awesome decree, for their own greed receive those our runaway people and peasants and cottars and refuse to investigate, and they don't return those our runaways to us, your slaves."[41] "And when we, your slaves, catch these our runaway people and peasants in flight and we take them to the chancelleries to the chancellery people, or to town governors and various chancellery people in the towns, . . . they do nothing for us, your slaves."[42]

In a series of petitions beginning in the 1650s (one perhaps dating as early as 1649), the gentry proposed a novel solution to the problem of enforcement. Whereas earlier petitions had agitated for diminishing the presence of the centralized chancelleries as much as possible, these petitions adopted precisely the opposite stance. They begged the state to take the responsibility for searching for runaways out of the hands of the individual landlord and to assume that burden itself. They envisioned a total process, in which state agents would take all initiative and responsibility, conducting ongoing searches for runaways without waiting for individual landlords to file missing-person reports (*iavki*). The investigators would be responsible for all stages of the process, from searching everywhere to interrogating witnesses, establishing ownership, carting the runaways back to their owners (at the harborers' expense), punishing the runaways, and, finally, exacting fines and penalties from the harborers.

In 1657, after describing how peasants and people fled from their estates while they themselves were away in the Sovereign's military service and how those runaways returned to burn down their estates and lure or force the few remaining peasants to leave with them, the "*dvoriane* and *deti boiarskie* of borderland towns and central Russian towns" complained that "in the towns and villages and hamlets the provincial governors and chancellery people won't help us against our destroyers and don't catch them." They begged the tsar to be merciful, and to order special gentrymen sent to conduct investigations "for us poor ones" in all towns throughout the land:

> And order [them], Sovereign, to investigate thoroughly about those our runaway people and peasants, [to find] which people and peasants turn up on whose *pomest'e* and *votchina* estates over and above [those listed in] the cadasters [*pistsovye* and *perepisnye knigi*], and to whom their fathers were registered. Order, Sovereign, [those gentrymen] to investigate about them and to question them [about] whose they are and whence they came, and according to that investigation, Sovereign, order them given back to us as previously in peasant status, and the bondsmen in slavery.

The petitioners foresaw the need to equip the special investigators with adequately armed soldiers if they were to have any effect in curbing the greed of the "strong people," so they requested that the tsar order the town governors and chancellery people in the towns to assign musketeers and petty officers to assist "those gentrymen who are sent out for the investigation."[43]

For the first time in the gentry's history of collective petitions, the 1657 petition solicited active involvement in local affairs by officials dispatched by the central chancelleries. The petitioners requested that the state assume the burden of combing the countryside to find their peasants and of prosecuting those found to be illegally harboring those peasants. Petitioners in 1658 even solicited state interference in traditionally ecclesiastical matters; they asked that the state impose fines, in addition to the canonical religious sanctions, on priests who concealed information about runaways, "so that all priests, because of the fear of God and of your sovereign sanctions, will not lie in their testimony."[44]

The same request for centralization of initiative and standardization of procedure characterized collective gentry petitions throughout the remainder of the century. In response to the gentry's petitions, the Sovereign agreed in 1658 to send *syshchiki* (special investigators) from Moscow to the provinces to search for runaways. The investigators were not sent to all towns, however, and responded only when individuals filed complaints about particular runaways rather than undertaking a general investigation. The gentry continued to complain that in some towns "there were no investigators" and to request that investigators be sent out to all towns to conduct all investigations about runaways. "Order, Sovereign, investigators sent to all of your Sovereign towns, and to villages and districts . . . with your powerful sovereign decree and [make the investigators take] your cross-kissed oath. And order, Sovereign, the investigators to search for our runaway slaves and serfs without our [having to] investigate and petition and without judicial red tape."[45] In a complete change of tack, the gentry now insisted on handing responsibility over to outsiders in the employ of the central state.

Displaying its attentiveness to and ability to understand Moscow politics, the gentry observed carefully and kept track of exactly what the policy on recovery of runaway serfs involved at any given time as well as what loopholes remained to allow peasants to take refuge in frontier regiments, in towns, or on the estates of the "strong people." On noticing a chink in the law, the gentry would promptly submit a new petition drawing the government's attention to the problem and recommending a practical policy solution. The first category addressed in the petitions was peasants and cottars who had left their masters between the two most recent censuses, the *pistsovye knigi*, begun after the Moscow fire of 1626 and completed in 1630, and the *perepisnye knigi*, compiled from 1646 to 1648. The *Ulozhenie* ruling on enserfment guaranteed perpetual ownership to those landlords registered in the new census books but did not look back to the old ones. The petitioners complained that

> [state officials refuse to return] peasants and cottars [who] left before the [later] cadasters, but who are recorded in the [earlier] cadasters as belonging to *pomeshchiki* and *votchinniki*, because in your Sovereign decree and in the Assembly of the Land *Ulozhenie* nothing is decreed about the ownership of those peasants and cottars, and they [the harborers of runaways] can own those, our peasants and cottars, from now on without fear and without any anxiety, because there has not been a single prohibition from you, Sovereign, [concerning this], nor does guilt lie [upon them].[46]

Likewise, neither the *Ulozhenie* nor subsequent decrees mentioned anything about the category of runaway household slaves, so landlords could not secure their return: "No one will give us our runaway household slaves without trial and without great Moscow red tape, because there has been not a single ban on owning them, nor is guilt assigned."[47] The gentry noticed another category of people that slipped through the cracks of existing legislation: hired laborers. In principle peasants needed to produce documentation showing that their landlords had approved their departure from their home estates to work as hired laborers, but the gentry petitioners complained that people were accepting runaways as hired hands without paying any attention to the necessary formalities: "Order, Sovereigns, all ranks of people to receive [peasants] as workers [only] with our documents giving them permission to work outside the estate, having confirmed that [the documents] are genuine, or with suretyship documents, and register those working and suretyship documents and those hired workers in the chancelleries in the towns."[48]

The demands set forth in these petitions, which span almost the entire second half of the century, echo some of the themes of the petitions of the first half but introduce new motifs as well. As noted in Chapter 7, before 1649 gentry petitioners had already displayed a surprising affinity for official paperwork and documentation as the grounds for securing their labor force when they demanded that peasants be bound to them "according to old cadaster books and excerpts from official documents." In the second half of the century, the gentry even more markedly cited official documentation as the only reliable means of establishing the truth. In 1682 petitioners requested that census records rather than the traditional religious procession be used to confirm the boundaries of their properties. Customary practice had employed longtime local residents as informed witnesses who would define property lines by walking them in solemn procession with a holy icon. By the time of this petition, gentry landlords had come to prefer the black and white evidence of chancellery records to the ambiguous testimony of local peasants: "In processions with icons and the lies of old-time residents much harm to the soul takes place."[49] This request demonstrates a preference for the cool, impersonal proof of official documentation and chancellery seals to the highly fallible traditional practice of having local peasants march off boundaries with clods of turf on their heads and icons in their hands. A 1691 petition spelled out the precise sequence of steps that the gentry suggested be substituted for icon procession, with the goal of establishing an adequate paper trail for proving legitimate ownership of peasants: special investigators from the central Moscow chancelleries were to question "people of all ranks" about runaways and write reports, "and [thcy] should bring those reports to Moscow to those chancelleries from which they have been sent."

> According to those reports and the investigation, [concerning] those, our runaway people and peasants and cottars wheresoever they may be found in the future, order, Sovereigns, that they, the special investigators, should take suretyship documents from those people where they are. And [they should] cart those, our runaway people and peasants and cottars, [back] to our *pomest'ia* and *votchiny* to their old plots. And when they are away from us, we and our estate agents will have official deeds of ownership [*otpisi*] and will bring those deeds of ownership to them, the special investigators, so that your great sovereign statute will be fearsome and effective with regard to all ranks of people, and so that, seeing [those documents], no one would, after your great sovereign prohibition, receive those our runaway people and peasants and cottars, nor harbor them for themselves.[50]

Far from attempting to eliminate the chancelleries from their lives, these later petitioners specifically request that their peasants' status and whereabouts be registered in both central and provincial chancelleries. These demands reflect a significant change in outlook among the gentry, a move toward accommodation to the newly bureaucratizing system, in which success would come to those who made good use of papers and chancelleries.

Official documents formed a critical and unavoidable aspect of daily life in seventeenth century Muscovy and bred their own varieties of veneration and abuse. A series of dishonor suits brought to Muscovite courts in the seventeenth century revolved around desecration of official documents or defamation of character through inappropriate (often inadvertent) recording of names, ranks, or status in official paperwork.[51] Official documents were necessary to sanction every aspect of life in seventeenth-century Russia. Travel passes authorized people to leave the province in which they were registered, special grants entitled them to postpone repayment of debt, immunity charters freed the peasants of certain privileged parties from communal service obligations. Any governmental document bore the sovereign's name and, like his palace and his city, shared his sacrosanct aura. To forge, tear, or deface a document thus dishonored the representation of the tsar and ultimately the tsar himself.[52] The gentry very practically analyzed the situation and incorporated documentary evidence as a powerful component of its effort to use governmental regulation to its own advantage. As E. P. Thompson says of laws, once ostensibly universal and egalitarian forms and rules are developed in a society, no matter whose interests they are initially developed to serve, they can be appropriated by the less powerful and deployed to serve the interests of the subjugated.[53]

The gentry's petitions of the 1650s through the 1690s raised another set of demands about fixing punitive penalties and exacting compensation from anyone who harbored runaways or any officials who failed to return known runaways. Nostalgically remembering a probably nonexistent golden age, the gentry "of all towns" petitioned Tsar Fedor Alekseevich in 1677, recalling the good old days under Tsar Aleksei when gentry-investigators had been sent out from Moscow and had actually tracked down and returned runaways and had extracted fines in cash and in kind (a set number of "penalty peasants" per peasant harbored) from the harborers.

> And those with whom our people and peasants lived after having run away had to pay residence fines and had to give [the money] to us, your slaves. And because of that ruling, our people and peasants, fearing and abiding by your great sovereign decree and punishment, fled from us but rarely. But now, Sovereign, in those towns and along the line there are no investigators, and our people and peasants run from us without any fear or apprehension. . . . And in towns, Sovereign, governors . . . [and other officials] hide our runaway people and peasants for their own greed and they collect from them great bribes and payoffs, because there are none of your sovereign fines or sanctions imposed upon governors

or . . . [other people], and residence fines and penalty peasants are not ordered collected from them.[54]

Without such penalties and deterrents to frighten them into line, powerful magnates and officials had little reason to abide by the new laws. The gentry had a strong interest in putting such penalties into effect. Thus once again the gentry petitioners in the second half of the century called on the state for more active intervention in protecting their privileges and in enforcing its own laws.

Novosel'skii makes the point that the "class struggle" dimension of the gentry's campaign against greedy magnates in the first part of the century was transformed in the second half to a regional struggle between the landholders of the more central provinces and those of the borderlands. The interests of these two regions were fundamentally at odds during this period, because the flow of peasant runaways headed ever southward, away from the enserfment and control of the older, more established regions to the freer, more open borderlands, where the need for ablebodied men was endless and opportunities for runaways abounded. The frontier itself shifted constantly farther to the south, pitting landholders in old frontier towns against those of the new outposts, which in turn drew peasants away from their earlier refuges. The loudest voices in the petitions about investigation and return of runaway serfs came from the eastern half of the old Zamoskov'e region, precisely the location of the Vladimir-Suzdal' provinces.[55] Of the several hundred names published by Novosel'skii of the gentrymen who signed the various petitions, 43 almost certainly came from one of the five Vladimir-Suzdal' provinces.[56] As Novosel'skii notes, primarily the "cream of local society" participated in the petition campaigns. Members of many of the leading families from the Vladimir-Suzdal' region appear among the signatories: Alalykin, Dolgovo-Saburov, Dubenskii, Golenkin, Kablukov, Kazimerov, Khmetevskii, Koisarov, Kolobov, Lazarev, Obolduev, Poroshin, Roganovskii, Stromilov, Tepritskii, Tregubov, Zhirovo-Zasekin. These are precisely the same people who participated most actively in local politics, men of high provincial and low Moscow rank who took upon themselves leading roles in provincial affairs. The same interests and practices that drove local politics moved these individuals to involve themselves in national policy issues as well.

The change of allegiances from anti- to proregularization and routinization of relationships and procedures that is evident in the collective petitions signifies a marked and pragmatic shift in the gentry's political conceptions from the earlier part of the century, but the shift was not abrupt or complete. It was an ongoing process, characterized by exceptions and ambivalence. The participation of the Vladimir-Suzdal' gentry in the campaigns for general searches epitomizes the equivocal stand of the gentry on the questions of state interference and impersonal routinization. Although their signatures on the collective petitions demonstrate that they wholeheartedly supported the general initiative of the gentry as a class to institutionalize the search for and recovery of runaway peasants, the gentry communities of the Vladimir-Suzdal' region also displayed a lingering affinity for the older, more flexible and personalized practices. The majority of gentry communities insisted that neither town governors nor *pistsy* (census takers) should conduct searches, the former because they were corrupt and in league with the "strong people" who harbored runaways, the latter because they were simply too busy and overloaded with work already. Of all Zamoskov'e, only three towns requested that the local town governors rather than special investigative agents from Moscow carry out the search for runaways in their districts. Those three towns were Vladimir, Shuia, and Uglich, and each one had its own reasons for resisting Moscow's interference. In February 1684, seventeen prominent landlords of Shuia Province (including four Koisarovs, three Kolobovs, two Obolduevs, and one Kazimerov) petitioned to have their own town governor conduct the search for runaways in place of the investigator sent from the central chancellery. The special investigator protested that the governor, Prince Nikita Petrovich Viazemskii, a man with strong roots in neighboring Vladimir and Iur'ev provinces, was colluding with the local gentry to block any honest investigation. The governor had refused to give him ink, paper, candles, wood, or people to send out on investigative business, "and thus he, the governor, has halted surveying and investigative business." Hindering the process still more, the governor and his friends refused to answer queries about runaways. Even when lesser landlords submitted specific accusations about runaways that were being harbored by particular people, the governor's supporters could rest secure in the knowledge that his search would turn up no fugitives on their estates. The issue thus pitted the leading members of the Shuia gentry community, the people of Moscow and highest provincial rank, against the petty gentry. The community leaders here assumed the role of "strong people" within the community, preying on the lesser gentry's peasants with impunity, knowing that their man in the governor's office would protect them. The special investigator reported ruefully, "They are defiant." Old patterns of local manipulation of central rules and the power of patronage networks in the provinces thus continued to shape the actual workings of administration on the local level. Local governors were more susceptible than special investigators to pressure from the leaders of the community. Manipulating the redundancy of officials and the overlap of jurisdictions in their province, influential Shuia landlords were able to accommodate the idea of general searches to their own agenda, blocking searches on their own estates and encouraging them on others.[57]

A petition from the Vladimir gentry tells a similar story. The landholders of Vladimir petitioned the tsar about their preference that the investigation of runaway peasants be carried out by the town governor, Prince Timofei Ivanovich Shakhovskoi, "a good man and knowledgeable and experienced and [who] has conducted many administrative matters," instead of by a special investigator. The latter, they feared, would ruin them and their peasants with his arbitrary demands.[58] Provincial landlords had good reason to fear the interference of outsiders, particularly when they resembled the incorruptible but arrogant special investigator D. I. Pleshcheev, whose self-righteous indifference to bribes made him invulnerable to the gentry's influence. Pleshcheev tracked down and returned thousands of runaway peasants, but he angered the magnates whose estates he raided, not only by confiscating their stolen peasants but also by boasting as he did to the archimandrite of the Monastery of the Caves, saying, "I blow my nose not only at you, Archimandrite, but also at all of the ecclesiastical authorities!"[59] This upright quality would not have endeared him to local landholders, who valued a pleasantly venal official.

Late in the century, between 1681 and 1685, another series of petitions expressed the provincial servitors' renewed anxiety about elite encroachment. The petitions spoke in the name of all provincial servitors, from *stol'niki* and *striapchie* to musketeers, dragoons, Cossacks, and the "poor, defenseless, and ruined to the utmost degree by strong people."[60] In its inclusion of lower-ranking servitors, its focus on the abuses inflicted by "strong people," and generally in its approach to political life, this set of petitions marks a partial return to the ideas and proposals of the petitions of the 1630s and

1640s. Novosel'skii identifies most of the more than 500 signatures on the two petitions of August 1682 as rank-and-file provincial *deti boiarskie* and lower-level infantrymen and gunners, especially from southern fortress towns. The petitions focused on the problems that arose constantly because the old survey books from the time of Tsar Mikhail Fedorovich were severely outdated. "Old boundary markers have been destroyed or are overgrown, and holes have been filled and in villages boundary markers and signs have been moved. . . . And rivers have altered their course and brooks have dried up."[61] The gentry consequently begged the government to carry out a general census of all provinces. For three years the government hedged and vacillated, promised to declare a general census, but did nothing. Partial measures and private surveys of disputed boundaries did not satisfy the provincial petitioners. In June 1684, 80 signatures endorsed another petition, which reminded the tsar of the promise he had made to carry out a universal census. The petitioners proffered precise suggestions about how an honest survey could be accomplished, suggestions which seemed in order since the government had proven incapable of orchestrating such a feat. In the place of unscrupulous, biased officials, the government should dispatch "good and God-fearing scribes" from the ministries. "And with them should be *dvoriane* and *vybornye* of those towns, two people per town." The sovereign firmly denied that particular request.[62]

The suggestion for community participation traced its lineage directly to the ill-fated 1637 and 1648 proposals for local selection of judges, which had been equally definitively rejected. Concepts of localism, personal relations, and the importance of local knowledge retained significant force in gentry political culture throughout the century, in spite of the gentry's accommodations and pragmatic appropriations of aspects of the new culture of paperwork and procedure and in spite of whatever setbacks the government dealt to proposals for local justice. Localism and community influence retained their significance and vibrancy while absorbing and making use of the new principles of state intervention and official regulation. The provincial gentry's two means of approaching politics continued to function interactively and to accommodate one another, but, as expressed by the gentry and by the tsarist regime, the emphasis gradually shifted toward the formal and official over the personal and particular.

The petitions of the second half of the century thus demonstrate that the gentry's attitude toward state intervention, regulation, and institutionalization evolved pragmatically in conjunction with the explosive growth of state control. Peter the Great's innovations did not come out of thin air, nor did he have to impose his interventionist, bureaucratizing, statist agenda on a stagnant, inflexible society. Specifically Western styles and manners had affected only a very small and very elite circle in Moscow prior to Peter's reforming crusade, but administrative routinization, depersonalization of relationships, and centralized regulation had all left their traces in the political culture of the provincial gentry. In the provinces, the gentry had been prepared for the Petrine reforms by fifty years of intensive bureaucratic buildup.

As do the 1648 petitions, some of the later petitions convey a sense of the deeper and broader vision of society and politics that informed the gentry's activity and expectations.[63] The gentry continued to subscribe to many of the traditional tenets of Muscovite political culture, including reliance on the tsar's personal mercy ("Be merciful, righteous Sovereign, to us, your slaves! Observe our terrible devastation!"[64]) and faith in his responsiveness to popular wishes ("In accordance with our, your slaves', signed petition, you Great Sovereign, favored us, your slaves."[65]). Also, as in earlier petitions, the petitioners insisted that the tsar live up to his end of the bargain. All of the petitions about the recovery of runaway serfs and slaves complained bitterly about the lack of tsarist sanctions against violators of the law. They admonished the tsar for the fact that magnates could freely harbor runaways, and officials could ignore the complaints of the real owners with impunity.[66] In 1657 the gentry of all towns wrote,

> Merciful Sovereign, Tsar and Grand Prince Aleksei Mikhailovich . . . favor your poor and utterly ruined slaves. Order, Sovereign, your merciful sovereign order carried out according to this our petition, so that we, your slaves, because of these our destroyers, will not utterly perish and [have to] miss your sovereign service. And so that when we, your slaves, are away on your sovereign service, those our destroyers won't utterly destroy what is left of our little homes and won't beat our wives and children to death.[67]

A tiny trace of a threat lurks in this otherwise pitiful statement: the gentry is willing to employ its primary point of leverage against the state by threatening to evade military service. Later in the century, when antiquated gentry cavalry service counted for less in the eyes of the state, laments about inability to pay taxes "from emptiness" carry the same hint of menace to the state coffers.

The inclination to reproach the tsar for failure to fulfill his obligations is clearly articulated in the famous 1658 petition, published by
V. N. Storozhev in 1892 and reprinted by Novosel'skii in 1975.[68] This
petition repeated many of the themes voiced in the 1648 petitions a
decade earlier. Reminding the tsar of his God-given status and obligation, the petitioners framed their requests in such a way that nothing
less than the preservation of God's order on earth was at stake in the
way the sovereign resolved the problem of runaway peasants:

> And order, Sovereign, your sovereign decree concerning those runaways
> implemented after due consideration, so that the Lord our God through
> you, the great sovereign, and through your mercifulness to us with righ-
> teous care and consideration, will implement all justice among us and rid
> us from such great and unendurable depredations and many years' fierce
> destruction and from our sin of feuding and fighting against each other.
> And even retroactively, Sovereign, your sovereign statute about enserf-
> ment in this matter forever would be immutable and no one would be
> tempted [to steal] God's gifts, and your ancient and eternal sovereign [land]
> grants would not be seized by force or greatness, by wealth or robbery, nor
> by any slyness or cunning would anyone [commandeer] other people's
> holdings, nor grow rich with ill-gotten gains. . . . So be, Great Sovereign,
> the righteous avenger for all of us who have been mistreated: to you is
> given from God judgment and correction and the sword of vengeance and
> the kindness of reason.

If the sovereign failed in his role as "righteous avenger" and stinted in
applying the God-given "sword of vengeance and kindness of reason," the petition implied, the idyllic picture of Christian peace and
plenty would be reversed, and the tsardom of Muscovy would topple
in a tidal wave of "great and unendurable depredations and many
years' fierce destruction and from our sin of feuding and fighting
against each other."

This rich and rather baroque passage clearly derived some of its inspiration from the 1648 templates, but new themes intertwined with
the familiar one of the tsar as protector of the defenseless and scourge
of the arrogant and greedy. A completely novel vision of social order,
perhaps derived from Western sources, appeared in this petition.

First, the petition developed the value of hard, honest labor. In the
ideal world, "No one would offend another in any way, and all people
would feed themselves by their own labor, according to God's com-
mandment, and military people of all ranks, great and small, when
they were at their homes, would be content with God's gifts and with
your tsarist grants and with their own quitrent [income], and [would

not covet] other people's holdings and profits." In the petitioners'
eyes, runaway peasants inverted the practices of honest folk when
they "rob and commit violence and drink and eat sweetly without
labor, and dress and shoe themselves with other people's possessions." The petitioners begged for "mercy," meaning tax exemptions,
for their few remaining peasants who "with their honest labor feed
themselves and pay both your sovereign taxes and our quitrent payments."[69] The value of conscientious labor was not unknown in
other sources, but it was usually framed in terms of patient endurance and dutiful service to the sovereign, not in terms of earthy
toil and sweat of the brow. Conventional formulations appealed to
the tsar's mercy in consideration of "the blood of our fathers, and
our wretched little service, and endurance," or condemned runaway
slaves who had fled to avoid their duty, "not wanting to accompany
us on your great sovereign service assignments nor to endure various
regimental hardships."[70] This new respect for hard work, perhaps
ahead of its time, anticipates (at a lower level and under different
influences) the reform projects of 1682, which substituted merit and
service for noble birth as the fundamental factors contributing to
social status and honor. The reform plan, if implemented, would
have established that "honors, in particular, and administrative
[posts] will be given to knowledgeable and needed people according
to [the degree of] reason and merit [that they have displayed] while
serving in all kinds of state business."[71] The abolition of the time-
honored system of *mestnichestvo* provoked no opposition, in part
because lesser gentry and even cadet branches of boyar families had
come to resent the lock on positions of authority and prestige that
the well-born had, regardless of talent or capability, and had come to
understand merit as a quality linked to hard work.

A second major innovation is introduced in the best known passage of the 1658 petition, a tiered, structured vision of society quite
at odds with conventional Muscovite formulations: "In your sovereign realm the people of God and of you, the sovereign, from each of
the four great orders—ecclesiastical and [military] service, trade and
agricultural—will uphold your statute and your tsarist order firmly
and unwaveringly." This statement depicts Muscovy as a Western-
style society of four orders. Society is divided by occupation, not by
rank, as is more usually the case in Muscovite rhetoric, and the new
social order, stratified and frozen into rigid categories by law, is natu-
ralized as a manifestation of divine as well as sovereign law.[72] Again,

this vision of a society divided into occupational groups places each individual's *work*, rather than birth or status, at the heart of his or her identity.

For all its subtlety and potential utility, this 1658 formulation was not repeated in later petitions. Although signed by 42 gentry servitors from various towns, including Vladimir and Iur'ev Pol'skii, this social vision may represent merely the idiosyncratic world view of its author. Nevertheless, arising as it did from the general cultural environment of the provincial gentry, the 1658 petition creatively combined the traditional Muscovite concept of a stern and merciful sovereign defending the poor and wretched of the earth with an innovative view of a social hierarchy based on occupation. In its peculiar synthesis, the petition allows us a glimpse of the process through which deeply rooted political cultures alter themselves in response to events and influences. Through a dynamic process of accretion and fusion, Muscovite political culture incorporated and reacted to changing legal, international, cultural, and administrative conditions and produced its own divinely inspired bureaucratism, long before the attempted reforms of 1682 or the more successful ones of Peter the Great.

Conclusion

In a powerfully influential article on dualism in old Russian culture, Tartu semioticians Jurij Lotman and Boris Uspenskij defined traditional Russian culture as sharply polarized, entertaining no grey zones, no middle ground, no purgatory between the extremes of heaven and hell.[1] By contrast, this is a book about grey zones and middle ground, about the ambiguous spaces between state and society, between the public and the private, and about the merging of such categories. With a focus on politics, the book responds to a call within the social sciences to "bring the state back in" to social and cultural history.[2] Yet the politics of the Muscovite provinces assumed forms that often fit only uneasily into ordinary understandings of the political and worked themselves out in the interstices of the autocratic state, where political life has been generally overlooked. Politics at the local level could mean scrambling for status and clients within the provincial community, asserting a claim to a particular sliver of abandoned land, or negotiating a favorable marriage for a son or daughter. But even these highly localized issues could never be divorced from matters of high politics and the state, from service rank, land entitlements, inheritance law, or relations with state and local officials. Thus the categories of local as opposed to central politics, of personal or kinship politics as opposed to traditionally conceived "high politics," blur to the point that such distinctions lose meaning.

The blurring of these categories is not coincidental, nor is it an

artifact of definition. Personal and institutional politics were insep-
arable and mutually constitutive in early-modern Russia. At least
until the burning of the *mestnichestvo* books in 1682, and in many
ways well beyond that date, kinship bonds and personal linkages
of protection and clientage remained the explicit and fundamental
principles on which the state functioned, while at the same time law
codes and court rulings asserted and upheld the opposite principle,
that of an equal, blind, impartial process of government. The rise of
the Muscovite state was not played out as a battle against particularist interests and patronage clusters. Rather, the two systems supported and built upon each other, with the personal lubricating the
functioning of the growing state administration, filling the gaps in
the understaffed bureaucracy, allowing for some play in a newly routinizing system. Patronage and kinship networks should be viewed
as an integral part of the state-building process in Muscovy, not as an
antiquated, medieval holdover against which the state had to battle.
Kinship and patronage groups served as partial equivalents to the
corporate groups, such as guilds, confraternities, municipalities, and
social estates, with which new monarchies of Western Europe dealt
and interacted, on which they relied, and from which they derived
income and support.[3]

Patronage and clientage flourished as expanding state power and
nascent institutional infrastructures provided lucrative sources for
patronage and distribution of posts and profits.[4] The great agnatic
clans of Muscovy by and large could not claim lineages dating back to
ancient Kiev. Instead, they traced their origins only to the fourteenth,
or even the fifteenth or sixteenth, century, when the Muscovite state
began its centralizing moves and the complex mythologies of patri-
lineal descent were invented.[5] The simultaneous growth of the Muscovite state and of clan-based politics suggests an intimate connection between the two. Kinship politics played an equally important
role but took on quite a different form in the provinces, where gentrymen and -women focused on the needs and interests of their immediate family members rather than on those of the broad, extended clan.
Through the intricacies of the service system, which determined
rank, landholding, and social status, family politics and state politics
intersected, providing the common ground for negotiation between
the state and its servitors.

More than just kinship and patronage bonds mediated relations
between the provinces and the center, however. In a wide array of

areas of provincial life, autonomous, unregulated activities were to some extent necessary and integral elements of successful governance.[6] Thus, once the independent appanages of Russian princes were incorporated into the Muscovite polity, the centralizing state fostered localism by creating provincial service registers and regiments, protecting gentry communities from the depredations of outsiders, and keeping careful track of gentrymen's regional affiliations. By granting *pomest'e* and *votchina* estates to its military servitors and allowing them some leeway in their home provinces, the state fostered the development of landed gentry with interests and wealth not tied directly to state service. The persistence of communities of landed gentry in the seventeenth century in turn contributed greatly to the state's control of the countryside, particularly of the peasantry. The tendency of those communities to absorb central chancellery officials into their own rhythms and politics helped rather than hindered the administrative process. Thus many of the currents of historical development that are usually viewed as antagonistic, particularly personal-patronage practices as opposed to routinized bureaucracy, displayed a high degree of compatibility as they worked themselves out in the chinks of tsarist rule.

Nonetheless, the symbiosis between the provincial gentry and the amorphous power of the state did not always proceed without glitches. The relationship was far from one-way, and the gentry, although to all appearances reverent and loyal subjects of the tsar, were fully capable of criticism, protest, and even resistance. The state made concessions to the gentry's demands throughout the century, such as calling Assemblies of the Land to discuss key issues, distributing of *pomest'e* land to poor gentrymen after the Time of Troubles, abolishing the statute of limitations on the recovery of runaway serfs, and initiating a new nationwide census in the 1680s. Such concessions should not be read as losses for the state, for autocratic power, or for the boyars, but rather as part of the consultative, responsive component of Muscovite autocratic rule. The relationship between gentry and the state was fluid and constantly renegotiated under ever-changing conditions.

The gentry's preference for personal mercy and the intercession of patrons rather than the impersonal mechanism of routinized administration continued unabated through the seventeenth century and well into the Imperial period. Despite such strong continuity, however, gentry political culture was fully capable of change and did accommodate itself to the growth of a depersonalized administrative apparatus in the decades following the 1649 *Ulozhenie*. The evolution of political thought and action among the provincial gentry in the second half of the seventeenth century, although rather subtle, opens up several important issues in the history of Muscovite political culture. First, the almost immediate evidence of a change in political strategy and understanding after the enactment of the new law code of 1649 suggests that codification and expansion of administrative authority had a dramatic effect in actual practice. This testifies to the efficacy and power of the Muscovite autocracy. Second, signs of change in political conceptualization at the level of the provincial gentry indicates that Russian society was far more responsive and far less entrenched in conservative traditionalism than has been assumed. Not only the few clean-shaven aristocrats in the capital were receptive to new ideas and responsive to changing conditions, but the middling social groups in the countryside were as well. However, despite their common receptivity to innovation, the origins and nature of the changes differed significantly between the two social groups. This contrast between high court elites and the petty provincial landholders raises a final issue of some importance: identifying the sources of change in Muscovite culture. While tsars, regents, and Moscow aristocrats responded to imported Western ideas and practices, petty gentry encountered and reacted to changes taking place within the tsardom, changes produced by the needs of a growing army, an insatiable state treasury, a swollen administrative and legal structure, and a fading cavalry militia. Much has been written about Peter the Great's reforms and how much or how little they departed from late Muscovite tradition, but most of the debate has focused on issues of administrative organization and elite culture.[7] At a lower and wider segment of society, the evolution of gentry political culture in the same period suggests that the gentry responded to, made sense of, and helped to shape the expansion of autocracy into provincial life. By preserving the precious interstitial spaces and assimilating officials into local communities, the gentry worked out a usable form of autonomy within autocracy. With its creative blend of institutionalism and personalism, the gentry contributed to the formation of a political culture resilient and strong enough to weather the changes of the eighteenth century.

*Epilogue: The Lesser Nobility and Cultural Change in
the Eighteenth Century*

With the reign of Peter the Great and the dawn of the eighteenth century, the explicit bases of Russian political culture shifted radically, and even reversed. Peter redefined the task of government, recasting it as a mission of secular transformation and worldly improvement rather than one of otherworldly salvation. Peter himself made inventive use of the dualities of Russian political culture, casting himself as first servant of the impersonal state and at the same time promulgating his personal image, filling every corner with his unmistakable likeness, playing up his reputation for tireless involvement in every detail of rule. Closely following Louis XIV's model based on the maxim *"l'état, c'est moi,"* Peter accomplished by dazzling sleight of hand the complete merger of his charismatic person with his state, and of the traditional tsar-sovereign with the radical imperial reformer.[8] Peter completed the reversal of acknowledged and subordinated values begun in the late seventeenth century. The language of his decrees and the thrust of his reforms ostentatiously privileged standardized procedure and general, impersonal routine over personalized, particularized processes. Yet Peter himself utilized the ongoing cultural force of personal connections and patrimonial rule, which is present as a powerful undercurrent in official rhetoric and Peter's self-presentation and even more powerfully in society at large.

The Petrine reforms, the introduction of the Table of Ranks, the increasing acceptance of administrative work as befitting the dignity of a nobleman, and the rising literacy rates all effected enormous changes in the cultural, social, and political lives of the gentry (usually called lesser nobility in the imperial era). In spite of a large and embarrassing corps of staunch parochials, who provoked the condescending ire of their more cultivated noble brethren, the eighteenth century witnessed the cultural transformation of the nobility as a whole.[9] The sweeping nature of Peter's cultural reforms is well known. He mandated change in every aspect of the elite's life, from requiring nobles to don Western clothing and shave their beards, to assigning and supervising attendance at parties in which men and women were forced to mingle, to asserting that young couples should be allowed to choose their own marriage partners. The changes mandated from above altered not only the nobility's dress and social life, but also the nature and focus of their service and political environment. In his book on Russian absolutism and the gentry, S. M. Troitskii sketches brief family histories of eighteenth-century nobles who were descended from petty provincial gentrymen of the previous century. He shows their rapid evolution from provincial landlords to educated, cultured participants in the great new administrative-military reforms of the Petrine era and after.[10]

The dramatic tempo and thoroughness of the change is reflected in the opening lines of Andrei Bolotov's memoirs, written in the second half of the eighteenth century:

> My whole life I have been annoyed that my ancestors were so negligent that they didn't leave behind them even the scantiest written information about themselves, and thus deprived us, their descendants, of that pleasant satisfaction of having even some small evidence and understanding about them and how they lived, and what happened in their lives. . . . I hold my forefathers responsible for this carelessness, and not wanting to make the same unforgivable mistake that they did and [suffer] the same complaints against me from my descendants, I decided to use the few holiday hours and other remaining free hours to describe all that happened to me in the whole duration of my life.[11]

Bolotov's ancestors never would have considered leaving such an account. They were generally scarcely literate and so lacked the technical skill to produce the family history that Bolotov craved. Furthermore, traditional, static ideas of time and circular, theocentric conceptions of history did not provide a fertile cultural setting to allow the memoirist's genre to flourish. Only in the eighteenth century, with the introduction of widespread literacy and at least passing familiarity with Western literary styles, did Bolotov's antiquarian urge make sense and his itch to record his experience for posterity become not only imaginable but even irresistible.[12]

For all the attempts at rationalization of the system and for all the stultifying growth of the central state bureaucracy, Russian gentry servitors retained the aversion to impersonal, abstract government that they manifested so clearly in their political behavior in the seventeenth century. Recent historians of the eighteenth century generally agree on this defining trait of the gentry's political style. John LeDonne describes court politics as the playing off of one kinship faction against another, with blood and marriage rather than substantive issues as the dividing line.[13] Wilson Augustine says that eighteenth-century Russian nobles conceived of power relations as personal and subjective. "For a Russian nobleman, 'good authority' (on the throne and elsewhere) was a duplication of the 'good father'— stern, loving, extending his patriarchal power over a numerous family."[14] The nobility viewed service as a personal debt to the tsar, not as service to an abstract state. The term "state service" was never employed; rather, contemporaries called their work simply "service" or "service to the sovereign."[15]

As in the seventeenth century, provincial landowners in the post-Petrine era focused most of their energies on local, particularist issues very similar to those of the previous century. They expressed concerns about reducing service requirements, restoring partible and female inheritance after Peter forced unigeniture on the country, and guaranteeing control over and economic viability of their peasants, the very issues over which they had fought and struggled in the seventeenth century. Given an opportunity to voice their most pressing demands during the confusing months of January and February 1730, at the time of the so-called "Constitutional Crisis," members of the guards regiments and lesser nobility agitated for the abolition of Peter's deeply hated law requiring that nobles practice unigeniture. "The seniority rule in matters of inheritance should be abrogated and complete freedom given to the parents; and, if there are no parents left, the inheritance is to be divided in equal shares."[16] Later in the century, strains of traditional Muscovite views toward politics and justice still surfaced just as strongly. In a study of the *nakazy* (reports) submitted to the Great Commission of 1767–68, Augustine finds the most common requests were for oral courts where judges who knew the community members would use their eyes and ears instead of relying solely on written law. In the last third of the eighteenth century, nobles still were articulating precisely the same notions about the nature and basis of justice as their great-great-grandfathers had in the petition campaigns of the 1630s and 1640s.[17]

On the other hand, principles of personalized kinship politics and patrimonial rule could not survive intact under the assault of change from the mid–seventeenth century onwards. Marc Raeff points to the acute confusion that resulted from the adulteration of the old system of personal loyalty to and dependence on the tsar with the new notions of nobility derived from merit, noble character, and moral and intellectual accomplishment, or, as we have seen among the gentry, hard work. According to Muscovite custom, the sovereign personally granted promotions to his servitors, but, by the new rules, any clerk could stamp the proper documents and approve a man's advancement up the Table of Ranks. Raeff maintains that Peter "brought into existence the Russian state, and the old personal relationship between subject and ruler was on the way to virtual disappearance." Muddying the waters still further, Raeff concedes, is the fact that the forceful personalities of Peter, Elizabeth, and Catherine all played on the traditional personal bonds of loyalty that rationalized administration claimed to eliminate.[18] Muscovite political culture thus survived and affected noble outlooks, values, expectations, and understandings of political life well into the eighteenth century, but in constant contact with changing political conditions and cultural currents, it also continued to adapt and evolve.

While the Muscovite personalist framework of political interaction may have clashed occasionally with the bureaucratizing, rationalizing impulses of the autocrats and their administrations, in general the two appear to have harmonized quite well in the minds and behavior of the nobility. Indeed, as Brenda Meehan-Waters observes, "A belief in the parental nature of authority ill fit an abstract state," and yet the two found common ground when the father-tsar declared himself also the embodiment of the state and when newly created administrative posts, expanding explosively under Catherine, provided ever richer bases for personal patronage and building of power bases. The nobility staffed the state administration and the military, while patronage, favoritism, and kinship bound individuals to the sovereign and to each other within the various branches of state service.[19] Personal and state interests were served simultaneously, without contradiction.

The "Constitutional Crisis" of 1730 provides a telling instance of the nobility's dual political outlook in the early eighteenth century. When the young emperor Peter II died abruptly on his wedding day, January 19, 1730, without having appointed a successor, the choice fell to the Supreme Privy Council, a small, elite body which had ruled the country under the weak leadership of the previous two monarchs. The Council invited Duchess Anna of Courland, niece of Peter the Great, to take the throne, but took the momentous step of issuing a set of conditions under which the new empress would rule. Hearing of the Council's conditions and of Anna's acceptance of them, the rank and file nobility, who had gathered en masse in Moscow for the intended wedding of the late emperor and had stayed on for the funeral, began drawing up its own counterproposals, mainly intended to limit the Council's oligarchical bid for power. Hundreds of noblemen (including a good number from Vladimir and Suzdal') affixed their signatures to the various plans.[20] Suspicion of the Council's scheme was so great that by the time Anna met with the assembled nobility and the guards regiments on February 25, Prince Ivan Iur'evich Trubetskoi submitted yet another petition, backed by the cries of the guards, imploring her to "graciously resume such *Autocratic* power as Your glorious and praiseworthy ancestors possessed and abrogate the article sent to Your Imperial Majesty by the Supreme Privy Council and signed by You."[21] The new empress called for the copy of the conditions that she had signed and dramatically ripped them up.

The Cherkasskii Petition, submitted directly to Empress Anna on the morning of February 25, is generally considered the beginning of the end of the effort at constitutional reform. It is condemned as the lesser nobility's retreat to the known and comfortable forms of autocracy, its willing acceptance of a return to tyranny. However, far from endorsing autocracy, the document proves to be a treasury of ambivalence and contradiction contained within a single framework. It begins as a traditional supplication, in the mode of Muscovite petitions, reminding the empress of her duty before God and people, who had jointly chosen her to rule: "Most glorious and most gracious Sovereign Empress! Although You have been elevated to the throne of the Russian Empire by the will of the Almighty and the unanimous consent of all the people, in testimony of Your high favor to the whole State, Your Imperial Majesty has deigned to sign the articles presented by the Supreme Privy Council, and we thank You most humbly for this gracious intent." In traditional manner the petition then lightly chided the ruler for being overly kind and generous, to the point of benefiting the wicked with her mercy: "However, most Gracious Lady, some of these articles raise such doubts that the majority of the people is in fear of future disturbances." The petition closed on a submissive note, agreeing to submit any plans for reform "for Your Majesty's approval," a direct parallel to the old Muscovite closing, "In this, Sovereign, as you decree." To this point, the petition clearly resembled its forebears and drew on old Muscovite traditions.

The concrete proposals offered in the petition, however, reflect anything but a traditional monarchist outlook and go far beyond anything produced in the previous century. The petition asked the Empress to permit an assembly broadly composed of "all general officers, officers, and noblemen, one or two from every family," whose task would be no less than "to devise a form of government for the state." The constituent assembly's decisions would be reached not by traditional consensus or by weight of rank and power but "on the basis of the majority's opinion," after examining all of "the opinions submitted by us and others" and investigating "all circumstances." Even the vision of the goal and purpose of government expressed in the Cherkasskii Petition demonstrates a marked change from Muscovite days. The traditional tsar had been responsible for maintaining piety and godliness in his earthly realm and conscientiously herding his flock to eternal salvation. By 1730, the petitioners endorsed quite a different understanding of the state's mission. They planned that there should "be devised a safe system of government for the peace and welfare of the state."[22] Although, as Nancy Kollmann has shown, notions of society as a collective entity and of governance for the common good had made their first tentative appearances in Muscovy in the late seventeenth century, their impact and acceptance then had been very limited.[23] But by 1730 those feeble first shoots had taken firm root. The petitioners during the Constitutional Crisis had no doubt about the social goals of good government. The Orthodox vision of statecraft had faded quickly from noble memory.

The events of 1730 provide an extraordinarily clear illustration of the amalgamation of levels and understandings of political and social life that had been characteristic of Muscovite political culture and that came to characterize noble Russian political culture in the eighteenth century. The nobles' plans expose the interpenetration and dynamic interplay of various planes of state and society, culture and politics. The significance of family politics did not preclude the participation of families in broader political endeavors. The lesser nobility's focus on family and inheritance in fact propelled that group onto the national political scene and forced it to express an abstract political vision. Although the traditional Muscovite framework of stern yet merciful parental rule continued to shape Russian understandings of relations of power as fundamentally personal, informal, and intimate, it would be misleading to describe an uninflected attachment on the part of the lesser nobility to the old, or an obstinate nostalgia for bygone ages. Instead of facing "a choice between two models of political authority—the European-rational-bureaucratic, and the native-Russian-traditional," the eighteenth-century Russian nobility maintained both, expressing a preference for the latter but making good use of the former when the need arose.[24] As in the seventeenth century, personal relations defined relations of power in the eighteenth century, but they also facilitated the fit between individual noblemen and the growing autocratic state. Family interests and state interests were not antithetical; rather they proved to be mutually constitutive.

Autocracy and Muscovite Political Culture

Dedicated to a patrimonial model of a divinely ordered household-state, the Muscovite gentry servitors of the first half of the seventeenth century conceived of relations of power within that model. They saw power as the prerogative of God and of the paternal ruler. Both of these relations were personal, sacred, and inviolable. Intercession and mercy were the fundamental characteristics of relations with both of these awesome figures and with lesser authorities. Caging relations of power within the cramping structures of institutions and relying on an abstract, impersonal foundation in written law or regulation directly violated the principles of Muscovite political thought. Yet, from at least the mid–sixteenth century, other principles of political legitimacy edged into Muscovite political culture. Concepts of broad consultation, of the initiative and wishes of "all the land," took their place along with divine will as sanctioning myths and modes of operation for the tsarist state. At the same time, impersonal bureaucratic regulation began to intrude into the lives of individuals on a grand scale, enveloping all aspects of human interaction in a web of paperwork. Adapting and modifying its political visions to fit emerging practical realities, the gentry developed a hybrid political culture, simultaneously rooted in the familial, paternalist, and divinely ordered traditions of the past and in the institutional, regularized, national procedures of the present.

Situating Muscovy in the context of its contemporary Western monarchies disperses some of the onus of "backwardness" from that "rude and barbarous kingdom." At the same time, scrutinizing Western monarchies in the context of Muscovite development may dim some of the glow of perfection attributed to the idealized West in Russian historiography, which traditionally views England as a fully democratic, constitutional monarchy from the signing of the Magna Carta. A comparative look at Muscovy in the context of early-modern Europe reveals far more similarities than differences. As it was in Western Europe, politics in Muscovy was broadly conceived as a divinely inspired process of reaching consensus and harmony. In parliamentary England as in autocratic Muscovy, contestation was viewed as a blight, a violation of the proper order of things. In early-modern Western monarchies as in Muscovy powerful myths about the past and the social order were freshly invented and endowed with the force of hallowed tradition, binding influential elites to the interests of the crown through concepts of lineage, clan, and service. As did other new monarchies, the Muscovite state spread its net of control by creative interplay between institutional and official supervision and local, personal connections and interests. As in all early-modern states, principles of pervasive control very poorly matched the realities of lax enforcement and autonomous local activity, and that very laxness and tolerance of localisms and personal patronage networks permitted the crown to succeed in matters essential to its governance. As it did in the West, a fundamental union of interests between Muscovite elites and the growing power of the crown welded those groups together in their domination of the peasantry.

Yet, in spite of all the similarities, Muscovy appeared barbaric, despotic, and fundamentally alien to Western observers. Although part of this sense of difference may be attributed to the generic tendency of travellers to view other societies as exotic and inferior, some of that sense of difference requires explanation. The primary difference sensed by the various travellers to Muscovy from England, France, and the German and Italian states in the seventeenth century derived from the difference in the public, acknowledged forms of government and relations of power. The tsar and his subjects represented their relations as based on mercy, personal intercession, and divine instruction. The fundamental processes of state and institution building, standardization, and paperwork were partially subordinated to and hidden beneath the privileged personalized forms of discourse. In France the King's mercy remained a crucial form of personal intercession and a last instance of appeal throughout the early-modern period, but it remained so as an addendum, a mitigation of a growing, acknowledged system of state officials and standardized institutions. From early in the seventeenth century, Louis XIII and his ministers deliberately attempted to define "state" or "public," as opposed to private, interests and to establish the moral and political priority of the former over the latter.[25] In England, parliamentary seats were still filled by whim of the local lord until the mid–seventeenth century, but the principle of election and the concepts of the body politic, the common good, and natural law were nonetheless highly developed in theoretical literature and political ritual. Meanwhile, in Muscovy, the rhetoric of power remained a highly personalized one, and until the late seventeenth century, more regularized, institutional relations of power grew largely unmentioned.

How much did this inversion of value hierarchies affect the actual conduct of politics? How much did the form shape the content? As the defining characteristics of Muscovite political culture, personalism and Orthodoxy set the parameters of the politically possible. Muscovy suffered its share of turmoil and rebellion in the seventeenth century, as did many Western states, but the elevation of a new autocrat after the Time of Troubles demonstrated that constitutional or parliamentary rule was not a viable option in Russia as it was for England or the Netherlands. Until the explicit values of the political culture were reversed by Peter the Great, politics could be conceived among the elite only along the axes of personal morality and Orthodox piety; other political visions were largely precluded. While individual tsars could be condemned, with very radical consequences, the divine tsarist order lay beyond question until other ideas of legitimacy trickled into Russian political culture in the eighteenth century.

Reference Matter

Appendix Tables

TABLE A.I
'Okladchiki' from the Vladimir-Suzdal' Provinces, 1628–52

Name	Date	Rank	Name	Date	Rank
From Vladimir			*From Suzdal' (continued)*		
Balakirev, I. M.	1648	selectman	Protopopov, A. V.	1648	selectman
Bologovskii, P.	1641	unknown	Protopopov, V. I.	1641	selectman
Iumatov, G. I.	1648	selectman	Sechenoi, A. F.	1641–48	*dvorovoi*
Kalitin, B. A.	1648	selectman	Sekerin, A. T.	1641	selectman
Pestroi, M. M.	1648	*gorodovoi*	Shishelov, S. I.	1648–52	selectman
Redrikov, V. G.	1648	selectman	Tregubov, A. A.	1648	selectman
Roganovskii, I. Ia.	1648	selectman	Tregubov, S. M.	1641	selectman
Vladykin, M.	1628	selectman	*From Iur'ev Pol'skii*		
Zlovidov, I. N.	1628	selectman	Iakshin, I. M.	1637	selectman
From Suzdal'			Miasoedov, F. F.	1637	selectman
Alalykin, V. L.	1648	selectman	Obukhov, F. D.	1637	*dvorovoi*
Alekseev, P. P.	1641	*dvorovoi*	Seletskii, Ia. I.	1637	*dvorovoi*
Bolotnikov, A. F.	1648	selectman	Selezenev, F. B.	1637	*gorodovoi*
Dolgovo-Saburov, I. F.	1648	selectman	Shalimov, M. I.	1637	*gorodovoi*
Dubenskii, I.	1628	selectman	*From Lukh*		
Gorin, D.	1628	selectman	Chernitsyn, A. B.	1637	selectman
Kazimerov, I. I.	1648	selectman	Iazykov, S. Z.	1637	selectman
Khmetevskii, M. A.	1648	selectman	Kolzakov, O. I.	1637	*dvorovoi*
Oshanin, F. M.	1648	selectman	Mukhanov, M. A.	1637	*dvorovoi*
Poroshin, M. G.	1641	selectman	Shulgin, F. F.	1637	selectman
			Zhukov, P. V.	1637	*dvorovoi*

SOURCES: *RGADA, f.* 210, *opis'* 4, *Dela desiaten'*, book 304, *ll.* 5–10, 24 ob, 45–57 (1648); *RGADA, f.* 210, *Vlad. stol, stlb.* 72, *ll.* 58–79 (1637/38), *stlb.* 33 (1628), *stlb.* 73, *ll.* 234–39, *stlb.* 101, *II.* 16, 17, 20; *SPbFIRI, f.* 62, *Koll. Kablukova,* no. 43 (1652).

TABLE A.2

Representatives at Assemblies of the Land, 1642, 1648, 1651, and 1653

Province	1642	Rank	1648	Rank
Vladimir	Pestroi, B. S.	(G/S)	Berechinskii, S. V.	(D)
	Vladykin, P. M.	(S)		
	Zinov'ev, L. M.	(S)		
Suzdal'	Tregubov, S. N.	(S)	Koisarov, I. I.	(D)
	Koisarov, G. B.	(S)	Protopopov, A. V.	(S/O)
	Sechenoi, O. F.	(D)		
Iur'ev Pol'skii	Iakshin, I. M.	(S)	Iakshin, I. M.	(S)
	Prokudin, P. E.	(S)	Miasoedov, F. F.	(S/O)
	Stromilov, Ia. F.	(D)		
	Brattsov, I. S.	(Zh)		
Lukh	Iazykov, S. Z.	(S)	Chernitsyn, A. B.	(S, ret.)
			Pivov, B. S.	(D?)

Province	1651	Rank	1653	Rank
Vladimir	Gorin, G. D.	(D)	Berechinskii, B. F.	(D)
	Vladykin, V. M.	(S)	Khonenev, I. S.	(S)
Suzdal'	Miakishev, I. G.	(D)	Koisarov, G. B.	(S)
	Nemtsov, I. K.	(S)	Alalykin, V. L.	(S/O)
Iur'ev Pol'skii	Kolachov, Ia. M.	(D)	Koisarov, B. I.	(U)
	Sechenoi, M. K.	(D)	Domogatskii, G. A.	(F)
			Stromilov, G. V.	(D/S)
Lukh	Pivov, I. S.	(D)	Pivov, B. S.	(D?)
	Kuchin, A. S.	(D)	Chernitsyn, O. B.	(S)

NOTE: Ranks and other identifying information are abbreviated as follows: D = *dvorovoi;* F = foreigner; G = *gorodovoi;* O = *okladchik;* S = selectman; U = unknown; Zh = *zhilets.*

SOURCES: For a list of men who attended the 1642 assembly, see Got'e, *Akty,* pp. 39–46. For 1648, see Tikhomirov and Epifanov, *Sobornoe Ulozhenie,* pp. 424–31. For 1651, see V. I. Latkin, *Materialy,* pp. 92–128. For 1653, see Kozachenko, "K istorii," pp. 223–27. Additional information on ranks derives primarily from muster rolls and may be found in *RGADA, Vlad. stol, f.* 210, book 4, *ll.* 68 ob, 77; *RGADA, f.* 210, *Vlad. stol, stlb.* 60, *l.* 153, *stlb.* 73, *ll.* 58, 59, 60, 64, 68, 78, 79, *stlb.* 82, *l.* 23, *stlb.* 101, *ll.* 1, 16, 18, *stlb.* 115, *ll.* 1, 2, 9, 17, 19, 30, 32, *stlb.* 132, *l.* 4, *stlb.* 40, *ll.* 10, 35, 93, 96; *RGADA, f.* 210, *opis'* 4, *Dela desiaten',* book 304, *ll.* 19 ob, 20, 45, 49, 217 ob, 218; *RNB, Ermitazhnoe sobranie,* no. 343/2, *l.* 10.

Glossary

beschest'e. Dishonor.

bit' chelom. To petition (literally, to beat one's forehead).

bobyl' (pl. *bobyli*). Cottar, landless peasant.

chelobit'e. Petition.

chelovek (pl. *liudi*). Person, often connoting a slave or bondsman.

chet' or *chetvert'* (pl. *cheti*). Standard unit of land, equivalent to 1.35 acres.

dacha. Actual amount of land or money held by servitors. Cf. *oklad*.

desiatni. Military muster rolls.

deti boiarskie (sing. *syn boiarskii*). Lesser gentrymen.

d'iak (pl. *d'iaki*). State secretary, administrator in charge of a chancellery or high in the chancellery system.

dumnyi d'iak. State secretary of the highest level, member of the consultative boyar duma; fourth duma rank, below boyar, *okol'nichii,* and *dumnyi dvorianin*.

dumnyi dvorianin. Third rank in the duma hierarchy, below boyar and *okol'nichii*.

dvoriane. Members of the gentry.

dvorianstvo. The gentry as a whole; both *dvoriane* and *deti boiarskie*.

dvorovoi. The middle ranks of provincial gentrymen (literally, "of the court").

gorod. Town, especially provincial town; sometimes interpreted as a gentry service corporation.

gorodovoi spisok. Provincial lists; lists of men who performed their military service from provincial towns rather than from Moscow.

gorodovoi syn boiarskii (pl. *gorodovye deti boiarskii*). Lowest-ranking provincial gentry.

guba. System of local administration, policing, and banditry control instituted under Ivan the Terrible, headed by locally selected elders, usually retired provincial gentrymen. *gubnoi*, adj.

kholop. Slave.

kniaz'. Prince; hereditary title given to all sons of princely families.

krest'ianin (pl. *krest'iane*). Peasant, serf.

mestnichestvo. System of precedence and rank order worked out according to principles of seniority within and among clans.

Moskovskii spisok. Moscow list; list of men who performed their military service from Moscow rather than from provincial towns.

namestnik (pl. *namestniki*). Vicegerent; a rank phased out in the mid–sixteenth century.

netchik (pl. *netchiki*). Military truant.

netstvo (or *v netakh.*) State of military truancy.

novik (pl. *noviki*). Novices; boys and young men newly enrolled in service (usually at age fifteen).

oklad (pl. *oklady*). The theoretical entitlement to an amount of land in accordance with service rank. Cf. *dacha.*

okladchik (pl. *okladchiki*). Local officers who helped supply information on the servicemen of a given province during military musters.

okol'nichii (pl. *okol'nichie*). The second highest noble title after boyar.

otvod. Separate registration for service, apart from family members.

palata. A chamber, often used to denote a high court or judicial body.

pistsovye and *perepisnye knigi.* Cadasters, census, and land-survey books.

pod'iachii (pl. *pod'iachie*). Clerk, clerical worker in chancellery system or governor's offices.

pomeshchik (pl. *pomeshchiki*). Holder of a *pomest'e.*

pomest'e (pl. *pomest'ia*). Property held in conditional tenure, granted by the state in return for service.

Pomestnyi prikaz. Chancellery of Service Lands.

prikaz (pl. *prikazy*). Chancellery. *prikaznyi*, adj.

prikazchik or *prikashchik.* Bailiff, estate overseer.

prikaznaia izba. Town hall, provincial governor's office.

prozhitochnoe (pl. *prozhitochnye*). Estate given to children or widows for lifetime maintenance; dowager's portion.

pustosh' (pl. *pustoshi*). Abandoned, unpopulated land.

raba. Female slave.

raspravnaia palata. High court of appeals.

Razboinyi prikaz. Chancellery of Brigandage Control.

razbor. Military muster.

Razriadnyi prikaz. Chancellery of Military Affairs.

reitar (pl. *reitary*). Horse guards; members of nonelite cavalry regiments, to which lesser gentrymen were demoted during the seventeenth century as their old-style cavalry formations grew obsolete. *reitarskii*, adj.

s"ezzhaia izba. Town hall, provincial governor's office.

sirota (pl. *siroty*). Orphan.

sluzhilye liudi po otechestvu. Service people by heredity or by patrimony; gentry servitors.

sluzhilye liudi po priboru. Service people by conscription; lower-level, nonelite servitors.

stan. District within a province.

stol'nik (pl. *stol'niki*). Court rank, below *duma* rank but above Moscow gentry.

strelets (pl. *strel'tsy*). Musketeer. *streletskii*, adj.

striapchii (pl. *striapchie*). A court rank, below *stol'nik*.

sudebnik. Law code; when capitalized referring specifically to those of 1497 and 1550.

syshchik (pl. *syshchiki*). Special investigator.

uezd (pl. *uezdy*). Province.

Ulozhenie. The 1649 Law Code.

usad'ba (pl. *usad'by*). Demesne land, manor estates, land, and houses belonging immediately to the gentry landholder.

verstanie. The process of assessing military service men and assigning them to service ranks and granting them remuneration rates.

voevoda (pl. *voevody*). Provincial governor or, in military contexts, general.

volokita. "Red tape"; bureaucratic delays.

volost'. District within a province.

votchina (pl. *votchiny*). Property held in outright tenure. There were three varieties of votchina: hereditary or clan votchina; earned votchina granted as a reward for meritorious servious; and purchased votchina. Different rules of inheritance and sale applied to each kind.

votchinnik (pl. *votchinniki*). The owner of a *votchina*.

vybor. Selection, especially that of men to serve in local offices or among the elite corps of provincial gentry cavalrymen.

vybornyi (pl. *vybornye*). Selectman, chosen to serve at the highest provincial rank in regimental or court service.

zamoskov'e. Central Russian region. (adj. *zamoskovnyi*).

zemskii (adj.). Civil, public; of or relating to the taxpaying population. Hence the *zemskii* system of local administration of tax collection and some municipal business.

zemskii sobor (pl. *zemskie sobory*). Assembly of the Land.

zhalovan'e. Grant, favor.

zhilets (pl. *zhil'tsy*). A transitional rank between provincial and Moscow rank; entry-level position.

Notes

The following abbreviations are used in the Notes. Complete authors' names, titles, and publication data are given in the Bibliography, pp. 335–62.

AAE   *Akty, sobrannye v bibliotekakh i arkhivakh Rossiiskoi imperii Arkheograficheskoiu ekspeditsieiu Imperatorskoi Akademii nauk.*

AI   *Akty istoricheskie, sobrannye i izdannye Arkheograficheskoiu kommissieiu.*

AIu   *Akty iuridicheskie ili sobrannye form starinnogo deloproizvodstva.*

AIuB   *Akty, otnosiashchiesia do iuridicheskago byta drevnei Rossii.*

AMG   *Akty Moskovskogo gosudarstva. Izdannye Imperatorskoiu akademieiu nauk.*

ChOIDR   *Chteniia v Obshchestve istorii i drevnostei rossiiskikh pri Moskovskom universitete. Sbornik.*

DAI   *Dopolneniia k aktam istoricheskim, sobrannye i izdannye Arkheograficheskoiu kommissieiu.*

DR   *Dvortsovye razriady, po vysochaishemu poveleniiu.*

PRP   *Pamiatniki russkogo prava.*

PSRL   *Polnoe sobranie russkikh letopisei.*

PSZ   *Polnoe sobranie zakonov Rossiiskoi imperii.*

RANION   *Rossiiskaia Assotsiatsiia Nauchno-Issledovatel'skikh Institutov Obshchestvennykh Nauk.*

RGADA   *Rossiiskii gosudarstvennyi arkhiv drevnikh aktov.*

RGB   *Rossiiskaia gosudarstvennaia biblioteka.*

RIB	*Russkaia istoricheskaia biblioteka.*
RNB	*Rossiiskaia natsional'naia biblioteka.*
SGGiD	*Sobranie gosudarstvennykh gramot i dogovorov.*
SPbFIRI	*Sanktpeterburgskii filial Instituta rossiiskoi istorii RAN.*
VGV	*Vladimirskiia Gubernskiia Vedomosti.*
Vremennik	*Vremennik Imperatorskogo obshchestva istorii i drevnostei*
IODR	*rossiskikh pri Moskovskom universitete.*

Preface

1. Borisov, *Opisanie* and *Starinnye akty; Pamiatniki delovoi pis'men-nosti.*

2. *AAE, AI, DAI, AMG, ChOIDR, Vremennik OIDR,* Khilkov, *Sbornik kniazia Khilkova, Opisanie dokumentov i bumag, VGV.* A very useful guide to published materials is Masonov, *Bibliografiia.*

3. See *RGADA, f. 210, opis' 4, Dela desiaten',* books 291, 299, 302, 304; *RGADA, f. 210, Vlad. stol,* books 4, 11, 15, and *stlb.* 40, 63, 72, 73, 82, 101, 115, 116; *RNB, Ermitazhnoe sobranie,* no. 343/2. For published *desiatni* see Storozhev, *Materialy.* On the landowners of the Suzdal' region, see Fomin, "Sotsial'nyi sostav."

4. Hellie, *Readings;* Novosel'skii, "Kollektivnye dvorianskie chelobitnye o syske"; Shakhmatov, "Chelobitnaia"; Smirnov, "Chelobitnyia"; Storozhev, "Dva chelobit'ia"; Stashevskii, *K istorii dvorianskikh chelobitnykh.*

5. *Alfavitnyi ukazatel';* Barsukov, *Spiski gorodovykh voevod; Dvortsovye razriady;* Golitsyn, *Ukazatel' imen lichnykh; Knigi razriadnyia;* Stashevskii, *Zemlevladenie;* Veselovskii, *D'iaki i pod'iachie.*

Introduction

1. Baron, *Travels of Olearius,* p. 173.

2. Ia. E. Vodarskii calculates that there were roughly 70,000 male *pomeshchiki* in 1678 and the same number in 1700. The number in the class as a whole, including women, children, retirees, and those who managed not to enroll in service, may have been two or three times that figure. To put this number in context, Vodarskii finds close to 5 million taxpayers in 1678. Male servitors, then, accounted for less than 1.5 percent of the population. See his *Naselenie Rossii,* pp. 64, 159. Yet secular landlords of less-than-boyar rank controlled 57 percent of all land in the tsardom and 67 percent in the Vladimir region in 1678, according to land census information, so they exerted great economic and social force as a group. See Vodarskii, *Dvorianskoe zemlevladenie;* Kliuchevskii, *Kurs russkoi istorii,* 3: 250. Hellie cites much lower figures. He says that in 1663 there were 39,757 men of the middle service class, in 1672 there were 37,859, and in 1681 only 9,712. These lower numbers must derive from a more restrictive definition based exclusively on service rank. *Enserfment,* p. 269.

3. Kollmann, *Kinship and Politics* and "Consensus Politics"; Crummey,

Aristocrats and Servitors and "Court Groupings and Politics"; Keenan, "Russian Political Folkways."

4. Henshall, *Myth of Absolutism*, pp. 1–2.

5. The complicated lineage of this trend in the historiography is discussed more fully in Chapter 2.

6. Dykstra and Silag, "Doing Local History," p. 421.

7. For example, see Pitt-Rivers, *People of the Sierra*.

8. For particularly interesting treatments of communities within broader societies, see Duara, *Culture*; Marriott, "Small Communities"; Sabean, *Power in the Blood*.

9. Rosen, "Alternative Courts," p. 558.

10. Duara, *Culture*, p. 5.

11. Lawrence Rosen points out that Americans have in fact grown less litigious as small communities have given way to large, impersonal cities. "Alternative Courts," pp. 563–64.

12. In an article on the political uses of territoriality, Richard M. Merelman says that contemporary polling finds that people define neighborhoods in purely territorial terms: "No matter where people live—whether in the center of large cities or in small towns—they define their neighborhood as a delimited area of approximately 125 acres immediately surrounding their domicile." "The Political Uses of Territoriality," p. 588, citing T. R. Lee, "Psychology and Living Space." In R. Downs and D. Stea, eds., *Image and Environment*. Chicago, 1973, pp. 87–109.

13. Pitt-Rivers, *People of the Sierra*, pp. 6–12.

14. Habermas, *Structural Transformation*, p. 3.

15. Ibid., p. xi.

16. Henshall also makes the case that autocracy and localisms could be compatible in his *Myth of Absolutism*. Nancy Shields Kollman applies this idea in a recent paper entitled "Terminology about Society."

17. On nationalism and its premodern or early modern manifestations, see B. Anderson, *Imagined Communities*; Hall, *States in History*. For a clear expression of Muscovite religious nationalism, see *AAE*, vol. 2, no. 188, pp. 319–20.

18. *AI*, vol. 2, no. 221, pp. 260, 261. See also Khilkov, *Sbornik*, no. 32, pp. 104–6.

19. Derzhavina and Kolosova, *Skazanie Avraamiia Palitsyna*, p. 137. My thanks to Edward Ponarin for his help in translating this passage.

20. Early theoretical work on political culture was done by Gabriel Almond, Lucian Pye, and Sidney Verba. Verba defines political culture as "the system of empirical beliefs, expressive symbols, and values which defines the situation in which political action takes place. It provides the subjective orientation to politics." See Verba, "Comparative Political Culture," p. 513. For more recent developments in historical application of the concept, see Baker, *Political Culture*; Ethington, *Public City*.

21. In my use of the term, I follow Keith Michael Baker, *Political Culture*, p. xii. Baker writes that "political culture is a historical creation, subject to

constant elaboration and development through the activities of the individuals and groups whose purposes it defines. As it sustains and gives meaning to political activity, so is it itself shaped and transformed in the course of that activity as new claims are articulated, old ones transformed."

22. Baron, *Travels of Olearius*, pp. 174–75.

23. Giddens, *Capitalism and Modern Social Theory*, p. 157; Weber, *Economy and Society*, 1: 231, 3: 1006–10. On the application of the patrimonial model to Muscovite society, see Kollmann, *Kinship and Politics*, esp. pp. 3–4.

24. This image of the king as merciful father persisted in the West as well, but was invoked only on particular occasions. Subjects turned to the king as source of unconditional pardon in only a few specific situations. According to Natalie Davis's work on France and other studies of English law, only certain categories of crimes qualified as pardonable. In other situations, evidently, appeal to the mercy of the sovereign was simply not considered. See, for instance, Davis, *Fiction in the Archives*.

25. Hellie, *Slavery in Russia*. Western European families were also highly patriarchal at this time, and patrimonial imagery cropped up in Western political writings, but the attachment to a patrimonial model of ruler as father and nation as family was fading in the West, whereas it remained in full force in Muscovy.

26. Baron, *Travels of Olearius*, p. 176.

27. Ibid., p. 174.

28. Rowland, "Muscovite Literary Ideology"; Paul of Aleppo, *Travels of Macarius*.

29. Hughes, *Russia and the West*, pp. 87–96; Kollmann, "Transformations," p. 25.

30. Smirnov, "Chelobitnyia dvorian i detei boiarskikh," p. 54; *SGGiD*, vol. 3, nos. 11, 12 (report of Assembly of the Land), pp. 46–55, no. 16 (coronation service of Mikhail Fedorovich), pp. 70–87.

31. *AAE*, vol. 2, no. 188, p. 320.

32. Rowland, "Problem of Advice," p. 276; Derzhavina and Kolosova, *Skazanie Avraamiia Palitsyna*, pp. 231–38.

33. This is also characteristic of Weber's patrimonial states: "Where patrimonial domination is exerted over large territories, however, a broader basis of recruitment [than just courtiers and household servants] is necessary, and frequently a tendency towards decentralisation of administration develops, providing a basis for a variety of tensions and conflicts between ruler and local patrimonial officials or 'notables.'" See Giddens, *Capitalism*, p. 157.

34. On the continuation of subordinated discourses and the inversion of acknowledged and suppressed cultural modes in Russia, see Lotman and Uspenskij, "Role of Dual Models," pp. 3–35.

35. For a very lucid account of the medieval development of ideas about kingship and different visions of the sources of royal legitimacy, see Kantorowicz, *King's Two Bodies*.

36. Konopczynski, "Une Antithèse," pp. 336–47; Subtelny, *Domination*.

37. Baron, *Travels of Olearius*, pp. 173, 176.
38. Das, "History Writing."
39. Beik, *Absolutism and Society*; Smith, "Culture of Merit," esp. pp. 25–30, 90–97.
40. Herrup, *Common Peace*, p. 193; Hay, *Albion's Fatal Tree*.
41. Anderson, *Lineages*, p. 29. Not all vestiges of "archaic" notions of political organization, such as morality, community, paternalism, and republicanism, went underground in the West during the early modern period. Quite the contrary; many of these held sway as important modes of conducting political life. Generally, however, even within these personalistic utopias, Western thinkers envisaged more formalized, institutionalized rights and responsibilities than their Russian counterparts. See Pagden, *Languages of Political Theory*, pp. 1–17.
42. Smith, "Culture of Merit," pp. 36, 266–67.
43. Hellie, *Muscovite Law Code*, ch. 10, art. 2, p. 23.
44. I have yet to find any convincing guidelines for selecting regions for local study. For a recent summary of monographic local studies in American history and the reasons behind the selection of the particular subject communities, see Dykstra and Silag, "Doing Local History," 411–25.
45. On the southern border areas, see Chistiakova, "Volneniia sluzhilykh liudei"; Davies, "Role of the Town Governors"; Stashevskii, *K istorii kolonizatsii Iuga*; Vazhinskii, *Zemlevladenie*; Vorob'ev and Degtiarev, *Russkoe feodal'noe zemlevladenie*. On Siberia, see Aleksandrov and Pokrovskii, "Mirskie organizatsii." On the north, see Bogoslovskii, *Zemskoe samoupravlenie*; Nosov, *Stanovlenie soslovno-predstavitel'nykh uchrezhdenii*.
46. Iu. G. Alekseev, *Agrarnaia i sotsial'naia istoriia*. See also Kiselev, "Feodal'noe zemlevladenie Iaroslavskogo uezda"; Kuznetsov, "Svetskoe feodal'noe zemlevladenie Kolomenskogo uezda"; Pozdniakov, "Sluzhilaia korporatsiia Maloiaroslavetskogo uezda"; Shvatchenko, *Svetskie feodal'nye votchiny*. A number of valuable collections of source materials from particular provinces have come out in recent years, such as Ermolaev, *Borovskii uezd*; Kozliakov, *Iaroslavskii arkhiv*.
47. For documents concerning the struggle over Vladimir between supporters of Tsar Vasilii Shuiskii and of the Second False Dmitrii, see *AI*, vol. 2, nos. 221–23, pp. 259–63; Khilkov, *Sbornik*, no. 12, pts. iii, xvi. Other documents about the fate of the region during the Time of Troubles include Khilkov, *Sbornik*, no. 12, pts. xxiv, xxvi, xli, xlii, xlvii, xlix, l, lii, lv, lvi, lxi, lxii, lxix; *ChOIDR*, 1847, no. 5, *Smes'* 21–24.
48. See Martin, "Novokshcheny of Novgorod," on Tatars and converts from Islam living in the Novgorod region. Got'e finds evidence of finnic settlement in Vladimir, but this seems hardly relevant by the sixteenth and seventeenth centuries. See *Zamoskovnyi krai*.
49. Vodarskii, *Dvorianskoe zemlevladenie*, p. 53.
50. Vodarskii, *Dvorianskoe zemlevladenie*, pp. 52–119. Documents from Iaroslavl', Galich, Pereiaslavl'-Zalesskii, Kostroma, Uglich, Romanov, Murom, Kolomna, Kashira, Tver, and Dmitrov, to name just a handful of the 50

provinces of the central region, all confirm the general outlines of provincial culture traced in the following pages. Of the 50 provinces of the central non–black earth region, 10 belong to the Moscow vicinity and so display quite a different population profile. Black-earth regions enjoyed rich, deep topsoil, while the non–black-earth areas had less fertile, shallower topsoil.

Chapter One

1. Smirnov, "Neskol'ko dokumentov," p. 6.
2. Pavlov-Sil'vanskii, *Gosudarevy sluzhilye liudi*, p. 82; Kliuchevskii, *Istoriia soslovii*, pp. 147, 156; Sergeevich, *Drevnosti russkogo prava*, 1: 396–97, 514. On the development of the *pomest'e* system, see Alekseev and Kopanev, "Razvitie"; Hellie, *Enserfment*, pp. 27–29. On the formation of the *deti boiarskie*, see also Bychkova, *Sostav klassa feodalov*, pp. 144–45; Uroff, "Kotoshikhin," pp. 70–71, 362–63; Veselovskii, *Feodal'noe zemlevladenie*, pp. 206, 214–15. On the evolution of the titles and roles, see Chernov, *Vooruzhennye sily*; Novitskii, *Vybornoe i bol'shoe dvorianstvo*.
3. Kalinychev, *Pravovye voprosy*, p. 80. The unit of a hundred probably often contained fewer than the requisite 100 men. The terms were organizational more than numerical indicators.
4. *TsGADA, f.* 210, *opis'* 4, *Dela desiaten'*, books 291, 299, 302; *opis'* 10, *Vlad. stol*, books 4, 11, 15, *stlb.* 40, 63, 72, 73, 82, 101, 115, 116; *RNB, Ermitazhnoe sobranie*, no. 343/2. Sample sizes: 69 *vybornye*, 32 *dvorovye*, 59 *gorodovye*.
5. *RGADA, f.* 210, *Vlad. stol, stlb.* 142, *l.* 58 (1658).
6. Chernov, *Vooruzhennye sily*, p. 125; Kalinychev, *Pravovye voprosy*, p. 40.
7. E.g., *RNB, Ermitazhnoe sobranie*, no. 343/2, *ll.* 16 v–17 (1626).
8. Novitskii, *Vybornoe i bol'shoe dvorianstvo*, pp. 10, 19; Novosel'skii, "Praviashchie gruppy," pp. 315–16, 318. A. A. Zimin questions whether Ivan's order was ever put into effect, but the practice of local *vybor* seems to date from about that time, whether or not the two phenomena were related. See *Reformy Ivana Groznogo*, pp. 366–71.
9. *RNB, Ermitazhnoe sobranie*, no. 343/2, *l.* 5-5v (1626).
10. According to S. B. Veselovskii, the term is derived from the word *zhit'*, to live, and originally implied residence in close proximity to the prince. Initially they filled the role of bodyguards. *Feodal'noe zemlevladenie*, p. 319.
11. Scholars have defined the origins, composition, and significance of the *zhil'tsy* in various contradictory ways, but the actual outlines of their service and status remain hazy. Kotoshikhin described the *zhil'tsy* as the entry-level rank for the sons of upper-level servitors. While it is true that some *zhil'tsy* were sons of Moscow-rank men, most were sons of successful provincial servitors. Uroff, "Kotoshikhin," pp. 70, 360; Chernov, *Vooruzhennye sily*, pp. 56–77; Veselovskii, *Feodal'noe zemlevladenie*, p. 318. Kliuchevskii asserted that provincial gentrymen gained promotion from the top

of the town lists into the *zhil'tsy*, and from there they ascended into the Moscow *dvoriane*. *Istoriia soslovii*, p. 142. Novosel'skii correctly maintained that *zhil'tsy* were invariably first-time servitors. "Praviashchie gruppy," p. 317.

12. Uroff, "Kotoshikhin," p. 69 (translation modified). In the seventeenth century, they numbered approximately 1,000 nationwide. Kliuchevskii refers to a *boiarskaia kniga* of 1627 that lists 826 *dvoriane moskovskie*. *Istoriia soslovii*, p. 142. Iakovlev shows 997 in 1638. *Prikaz sbora ratnykh liudei*, p. 259.

13. Stashevskii, *Ocherki*, pp. 121–32.

14. Got'e, *Zamoskovnyi krai*, pp. 326–38, 428. Got'e says that servitors' landholdings increased overall throughout the seventeenth century, but the effects of the increase were vitiated by the simultaneous rise in the gentry population and by the inordinately large holdings of boyars and royal favorites (p. 383).

15. The petition was submitted by "*stol'niki* and *striapchie* and Moscow gentry and *zhil'tsy* and *dvoriane* and *deti boiarskie* and Suzdal' *zhil'tsy* and *pomeshchiki* and *votchinniki* who have *pomest'ia* and *votchiny* in Suzdal' Province." *AMG*, vol. 2, no. 792, pp. 481–82.

16. On the boyar aristocracy, see Crummey, *Aristocrats and Servitors*.

17. Hellie, *Enserfment*, p. 200, citing Stashevskii, *Smeta voennykh sil*, pp. 13–14.

18. Crummey, *Aristocrats and Servitors*, p. 14.

19. Smith, *De Republica Anglorum*, p. 73.

20. Quoted in Wrightson, *English Society*, p. 17.

21. Ibid., p. 25. On definitions of nobility or gentility in early modern France, where concepts of birth and "virtue" were inseparably linked, see J. M. Smith, "Culture of Merit," pp. 7–10.

22. On the "particular ideal of manliness of the Anglo-Saxon gentleman," "a stratum of notables of decidedly manorial character," and its links to the creation of a system of voluntary cooperation of free members of a political association, see Weber, *Economy and Society*, 3: 1063.

23. Nikol'skii, "Rifmovannoe poslanie," pp. 279–81.

24. "Skazanie o roskoshnom zhitii i veselii," in Adrianova-Perets, *Russkaia demokraticheskaia satira*, p. 32. My thanks to Michael Khodarkovsky for his help in translating this and the following passage.

25. "Povest' o Fome i Ereme," in Adrianova-Perets, *Russkaia demokraticheskaia satira*, pp. 34–36.

26. Acknowledging the vastly different cultural milieu of the Muscovite provinces and the absence of detectable "gentleness" or "gentility," I have avoided using the term *gentleman*. I have substituted instead the term *gentryman*.

27. Berry and Crummey, *Rude and Barbarous Kingdom*, p. 177.

28. Fletcher's description overlooks the existence of non-"gentle" military servitors, such as the musketeers, who already played a significant role

under Ivan IV. Conscription and lower-service-class regiments increased in importance in the seventeenth century, after Fletcher's visit.

29. Kliuchevskii, *Istoriia soslovii,* p. 162.

30. Pavlov-Sil'vanskii, *Gosudarevy sluzhilye liudi,* pp. 153, 201. Kliuchevskii also presented the boyars as a failed aristocracy, although he later tempered his view with an appreciation of the consensual nature of Muscovite politics. *Boiarskaia duma,* chapts. 5–7, 9–20. See also Novitskii, *Vybornoe i bol'shoe dvorianstvo,* pp. 68–71; Novosel'skii, "Praviashchie gruppy," pp. 315–35. The debate over the ratio of birth to service in working up the ranks continues in recent works, primarily about the boyars. For arguments emphasizing service, see Kleimola, "Military Service and Elite Status," and "Up Through Servitude"; Zimin, "Sostav boiarskoi dumy." For an opposing view emphasizing birth, see Kollmann, *Kinship and Politics.*

31. Mousnier, *Social Hierarchies,* pp. 115–25.

32. *AMG,* vol. 2, no. 435; Novosel'skii, "Praviashchie gruppy," p. 318.

33. *Vremennik OIDR* 1851, book 11, *Smes',* p. 24.

34. *RGADA, f.* 210, *Vlad. stol, stlb.* 82, *l.* 35.

35. Ibid., *stlb.* 132, *ll.* 146, 149, 162.

36. *RIB,* 10: 241. Cited in Novosel'skii, "Praviashchie gruppy," p. 318. Emphasis added.

37. *RGADA, f.* 210, *Vlad. stol, stlb.* 132, *l.* 131–131 v.

38. Ibid., *stlb.* 72, *l.* 68. For other cases where sons received rewards for their fathers' service, see *RGADA, f.* 210, *Dela desiaten',* book 304, *l.* 72 v (1648); *RGADA, f.* 210, *Vlad. stol, stlb.* 132, *l.* 141 (1648); *RGADA, f.* 210, *Bezglasnyi stol,* no. 177, *ll.* 217–222 (1699).

39. Novosel'skii, "Praviashchie gruppy," p. 320; Kalinychev, *Pravovye voprosy,* pp. 54–57.

40. Davies, "Role of the Town Governors," p. 327. See also a useful discussion in Keep, *Soldiers of the Tsar,* p. 42.

41. *PSZ,* vol. 2, no. 744, pp. 186–92.

42. *RNB, Ermitazhnoe sobranie,* no. 343/2, *ll.* 2-2 v.

43. *Voronezhskie akty,* vol. 3, no. 173. Quoted in Davies, "Role of the Town Governors," p. 341.

44. *RGADA, f.* 210, *Prikaznyi stol,* no. 561, *ll.* 598–600 (1647).

45. Hellie, *Enserfment* pp. 214–25. For evidence of gentry resistance to registration in lower units, see *AMG,* vol. 2, no. 1126, p. 659 (1659).

46. *RGADA,* f. 210, *Vlad. stol, stlb.* 63, *l.* 195. The Iur'ev muster roll of 1667/68 included twelve gentrymen who had been shifted to *reitar* regiments: ibid., book 4, *ll.* 76–76 v.

47. Keep, *Soldiers of the Tsar,* p. 51 (his emphasis).

48. *AMG,* vol. 1, no. 322, p. 341 (1632); *PSZ,* vol. 1, no. 100, p. 201 (1653).

49. Hellie, *Muscovite Law Code,* chapt. 7, art. 17, p. 14, chapt. 16, art. 61, p. 119; *PSZ,* vol. 1, nos. 155, 158, 177, 186, 208, 269, 280, 347, 353; Kalinychev, *Pravovye voprosy,* pp. 58–59.

50. On the new solidarity between the *boiarstvo* and the gentry, see a most intelligent account by Vysotskii, "Kollektivnye dvorianskie chelobitnye."

51. Miliukov, *Ocherki*, 1: 130; Chernov, *Vooruzhennye sily*, pp. 161–62; Hellie, *Enserfment*, pp. 221, 223.

52. Hellie, *Enserfment*, p. 189, citing Mikhnevich and Il'enko, "Glavnyi shtab," p. 8.

53. *AI*, vol. 4, no. 70; Sh., "Dvorianstvo"; *AMG*, vol. 2, no. 1089; vol. 3, nos. 49, 301, 520; *PSZ*, vol. 1, no. 246, p. 483 (Feb. 21, 1659). All cited in Hellie, *Enserfment*, pp. 211–21.

54. Denisova, "Pomestnaia konnitsa," p. 44; Vodarskii, *Naselenie Rossii*, p. 193; Ivanov, *Opisanie gosudarstvennogo Razriadnogo arkhiva*, "Prilozhenie"; Kalinychev, *Pravovye voprosy*, pp. 44–45.

55. Novosel'skii, "Feodal'noe zemlevladenie," p. 154.

56. *AIu*, no. 407, p. 428.

57. Ibid., no. 399, pp. 421–22.

58. Ibid., no. 403, p. 425. Sometimes marriage agreements stated that the woman should return to her former master upon the death of her husband. See ibid., no. 402, IV, pp. 424–25.

59. Levin, *Sex and Society*, p. 101.

60. Dewey, *Muscovite Judicial Texts*, art. 62, p. 62.

61. *AAE*, vol. 3, no. 174, p. 257 (1628). On tax collection, peasant indebtedness, and jurisdiction, see Blum, *Lord and Peasant*, esp. 234–35.

62. For examples showing landlords' involvement with their estates, see *AIu*, nos. 395, 425–26, pp. 419–20, 460–61; *AIuB*, vol. 3, no. 305, cols. 118–20; *AAE*, vol. 3, no. 174, p. 257; *ChOIDR*, 1847, no. 5, *Smes'*, 21–24; and many others.

63. Got'e, *Zamoskovnyi krai*, p. 68; Vodarskii, *Dvorianskoe zemlevladenie*, pp. 65–66.

64. A similar degree of overlap and intermarriage can be observed with other neighboring provinces as well: between Suzdal' and Nizhnii Novgorod, Vladimir and Murom, Iur'ev and Rostov. However, the five I have chosen form a coherent whole and avoid the problems that arise when one incorporates Nizhnii Novgorod in particular, with its sizable Turkic population and its very different, trade-based economy.

65. Baron, *Travels of Olearius*, p. 291.

66. Newey, "Vegetation and Soil," p. 42.

67. Veselovskii, *Feodal'noe zemlevladenie*, p. 157.

68. Extracting information from Muscovite census books, the historian Rozhkov studied soil types of various provinces. In census books, land was recorded according to a four-tiered ranking system as good, average, poor, and very bad (*dobrekhudaia*). Within central Russia, the extremes of quality were found in Dmitrov *uezd*, where registrars considered 100 percent of a large sample of recorded land to be poor quality, and in Nizhnii Novgorod, where 86 percent was deemed good, 12 percent average, and 2 percent poor. Iur'ev Pol'skii approached Nizhnii Novgorod's high: two-thirds of the land recorded was labeled good and the remaining third was average. Vladimir census books showed two-thirds average land and one-third poor. In Suzdal'

approximately half of the land was categorized as good or average and half as poor. Rozhkov, *Sel'skoe khoziaistvo*, pp. 36–37, 41.

69. Novosel'skii, *Votchinnik*, p. 98.

70. Ibid., p. 33.

71. Ibid., esp. pp. 33, 45. See also Aleksandrov, "Pamflet na rod Sukhotinykh (XVII v.)"; Stashevskii, *K istorii kolonizatsii Iuga*. On regional differences, see Blum, *Lord and Peasant*, esp. pp. 199–218.

72. Novosel'skii, *Votchinnik*, p. 99; Veselovskii, *Feodal'noe zemlevladenie*, pp. 152–54.

73. According to Vodarskii's study of land cadastres of the late seventeenth century, in the Vladimir region, which included Vladimir, Shuia, Suzdal', and Iur'ev Pol'skii, as well as six other provinces, only 4 percent of all arable land and 5 percent of all arable land held in estates, was left unplowed. Suzdal' had the highest rate of unplowed arable land at 10 percent, while Vladimir had a negligible 8 *cheti* of arable land left uncultivated, less than 1 percent. *Dvorianskoe zemlevladenie*, pp. 65–72.

74. Iakovlev, *Prikaz sbora ratnykh liudei*, p. 260; Veselovskii, "Smety voennykh sil," p. 5. I am a bit suspicious of their figure, because both men assume that widows and adolescent boys held "exactly the same" property and wealth as the servicemen, their husbands and fathers, themselves. Iakovlev's figure derives from a census of peasant households owned exclusively by widows and boys. But because estates were divided among all adult heirs, women and boys tended to own smaller estates than their husbands and fathers. Therefore, figures on serf holding may be more in line with the numbers I have found in Vladimir-Suzdal'.

75. Author's compilation and Iakovlev, *Prikaz sbora ratnykh liudei*, p. 262. Lukh had an exceptionally high proportion of landlords reporting that they owned no peasant households at all. Due to the survival of a document that recorded only peasantless landlords this result may be artificially low. *RNB, Ermitazhnoe sobranie*, no. 343/2 (Lukh muster roll from 1626).

76. According to Hellie, servitors claimed to require a minimum of 50 households to support their military service. Hellie, *Enserfment*, p. 50, citing Presniakov, "Moskovskoe gosudarstvo pervoi poloviny XVII veka," 1: 65.

77. According to Alekseev's estimates, 20 percent of the rent a landlord could exact from a 100-*cheti pomest'e* went to support his service, that is, to buy the necessary horses, weapons, and equipment and food supplies to feed man and horse during campaigns. Alekseev, "15 rublevyi maksimum," pp. 110–17.

78. This average was derived from 175 cases in the five provinces in which complete landholdings were recorded in descriptions of an individual's properties. The numbers reflect the number of *cheti* in conditional *pomest'e* and outright *votchina* holdings combined. Estate measurements were listed by the amount in one field, assuming a three-field rotation system. The average *pomest'e* size throughout the *Zamoskov'e* region seems to have been fairly standard. In Kolomenskoe *uezd*, for instance, *pomest'ia* averaged 179.6 *cheti* in the sixteenth and seventeenth centuries. See Kuznetsov, "Svetskoe feo-

dal'noe zemlevladenie," p. 9. Average estates were larger in some regions outside *Zamoskov'e* and smaller in others. For instance, Vorob'ev and Degtiarev say that the average in the Novgorod area in 1615 was 516 *cheti* in one field (*Russkoe feodal'noe zemlevladenie*, p. 137). In the southern border provinces of Kozlov, Iablonov, and Userd, town servitors averaged only between 25 and 60 *cheti* per field. Vazhinskii, *Zemlevladenie*, p. 112.

79. Vodarskii, *Dvorianskoe zemlevladenie*, p. 72.

80. Got'e, *Zamoskovnyi krai*, pp. 317–18.

81. *RNB, Ermitazhnoe sobranie*, no. 343/2 (1626).

82. Ibid., *l.* 23.

83. *AMG*, vol. 2, no. 231, pp. 145–46 (1645).

84. Nonetheless, some of the gentry of the area somehow acquired quite impressive material wealth. See for instance the lists of lost items listed in reports of the theft or fire, or in wills. E.g., "Chelobitnaia boiarskogo syna Sakharov 1637 g. o pokrazhe u nego raznogo imushchestva," *VGV*, 1857; "Chelobitnaia Dmitriia Kaisarova," *VGV*, no. 28, 1857; "Akty o kabal'nykh liudiakh XVII v.," *VGV*, no. 6, 1858; "Chelobitnaia Vasiliia Sobakina 1644 g.," *VGV*, no. 7, 1856; *VGV*, no. 32, 1865.

85. Borisov, *Starinnye akty*, no. 79, p. 146.

86. Andreev, "Sil'nye liudi"; Smirnov, "Chelobitnyia," pp. 1–73; Stashevskii, *K istorii dvorianskikh chelobitnykh.*

87. *RGADA* f. 210, *Vlad. stol*, no. 62, *l.* 112, cited in Andreev, "Sil'nye liudi," p. 78.

88. Cited in Andreev, "Sil'nye liudi," p. 78.

89. Ibid.

90. Storozhev, "Dva chelobit'ia," p. 12.

91. For instance, Bakhrushin, "Moskovskoe vosstanie 1648," pp. 46–91; Cherepnin, *Zemskie sobory*, pp. 260–62, 394–95; Orlov, "Voprosy sotsial'no-ekonomicheskoi istorii," pp. 149–61; Smirnov, "Chelobitnyia," pp. 6–7; Vodarskii, *Naselenie Rossii*, p. 62. Soviet historians of the poor southern gentry tend to be more sympathetic to their class interests and problems; see Vazhinskii, *Zemlevladenie*, pp. 24–25.

92. *AMG*, vol. 2, no. 285, p. 178 (1647), no. 382, p. 241 (1649).

93. Hellie, *Enserfment*, pp. 211–25. Iakovlev, *Prikaz*, pp. 70–75; Novosel'skii, "Praviashchie gruppy," pp. 315–35, and "Feodal'noe zemlevladenie," pp. 139–56.

94. Gramsci, *Selections from the Prison Notebooks*, p. 238. See also Raeff, *Well-Ordered Police State*, p. 234; and Pipes, *Russia Under the Old Regime*, esp. such revealing chapter titles as "Absence of Corporate Institutions and Spirit."

95. Rowland, "Problem of Advice," p. 281.

96. Smirnov, "Chelobitnyia," p. 53; Stashevskii, *K istorii kolonizatsii Iuga*, p. 19.

97. On class as cultural construct, see among others Suny, *Revenge of the Past*; Duara, *Culture*, esp. p. 270, n. 9.

Chapter Two

1. Haxthausen, *Studies*, p. 250.
2. Romanovich-Slavatinskii, *Dvorianstvo*, p. 402 (his emphasis). See also Got'e, *Zamoskovnyi krai*, pp. 421–22; Rozhdestvenskii, *Sluzhiloe zemlevladenie*, pp. 228–29. One of the few historians to notice the frequent presence of landlords on their estates, even in the sixteenth century, was Ivanchin-Pisarev; see his "O starinnoi sluzhbe russkikh dvorian."
3. An opposing historiographic approach postulates the existence of "service cities" or "gentry corporations," which flourished from the mid-sixteenth to mid–seventeenth centuries and then fell apart. See Novosel'skii, "Praviashchie gruppy," "Raspad," and "Feodal'noe zemlevladenie."
4. Raeff acknowledges that provincial servicemen returned to their homes to manage their estates between campaigns and that serving in territorial units fostered an esprit de corps among them. Raeff, *Origins*, pp. 23, 29–30. Quote on p. 30. Similar views expressed in Keep, *Soldiers of the Tsar*, pp. 40, 44–45; Pipes, *Russia Under the Old Regime*, pp. 98, 107; Rozhdestvenskii, *Sluzhiloe zemlevladenie*, pp. 217–31.
5. *RGADA, f.* 210, *op.* 18, no. 54, *l.* 1.
6. Bychkova, *Sostav klassa feodalov*, pp. 78–174. For the earlier history of the region, see Kobrin, "Zemlevladel'cheskie prava," and "Iz istorii pravitel'stvennoi politiki."
7. Fomin, "Sotsial'nyi sostav," pp. 89–94.
8. Ibid., pp. 90–91; Veselovskii, *Feodal'noe zemlevladenie*, pp. 289–94, 323. On the controversy over this event, see Zimin, *Reformy Ivana Groznogo*, pp. 366–71, and his edition of *Tysiachnaia kniga*.
9. The range of numbers reflects the uncertain link of seven seventeenth-century individuals or families to those in the sixteenth century. For the names and survivors, see Fomin, "Sotsial'nyi sostav." Fifteen more families residing in or serving from the broader Vladimir-Suzdal' area in the sixteenth and into the seventeenth century can be added to Fomin's list: Chelishchevs, Dubenskiis, Glotovs, Golenkins, Khmetevskiis, Kolokoltsovs, Koriakins, Kuzminskiis, Linevs, Manuilovs, Mikitins, Novikovs, Oborins, Stromilovs, Zasekins. These additions do not alter the overall persistence rate significantly: it increases to approximately 53 percent.
10. These percentages are the same whether or not the uncertain cases are included in the calculations.
11. Bush, *Rich Noble, Poor Noble*, p. 97. Bush criticizes the method of charting survival by tracing family names forward from a given starting date because this method does not take into account the proliferation of family names from common ancestors. His point is very well taken, but I am more concerned here with families than with clans, as will be discussed below. In addition, Fomin conscientiously indicates which clans spawned which offshoots, alleviating some of the difficulty.
12. Stone, *Crisis of the Aristocracy*, pp. 37, 79.
13. Vorob'ev and Degtiarev, *Russkoe feodal'noe zemlevladenie*, pp. 123–

27; Alekseev, *Agrarnaia i sotsial'naia istoriia*, pp. 188, 211–12; Got'e *Zamo-skovnyi krai*, pp. 245–58; Fomin, "Sotsial'nyi sostav," pp. 93–94.

14. Fomin writes that 43 families disappeared altogether from Suzdal' during the *Oprichnina*, but at least 11 of them eventually resurfaced either in Suzdal' itself or in one of the neighboring provinces during the course of the seventeenth century. Some reappeared late in the century, making continuity uncertain. The 11 families that Fomin says disappeared but who reappear in the area are: Aksakovs (in Suzdal' by 1663/4); Belyis (in Lukh by 1625/6); Bestuzhevs (in Vladimir by 1637/8); Iz"edinovs (in Vladimir by 1675/6); Kurovs (in Iur'ev Pol'skii by 1630); Prokof'evs (in Vladimir by 1637/8); Sushchevs (in Vladimir by 1620/21); Teliatevs (in Suzdal' by 1630); Tiutchevs (in Vladimir by 1641); Toporkovs (in Suzdal' prior to 1648); Vlady-kins (in Vladimir by 1611). Other possible reappearances are made by Lukin and by Rusanovs (one Lukin and two Rusanovs in Vladimir in 1637/8).

15. *RGADA, f. 210, Vlad. stol, stlb. 82, ll. 11–14*. Those promoted from *pod'iachie* whose names never reappeared: Babkov, Belyshev, Borestov, De-riabin, two Dubinin brothers, Kilemin, Kovrin, Kushinkov, Liutov, Neliu-bov, Nemirov, Okatov, two Posnikovs, two Pustoshnikovs, three Rakovskii brothers, two Rusinovs, Shein, Simianskii, Ziabloi. Those who bore old local gentry names: Aigustov, Khvitskoi, Kishkin, Lukin, Redrikov, two Rusinovs, Shulepov. A Fedorov family may begin in Vladimir and Shuia starting with the promotion of Selivestr Ivanov Fedorov.

16. Many published genealogies contain lists of "people who did not fit into any list." These people pose a serious problem to family reconstruction.

17. *AMG*, vol. 2, no. 392, p. 248.

18. Zhadovskii: *SPbFIRI, f. 62, Koll. Kablukova*, nos. 31, 142. Similarly, all of the Klishovs were affiliated with Iur'ev. *RGADA, f. 210, Smotrennye knigi* no. 55, *l.* 170; *RGADA, f. 210, Vlad. stol, stlb.* 72, *l.* 66, *stlb.* 40, *l.* 45, book 4, *l.* 73; *RGADA, f. 210, op. 4, Dela desiaten',* book 291, *l.* 9.

19. Karpovs: *RGADA, f. 210, Vlad. stol, stlb.* 159, *l.* 3, *stlb.* 115, *ll.* 25, 32, *stlb.* 101, *ll.* 24, 30a, 33, *stlb.* 40, *ll.* 35–37, 122–23, *stlb.* 82, *ll.* 30, 40, 43, 48, 56, *stlb.* 63, *l.* 164; *RGADA, f. 210, Prikaznyi stol*, no. 273, *ll.* 986–986 v, no. 784, *ll.* 91–97; *RNB, Sobranie Zinchenko, f.* 299, no. 1017; *SPbFIRI, f.* 21, *Koll. Borisova*, nos. 70, 141, 264; *RGADA, f. 210, op. 4, Dela desiaten',* book 304, *l.* 80.

20. Rummel' and Golubtsov, *Rodoslovnyi sbornik*, vol. 2, pp. 194–205. I have not found any service record or regional affiliation for a number of the Obukhov men. Some of them must have died young, before establishing a record.

21. Ibid., vol. 1, pp. 393–98.

22. Of the prolific Voeikov clan, in which each male produced on average four or five sons, three brothers made their way to Vladimir and Suzdal', along with one cousin. With 88 men in a single generation, the clustering of a tiny group of three brothers on a massive chart vividly underscores the way in which small family groups, rather than whole clans, often moved together and functioned as independent units. The Voeikov chart is far too large

to reproduce here. See Dolgorukov, *Rossiiskaia rodoslovnaia kniga*, pt. 4, pp. 335–47 (Voeikovs); Rummel' and Golubtsov, *Rodoslovnyi sbornik*, vol. 2, pp. 657–79 (Chelishchevs).

23. Tregubov, *Alfavitnyi spisok*. Again, compare this with survival statistics reported by Bush and Stone for other European aristocracies. Bush, *Rich Noble, Poor Noble*, p. 97; Stone, *Crisis of the Aristocracy*, pp. 37, 79.

24. *RGADA, f. 210, op. 18, Rodoslovnye rospisi*, no. 29 (Bludovy); Bychkova, "Iz istorii sozdaniia rodoslovnykh rospisei."

25. Fomin, "Sotsial'nyi sostav," p. 91. Shiriai Bludov held local office as *guba* elder in Suzdal' in 1577/8, when he certified a land grant to the Golenkin family, as cited in the Golenkin genealogical list. See *RGADA, f. 210, op. 18, Rodoslovnye rospisi*, no. 54, *l.* 2. For a fascinating discussion of the creative fabricating of ancestral glories, see Bychkova, "Iz istorii sozdaniia rodoslovnykh rospisei."

26. *RGADA, f. 210, op. 18, Rodoslovnye rospisi*, no. 29, *l.* 3.

27. *RGADA, Dela desiaten'*, book 304, *ll.* 80 v, 81, 82 v; *RGADA, f. 210, Vlad. stol, stlb.* 82, *ll.* 43–44; *stlb.* 116, *l.* 227. R. M. Bludov's promotion to *zhilets* is found in *RGADA, f. 210, op. 5, Smotrennye knigi*, no. 55, *l.* 37 v.

28. *RGADA, f. 210, Vlad. stol, stlb.* 159, *l.* 34 (1677).

29. Documents on the Kablukov family are concentrated in the Borisov Collection (*SPbFIRI, f. 21*) and the Kablukov Collection (*SPbFIRI, f. 62*) as well as in the two volumes of sources published by V. B. Borisov, but the name crops up frequently in any collection of documents relating to Suzdal' or Shuia in the period. Borisov, *Opisanie* and *Starinnye akty*.

30. *RGADA, f. 210, op. 18, Rodoslovnye rospisi*, no. 53, *l.* 1; Bychkova, "Iz istorii sozdaniia rodoslovnykh rospisei," p. 104; Fomin, "Sotsial'nyi sostav," p. 90. By the seventeenth century the Deminskii district was considered part of Suzdal' rather than Shuia.

31. Fedor Vasil'evich's wife Maria appears alternately as the daughter of Osip Kuz'mich Tepritskii and of Kuz'ma Tepritskii. Ikonnikov, *Noblesse de la Russe*, vol. Y, pp. 227–35, cites Kablukov family documents published in *Letopisi Zaniatii Arkheograficheskoi komissii*, facs. XXVI. Unfortunately, I have not been able to find a copy of this undoubtedly rich source. See also *SPbFIRI, f. 62, Koll. Kablukova*, no. 65 (1660), where Aleksei Fedorovich's mother is called "Maria Kuz'mina doch'."

32. For information on land allotment and actual grant from a *vvoznaia gramota* (listing of lands and peasants given to owner to replace lost original) from 1638, see *SPbFIRI, f. 252, Suzdal'skie akty*, no. 13. The petition for cousin's land is in ibid., no. 16 (1657).

33. He had ongoing feuds with the Boriatinskii princes and the Nainarovs as well as with the Tepritskiis. *SPbFIRI, f. 62, Koll. Kablukova*, nos. 13, 16, 18, 36, 40, 42, 44, 47, 115, 119, 149, 159.

34. Ibid., nos. 51–56.

35. Ibid., no. 51.

36. Hellie, *Muscovite Law Code*, chapt. 16, art. 32, p. 109.

37. *SPbFIRI, f. 62, Koll. Kablukova*, no. 65 (1660).

38. *RGADA, f.* 210, *Prikaznyi stol*, no. 863, *ll.* 118–38.

39. Court disputes over A. F. Kablukov's will are documented in *SPbFIRI*, *f.* 62, *Koll. Kablukova*, nos. 243, 245, 257, 258, 260, 265, 273, 276, 283, 293, 294 (1688–91).

40. "*On sam gramote ne umeet*": ibid., no. 117 (1670), *l.* 1 v; Aleksei's signature: ibid., no. 57 (1660).

41. Bolotov marriage: Ikonnikov, *Noblesse de la Russe* vol. Y, p. 228. Mishukov marriage: *SPbFIRI, f.* 62, *Koll. Kablukova*, no. 138.

42. *SPbFIRI, f.* 21, *Koll. Borisova*, no. 500 (1674).

43. *SPbFIRI, f.* 62, *Koll. Kablukova*, nos. 48, 186, 188, 192.

44. Ibid., no. 248 (1686/87).

45. *Zhilets* N. A. Kablukov heads a regiment of *zhil'tsy* in 1678: ibid., no. 142. He is still called *zhilets* in an extract from Shuia census books in 1681: ibid., no. 170. Listed as Moscow *dvorianin* in 1691/2: *Alfavitnyi ukazatel'*, p. 168.

46. *SPbFIRI, f.* 62, *Koll. Kablukova*, nos. 155, 196–97, 208, 210–13, 216, 218, 221, 273, 278, 298, 323; *RGADA, f.* 210, *Vlad. stol, stlb.* 159, *ll.* 12, 18, 35; *VGV*, 1852, no. 29.

47. *SPbFIRI, f.* 62, *Koll. Kablukova*, nos. 243, 245, 257, 258, 260, 265, 267, 273, 276, 283, 293, 294 (1688–91).

48. Ibid., nos. 107, 170 (1667).

49. Ikonnikov, *Noblesse de la Russe* vol. Y, p. 229; *Alfavitnyi ukazatel'*, p. 417.

50. *SPbFIRI, f.* 62, *Koll. Kablukova*, no. 261 (1689). Family members also appear in the *desiatni* of Suzdal' from the 1630s through the end of the century.

51. *SPbFIRI, f.* 62, *Koll. Kablukova*, nos. 127, 132 (1675–76).

52. *VGV*, 1854, no. 21. The documents do not provide Marfa's secular name. She could have been Aleksei Kablukov's mother, Maria, who took the monastic name Marfa and died a nun, but she would have lived an extraordinarily long time. She might also have been Aleksei's daughter Maria, who married S. S. Boldyrev in 1671.

53. Grigorii predeceased his father, dying in 1687 (*SPbFIRI, f.* 62, *Koll. Kablukova*, no. 228). Ivan's fate is more difficult to determine. He probably died in 1679, when his land was transferred to his son, Konstantin (ibid., no. 225). He was not a beneficiary of his father's will in 1688, although his son Konstantin was (ibid., nos. 234, 245, 257, 258, 260, 265, 267, 273, 276, 283, 293, 294). On the other hand, an Ivan Alekseevich Kablukov appears in *boiarskie spiski* and other documents as a *stol'nik* in 1690 and 1692 (ibid., no. 306, and *Alfavitnyi ukazatel'*, p. 168). Ikonnikov *Noblesse de la Russe*, assumes that this *stol'nik* is the same Ivan Alekseevich (vol. Y, p. 228).

54. Konstantin was recorded as a *striapchii* in 1680/81, advancing to *stol'nik* in 1686/87. Matvei appeared on a list of Moscow gentry in 1691/92 and Roman as a *striapchii* in 1691/92. *Alfavitnyi ukazatel'*, p. 168.

55. Ivan Alekseevich's daughter married F. A. Volkov, a *d'iak* in Moscow but derived from an old Suzdal' family. Konstantin Ivanovich's daughter mar-

ried *stol'nik* F. I. Durnovo, whose family had lived in Suzdal' and Vladimir since at least the 1630s and who held land himself in Suzdal'. One of Lev Nikitich's daughters (Vasilissa) married a Kolzakov, from a large Vladimir family, while another (Daria) married a Sobolev, another family with roots in Vladimir-Suzdal' dating back to the sixteenth century. Ikonnikov, *Noblesse de la Russe,* vol. Y, p. 229.

56. Meehan-Waters, *Autocracy and Aristocracy,* p. 2. For another statement of similar ideas, see Stashevskii, "Sluzhiloe soslovie," p. 22.

57. Crummey, *Aristocrats and Servitors,* pp. 107–34; Novosel'skii, *Votchinnik;* Petrikeev, *Krupnoe krepostnoe khoziaistvo;* Rozhdestvenskii, *Sluzhiloe zemlevladenie,* pp. 217–31, esp. 228; Vodarskii, "Praviashchaia gruppa"; Zabelin, "Bol'shoi boiarin"; Zaozerskii, *Tsarskaia votchina.*

58. Servitors on average held less than half of their *oklady.* On assigning rank and *oklady* and conferring *pomest'ia,* see Davies, "Role of the Town Governors," pp. 327–66; Kalinychev, *Pravovye voprosy,* pp. 54–61; Stashevskii, "Sluzhiloe soslovie," pp. 14–31.

59. *RGADA, f.* 1112, *opis'* 1, no. 72.

60. Ibid., no. 69.

61. See, for example, *RNB, f.* 649, Rokotov, nos. 5, 15, 16, 32.

62. See Sedashev, *Ocherki,* pp. 108–9, for an early decree dating from 1576; Shumakov, *Sotnitsy, zapisi i gramoty,* 4: 130–31, for a decree of 1634. Discussed in Novosel'skii, "Raspad," pp. 247–48, and "Feodal'noe zemlevladenie," pp. 143–44.

63. *RNB, Ermitazhnoe sobranie,* no. 343/2, *l.* 3 v (1625/26).

64. *RGADA, f.* 210, *Vladimirskii stol, stlb.* 132, *l.* 80 (1648).

65. *SPbFIRI, f.* 252, *Suzdal'skie akty,* no. 42.

66. *RNB, Ermitazhnoe sobranie,* no. 343/2, *ll.* 29 (1625/26).

67. *RGADA, f.* 1112, *opis'* 1, no. 56.

68. Vorob'ev and Degtiarev, *Russkoe feodal'noe zemlevladenie,* p. 141; Vodarskii, *Naselenie Rossii,* p. 75.

69. Novosel'skii, "Raspad," p. 232 (his parentheses).

70. See, for example, *RNB, Ermitazhnoe sobranie,* no. 343/2, *ll.* 25–25 v (1626).

71. *RGADA, f.* 210, *Vlad. stol, stlb.* 73, *l.* 253–55.

72. Ibid., *stlb.* 132, *l.* 135.

73. Ibid., *stlb.* 73, *l.* 209. See also *AMG,* vol. 2, no. 307, p. 190.

74. Sergeevich, *Drevnosti,* 1: 298–302; Vladimirskii-Budanov, *Obzor,* pp. 388–89.

75. The more important families include Kablukov, Kazimerov, Korobov, Kochiukov, Oshanin, Volkov, Kozynskii, Mishukov, Voeikov, Koisarov, and Khonenev. Lesser families include Taneev, Orlov, Bologovskii, Koptev, and Durnoi.

76. *RGADA, f.* 1112, *opis'* 1, no. 133, 8 *ll.*

77. *RNB, Ermitazhnoe sobranie,* no. 343/2, *ll.* 12 v–13 v.

78. *RGADA, f.* 1112, *opis'* 1, no. 154 (1697/98). For other examples of

foreclosure, see ibid., no. 19 (1696/97), no. 141 (1649/50), *RNB, f.* 532, no. 2383, *ll.* 13–15 (1678–1704).

79. *SPbFIRI, f.* 21, *Koll. Borisova,* no. 136.

80. "Chernovaia chelobitnaia tsariam," *Sbornik starinnykh bumag,* pt. 2, 1897, pp. 157–59. For other examples, see *RGADA, f.* 210, *Prikaznyi stol,* no. 161, *ll.* 38–42; *RGADA, f.* 1112, *opis'* 1, no. 44 (1679/80).

81. Novosel'skii, *Votchinnik,* pp. 40, 41.

82. *SPbFIRI, f.* 62, *Koll. Kablukova,* no. 261 (buys from sister); no. 206 (buys from and trades with Suponovs); no. 280 (buys from Danilo Mishukov); no. 99 (trades with Redrikov); no. 195 (buys from Vysotskii); no. 129 (trades with Kolobov); no. 151 (trades with Babkins); no. 167 (trades with Kozynskii); no. 170 (trades with Kolobov and with Babkins); no. 198 (trades with Babkins); no. 203 (trades with Kozynskii); no. 210 (trades with Kozynskii); no. 241 (trades with Koisarov); no. 242 (trades with Koisarov); nos. 262–64 (trades with Dolgovo-Saburov); no. 277 (trades with Mishukov); no. 303 (trades with Iuren'ev); no. 304 (trades with Priklonskiis); no. 309 (trades with Tepritskii); no. 333 (trades with Volkov).

83. *RGADA, f.* 1112, *opis'* 1, no. 109.

84. Ibid., no. 17.

85. For examples of exchanges, see *RNB, f.* 532, nos. 1061, 1062, 1085, 318, 4738; *RNB, f.* 649, Rokotov, nos. 5, 15, 16, 32; *SPbFIRI, f.* 21, *Koll. Borisova,* no. 370; *SPbFIRI, f.* 252, *Suzdal'skie akty,* no. 17; *SPbFIRI, f.* 62, *Koll. Kablukova,* nos. 222, 126, 162, 168; *VGV,* 1880, no. 1; *Pamiatniki delovoi pis'mennosti,* no. 4, pp. 15–16; *RGADA, f.* 1112, *opis'* 1, *ed. khr.* 109, 166, 4, 59, 90, 84, 164. For examples of sales, see *RNB, f.* 532, no. 684; *RGADA, f.* 1112, *opis'* 1, *ed. khr.* 3, 44, 59, 62, 154; *VGV,* 1847, no. 1.

86. Weickhardt, "Pre-Petrine Law."

87. Got'e, *Zamoskovnyi krai,* p. 422.

88. In Teleshovskaia *volost',* see *SPbFIRI, f.* 62, *Koll. Kablukova,* nos. 228, 137, 243, 191, 129, 170, 198, 199, 210, 203, 241, 242, 243, 245, 249, 257, 258, 262, 263, 264, 269, 265, 267, 273, 276, 283, 293, 294; *SPbFIRI, f.* 252, *Suzdal'skie akty,* no. 42.

In Deminskii *stan,* see *SPbFIRI, f.* 252, *Suzdal'skie akty,* nos. 13, 17, 20, 168, 243, 245, 257, 258, 265, 267, 269, 273, 276, 283, 293, 294; *SPbFIRI, f.* 62, *Koll. Kablukova,* nos. 117, 151, 262, 263, 264; *RGADA, f.* 210, *Prikaznyi stol,* no. 863, *ll.* 118–38.

In Opol'skii *stan,* see *SPbFIRI, f.* 62, *Koll. Kablukova,* nos. 243, 245, 257, 258, 260, 265, 267, 273, 276, 283, 293, 294. In Talitskii *stan,* Suzdal', see *SPbFIRI, f.* 252, *Suzdal'skie akty,* no. 16. In Borisoglebskaia *volost',* Shuia, see *SPbFIRI, f.* 62, *Koll. Kablukova,* nos. 191, 225. In Starodub-Riapolovskii *stan,* see *SPbFIRI, f.* 62, *Koll. Kablukova,* no. 167.

89. *RGADA, f.* 1112, *opis'* 1, no. 99, *l.* 5 (Vladimir, 1634).

90. Ibid., no. 51, *l.* 3 (Vladimir, 1658).

91. Ibid., no. 72, 130, 154, 165. *VGV,* 1880, no. 1.

92. *RNB, f.* 649, Rokotov, nos. 5, 15, 16, 32.

93. *RGADA, f.* 1112, *opis'* 1, no. 59 (1696).

94. Ibid., no. 166. For other examples of consolidation, see *SPbFIRI, f.* 62, *Koll. Kablukova,* nos. 146, 183; *SPbFIRI, f.* 21, *Koll. Borisova,* no. 136; *RNB, f.* 532, no. 1085; *Pamiatniki delovoi pis'mennosti,* no. 4, pp. 115–16. For cases showing division rather than consolidation, see *VGV,* 1857, no. 11; *RGADA, f.* 1112, *opis'* 1, *ed. khr.* 17, 84.

95. On the Mishukov-Kablukov marriages: A. M. Mishukov married F. V. Kablukov's widow, Maria, as seen by squabbles over Mishukov's will; *SPbFIRI, f.* 62, *Koll. Kablukova,* nos. 51–56 (1657–58). D. F. Mishukov married N. A. Kablukov's sister or daughter, as seen by a receipt that Mishukov gave Kablukov for the dowry as agreed; ibid., no. 138 (1677).

96. Ibid., no. 225 (1685/86). The details of the transaction survive because ultimately the state confiscated the Orlov properties from Miachin and handed them over to Ivan Alekseevich Kablukov. A deed given to Ivan Kablukov's son-in-law when he received those lands as part of his bride's dowry preserved the history of ownership of those particular pieces of land.

97. *SPbFIRI, f.* 21, *Koll. Borisova,* no. 494 (1673). It is not entirely clear from the document whether the groom already had purchased the land before the marriage or whether he bought it later to consolidate his holdings. In either case, the union resulted in the entire village ending up in their hands. The document is a complaint by A. V. Kozynskii against his mother-in-law, the widowed Ustina Durnaia, for failure to register a sale of land to him. The complaint lists the past ownership history of the land in question.

98. M. V. Miloslavskii, a Moscow gentryman with *votchina* estates in Suzdal', requested leave to return home to Suzdal', where his wife had died, in order to bury her in the Suzdal' Pokrovskii Convent as she had requested. His request was granted. *RGADA, f.* 210, *Vladimirskii stol, stlb.* 73, *l.* 345.

99. See *SPbFIRI, f.* 21, *Koll. Borisova,* nos. 143, 144 (1624) for the case of Frol Kishkin against his daughter-in-law Maria and her peasants. For widows as litigants in court because their peasants were beaten or their property damaged, see *SPbFIRI, f.* 21, *Koll. Borisova,* no. 123 (1640), no. 218 (1645); *RGADA, f.* 210, *Prikaznyi stol,* no. 740, *ll.* 4–65 (1678); *RGADA, f.* 210, *Vlad. stol, stlb.* 63, *l.* 65 (1663), *stlb.* 159, *l.* 33 (1677). On widows as defendants against complaints about beatings or damage inflicted by their peasants or slaves, see *SPbFIRI, f.* 21, *Koll. Borisova,* no. 135 (1635), no. 393 (1663), no. 396 (1662), no. 668 (1700). On widows and wives as bandits, see *RGADA, f.* 210, *Vlad. stol, stlb.* 63, *l.* 52–53, 65, 70 (1663).

100. *RGADA, f.* 210, *Prikaznyi stol,* no. 273, *ll.* 972–989 v (1651), no. 740, *ll.* 4–65 (1677).

101. "The Life of Yuliania Lazarevsky," in Zenkovsky, *Medieval Russia's Epics, Chronicles, and Tales,* p. 392 (spelling modified here). For a Russian version, see "Povest' ob Ul'ianii Osor'inoi," pp. 98–104.

Chapter Three

1. Jefferson, 1: 49, 68–69; quoted in J. P. Cooper, "Patterns of Inheritance," p. 195.

2. Wives rarely named husbands as heirs in their wills, possibly because women tended to live longer or because surviving husbands would be assumed as heirs. Kaiser, "Women's Property," pp. 2–3. I would like to thank Daniel Kaiser for his helpful comments and for generously allowing me to use his unpublished work on women and property.

3. Muscovite aristocrats had so many friends, relatives, affines, and clients to choose from that blood alone did not serve as the unique determinant of association. Crummey, *Aristocrats and Servitors*.

4. Keenan, "Muscovite Political Folkways," esp. p. 132; Crummey, *Aristocrats and Servitors*; Kollmann, *Kinship and Politics*; Veselovskii, *Issledovaniia po istorii klassa sluzhilykh zemlevladel'tsev* and *Issledovania po istorii oprichniny*.

5. Robert Crummey makes the same point in "Origins of the Noble Official," p. 50. See also his *Aristocrats and Servitors*, pp. 68–69. For strict definitions of *family*, *clan*, and *lineage*, see Goody, *Development of the Family and Marriage*, pp. 222–39. In the Muscovite context, *rod* is generally translated as *clan*, as I am doing here, although such a translation does not match Goody's anthropological definition of a clan as the largest kinship unit having members who acknowledge common descent but do not know the exact genealogical nature of their ties. *Rod* matches more closely the terms *lineage*, a more restricted unit with an unambiguous membership linked by specific, known, genealogical ties.

6. For examples of provincial families' genealogies, see *RGADA f.* 210, *opis'* 18, *Rodoslovnye rospisi*, no. 53, *l.* 1 (Kablukovs), no. 29 (Bludovs), no. 54, *l.* 1 (Golenkiny). On genealogies in general, see Bychkova, "Iz istorii sozdaniia rodoslovnykh rospisei" and *Rodoslovnye knigi*.

7. *RGADA, f.* 210, *Prikaznyi stol, stlb.* 1151, *ll.* 55–60 v.

8. *SPbFIRI, f.* 252, *Suzdal'skie akty*, no. 16 (1657).

9. Bourdieu, *Outline of a Theory of Practice*, p. 35. Emphasis in original.

10. *RGADA, f.* 1112, *opis'* 1, no. 99 (1634).

11. Ludwig Steindorff finds similar patterns in his unpublished study "Donations, Charity, and Commemorations." My thanks to him for permission to cite this paper.

12. Hellie, *Muscovite Law Code*, chapt. 16, art. 34, p. 109.

13. *RGADA, f.* 1112, *opis'* 1, no. 116.

14. Ibid., no. 163.

15. Daughters were problematic in Western European practice as well, where formal systems of agnatic lineages often gave way in practice to the wishes of parents to secure their childrens' future by leaving their property to their direct descendants rather than their collateral kinsmen. Among others, see Cooper, "Patterns of Inheritance"; Goody, "Inheritance, Property and Women," pp. 10–36.

16. Kaiser, "Women, Property and the Law," p. 9. My thanks to him for allowing me to use this unpublished work. Kleimola, "In Accordance with the Canons," pp. 204–29. See also Vladimirskii-Budanov, *Obzor*.

17. Kleimola, "In Accordance with the Canons." On women's property

holding in medieval and early-modern Russia, see also Levy, "Women and the Control of Property."

18. *RNB, f.* 532, no. 668 (1630).

19. *RGADA, f.* 1112, opis' 1, no. 10 (1679).

20. *SPbFIRI, f.* 252, *Suzdal'skie akty*, no. 20.

21. *SPbFIRI, f.* 62, *Koll. Kablukova*, no. 170.

22. *SPbFIRI, f.* 252, *Suzdal'skie akty*, no. 27. The document containing this information, a rescript from the official confirmation of the transfer of title, leaves some uncertainty about whether this property comprised the entire inheritance or just one part of it.

23. *RGADA, f.* 1112, *opis'* 1, no. 133, 8 *ll.*

24. Ibid., no. 142.

25. *RNB, Ermitazhnoe sobranie*, no. 343/2, *l.* 29.

26. *RGADA, f.* 1112, *opis'* 1, no. 103 (1677). In Iur'ev, Alena Kipreianov split her late husband's *pomest'ia* with her late husband's brother, each getting half (150 *cheti*), but the widow also received an additional grant of 70 *cheti* to support her and her three children. *Pamiatniki delovoi pis'mennosti*, no. 10, pp. 21–23 (1632).

27. *RGADA, f.* 1112, *opis'* 1, no. 56.

28. Hellie, *Muscovite Law Code*, chapt. 16, arts. 30–32, p. 109.

29. *RGADA, f.* 1112, *opis'* 1, no. 63 (A) (1677).

30. The single clear exception was found in "Riadnaia rospis' pridanomu," pp. 269–70. Also possibly *RGADA, f.* 1112, *opis'* 1, no. 51 (1659).

31. *SPbFIRI, f.* 62, *Koll. Kablukova*, nos. 191, 225 (1683, 1685/86).

32. E.g., *RGADA, f.* 1112, *opis'* 1, no. 114 (1690).

33. Some of these documents were denied to me in 1986 on various grounds, primarily that they were too dilapidated to use, so I do not know if some of them record actual amounts of land given to each son. On the division of N. A. Kablukov's estate and the disputes over it, see *SPbFIRI, f.* 62, *Koll. Kablukova*, nos. 339, 340, 342, 343, 347, 349. On the average number of peasants, see Chapter 1.

34. *RGADA* f. 1112, *opis'* 1, no. 161. For other examples, see ibid., no. 2 (1683), no. 77 (1671); *VGV* (1858), no. 11.

35. Giles Fletcher, "Of the Russe Commonwealth," p. 145. Cf. the work of Marshall Poe, "Russian Despotism," who finds that the notion of "feudalism" similarly gave Western elites a sense of itself and of its rights and freedoms as opposed to other places, which were defined as nonfeudal and hence "barbaric."

36. See below, pp. 114–15.

37. *PSZ*, 1st series, vol. 5, no. 2789, pp. 91–94. Translation from Dmytryshyn, *Imperial Russia*, p. 16.

38. Collins, *Present State of Russia*, pp. 64, 68, 70.

39. The literature on Western European inheritance patterns is enormous, but surprisingly little has been written specifically on the gentry or lesser nobility. Most concentrates on either great lords or peasants. See, among others, Bush, *Rich Noble, Poor Noble*, esp. pp. 1–6, 30–45; J. P. Cooper,

"Patterns of Inheritance"; Klapisch-Zuber, *Women, Family, and Ritual*; Thirsk, "European Debate." On England, see Bonfield, *Marriage Settlements*; Slater, *Family Life in the Seventeenth Century*; Staves, *Married Women's Separate Property*; Stone and Stone, *An Open Elite?* pp. 105–47.

40. Aylmer, *Harborowe for faithfull and Trewe subjectes*; quoted in J. P. Cooper, "Patterns of Inheritance," p. 194.

41. I have modernized the English of this passage. Starkey, *A Dialogue Between Pole and Lupset*, pp. 73–74.

42. Alef, "Crisis of the Muscovite Aristocracy," pp. 34, 58. For other discussions of the effects of partible inheritance, see Keep, *Soldiers of the Tsar*, p. 45; Pipes, *Russia under the Old Regime*, pp. 41–42, 176–77; Raeff, *Origins*, pp. 16–17; Rozhdestvenskii, *Sluzhiloe zemlevladenie*, pp. 63–78; Uroff, "Kotoshikhin," pp. 70–71.

43. *Pamiatniki delovoi pis'mennosti*, no. 8, pp. 19–20.

44. *RGADA, f.* 1112, *opis'* 1, no. 93 (1647/48).

45. *SPbFIRI, f.* 62, *Koll. Kablukova*, no. 170. For similarly mysterious cases of disappearing landlords, see *RGADA, f.* 1112, *opis'* 1, no. 3 (1695), no. 68 (1672), *Pamiatniki delovoi pis'mennosti*, no. 6, pp. 17–18; *RNB, f.* 532, no. 302 (1625/26); *AIu*, no. 29.

46. *RGADA, f.* 210, *Vlad. stol., stlb.* no. 73, *l.* 229.

47. Ibid., *l.* 236. The 30 impoverished Suzdalians were P. P. Aleksin, I. K. Durnoi, L. G. and Z. G. Ershovskii, A. Golenkin, G. Ia. Iaryshkin, A. F. Kablukov, I. Ch. Karastilov, F. B. and F. M. Kazimerov, L. O., P. S., and S. I. Kolobov, M. Kolokoltsov, A. A., I., and L. P. Kozlov, I. G. and P. G. Miakishev, D. G. Molchanov, M. and P. Opranin, D. A. Sekerin, G. I. and I. G. Shafrov, I. Surovtsov, and four sons of Nikita Tregubov. The 18 Vladimirtsy were D. K. and I. R. Bakin, three sons of Maksim Balakirev, A. I. Basargin, O. V. Berechinkov, N. O. Bolotovskii, A. F. and I. Iazykov, F. B. Kuchin, two Nougorodovs, S. and V. Z. Pevtsov, A. L. Salmanov, P. G. Serbenin, and M. M. Simanov.

48. At military musters, *okladchiki* reported that former gentrymen had become bandits or slaves, had fallen into poverty or were serving in the lower-ranking service regiments as infantrymen or non-noble cavalrymen: *RGADA, f.* 210, *Dela desiaten'*, book 304, *ll.* 75, 78–78 ob, 80–81 ob (1648); *RGADA, f.* 210, *Vladimirskii stol, stlb.* 63, *ll.* 195, 211 (1664), *stlb.* 72, *ll.* 68, 79 (1636/37), *stlb.* 82, *l.* 43 (1637/38), book 4, *l.* 76 (1667/8); *RNB, Ermitazhnoe sobranie*, no. 343/2, *l.* 22 ob (1626); *AMG*, vol. 1, nos. 256, pp. 270–71.

49. These statistical means are derived from a pool of 718 men and women, 188 of whom held Moscow rank and 530 of whom held provincial rank. The information on these subjects dates from 1600 through 1700, with the least amount of data in the first 20-year period.

50. Hellie, *Enserfment*.

51. Not all historians agree about which laws favored which category. See Kaiser, "Women, Property and the Law"; Kleimola, "In Accordance with the Canons"; Kobrin, *Vlast' i sobstvennost'*; Weickhardt, "Pre-Petrine Law."

52. For an example of a young woman receiving her grandfather's earned

votchina as dowry, see *SPbFIRI, f. 21, Koll. Borisova,* no. 496, (1673). For an example of a father giving his daughter part of his earned *votchina* (in 1626, before the new law?), see *RNB, Ermitazhnoe sobranie,* no. 343/2, *l.* 29. In his property statement in 1632, Vasilii Alekseev Tepritskii claimed earned *votchina* land in Suzdal' that came to him from his father-in-law, and so through the female line; see Stashevskii, *Zemlevladenie,* no. 511, p. 202.

53. *SPbFIRI, f. 62, Koll. Kablukova,* no. 117 (1670). For other dowries specifying the transfer of manor houses and household plots to brides, see the Kazimerov-Lazarev marriage of 1673 (*SPbFIRI, f. 21, Koll. Borisova,* no. 496); Kablukov-Volkov marriage of 1683 (*SPbFIRI, f. 62, Koll. Kablukova,* no. 191); Rchinov-Sontsev Zasekin marriage, 1685/6 (*RGADA, f. 1112, opis'* 1, *ed. khr.* 83); Kazimerov-Oshanin marriage of 1681 (*VGV,* 1856, no. 29).

54. Kaiser, "Women's Property," p. 10.

55. *RGADA, f. 1112, opis'* 1, no. 67 (1700/1701). The other case is in *RGADA, f. 210, Vlad. stol, stlb.* 132, *l.* 86 (1648).

56. On clerical attitudes toward remarriage, see Levin, *Sex and Society* pp. 79–135. On legal statutes on property transfer and remarriage, see Hellie, *Muscovite Law Code,* ch. 17, arts. 1–2, 7–8, pp. 121–123, 124–25.

57. *SPbFIRI, f. 62, Koll. Kablukova,* no. 225.

58. *RGADA, f. 1112, opis'* 1, no. 165. For other examples of remarriage and expanded dowry, see also ibid., no. 17 (1696/97), no. 67 (1700/1701).

59. Ibid., no. 108 (1672).

60. Ibid., no. 106 (1691). Isai Petrovich Beklemishev is listed as a *striapchii* in 1675/76; *Alfavitnyi ukazatel',* p. 26.

61. Cases in which widows left land to male relatives in their own line (usually nephews) were more likely to be contested by their late husbands' relatives than were remarriage cases. For examples of women ceding property to their own male relatives, see *RGADA, f. 1112, opis'* 1, no. 77 (1671/72). See also ibid., no. 141 (1697), no. 139 (1690/91); *RNB, f.* 532, no. 486 (1641); *SPbFIRI, f. 21, Koll. Borisova,* no. 370 (1660).

62. *RGADA, f. 1112, opis'* 1, no. 99 (1634).

63. Author's data base; Stashevskii, *Zemlevladenie.* These figures do not necessarily represent the total landholdings of these 718 individuals.

64. Kaiser, "Women's Property," p. 10.

65. *SPbFIRI, f. 21, Koll. Borisova,* no. 496 (1673); *RNB, Ermitazhnoe sobranie,* no. 343/2, *l.* 29; Stashevskii, *Zemlevladenie,* no. 511, p. 202.

66. Klapisch-Zuber, *Women, Family, and Ritual,* pp. 117–31. Quote from 117.

67. Lockridge, *Sources of Patriarchal Rage.*

68. Grossman, "Feminine Images"; Kollmann, "Women's Honor," pp. 60–61; McNally, "From Public Person," pp. 102–41.

69. Because the sources that I examined all related to the five Vladimir-Suzdal' provinces, a potential bias towards endogamy may enter the equation. However, since I recorded *all* documented marriages involving any individual from the region, marriage out of or into the community should show up proportionally to actual occurrence.

70. The bride's maiden name and father or brothers can be established in 62 cases. In an additional 10 cases, widows remarried and their first husbands' names are recorded. In 4 cases, kinship through marriage is noted without listing any particulars of the relationship. Service with one of the five towns, evidence of land ownership in the area, or mention in documents of the region antedating the marriage here establish connection to a region. Information on the marriages is taken from the following: *RGADA, f.* 1112, *opis'* 1, nos. 10, 17, 44, 51, 55, 57, 63 (A), 63 (B), 67, 69, 77, 81, 103, 106, 107, 108, 111, 114, 131, 139, 142, 165, 166; *RGADA, f.* 210, *Prikaznyi stol,* no. 273, fols. 972–89 v; *SPbFIRI, f.* 62, *Koll. Kablukova,* nos. 51, 52–56, 63, 100, 117, 127, 138, 181, 191, 200, 225, 261; *SPbFIRI, f.* 21, *Koll. Borisova,* nos. 496, 553, 626; *RNB, f.* 532, nos. 447, 668, 829, 1717, 3055; *RNB, Ermitazhnoe sobranie,* no. 343/2, *l.* 29; *AIuB,* vol. 3, no. 334, pt. ix–x; Ikonnikov, *Noblesse de la Russe,* vol. Y, pp. 227–35; "Riadnaia rospis'"; *VGV,* 1856, no. 29.

71. Quoted in Iakovlev, *Prikaz sbora ratnykh liudei,* p. 71.

72. Kaiser finds that women donated more to the church than men did, but they gave primarily movable property; see "Women's Property," pp. 7–9.

73. *RNB, Ermitazhnoe sobranie,* no. 343/2, *ll.* 30–31. For other examples of surveys of women's landholding status, see *RNB, Muzeinoe sobranie, f.* 178, no. 1393, *ll.* 10–13 (1646, Suzdal').

74. *RNB, Ermitazhnoe sobranie,* no. 343/2, *l.* 21.

75. On the widow Lukeria Dolgovo-Saburova selling land to her brother N. A. Kablukov in 1689/90, see *SPbFIRI, f.* 62, *Koll. Kablukova,* no. 261. Lukeria's son traded pieces of land and peasants in Shuia with his uncle N. A. Kablukov according to a trade agreement, which is in ibid., no. 262 (1689/90). P. N. Kablukov's report on the previous owners of his peasants is found in *SPbFIRI, f.* 252, *Suzdal'skie akty,* no. 42 (1699). N. A. Kablukov's will left the village he had regained from the Dolgovo-Saburov relatives to his sons; see *SPbFIRI,* see *f.* 62, *Koll. Kablukova,* no. 349 (1699).

76. For the marriage agreement of Praskovia Pimenovna and Iu. A. Vysotskii, see *SPbFIRI, f.* 62, *Koll. Kablukova,* no. 187. For Vysotskii ceding his peasants to Kablukov, see ibid., no. 218.

Chapter Four

1. Braddick, "State Formation," p. 1.

2. Mann, *Sources of Social Power,* 1: 461–62.

3. Habermas, *Structural Transformation,* p. 3.

4. "1550 Sudebnik," art. 64, in Dewey, *Muscovite Judicial Texts,* p. 63: "And vicegerents shall [have jurisdiction to] try petty boyars in all cities in accordance with the general charters of grant [*zhalovannye vopchie gramoty*] of the Tsar and Sovereign which are now in force."

5. Governors were sometimes appointed by the Chancellery of Military Affairs and sometimes by the *chetverti.* Shumilov and Cherepnin, *Knigi moskovskikh prikazov,* pp. 13, 28.

6. For a convenient outline of the functions and chronological develop-

ment of the various chancelleries, see Brown, "Muscovite Government Bureaux." For more extensive coverage of the bureaux and of bureaucratic process, see his dissertation, "Early Modern Russian Bureaucracy." Kniaz'kov says that the judicial chancelleries judged cases involving not only military servitors but also their peasants and slaves. Kniaz'kov, "Sudnye prikazy." Most studies say that provincial servitors went to the Moscow Judicial Chancellery while those of Moscow rank went to the Vladimir Judicial Chancellery.

7. A series of decrees limited governors' interactions with local economies, and in 1672 governors were prohibited from owning land within their jurisdictions. *AAE*, vol. 3, no. 115, pp. 159–60. Chicherin, *Oblastnye uchrezhdeniia*, pp. 302–3. *PSZ*, vol. 1 no. 508, p. 875.

8. Davies, "Role of the Town Governors," p. 39; Novitskii, *Vybornoe i bol'shoe dvorianstvo*, p. 95.

9. Stashevskii argues that landholding could not support gentrymen adequately, mainly because of the severe lack of peasants to work the land. He suggests that administrative posts provided the mainstay of gentry economic survival. Stashevskii, *Zemlevladenie*, pp. 31–32.

10. *PSZ*, vol. 1, no. 295, pp. 528–29 (1661).

11. *RGADA, f. 210, Knigi zapisnye*, book 11, *l.* 8.

12. *RGADA, f. 210, Vlad. stol, stlb.* 132, *ll.* 148–148 ob.

13. *RGADA, f. 210, Prikaznyi stol, stlb.* 51, *l.* 543.

14. Chicherin, *Oblastnye uchrezhdeniia*, pp. 125–29; Gradovskii, *Istoriia*, p. 311.

15. Chicherin, *Oblastnye uchrezhdeniia*, pp. 127–28; Davies, "Role of the Town Governors," pp. 10–11, 138–39.

16. *RGADA, f. 210, Prikaznyi stol, stlb.* 740, *ll.* 18–23.

17. Ibid., *stlb.* 51, *ll.* 299–300.

18. Solov'ev, quoted in Kizevetter, *Mestnoe samoupravlenie*, p. 58 (no citation).

19. *RGADA, f. 210, Vlad. stol, stlb.* 146, *l.* 124 (1663/4).

20. *RGADA, f. 210, Prikaznyi stol*, no. 384, *ll.* 422–24 (1666).

21. *RGADA, f. 210, Vlad. stol, stlb.* 146, *ll.* 1, 36, 79.

22. Davies, "Role of the Town Governors," pp. 10–11, 138–39.

23. For example, see Kliuchevskii, *Kurs*, 3: 158–60; Kizevetter, *Mestnoe samoupravlenie*, pp. 58–70.

24. Kizevetter, *Mestnoe samoupravlenie*, pp. 53–71.

25. Borisov, *Opisanie* no. 39.

26. For instance, see *RGADA, f. 210, Prikaznyi stol, stlb.* 314, *ll.* 206–207 (Iur'ev Pol'skii, 1659/60); *RGADA, f. 210, Vlad. stol, stlb.* 33, *ll.* 304–306.

27. *RGADA, f. 210, Vlad. stol, stlb.* 142, *l.* 92, *l.* 50; *stlb.* 63, *l.* 162.

28. Solov'ev, *Istoriia Rossii*, vol. 13, chapt. 1.

29. *RGADA, f. 1112, opis'* 1, no. 130.

30. Ibid., no. 70.

31. *SPbFIRI, f. 21, Koll. Borisova*, no. 569.

32. For the standard view of the separation between governors and local gentry, see Kizevetter, *Mestnoe samoupravlenie*, pp. 58–59; Kliuchevskii, *Kurs*, 3: 158–60. An exception to the general trend among historians is Brian Davies, who notes that governors frequently favored supplicants on the basis of blood ties or patronage: "Role of the Town Governors," pp. 47–48. The same techniques were employed in France and in colonial New England to limit the connections of *intendants* and colonial governors to their subject populations.

33. Fletcher, "Of the Russe Commonwealth," p. 150.

34. Baron, *Travels of Olearius*, p. 177.

35. On the 1620 edict, see *AAE*, vol. 3, no. 115, pp. 159–60. On contracts, see Hellie, *Muscovite Law Code*, chapt. 20, art. 58 p. 177; *AI*, vol. 4, no. 209; *DAI*, vol. 3, no. 83; *PSZ*, no. 1579. See also Chicherin, *Oblastnye uchrezhdeniia*, p. 302.

36. *PSZ*, vol. 1, no. 508, p. 875.

37. The list of town governors linked by land, kinship, and service to one or more of the five towns in the region includes many of the most prominent names of the area: Kablukov, Kashintsov, Kazimerov, Koisarov, Sekerin, Obukhov, Prokudin, Alalykin, Roganovskii, Novokshchenov, Tregubov, and the princes Drutskoi. It is interesting to note that Iu. V. Got'e finds very similar figures in his study of provincial and town *voevody* in the second quarter of the eighteenth century. Just under one-third of those in his study served in the *uezd* adjacent to their own, while more governed in *uezdy* nearby but not adjoining the *uezd* where they had their permanent residence and owned property. Ten percent served in their own *uezdy*. Got'e explains that these figures are remarkable, since the government continued to issue edicts prohibiting *voevody* from administering their own provinces; *Istoriia oblastnogo upravleniia*, 1:221–23.

38. On the Volkovs in the sixteenth century, see Fomin, "Sotsial'nyi sostav," p. 93. On Karp and Stepan as *deti boiarskie*, see Khilkov, *Sbornik*, pp. 67–69. On Karp as *vybornyi*, see Storozhev, *Materialy*, p. 95; as *voevoda*, see *RGADA*, f. 210, *Vlad. stol*, stlb. 33, Barsukov, *Spiski*, p. 45. On F. A. Volkov's marriage to Kablukova (land document/dowry information), see *SPbFIRI*, f. 62, *Koll. Kablukova*, no. 225. For other examples of the Volkovs' continuing presence, see an agreement between two Volkov brothers in 1651/52 (*VGV*, 1876, no. 27) and an agreement with yet another brother in 1669 (*VGV*, 1876, no. 30).

39. *SPbFIRI*, f. 62, *Koll. Kablukova*, no. 298 (1690/91). On Kashintsov, see below, Chapter 5.

40. The Obukhovs were affiliated with Iur'ev Pol'skii at least since 1577, according to Rummel' and Golubtsov, *Rodoslovnyi sbornik*, 2: 194–205. On Obukhov's appointment, see *RGADA*, f. 210, *Vlad. stol*, stlb. 142, *l.* 47. On the Kuroedov-Obukhov case, *RGADA*, f. 210, *Prikaznyi stol*, no. 314, *ll.* 88–90.

41. *SPbFIRI*, f. 21, *Koll. Borisova*, no. 487.

42. Ibid., no. 569.

43. Bogoslovskii, *Zemskoe samoupravlenie*; Chicherin, *Oblastnye uchrezhdeniia*, pp. 449–504; Gradovskii, *Istoriia*; Keep, "Bandits"; Kizevetter, *Mestnoe samoupravlenie*; Nosov, *Ocherki po istorii mestnogo upravleniia*; Zimin, *Reformy Ivana Groznogo*, p. 255.

44. *PRP*, 4: 176–79; translation from Dewey, "Beloozero Anti-Brigandage Charter, October 23, 1539," in *Muscovite Judicial Texts*, p. 33.

45. Dewey, *Muscovite Judicial Texts*, p. 34.

46. Davies, "Role of the Town Governors," p. 24; Keep, *Soldiers of the Tsar*, pp. 29–30 and "Bandits," p. 221. Chicherin, *Oblastnye uchrezhdeniia*, p. 471, says that except for the post of *guba* elder, all elective positions were burdensome responsibilities. See also Kizevetter, *Mestnoe samoupravlenie*, pp. 43–52.

47. E.g., in 1663 the townspeople of Iur'ev Pol'skii complained that the governor had appointed *tseloval'niki*, or assistants to the elders (in this case tax-collection or *zemskie* officials rather than *guba*), instead of allowing the people to select them. *RGADA*, f. 210, *Vlad. stol, stlb*. 63, *ll*. 42–43. In 1613/14, the people of Shuia asked permission to select their own local judges to replace the corrupt governor who had been abusing the legal system. Borisov, *Opisanie*, no. 3, pp. 239–40. For another example of community preference for *guba* over *voevoda*, see *AMG*, vol. 2, no. 269, pp. 170–71.

48. Kishlansky, *Parliamentary Selection*, pp. 5–7, 73–101. Kishlansky attributes the change from selections to elections to the political divisions of the revolutionary period in England. For a very interesting discussion of the ideological prerequisites for representative government, see Major, *Estates General*, pp. 3–15.

49. Chicherin, *Oblastnye uchrezhdeniia*, p. 455; Hellie, *Muscovite Law Code*, chapt. 21, art. 4, p. 195.

50. Translation adapted from Hellie, *Muscovite Law Code*, chapt. 21, art. 4, p. 195.

51. By the 1660s and 1670s most of the gentrymen of the region could sign their own names. On literacy, see Stevens, "Belgorod."

52. See the statute book of the Office of Brigand Control, *PRP*, 4: 356–70, and texts in Iakovlev, *Namestnich'i, gubnye i zemskie ustavnye gramoty*.

53. For early dates of decline see Bogoslovskii, *Zemskoe samoupravlenie*; Bogoiavlenskii and Veselovskii, "Mestnoe upravlenie," p. 386. For a later estimate, see Demidova, "Gosudarstvennyi apparat," p. 132. Chicherin expresses contradictory views; *Oblastnye uchrezhdeniia*, pp. 451, 484.

54. *RGADA*, f. 210, *Prikaznyi stol, stlb*. 1434, *ll*. 348–49.

55. The formal abolition evidently engendered real changes in the administration of the provinces, as is clear from two petitions from Shuia governor Lopukhin of 1681. One notes the shift of jurisdiction in *guba* matters to the governor; the other notes that the *guba* building no longer serves any purpose and should be converted to some other use. Borisov, *Opisanie*, no. 59, pp. 365–68. On abolition in 1679, see *PSZ*, nos. 779, 219–20. On revival in 1684, see *PSZ*, no. 1062 (Feb. 18, 1684). On abolition in 1702, see Chicherin,

Oblastnye uchrezhdeniia, p. 147; *PSZ*, no. 1900 (March 10, 1702). For a good review of legislation, see Vladimirskii-Budanov, *Obzor*, pp. 195–98.

56. Hellie, *Muscovite Law Code*, chapt. 21, art. 3, p. 195. Cf. the charter of the *Razboinyi prikaz* in *PRP* 4:356–60.

57. Borisov, *Opisanie*, no. 4, pp. 241–42 (1613/14).

58. Ibid., no. 5, pp. 243–45 (1613/14).

59. *Pamiatniki delovoi pis'mennosti*, no. 115, p. 155.

60. Borisov, *Opisanie*, no. 12, pp. 263–64. Other extreme cases of *guba* corruption are found in *Pamiatniki delovoi pis'mennosti*, no. 111, pp. 152–53; *SPbFIRI, f.* 21, *Koll. Borisova*, no. 55; *RGADA, f.* 210, *Prikaznyi stol*, no. 314, *ll.* 88–90.

61. On routine business, see Borisov, *Opisanie*, no. 14, pp. 267–68 (1624); *SPbFIRI, f.* 21, *Koll. Borisova, f.* 21, no. 129 (1634). On the new corruption suit, see Borisov, *Opisanie*, no. 18, pp. 278–79.

62. On Liubim Vasil'evich, see *Pamiatniki delovoi pis'mennosti*, no. 153, pp. 179–80. On Semen in Iur'ev, see ibid., no. 4, pp. 15–16, no. 11, pp. 23–24. On Moisei, see *RGADA, f.* 210, *Vlad. stol, stlb.* 73, *l.* 460. On Semen Frolov, see *SPbFIRI, f.* 21, *Koll. Borisova*, nos. 184, 189.

63. *RGADA, f.* 210, *Belgorodskii stol, stlb.* 542, *ll.* 165–75. I am grateful to Nancy Kollmann for this reference.

64. On Temka Belenikhin, see *RNB, Ermitazhnoe sobranie*, no. 343/2, *l.* 25 v (1626). On Ivan Chertov, see *RGADA, f.* 210, *Prikaznyi stol*, no. 51, *ll.* 207–11 (1630). On Kishkins, see notes 61 and 62 above. On Aleksei Kuroedov, see *RGADA, f.* 210, *Vlad. stol, stlb.* 63, *ll.* 53–60. Kostentin Karpov Golenkin, *guba* elder in Vladimir in 1676, may have come from a family of poor *gorodovoi* and *dvorovoi deti boiarskie* from Suzdal', but he does not appear on the genealogy that family submitted to the Heraldic Chancellery in the 1680s. There the family claims that it has no kin in any other province. On Karp as elder, see *RGADA f.* 210, *opis'* 4, *Dela desiaten'*, book 291, *l.* 1 v. For the Golenkin genealogy, see *RGADA f.* 210, *opis'* 18, *Rodoslovnye rospisi*, no. 54.

65. *SPbFIRI, f.* 21, *Koll. Borisova*, no. 189.

66. On Abram as *voevoda*, see Barsukov, *Spiski*, p. 277; Borisov, *Opisanie*; *DAI*, vol. 5, no. 61. On Abram Mishukov as *dvorovoi*, see *RGADA, f.* 210, *Vlad. stol, stlb.* 40, *l.* 116; as *vybornyi*, see ibid., *stlb.* 82, *l.* 21; as *guba* elder, see ibid., *stlb.* 116, *ll.* 367–68. On his marriage to M. Kablukova, see *SPbFIRI, f.* 62, *Koll. Kablukova*, nos. 51–56. On Danilo as *zhilets*, see *RGADA, f.* 210, *Dela desiaten'*, book 291, *l.* 53 v; *SPbFIRI, Koll. Kablukova*, no. 142. On his marriage to a Kablukova, *Koll. Kablukova*, no. 138.

67. Gradovskii, *Istoriia*, pp. 23–28. Enthusiastic descriptions of local self-government are found in Slavophile writings, e.g., Beliaev, *Lektsii po istorii russkago zakonodatel'stva*, pp. 40–43.

68. Nosov, *Stanovlenie*, 527–37. Other Soviet writers display the same viewpoint, e.g., Bogoiavlenskii and Veselovskii, "Mestnoe upravlenie," p. 384; Eroshkin, *Istoriia gosudarstvennykh uchrezhdenii*, p. 45.

69. Torke, *Die staatsbedingte Gesellschaft*, Chapter 4. Keep says that

although established for governmental reasons, the *guba* system initially had "a certain popular flavour which it lost when it later became bureaucratised." See "Bandits," p. 204.

70. Dewey, "Charters," pp. 16–20.

71. Pocock, "Virtue, Rights, and Manners," p. 41.

72. On participation through advice in Muscovy, see Rowland, "Problem of Advice."

73. Braddick, "State Formation," p. 2.

74. Beik, *Absolutism and Society*, p. 99. See also Armstrong, "Old-Regime Governors." For a different view, see Giesey, "State-Building in Early Modern France," esp. pp. 197–98, n. 14. Also on the dual nature of local officials, as representatives of the state and of the locals, see, e.g., Major, "Noble Income," pp. 21–48; Mann, *Sources of Social Power*, 1: 461–62; Parker, "French Absolutism, the English State," esp. p. 298, and "Social Foundations of French Absolutism," pp. 67–89.

Chapter Five

1. On new feudalism, see Major, "Crown and Aristocracy."

2. Mann, *Sources of Social Power*, 1: 458.

3. Kettering, *Patrons, Brokers, and Clients*, p. 5. See also Mann, *Sources of Social Power*, 1: 32, 436.

4. S. N. Eisenstadt describes this as an inherent contradiction faced by "historical bureaucratic empires" in his *Political Systems of Empires*, pp. 22–25; see also Abrams, *Historical Sociology*, pp. 182–83.

5. Weber, *Economy and Society*, 3: 974–75; Giddens, *Capitalism and Modern Social Theory*, pp. 159–60.

6. Armstrong, "Old-Regime Governors."

7. Cf. Beik's description of France: "Personal ties were central to the functioning of seventeenth-century absolutism on every level of government and remained so throughout the period. They provided contacts between institutions as well as the means to assure that petitions would be favorably received, law suits would be brought to a satisfactory conclusion, and expressions of support would be generated in the proper places at the proper times." Beik, *Absolutism and Society*, p. 243.

8. On the secular servitors of the monastic and patriarchal institutions, see Liutkina, "Gosudarstvo."

9. On Kurbatov as clerk in the Suzdalian governor's office, see *RGADA*, f. 210, *Prikaznyi stol*, no. 993, *ll.* 35–107 (1666). For his listing as secretary of the Chancellery of Service Lands from 1671/72 to September 1672 and again in 1682, see Veselovskii, *D'iaki i pod'iachie*, p. 278.

10. *Pamiatniki delovoi pis'mennosti*, no. 257, p. 250. Veselovskii, *D'iaki i pod'iachie*, p. 170, lists Evstaf'ev as a *d'iak* first in 1672, so the correspondence most likely dates from the 1670s.

11. *Pamiatniki delovoi pis'mennosti*, no. 261, pp. 252–53. Fefanov served as *d'iak* at the Printing Office in 1672/73, confirming the date of the corre-

spondence; Veselovskii, *D'iaki i pod'iachie*, p. 546. Veselovskii, p. 34, lists Pavel Mikhailovich "Astaf'ev" (Ostaf'ev) as a *dumnyi d'iak* in 1683/84 and 1687/88; he presumably occupied a somewhat lower office a decade earlier. Emel'ian Telitsyn was a *pod'iachii* active in the 1670s (Veselovskii, p. 511). The Belin family's friendship with the Telitsyns is evident in their visits to each others' houses in Suzdal' in *Pamiatniki delovoi pis'mennosti*, no. 264, p. 254.

12. *Pamiatniki delovoi pis'mennosti*, no. 260, pp. 251–52.

13. Ibid., no. 264, p. 254.   14. Ibid., no. 261, pp. 252–53.

15. *Gramotki*, no. 213, p. 116.   16. Ibid., no. 210, pp. 114–15.

17. Ibid., no. 213, p. 116.

18. Four delegates to Assemblies of the Land had houses in Moscow: Ivan Stepanov Brattsov, Savva Zakhar'ev Iazykov, Ivan Grigor'ev Miakishev, Ivan Karpov Nemtsov. Campbell, "Composition," pp. 252, 276, 304, 310.

19. *Gramotki*, no. 144, p. 80.

20. Ibid., no. 260, p. 141.

21. On difficulty of establishing lines of patronage, see Crummey, *Aristocrats and Servitors*, pp. 82–83.

22. A hint of such a relationship between Bogdan Miachin and Ia. K. Cherkasskii is found in *SPbFIRI, f. 21, Koll. Borisova*, no. 281. See also suggested links between P. G. Kashintsov and A. Matveev, this chapter.

23. *Pamiatniki delovoi pis'mennosti*, no. 262, p. 253.

24. Torke, "Continuity and Change," p. 472.

25. For a sample of petitions complaining about administrative and judicial corruption from the Vladimir-Suzdal' region, see *RGADA, f. 210, Vlad. stol, stlb. 33, stlb. 63, ll. 23 ff., 53, 76–111; Prikaznyi stol, stlb. 1434, ll. 302–05; RGADA, f. 1112, opis' 1, no. 103; SPbFIRI, f. 21, Koll. Borisova*, nos. 11, 234, 487, 553, 556, 557; *f. 62, Koll. Kablukova*, no. 211; *RNB, f. 532*, no. 3595; *Pamiatniki delovoi pis'mennosti*, no. 108, p. 151, no. 111, pp. 152–53, no. 115, p. 155. On nationwide petitions against corruption, see Chapter 7.

26. Davies, "Politics of Give and Take," p. 12. My thanks to Brian Davies for permission to cite this unpublished work.

27. Russia was not alone in picturing a heavenly hierarchy analogous to the secular bureaucracy. On Chinese parallels between the supernatural and imperial bureaucratic hierarchies, Duara writes, "It was as if, by co-opting the hierarchical symbolism of the supernatural, the imperial state extended its authority through the ritual medium into village society." Duara, *Culture, Power, and the State*, p. 34.

28. Information on rank comes from the case itself and from *Alfavitnyi ukazatel'*, p. 169.

29. Petr Kashintsov's sureties on June 6, 1677, were Ignatei and Petr Fedorovich Parfen'ev (both *striapchie*), Vasilii Petrovich Fedorov (*striapchii*), Ivan Rodionov Chirikov (*zhilets*), Andrei Ivanovich Narmatskoi (*striapchii*), Nikon Iur'ev Karapiperov (*striapchii*), Alferii Sergeev Stroev (*striapchii*), Fedor Fedorov Ivanov (*zhilets*), Petr Iakov Bastanov (*zhilets*), Fedor Priklonskoi (*zhilets*), and Gavrilo Iur'ev Aksakov-Moskva. Of these, Chirikov,

Aksakov-Moskva, and Bastanov came from established Suzdal' families, but of these three men, only P. Ia. Bastanov appears personally in other Suzdalian documents. Aksakov's hyphenated name emphasizes his Moscow affiliation.

30. Even Petr's widowed mother accumulated a bad record, although at a later date. In 1699 the bailiff of a Suzdal' landlord accused her bondsmen of having beaten him up. See *SPbFIRI, f. 21, Koll. Borisova,* no. 668. On the grandfather and the priest, see ibid., no. 97 (which document was denied me at the archive). On the brothers' misconduct, see ibid., *no.* 233 (1649/50); *RGADA, f. 210, Vlad. stol, stlb.* 159, *l.* 17 (1675); Borisov, *Opisanie,* no. 58: 362–64 (1682). On the father's abuses, see *SPbFIRI, f. 21, no.* 204 (1643); Borisov, *Opisanie,* no. 41, pp. 330–31 (1666).

31. *SPbFIRI, f. 21, Koll. Borisova,* no. 553.

32. Ibid.

33. On poultry theft, see *Pamiatniki delovi,* no. 185, pp. 203–4 (1681/82).

34. Townspeople, of course, may have had a very different impression of him than did his peers in the province. A few local gentrymen did sign for him, as noted above.

35. Borkov's sureties were *pod'iachii* of the Chancellery of the *Sytnyi Dvor* (Beverage Court) Ivan Andreev, *striapchii* of the *Sytnyi Dvor* Mikhail Ivanovich Borkov (his son?), *puteinyi kliuchnik* (supervisor) of the *Khlebennyi Dvorets* (Grain Court) Lev Petrovich Kruglikov, *striapchii* of the *Sytnyi Dvor* Konstentin Fedorovich Borkov (relation?), *zhilets* Andrei Fedorov Zakharin, *puteinyi kliuchnik* Nikifor Fedorovich Borkov (relation?), *stol'nik* Ofonasii Denisovich Fanvisin-Moskva, Boris Shcherbachev, *stol'nik* Aleksandr Vasil'evich Lepunov.

36. *RGADA, f. 210, Prikaznyi stol,* no. 740, *ll.* 4–65; *SPbFIRI, f. 21, Koll. Borisova,* nos. 510, 553; Borisov, *Opisanie,* no. 54, pp. 352–54 (1677).

37. *Alfavitnyi ukazatel',* p. 179; *SPbFIRI, f. 62, Koll. Kablukova,* no. 298.

38. *SPbFIRI, f. 21, Koll. Borisova,* no. 553.

39. Ibid.

40. See Eisenstadt's general observations on the activities of gentries in traditional-bureaucratic empires in *Political Systems of Empires,* p. 206.

41. Among the "top families" I include those with members holding Moscow rank, or at least the highest provincial ranks (selectmen, *okladchiki*), and distinguished by wealth and influence locally.

42. *SPbFIRI, f. 62, Koll. Kablukova,* nos. 30, 47 (dividing estate), 44 (wrecking fields), 42 (arbitration).

43. Ibid., no. 309; *RGADA, f. 210, Prikaznyi stol,* no. 863, *ll.* 118–38.

44. *SPbFIRI, f. 62, Koll. Kablukova,* no. 63.

45. Ibid., nos. 63, 113, 131, 181, 196, 211, 212, 213, 241, 242.

46. On Kablukov, see ibid., no. 306 (1692). On Volzhinskii, see *RGADA, f. 210, Vlad. stol, stlb.* 159, *l.* 34. On the monk, *SPbFIRI, f. 21, Koll. Borisova,* no. 82.

47. *SPbFIRI, f. 21, Koll. Borisova,* no. 99 (1630).

48. *RGADA, f. 210, Prikaznyi stol, stlb.* 740, *l.* 10.

49. Ibid.

50. *RGADA, f.* 1112, *opis'* 1, no. 165 (1692). This phrase could be interpreted as a bid for contiguous property with the goal of consolidating landholdings, but the context of previous hostilities lends it the sense I have given it in translation. See also Kolechenikova, "K voprosu o sosedakh." For other cases concerning trespassing and neighborly enmity, see *SPbFIRI, f.* 21, *Koll. Borisova,* nos. 315, 317 (1652); *f.* 62, *Koll. Kablukova,* no. 43; *RGADA, f.* 210, *Vlad. stol, stlb.* 60, *l.* 153 (1641); Borisov, *Opisanie,* no. 2, pp. 234–38.

51. *SPbFIRI, f.* 62, *Koll. Kablukova,* nos. 160, 162, 183, 275, 332, 334, 336; *Gramotki,* nos. 210–13, pp. 114–16.

52. *Gramotki,* no. 212, p. 115.

53. *SPbFIRI, f.* 62, *Koll. Kablukova,* no. 169, no. 221, no. 252, *l.* 1 (undated), no. 334 (which document was denied me because it was "dilapidated"); *Gramotki,* no. 211, p. 115.

54. Letter written jointly with Lev Zvorykin. *Gramotki,* no. 213, p. 116; *SPbFIRI, f.* 62, *Koll. Kablukova,* no. 332, *ll.* 1–1 v. "*A po tom tebe gsdr' malo pishem a mnogo chelom b'em da litsa zemnaga.*"

55. *Gramotki,* no. 210, pp. 114–15.

56. In some contexts, *zakup* can mean hired laborer, but in the context of patronage it clearly connotes people who have been bribed or bought off.

57. Obrazets Afanas'evich Kablukov was Aleksei's third cousin once removed: *SPbFIRI, f.* 62, *Koll. Kablukova,* no. 22 (1643/44), no. 25 (1644/45). Afanasii Il'ich was his third cousin: *SPbFIRI, f.* 252, *Suzdal'skie akty,* no. 16 (1657). See Figure 2.6.

58. Hellie, *Slavery.*

59. *Khrebet* means spine or spinal column in modern Russian. For use of the term see *SPbFIRI, f.* 21, *Koll. Borisova,* no. 184 (1639/40): "Tsar's order to the *gubnoi starosta* of Shuia to send to Moscow all masons and brickmakers, both monastic and those living with townspeople as *zakhrebetniki.*"

60. *VGV,* 1862, no. 43.

61. Crummey, *Aristocrats and Servitors,* p. 106.

62. Major, "Crown and Aristocracy," pp. 635–36. Another difference from the Western model described by Major is that Muscovite clients did not follow their patrons to battle; military recruitment and service for members of the nobility was all organized at the national level on an individual basis. Wealthy landholders were expected to provide extra armed men, but their retinues were generally composed of slaves.

63. *SPbFIRI, f.* 21, *Koll. Borisova,* no. 136. For other examples, see F. A. Mishukov's suit against V. G. Kozynskii's sons for beating his peasants in ibid., no. 398 (1662); *stol'nik* S. V. Sobakin's and *zhilets* N. A. Kablukov's suit and countersuit for beating each other's peasants and stealing each other's horses in *RGADA, f.* 210, *Vlad. stol, stlb.* 159, *l.* 35 (1677). See also *SPbFIRI, f.* 21, *Koll. Borisova,* nos. 214, 372; *RGADA, f.* 210, *Vlad. stol, stlb.* 60, *l.* 153; *VGV,* 1857, no. 28.

64. Hellie, *Muscovite Law Code,* chapt. 10, arts. 122, 138–41, pp. 42, 48–50. Most of these articles refer to slaves or *liudi* (people) rather than peasants.

65. For another case in which the authorities tried to hold peasants as substitutes for their master, see *RGADA, f.* 210, *Prikaznyi stol., stlb.* 273, *ll.* 972–89.

66. *SPbFIRI, f.* 21, *Koll. Borisova,* no. 167 (1637). For more on Shalimov's feuds with his neighbors, see ibid., nos. 135 (1634), 212 (1644), 217 (1644).

67. *VGV,* 1857, no. 28.

68. Hellie, *Muscovite Law Code,* chapt. 10, art. 1, p. 23. The same wording was used well before the 1649 *Ulozhenie.* For instance, a clerk took an oath of office in Lukh in 1631 promising not "to favor a friend or take vengeance on an enemy or to favor anyone in anything." *RGADA, f.* 210, *Prikaznyi stol,* no. 51, *l.* 284.

69. "Vladimirite Boris Serbin called their father's uninhabited *pomest'e* Mikhailevo by another name, 'Serkovo,' and the village and cultivated fields of Grigor'evo [he called] *pustosh'* [uninhabited plot] 'Okulino.'" His supporters are called "*khleboiazhtsy, zakupaiachie, druz'ia.*" *RGADA, f.* 1112, *opis'* 1, no. 15.

70. Hellie, *Muscovite Law Code,* chapt. 10, art. 161, p. 56.

71. *SPbFIRI, f.* 21, *Koll. Borisova,* no. 320. For another illustrative case see *RGADA, f.* 1112, *opis'* 1, *ed. khr.* 103, *ll.* 4–5.

72. *RGADA, f.* 210, *Prikaznyi stol,* no. 993, *ll.* 1–107.

73. Veselovskii, *Prikaznyi stroi,* p. 22.

74. My thanks to Dan Kaiser, who posed these questions in his response to an earlier draft.

75. Kollmann, "Honor and Dishonor"; Crummey, "Reflections on *Mestnichestvo.*"

76. According to David Bien, a similar contradiction arose in France in the eighteenth century. In the pursuit of professionalization, French nobles, like Muscovites, believed that "sons succeeding fathers in the same occupations . . . was a good thing in itself. Generally it was best to recruit from professional 'insiders,' from families where the flow of helpful impressions was already established at home." Bien, "Aristocracy," and "Army in the French Enlightenment."

77. Das, "History Writing," pp. 508–09. Kollmann argues, contrary to all accepted wisdom about Muscovite culture, that the society had traditionally placed a high value on individual worth, as evident in the practice of suing for dishonor. See her "Honor and Dishonor," esp. pp. 143, 145–46.

78. Das, "History Writing," p. 508, no. 30. Das refers to similar transformations in the aristocratic cultures of Western European courts. See also Bien, "Army in the French Enlightenment"; J. M. Smith, "Culture of Merit."

79. *Pskovskaia sudnaia gramota,* pp. 132–78. Translation from Weickhardt, "Due Process," p. 467.

Chapter Six

1. See *Gramotki,* nos. 45, 59–62, 114–16, 144, 203, 210–14, 259, 445–46; *Pamiatniki delovoi pis'mennosti,* nos. 256–323, pp. 249–88.

2. See James C. Scott's concept of "hidden transcripts" in his *Domination and the Arts of Resistance*.

3. See Dewey, *Muscovite Judicial Texts*, arts. 8–11, pp. 48–49.

4. Ibid., art. 15, p. 50. On judicial duels, see Dewey, "Trial by Combat." On the risks of being a witness, see Kaiser, *Growth of the Law*, pp. 128–48. On ordeals, see Kaiser, *Growth of the Law*, pp. 148–52.

5. Berry and Crummey, *Rude and Barbarous Kingdom*, p. 177.

6. Baron, *Travels of Olearius*, p. 227. Baron notes that Olearius was wrong about the lack of laws prior to the *Ulozhenie*, but Olearius' qualitative impression of change surely was accurate. In 1671 Samuel Collins still insisted that the Russians had "very few written laws." *Present State of Russia*, p. 43.

7. Adapted from Hellie, *Muscovite Law Code*, chapt. 10, art. 217, p. 70.

8. Klokachev's peasants countersued, accusing Tret'iakov of beating them, chasing them with a saber (which he claimed he did not have at the time), and threatening them. *SPbFIRI, f.* 21, *Koll. Borisova*, nos. 315, 317 (1652).

9. *RGADA, f.* 210, *Prikaznyi stol*, no. 993, *l.* 26.

10. Ibid., *stlb.* 273, *ll.* 972–89.   11. Ibid., *l.* 975.

12. Ibid., *ll.* 981.   13. Ibid., *l.* 982.

14. Ibid., *l.* 983.

15. Ibid., *l.* 986. Miachin's sureties were *suzdal'tsy* (Suzdal' gentrymen) Fedor Ivanov Chelishchev-Moskva, Mikita Ivanov Karpov, Osip Borisov Karpov, Mikhail Borisov Kolokol'tsov, Mikifor Kalistov Kozynskii, and Suzdal' *zhilets* Sotnik Kalistov Kozynskii.

16. Ibid., *ll.* 988–89.

17. Ibid., *l.* 986.

18. *SPbFIRI, f.* 21, *Koll. Borisova*, no. 320. Zakharii is called a *sotnik* or regimental captain in the document. Most *sotniki* in my sample were simultaneously listed as selectmen.

19. In 1648, just three years before the first incident, Bogdan appeared on the Suzdalian muster roll as a *gorodovoi syn boiarskii z gorodom* with a service compensation rate of 350 *cheti; RGADA, f.* 210, *opis'* 4, *Dela desiaten'*, book 304, *l.* 63 v.

20. *RGADA, f.* 210, *Prikaznyi stol*, no. 314, *l.* 88 (1658/59).

21. Ibid., *ll.* 206–7 (1659/60).

22. Ibid., no. 561, *ll.* 598–600.

23. *RGADA, f.* 210, *Vlad. stol, stlb.* 146, *ll.* 165–75.

24. Describing provincial administration in the eighteenth century, John LeDonne writes that the men who filled local administrative posts "determined the limits of power." "Orders were executed if they fell within the 'zone of acquiescence' which the personal interests of these men and the collective experience of their communities had gradually defined and kept defining in response to external challenges." *Ruling Russia*, p. 54.

25. Scott, *Weapons of the Weak*. For a pointed critique of Scott's ideas, see Ortner, "Resistance."

26. The results described here certainly are shaped in part by the sources available. In addition to scattered references, I have extensive lists of *netchiki* from 1629 (20 *netchiki*), 1640/41 (35), 1644 (11), 1645 (53), 1648 (35), and 1674 (12). *AMG*, vol. 1, nos. 233, 256 (1629); *RGADA, f.* 210, *Vlad. stol, stlb.* 73, *ll.* 98–140 (1640/41); *RGADA, f.* 210, *Prikaznyi stol,* no. 585, *ll.* 87–90 (1644); *RGADA, f.* 210, *Vlad. stol, stlb.* 116, *ll.* 225–27 (1645); *RGADA, f.* 210, *opis' 4, Dela desiaten',* book 304, *ll.* 21–86 (1648); *AMG,* vol. 2, no. 458 (1650/51).

27. *RGADA, f.* 210, *Vlad. stol, stlb.* 72, *l.* 76.

28. Ibid., *stlb.* no. 63, *l.* 149 (1663). Another young man combated a false charge of *netstvo* by proving that he was not evading service in Iur'ev but instead was serving dutifully from the Smolensk lists. *RGADA, f.* 210, *Prikaznyi stol,* no. 863, *ll.* 118–38 (1659), no. 161, *ll.* 38–42 (1644).

29. *AMG,* vol. 1, no. 256, pp. 270–71.

30. *RGADA, f.* 210, *Vlad. stol, stlb.* 63, *l.* 211. In a similar case during the July 1648 muster in Vladimir, *okladchiki* excused the absences of fourteen men who initially had been listed as truants: one was serving as town governor elsewhere, one was serving in a state chancellery, one was in a monastery, ten were in active duty along the southern frontier, and for one the local witnesses simply asserted that he had a legitimate excuse. *RGADA, f.* 210, *opis' 4, Dela desiaten',* book 304, *ll.* 5–5 ob, 7, 8 ob, 19 ob–23 ob, 25.

31. *RGADA, f.* 210, *Vlad. stol, stlb.* 63, *l.* 211 (1664); *RGADA, f.* 210, *opis' 4, Dela desiaten',* book 304, *l.* 23 ob (1648).

32. *RGADA, f.* 210, *Vlad. stol, stlb.* 73, *l.* 133; *RGADA, f.* 210, *opis' 4, Dela desiaten',* book 304, *l.* 22.

33. *RGADA, f.* 210, *Vlad. stol, stlb.* 116, *l.* 226; *RGADA, f.* 210, *opis' 4, Dela desiaten',* book 304, *ll.* 55, 79.

34. Prince S. S. Gundarov, I. S. and Ia. S. Elchaninov were judged too poor to serve; *RGADA, f.* 210, *Vlad. stol, stlb.* 116, *l.* 226; *RGADA, f.* 210, *opis' 4, Dela desiaten',* book 304, *ll.* 81–83. Semen Pavlov was judged too sick to serve; *RGADA, f.* 210, *opis' 4, Dela desiaten',* book 304, *l.* 76 ob; *RGADA, f.* 210, *Vlad. stol, stlb.* 115, *l.* 24, *stlb.* 116, *l.* 226.

35. On V. A. Lazarev as *netchik,* see *RGADA, f.* 210, *opis' 4, Dela desiaten',* book 304, *ll.* 82 ob–83 (1648); as a seven-year-old in 1637/38, see *RGADA, f.* 210, *Vlad. stol, stlb.* 82, *l.* 51; as a Moscow *dvorianin,* see *RGADA, f.* 210, *opis' 4, Dela desiaten',* book 291, *l.* 51 ob; *Alfavitnyi ukazatel',* p. 223.

36. *AMG,* vol. 1, no. 256, pp. 270–71.

37. On A. F. Kablukov, see *RGADA, f.* 210, *Prikaznyi stol,* no. 863, *ll.* 118–38. On I. F. Shafrov, see *RGADA, f.* 210, *Vlad. stol, stlb.* 73, *l.* 460.

38. *RGADA, f.* 210, *Prikaznyi stol,* no. 585, *ll.* 87–90.

39. On the supposedly high level of absenteeism, see Chistiakova, *Gorodskie vosstaniia,* p. 21; Hellie, *Enserfment,* pp. 216, 218–19, Iakovlev, *Prikaz sbora ratnykh liudei,* p. 82. In the south, where conditions were even harsher, absenteeism was apparently much higher.

40. E.g., Aleksei Ivanov Golenkin and Fedor Mikhailov Zabelin, both of Suzdal', were transferred from the list of minors (*nedorosli*) to service ranks "by petition" in 1644/45; *RGADA, f.* 210, *Vlad. stol, stlb.* 115, *l.* 27. For other petitions to enter service ranks, see *RGADA, f.* 210, *Bezglasnyi stol*, no. 177, *ll.* 135–37, 208a–11, 217–22 (1695); *RGADA, f.* 210, *Vlad. stol, stlb.* 116, *l.* 316 (1644).

41. *RGADA, f.* 210, *Vlad. stol, stlb.* no. 132, *ll.* 58, 125 (1648).

42. E.g., ibid., *stlb.* no. 73, *l.* 206 (Suzdal', 1642/43); *RGADA, f.* 210, *Prikaznyi stol*, no. 161, *ll.* 38–42 (Iur'ev Pol'skii, 1644).

43. In one such case, M. I. Maslov received a charter converting 40 *cheti* in Kostroma and Vladimir Provinces from *pomest'e* to *votchina*; *RNB, f.* 532, no. 2895 (1682).

44. *AMG*, vol. 1, no. 182. See also nos. 183, 184, pp. 197–99.

45. *RNB, Ermitazhnoe sobranie*, no. 343/2, *ll.* 12 ob–13 ob.

46. *RGADA, f.* 210, *opis'* 4, *Dela desiaten'*, book 304, *l.* 5. On selectmen and *okladchiki*, see Novosel'skii, "Praviashchie gruppy," pp. 316, 322–23, 325–27.

47. Of the 38 *okladchiki* recorded from the Vladimir-Suzdal' area between 1627/28 and 1651/52, 27 were selectmen. Of the remainder, 7 were *dvorovye deti boiarskie* and came from large, well-established local families. *RGADA, f.* 210, *opis'* 4, *Dela desiaten'*, book 304, *ll.* 5–10, 24 ob, 45–57 (1648); *RGADA, f.* 210, *Vlad. stol, stlb.* 72, *ll.* 58–79 (1637/38), *stlb.* 33 (1628), *stlb.* 73, *ll.* 234–39, *stlb.* 101, *ll.* 16, 17, 20; *SPbFIRI, f.* 62, *Koll. Kablukova*, no. 43 (1652).

48. *SPbFIRI, f.* 62, *Koll. Kablukova*, no. 43. See also Novosel'skii, "Praviashchie gruppy," p. 327.

49. For examples, see Campbell, "Composition," p. 46.

50. Of the remaining three, one was a foreigner, one was unknown, and one, B. S. Pivov of Lukh, was a lowly *gorodovoi syn boiarskii* who, strangely enough, served twice, in 1648 and 1653. For a list of men who attended the 1642 assembly, see Got'e, *Akty*, pp. 39–46. For 1648, see Tikhomirov and Epifanov, *Sobornoe Ulozhenie*, pp. 424–31. For 1651, see V. I. Latkin, *Materialy*, pp. 92–128. For 1653, see Kozachenko, "K istorii," pp. 223–27. Additional information on ranks derives primarily from muster rolls and may be found in *RGADA, f.* 210, *Vlad. stol*, book 4, *ll.* 68 ob, 77; *RGADA, f.* 210, *Vlad. stol, stlb.* 60, *l.* 153, *stlb.* 72, *ll.* 58, 59, 60, 64, 68, 78, 79, *stlb.* 82, *l.* 23, *stlb.* 101, *ll.* 1, 16, 18, *stlb.* 115, *ll.* 1, 2, 9, 17, 19, 30, 32, *stlb.* 132, *l.* 4, *stlb.* 40, *ll.* 10, 35, 93, 96; *RGADA, f.* 210, *opis'* 4, *Dela desiaten'*, book 304, *ll.* 19 ob, 20, 45, 49, 217 ob, 218; *RNB, Ermitazhnoe sobranie*, no. 343/2, *l.* 10. Delegates to Assemblies of the Land from all of Muscovy share these characteristics. See Campbell, "Composition" (esp. his useful appendix with names and biographical information on the individuals who attended Assemblies of the Land: pp. 238–362); Novosel'skii, "Praviashchie gruppy," p. 334.

51. *RGADA, f.* 210, *Prikaznyi stol*, no. 51, *ll.* 340–43 ob.

52. *AMG*, vol. 2, no. 20, p. 9.

53. *RGADA, f.* 210, *Vlad. stol, stlb.* 63, *l.* 23 ff.

54. *RGADA, f.* 210, *Prikaznyi stol,* no. 784, *ll.* 91–97 (Nov. 9, 1678, and Jan. 16, 1679), no. 819, *ll.* 125–28 (Jan. 10, 1682).

55. There were 62 signers, including 14 of the 42 who had signed the 3 earlier petitions about Manat'in. Families and rank profiles were very much the same. *RNB, Sobranie Zinchenko, f.* 299, no. 1017.

56. Novosel'skii, "Feodal'noe zemlevladenie," pp. 152–53.

57. Novosel'skii, "Raspad." The Soviet (and now Russian) use of the terms *corporation* and *service city* exaggerate the formal, institutional nature of gentry communities. On the term *gorod* (city), see Sakharov, "O termine 'gorod'."

58. Even without a systematic examination of sixteenth-century sources, I find that 20 percent of those elevated to Moscow rank after 1665 had kinsmen in the region prior to 1605, which leads me to believe that with further investigation a sizable fraction of the families concerned could be dated back that far.

59. Moscow-rank families with enduring local ties in the Vladimir-Suzdal' region included Bolotovskiis, Fefilatevs, the princes Gundarov, Kazimerovs, Khmetevskiis, Kochiukovs, Kolobovs, Kolokoltsovs, Koriakins, Korobovs, Lazarevs, Simanovs, Taneevs, Tepritskiis, Voronovs, the princes Boriatinskii, Bratsovs, Buturlins, Iaryshkins, Izmailovs, Ketevs, Kozlovskii princes, Kruglikovs, Lodygins, Molvianinovs, Oshanins, Pushkins, and Tolstois.

60. *RGADA, f.* 210, *opis'* 5, *Smotrennye knigi,* no. 55, *l.* 1.

61. Ibid., *ll.* 1–75. The reference to Kuzminskii is on *l.* 25 ob.

62. Ibid., *ll.* 76–174 ob. My emphasis.

63. On consolidation, see Chapter 2.

64. An illustration of this principle is seen in the strategem of Fedosia Kopteva, who traded her dowager's *pomest'e* in Iaroslavl' *uezd* for a *votchina* property in Vladimir *uezd* but retained the option of removing the peasants from the Iaroslavl' estate and relocating them where she pleased; *RNB, f.* 532, *Obshchee sobranie,* no. 1062 (Vladimir, 1677). On *votchina* and *pomest'e* see Got'e, *Zamoskovnyi krai,* pp. 393–94, 416–20, 428; Kuznetsov, "Svetskoe feodal'noe zemlevladenie," pp. 12–14; Rozhkov, *Sel'skoe khoziaistvo,* pp. 448–55. Zimin found, on the contrary, that *pomest'ia* were no less profitable for landlords than were *votchiny; pomest'ia* labor regimes were simply harder on the peasants; see his "O politicheskikh predposylkakh." For the *Ulozhenie* statutes on the two kinds of property, see Hellie, *Muscovite Law Code,* chapts. 16 (Service Lands), 17 (Hereditary Estates), pp. 103–40.

65. On enserfment, see Chapter 7; Hellie, *Enserfment.*

66. *RNB, f.* 299, *Sobranie Zinchenko,* no. 1017 (1686); *RNB, f.* 532, *Obshchee sobranie,* no. 2018 (1673); *VGV,* 1879, no. 51 (1635); *SPbFIRI, f.* 62, *Koll. Kablukova,* nos. 17 (1642), 27 (1645), 169 (1680/81), 221 (1686), 337 (1696); *SPbFIRI, f.* 21, *Koll. Borisova,* nos. 169 (1638), 433–34, 442 (1666), 607

(1685/86); *Pamiatniki delovoi pis'mennosti*, no. 109, p. 152 (1614), no. 188, p. 210 (1688); Borisov, *Opisanie*, no. 2, pp. 234–38 (1606).

67. On honor in Muscovy, see Kollmann, "Honor and Dishonor"; Crummey, "Reflections on *Mestnichestvo*"; Dewey, "Old Muscovite Concepts of Injured Honor."

68. Berry and Crummey, *Rude and Barbarous Kingdom*, p. 145.

69. Baron, *Travels of Olearius*, p. 221.

70. *SPbFIRI, f. 62, Koll. Kablukova*, nos. 30, 31, 47.

71. Ibid., nos. 17, 42.

72. Ibid., no. 30. On laws concerning arbitration, see the 1637 law in *AAE*, no. 277, pp. 420–21; the 1649 law, Hellie, *Muscovite Law Code*, chapt. 15, art. 5, p. 102.

73. *SPbFIRI, f. 62, Koll. Kablukova*, no. 63 (1660).

74. On issues of women's honor, see Kollmann, "Women's Honor."

75. Kollmann's study of the role of honor in Muscovite society in the sixteenth and seventeenth centuries confirms that physical assault alone did not constitute dishonor. An added ingredient of verbal or symbolic indignity distinguished dishonor complaints from ordinary suits over assault or physical offense. She derives these findings from a collection of 617 cases; "Honor and Dishonor," p. 139.

76. *SPbFIRI, f. 21, Koll. Borisova*, no. 487. Other than those described below, see *SPbFIRI, f. 62, Koll. Kablukova*, nos. 41, 115, 197, 216.

77. Khilkov, *Sbornik*, no. 54, pt. 2, p. 146. Kollmann finds a "rash of cases for dishonor caused by scribal error from the 1660s and 1670s"; "Honor and Dishonor," n. 63.

78. Kollmann, "Honor and Dishonor," p. 142.

79. *VGV*, 1876, no. 27. Aleksei Kablukov sued O. F. Bolotnikov in 1651/52 for swearing at him and dishonoring his wife and children; *SPbFIRI, f. 62, Koll. Kablukova*, no. 40.

80. *SPbFIRI, f. 62, Koll. Kablukova*, no. 208.

81. *SPbFIRI, f. 62, Koll. Kablukova*, no. 323.

82. Hellie, *Muscovite Law Code*, chapt. 7, art. 32, chapt. 10, arts. 27–99, pp. 17, 29–36.

83. *SPbFIRI, f. 62, Koll. Kablukova*, no. 43.

84. *RGADA, f. 210, opis' 4, Dela desiaten'*, book 304, l. 79 ob.

85. Ibid., l. 76 ob.

86. *RGADA, f. 210, Vlad. stol, stlb.* 115, l. 24, *stlb.* 116, l. 226.

87. Khilkov, *Sbornik*, no. 54, pt. 1, pp. 145–46. For other examples of slanderous accusations of nonservice, see *RGADA, f. 210, Vlad. stol, stlb.* 73, l. 206 (1642/43), l. 460; *RGADA, f. 210, Prikaznyi stol*, no. 161, ll. 38–42.

88. Arendt, *On Violence*, p. 44; Habermas, "Hannah Arendt's Communications Concept of Power," pp. 4–5.

89. Mann, *Sources of Social Power*, 1: 7.

90. P. Anderson, *Lineages*, p. 41.

91. Ibid., p. 212.

Chapter Seven

1. Material in this and the following chapter originally appeared in Kivelson, "Devil Stole His Mind."

2. For instance, the Vladimir gentry's instructions to its delegate to the Assembly of the Land in June 1648 discusses abolition of the statute of limitations on the recovery of runaway peasants, reform of the judicial system, and abolition of tax-exempt districts. *SPbFIRI, Sobranie Artem'eva,* no. 2.

3. Marshall Poe explores the intellectual genealogy of this idea in his dissertation, " 'Russian Despotism.' "

4. Recent works that look seriously at the vocabulary and imagery used in Muscovite literature and in court ritual include Bushkovitch, "Epiphany Ceremony"; Flier, "Breaking the Code" and "Iconology of Royal Ritual"; Kollmann, "Pilgrimage"; Rowland, "Biblical Military Imagery" and "Muscovite Literary Ideology."

5. See discussion of this debate in Nosov, *Zakonodatel'nye akty,* pp. 6–9.

6. Crummey, "Court Spectacles," p. 137. See also Kollmann's evidence of collective rule in an earlier period (to 1547), in her *Kinship and Politics.*

7. Rowland, "Problem of Advice," p. 279.

8. Rowland, "Artist's View of Politics," p. 2. Divine selection did not entail a concept of tsar as a divinity, which would have been considered heretical. Divine right did not enter Russian political theory until the eighteenth century. See Baehr, *Paradise Myth,* pp. 14–40; Whittaker, "Reforming Tsar."

9. Rowland, "Problem of Advice," pp. 271–72.

10. *AMG,* vol. 2, no. 264, pp. 167–68; Novombergskii, *Slovo i delo gosudarevy,* no. 211, pp. 369–72.

11. Nosov, *Zakonodatel'nye akty,* no. 76, p. 84.

12. Ibid., no. 87, p. 95.

13. Hellie, *Muscovite Law Code,* pp. 1, 2.

14. I. L. Andreev, "Sil'nye liudi"; Hellie, *Enserfment* pp. 48–74, 123–40; Smirnov, "Chelobitnyia."

15. Ditiatin, *Rol' chelobitii.*

16. For the petition of February 25, 1608, see *PRP,* vol. 4, pp. 377–79, 403–4; *AI,* vol. 2, no. 85, pt. 2. For that of 1611, see *PSRL (Novyi letopisets),* vol. 14, p. 112. For that of 1614/15 (which may not refer to a collective petition), see Nosov, *Zakonodatel'nye akty,* no. 76, p. 84. For that of 1619, see Nosov, *Zakonodatel'nye akty,* no. 87, pp. 94–95.

17. *PSRL (Novyi letopisets),* vol. 14, p. 112.

18. Smirnov, "Chelobitnyia"; Novosel'skii, "Kollektivnye dvorianskie chelobit'ia po voprosam mezhevaniia," pp. 103–8, and "Kollektivnye dvorianskie chelobitnye o syske beglykh krest'ian," pp. 303–43; Storozhev, "Dva chelobit'ia," pp. 8–15.

19. For the earlier decades, no signatures or parallel petitions from particular local regions survive, but the 1648 instructions to the Vladimir dele-

gate repeat the primary concerns of the earlier decades. *SPbFIRI, Sobranie Artem'eva*, no. 2. After midcentury, lists of gentrymen who signed the petitions give ample evidence of participation from the Vladimir-Suzdal' region. Novosel'skii, "Kollektivnye dvorianskie chelobit'ia po voprosam mezhevaniia" and "Kollektivnye dvorianskie chelobitnye o syske beglykh krest'ian."

20. Smirnov, "Chelobitnyia," pp. 38–41.

21. Ibid., pp. 41–47.

22. I. L. Andreev, "Sil'nye liudi," p. 83.

23. Ibid.

24. Ibid.

25. According to Smirnov, the February 1637 petition, probably the first of its kind, requested the complete elimination of the statute of limitations, but Stashevskii notes that one of the two petitions submitted at that time requested lengthening rather than abolishing the limit on recovery period. I prefer Smirnov's reading. Smirnov, "Chelobitnyia," p. 8; Stashevskii, *K istorii dvorianskikh chelobitnykh*, p. 8.

26. Stashevskii, *K istorii dvorianskikh chelobitnykh*, p. 20. For a slightly different reconstruction of the text, see Smirnov, "Chelobitnyia," p. 38. It is important to remember that although the pathos of the gentry's language and the outright nastiness of the bullying "strong people" may engage the sympathies of the reader, the property in question here was human beings, whose freedom neither side took into account.

27. *SPbFIRI, Sobranie Artem'eva*, no. 2.

28. I. L. Andreev, "Sil'nye liudi," p. 77.

29. Smirnov, "Chelobitnyia," pp. 14–15.

30. Ibid., pp. 49–50. This petition also survives only in fragments incorporated into official responses.

31. Hellie, *Enserfment*, p. 134. I. L. Andreev asserts that the state intended to fulfill its promise; "Sil'nye liudi," pp. 84–85.

32. *SPbFIRI, Sobranie Artem'eva*, no. 2.

33. I. L. Andreev, "Sil'nye liudi," p. 85.

34. This version is a seventeenth-century English translation; Loewenson, "Moscow Rising"; p. 153.

35. Baron, *Travels of Olearius*, p. 209.

36. On the distribution of monetary grants to provincial servitors in Vladimir, Suzdal', Iur'ev Pol'skii, and Lukh, see *RIB*, vol. 10, pp. 428–39, 445–47, 476–83.

37. Chistiakova, *Gorodskie vosstaniia*, pp. 98–99.

38. Bazilevich, *Gorodskie vosstaniia*, p. 40 (Pommerening). Chistiakova cites an interesting document from December 1649, which she describes as the final report on the investigation into the rebellion. It lists people charged with "stealing" and "knavery," but a note on the back mentioning "musketeers who agitated" ties it to the rebellion. Hence Chistiakova's evidence confirms Pommerening's that rebels were not charged directly with mutiny. Chistiakova, *Gorodskie vosstaniia*, pp. 100–1.

39. Shakhmatov, "Chelobitnaia," p. 11; Smirnov, "Chelobitnyia," pp. 50, 59. Smirnov is probably right when he speculates that the original would have included the more conventional listing of all ranks of people: "Moscow *dvoriane,* and *zhil'tsy,* and *dvoriane* and *deti boiarskie* of various towns, and foreigners, and leading merchants, and merchants of all and various guilds and tax-exempt trading people."

40. Vysotskii, treating the Smirnov and Shakhmatov versions as a single document, says that it must have been written by someone from high church circles: "Kollektivnye dvorianskie chelobitnye," p. 136. It does contain more religious imagery than previous gentry petitions but clearly represents gentry conceptions and interests.

41. Smirnov, "Chelobitnyia," pp. 50–60. Smirnov also published the Swedish version; ibid., pp. 61–65. It is also available in English in Hellie, *Readings,* pp. 198–205.

42. Ellersieck, "Russia Under Aleksei Mikhailovich," pp. 6–29, 79–89. My thanks to David Ransel for this reference.

43. The instructions paraphrase Psalm 72, as do the Pommerening and Shakhmatov petitions. *SPbFIRI, Sobranie Artem'eva,* no. 2.

44. Edward L. Keenan, personal communication, September 28, 1991. Chistiakova also thinks they are the same; *Gorodskie vosstaniia,* pp. 78–79. See Shakhmatov's argument for the distinctiveness of the two; "Chelobitnaia,".pp. 5–6. A debate continues in the literature about the precise dating of the various petitions. See Hellie, *Enserfment,* pp. 135–36; Smirnov, "O nachale Ulozheniia," p. 45; Chistiakova, *Gorodskie vosstaniia,* p. 78.

45. Shakhmatov, "Chelobitnaia," p. 20; Smirnov, "Chelobitnyia," p. 60. For earlier petitions, see also, Stashevskii, *K istorii dvorianskikh chelobitnykh,* pp. 20–21; Smirnov, "Chelobitnyia," pp. 38–60. For an English version of the 1637 petition, see Hellie, *Readings,* pp. 167–76, esp. p. 171.

46. Ibid.

47. Ibid., p. 39. My emphasis.

48. Ibid., p. 43. On p. 13 Smirnov suggests that the 1641 petitioners probably envisioned the same proposal for local selection of judges, which somehow dropped out of the surviving account of it.

49. Shakhmatov, "Chelobitnaia," p. 20; Smirnov, "Chelobitnyia," p. 60. For earlier petitions, see also, Stashevskii, *K istorii dvorianskikh chelobitnykh,* pp. 20–21; Smirnov, "Chelobitnyia," pp. 38–60. For an English version of the 1637 petition, see Hellie, *Readings,* pp. 167–76, esp. p. 171.

50. Smirnov, "Chelobitnyia," p. 60.

51. Ibid., pp. 9–10.

52. Bazilevich, *Gorodskie vosstaniia,* p. 74 (*Sbornik* of Leningrad Public Library). The story is confirmed in Pommerening's account of Pleshcheev's malfeasance (Ibid., pp. 38–39), and in Olearius. See Baron, *Travels of Olearius,* p. 205.

53. Bakhrushin, "Moskovskoe vosstanie 1648," p. 49; Baron, *Travels of Olearius,* pp. 203–14.

54. Shakhmatov, "Chelobitnaia," p. 18. During the uprisings of 1662 and 1682, rebels accused "strong people" of corruption in almost identical terms.

55. Ibid., p. 13.

56. Hellie, *Enserfment.*

57. Smirnov considers this passage, from a 1642 petition, closer to the original text of the 1648 petition than Pommerening's scrambled Swedish version. Smirnov, "Chelobitnyia," p. 53, n. 39, quotes *SGGiD*, vol. 3, no. 113. The Shakhmatov text is very similar to the 1642 version; "Chelobitnaia," p. 13. This same complaint of grandeur above their station was leveled against coiners and metal smiths in 1662; Uroff, "Kotoshikhin," pp. 188–89.

58. Smirnov, "Chelobitnyia," p. 53; Shakhmatov, "Chelobitnaia," p. 13.

59. Demidova, "Prikaznye liudi XVII v.," p. 347. See also Zimin, "O slozhenii prikaznoi sistemy."

60. Marker, *Publishing*, p. 19.

61. Shakhmatov, "Chelobitnaia," p. 15.

62. Ibid., p. 18. Emphasis added.

63. Smirnov, "Chelobitnyia," p. 43.

64. For an entertaining discussion of this phenomenon, see Perrie, *Image of Ivan the Terrible*.

65. Smirnov, "Chelobitnyia," pp. 51–54. Translation taken in part from Hellie, *Readings*, pp. 199–200.

66. In 1641, and perhaps in 1619, the gentry had requested that the government *establish* a boyar commission as an appeals court in order to remove appeals in cases against "strong people" from the jurisdiction of the corrupt chancellery courts. Nosov, *Zakonodatel'nye akty*, no. 87, p. 95; Smirnov, "Chelobitnyia," pp. 42, 43, 45, 46. By 1648 the petitioners had given up on the idea of a boyar court of appeals, although the Vladimir petition still retained that concept. *SPbFIRI, Sobranie Artem'eva*, no. 2.

67. Smirnov, "Chelobitnyia," p. 60. The Shakhmatov petition also promised that when the boyars were removed from service in the Supreme Judicial Commission (*Raspravnaia Palata*) "all [their time would be free] for their own domestic administration." Shakhmatov, "Chelobitnaia," p. 20.

68. Hellie, *Muscovite Law Code*, ch. 10, art. 2, p. 23. The Vladimir gentry had endorsed this solution in late June 1648 in its instructions to its delegate to the Assembly of the Land. *SPbFIRI, Sobranie Artem'eva*, no. 2.

69. See Kaiser, *Growth of the Law*.

70. Smirnov, "Chelobitnyia," p. 42.

71. Ibid., p. 39. Emphasis added.

72. Ibid., p. 43.

73. *SPbFIRI, Sobranie Artem'eva*, no. 2.

74. On the compilation of the *Ulozhenie*, see Hellie, "Ulozhenie Commentary—Preamble," and Smirnov, "O nachale Ulozheniia."

75. Smirnov, "Chelobitnyia," p. 57.

76. Ibid., p. 57.

77. Ibid., p. 56; translation modified from Psalm 72, *Orthodox Study Bible*, pp. 692–93. Where the Smirnov text says, "*Iako izbavi nishcha ot silna*," ("For He will deliver the needy *from the powerful*"), the Psalm translation reads, "For He will deliver the needy when he cries."

78. The Vladimir gentry's instructions to the assembly delegate uses passages from the same Psalm, to similar effect: "And the Sovereign would

establish among us his righteous judgment. . . . And the sovereign's name would be acclaimed in all surrounding countries and kingdoms because truth would be established by him after many years." *SPbFIRI, Sobranie Artem'eva,* no. 2. Cf. Psalm 72, *Orthodox Study Bible,* p. 693.

79. Shakhmatov, "Chelobitnaia," pp. 18–19. Other reports confirm that the petitioners called for a meeting with the tsar, not for a law code; see Smirnov, "Neskol'ko dokumentov," p. 6. See also Pommerening's comparable report in Bazilevich, *Gorodskie vosstaniia,* pp. 37–38.

80. Eventually S. V. Berechinskii was chosen as Vladimir's delegate. Campbell, "Composition, Character and Competence," pp. 247–48. On the Berechinskii family, see *Tysiachnaia kniga,* pp. 155, 157; *RGADA, f.* 210, *Vlad. stol, stlb.* 40, *ll.* 35 (1630), *stlb.* 73, *l.* 238, *stlb.* 82, *l.* 2 (1638), *stlb.* 101, *ll.* 11, 31 (1639/40), *stlb.* 115, *ll.* 9, 33 (1644/45).

81. The Vladimirites must have used the earlier petitions as their model in composing this one. Cf. passages in the Shakhmatov petition predicting that "all pestilence will decrease and your kingdom will last for ages and expand, and the earth will give abundant fruits in due time"; Shakhmatov, "*Chelobitnaia,*" p. 17. The themes, again, come from Psalm 72.

82. Smirnov, "Neskol'ko dokumentov," p. 6.

83. Ibid. Two separate assemblies met in the wake of the uprising, first in July and then in September 1648. The latter remained in session for many months while the law code was worked out fully.

84. Smirnov, "Chelobitnyia," pp. 45, 46.

Chapter Eight

1. Shakhmatov, "Chelobitnaia," p. 12. See also Smirnov, "Chelobitnyia," p. 51. Emphasis added.

2. Hellie, *Muscovite Law Code,* chapt. 10, art. 20, p. 27.

3. Ibid., chapt. 1, arts. 8–9, p. 4. Prohibitions on petitioning the tsar directly were repeated periodically, presumably without success, at least until 1767. For instance, see *PSZ,* no. 1092 (1684).

4. The sources are unclear about whether the tsar himself refused the petition on June 2 or whether his musketeer bodyguard or even his boyar entourage was responsible. Pommerening says that "his tsarist majesty himself did not want to accept the petition himself" (Bazilevich, *Gorodskie vosstaniia,* p. 35). The anonymous Swede is vague on the subject: "Not only was [the crowd] not heard out, but the musketeers even chased them away with shots" (ibid., p. 53). The Leyden Brochure says that "the Bojates, environing his imperiall Majestie, got these petitions, tore ye same not onely into pieces, flung the pieces into the petitioners faces, rayling at them mightilie" (Loewenson, "Moscow Rising of 1648," p. 153).

5. The refusal of petitions triggered the 1648 Tomsk uprising and also figured prominently in complaints leveled against Patriarch Nikon. On Tomsk, see Pokrovskii, "Nachal'nye chelobitnye" and "Sibirskie materialy," esp. p. 48.

6. Terdiman, *Discourse/Counter-Discourse.*
7. Shakhmatov "Chelobitnaia," p. 14.
8. Smirnov, "Chelobitnyia," p. 54.
9. Quoted in Kliuchevskii, *Kurs,* vol. 3. Translation from Kliuchevsky, *Course in Russian History,* p. 346.
10. Smirnov, "Chelobitnyia," p. 56.
11. Ibid., p. 54.
12. Shakhmatov, "Chelobitnaia," p. 15. See also Smirnov, "Chelobitnyia," p. 55. Although this passage uses a standard trope to lay some of the blame on evil advisers, it points out that these hated administrators and advisers have almost succeeded in their task of alienating the tsar himself from his people, thus making him part of the problem.
13. Smirnov, "Chelobitnyia," p. 57.
14. Ibid., pp. 55–56.
15. Ibid., p. 55. The Vladimir gentry's instructions to the 1648 Assembly of the Land delegate contain a similarly subtle condemnation of the tsar. If the sovereign would follow the Vladimirites' suggestions, all would praise him for establishing justice "after many years." This final phrase indicates that for many years, including the present, justice has not been well served. *SPbFIRI, Sobranie A. M. Artem'eva,* no. 2.
16. Thanks to Dan Kaiser for this observation.
17. Smirnov, "Chelobitnyia," pp. 56–57.
18. Shakhmatov, "Chelobitnaia," pp. 19–20. Also Smirnov, "Chelobitnyia," pp. 59–60.
19. See Rowland, "Muscovite Literary Ideology," pp. 125–55; Lotman and Uspenskij, "Role of Dual Models," pp. 3–35. Cherniavsky makes a strong case using this biblical dualism in views of the tsar to explain the intensity of the church schism that divided Russian Orthodoxy in the late seventeenth and early eighteenth centuries ("Old Believers and the New Religion").
20. Iakovlev, *Prikaz sbora ratnykh liudei,* p. 36.
21. P. Anderson, *Lineages.*
22. Avrich, *Russian Rebels,* pp. 50–130; Buganov, "O sotsial'nom sostave"; Khodarkovsky, "Stepan Razin Rebellion."
23. In my understanding of the nature of resistance, a number of works have been particularly useful: Burke, "Reactionary Rebels?" F. Cooper, "Dialectics of Decolonialization"; Guha, "Prose of Counter-Insurgency"; Kelley, "'We Are Not What We Seem'" and "Archaeology of Resistance"; Ortner, "Resistance"; Scott, *Weapons of the Weak* and *Domination and the Arts of Resistance.*
24. Much of the material in this discussion comes from Kollmann, "Transformations." See also Hughes, *Russia and the West* and *Sophia;* Volkov, "Ob otmene mestnichestva." There was a prior tradition of miniature illustrations in histories, chronicles, and saints' lives, which sometimes came close to secular art.
25. Volkov, "Ob otmene mestnichestva."
26. Hellie, "Material Culture."

27. On the new Monasterial Chancellery, see Hellie, *Muscovite Law Code*, chapt. 13, pp. 95–97; on the prohibition against working on Sundays, see ibid., chapt. 10, art. 26, p. 29. See also Kollmann, "Transformations," pp. 19–20.

28. *PSZ*, vol. 1, no. 453, p. 825; Kollmann, "Transformations," p. 20.

29. Hellie, *Muscovite Law Code*, chapt. 10, arts. 281–84, pp. 84–85.

30. *PSZ*, vol. 2, no. 1181; Kollmann, "Transformations," pp. 20–21.

31. Brown, "Early Modern Russian Bureaucracy"; Demidova, *Sluzhilaia biurokratiia*.

32. Kollmann notes that in the 1660s the boyar council, which had met informally with the tsar for centuries, found itself institutionalized with set hours for consultation with the tsar. The hours during which state secretaries should work were also established by law. "Transformations," p. 20; *PSZ*, vol. 1, nos. 237, 461, 582, vol. 2, no. 621.

33. Novosel'skii, "Kollektivnye dvorianskie chelobitnye o syske," p. 321.

34. Ibid., pp. 342–43; Novosel'skii, "Pobegi krest'ian," p. 343.

35. Novosel'skii, "Kollektivnye dvorianskie chelobitnye o syske," p. 323.

36. Vysotskii, "Kollektivnye dvorianskie chelobitnye," p. 133.

37. Novosel'skii, "Kollektivnye dvorianskie chelobitnye o syske," p. 314.

38. Ibid., pp. 320, 325.

39. *RGADA, f. 210, Vlad. stol, stlb. 142, l. 110.*

40. Novosel'skii, "Pobegi krest'ian," p. 334.

41. Novosel'skii, "Kollektivnye dvorianskie chelobitnye o syske," p. 314.

42. Ibid., p. 331.

43. Both Novosel'skii and Storozhev print the petition from the landholders of Galich and other towns, but both note that the *dvoriane* and *deti boiarskie* of "borderland and central Russian towns" submitted an identical petition in the same year. Storozhev, "Dva chelobit'ia," pp. 8–10; Novosel'skii, "Pobegi krest'ian," p. 328, and "Kollektivnye dvorianskie chelobitnye o syske," pp. 305–6 (from which the passage in quotes was taken).

44. Novosel'skii, "Kollektivnye dvorianskie chelobitnye o syske," p. 311.

45. Ibid., pp. 308, 310.

46. Ibid., p. 309. On cadasters, see Veselovskii, *Soshnoe pis'mo*. For a useful historiographic overview, see Kochin, "Pistsovye knigi."

47. Novosel'skii, "Kollektivnye dvorianskie chelobitnye o syske," p. 309.

48. Ibid., p. 332. Elsewhere the same petition describes cases similar to those that I have categorized in Chapter 6 as hyperlegalist: in employing laborers, people "claim they live with them on hire as workers according to the decree."

49. Novosel'skii, "Kollektivnye dvorianskie chelobit'ia po voprosam mezhevaniia," p. 106. On boundary demarcation processions see Dewey and Kleimola, *Russian Private Law*, pp. 83–89.

50. Novosel'skii, "Kollektivnye dvorianskie chelobitnye o syske," pp. 337–38.

51. Kollmann, "Honor and Dishonor," p. 142.

52. For the laws that regulated the production of official documents, see

Hellie, *Muscovite Law Code*, chapt. 4, pp. 9–10. Instead of encouraging orderly control over provincial backwaters, the emphasis on the written word gave rise to its own genre of confrontation and negotiation between provincial servitors and representatives of the state. For Suzdalian examples of "white collar crime," abuse of official documents, see *RGADA, f.* 210, *Prikaznyi stol, stlb.* 384, *ll.* 422–24 (1667), *stlb.* 788, *ll.* 113–35 (1678). I am grateful to Nancy Kollmann for this reference.

53. Thompson, *Whigs and Hunters*, pp. 265–69.

54. Novosel'skii, "Kollektivnye dvorianskie chelobitnye o syske," p. 317. For a discussion of government policy on deterrents and fines, see Novosel'skii, "Pobegi krest'ian," and for summary of legislation, see Novosel'skii, "Kollektivnye dvorianskie chelobitnye o syske," pp. 342–43.

55. Novosel'skii, "Pobegi krest'ian," p. 332.

56. Another 51 seem likely candidates. Novosel'skii, "Kollektivnye dvorianskie chelobitnye o syske."

57. Novosel'skii, "Pobegi krest'ian," pp. 348–50.

58. Ibid., p. 349.

59. Ibid., p. 348.

60. Novosel'skii, "Kollektivnye dvorianskie chelobit'ia po voprosam mezhevaniia," p. 105.

61. Ibid., p. 107. Gentry landholders had been asking for a new census since 1648, as evident in the Vladimirites' instruction to their delegate to the Assembly of the Land in June of that year: "He is to speak about the peasant years and firmly demand that the sovereign order census books without statute of limitations." *SPbFIRI, Sobranie Artem'eva*, no. 2.

62. Novosel'skii, "Kollektivnye dvorianskie chelobit'ia po voprosam mezhevaniia," p. 107.

63. Other studies have very fruitfully examined the gentry's consolidation as an estate and its interactions with other classes, subclasses, and the state. Therefore, I have chosen not to discuss these issues here. See I. L. Andreev, "Sil'nye liudi" and "Urochnye leta"; Hellie, *Enserfment*; Kosheleva, "Kollektivnye chelobit'ia"; Vysotskii, "Kollektivnye dvorianskie chelobitnye," pp. 134, 138.

64. Novosel'skii, "Kollektivnye dvorianskie chelobitnye o syske," p. 305.

65. Ibid., p. 319.

66. Magnates could transgress and bully "without apprehension and without any kind of fear, because there is not a single prohibition from you, Sovereign, nor does any guilt lie on them." Ibid., pp. 309, 316.

67. Ibid., p. 306.

68. Storozhev, "Dva chelobit'ia," pp. 10–15; Novosel'skii, "Kollektivnye dvorianskie chelobitnye o syske," pp. 308–13.

69. Novosel'skii, "Kollektivnye dvorianskie chelobitnye o syske," pp. 312, 310.

70. Ibid., pp. 310, 335.

71. Volkov, "Ob otmene mestnichestva," p. 57.

72. Vysotskii, "Kollektivnye dvorianskie chelobitnye," pp. 137–38.

Conclusion

1. Lotman and Uspenskij, "Role of Dual Models."

2. Skocpol, *Bringing the State Back In.*

3. For instance, see David Bien on the rise of corporate bodies in the early-modern, rather than medieval, period and the state's reliance on them: "Offices, Corps, and a System of State Credit" and *"Secrétaires du Roi."*

4. In his study of Russian administration in the eighteenth century, LeDonne describes the remarkable "absorption of the procuracy by local society and the undermining of its chief activity as guardian of the law, its transformation into yet another source of patronage"; *Ruling Russia,* p. 78. Cf. Mann, *Sources of Social Power,* 1: 458.

5. Kollmann, *Kinship and Politics;* Bychkova, "Idei vlasti"; Nazarov, "Genealogiia Koshkinykh-Zakhar'inykh-Romanovykh"; Kleimola, "Who We Are or Who We Wish We Were."

6. At the NEH conference on cultural identity in a multicultural state in Los Angeles, March 1994, Maurene Perrie raised the question of how to measure the success of a dynasty's rule. Is the mere fact of the 300-year survival of the Romanov monarchy sign enough of success? I would say that the Romanovs did more than merely survive. They managed to construct a powerful state machine, bolstered by effective legitimizing myths, which successfully extracted resources, conducted wars, and defended Muscovy's status domestically and internationally. This is not an insignificant measure of success, given the rate at which neighboring states (notably Poland) folded during these centuries.

7. There are a few exceptions. Paul Bushkovitch, *Religion and Society,* suggests that an internal, moral, individual spirituality had arisen in the late seventeenth century that prepared the ground for Peter's church reforms.

8. J. M. Smith writes that Louis XIV's phrase *"L'état, c'est moi"* was emblematic of his regime not because of his megalomania but because it suggests that he promoted an ethic of state service that was framed largely in traditionally personal terms. Of Louis's practice of broadcasting his image (as Peter the Great did), Smith writes, "By routinizing his own presence, Louis XIV would build on a central assumption of the 'personal' modality of service." See J. M. Smith, "Culture of Merit," pp. 96–97, 125, 128–30. On Peter's image as tsar-transformer or tsar-savior, see Whittaker, "Reforming Tsar."

9. Eighteenth-century playwright Denis I. Fonvizin satirized both the backward obscurantism of the *glushch'* (provincial backwaters) and the ignorant ostentation of people who grasped too eagerly at all that was new. For example, see Fonvizin, *The Minor,* p. 91. See also Romanovich-Slavatinskii's description of gradual change in *Dvorianstvo,* pp. 9–11.

10. Troitskii, *Russkii absoliutizm.*

11. Bolotov, *Zhizn',* p. 5.

12. On the state of Muscovite historiography in the late seventeenth century, see Das, "History Writing." Isolated Muscovite individuals left autobio-

graphical and biographical sketches. Avvakum, for instance, left his remarkable autobiography, and *someone* wrote the Ivan-Kurbskii correspondence. B. N. Morozov is currently working on some autobiographical material written by a late-sixteenth-century clerk. Daniel Kaiser has informed me that Dmitrii Rostovskii kept a journal of sorts in the 1690s.

13. LeDonne, "Ruling Families." LeDonne suggests elsewhere that Catherine II's reforms can be seen as fundamentally *anti*bureaucratic. By destroying the central colleges and shifting authority to local elected bodies and governors, by allowing governors to bypass any regularized procedures or institutions and giving them direct access to her, Catherine returned to a more personalized, uninstitutional politics. *Ruling Russia*, pp. 77–79.

14. Augustine, "Notes," p. 384.

15. Meehan-Waters, *Autocracy and Aristocracy*, p. 69. The same terminology applied in the seventeenth-century vocabulary as well.

16. Raeff, *Plans for Political Reform*, p. 50; translation of Kashpirev, *Pamiatniki novoi russkoi istorii*, pp. 7–8. Another noble proposal, the Project of Grekov, expresses similar concerns: "Make an examination of retirement and inheritance [rules], and of what is to be done about them in the future." Raeff, *Plans for Political Reform*, p. 49; translation of Kashpirev, *Pamiatniki novoi russkoi istorii*, p. 5.

17. Augustine, "Notes," p. 384. LeDonne makes a useful distinction between administrative and legislative modes of understanding: "Much of the political function was still expressed in administrative terms, i.e., in the modalities by which an agreed-upon program was carried out, rather than in legislative terms establishing substantive norms of political action"; *Ruling Russia*, p. 13.

18. Raeff, *Origins*, pp. 53–56. See also Raeff, *Well-Ordered Police State*, pp. 207–8.

19. Meehan-Waters, *Autocracy and Aristocracy*, p. 69–70. On the burgeoning of administrative posts, see Le Donne, *Ruling Russia*.

20. Signers of the Sekiotov or "Majority" Project included prominent Suzdal' names such as Khmetevskii (Ivan), Koisarov (Lev and Mikhail), Lazarev (Andreian), Meshcherskii (Princes Boris Vasil'evich, Vasilii Alekseevich, Ivan Alekseevich, Ivan Vasil'evich, and Mikhail Ivanovich), Solntsev-Zasekin (Princes Andrei and Fedor), Tregubov (Andrei and Mikhail), as well as a number of families with possible or probable Vladimir-Suzdal' connections: Bezobrazov, Vel'iaminov, Princes Viazemskoi, Dubenskii, Durnovo, Zagriazhskii, Princes Zasekin, Zasettskii, Zinov'ev, Matrunin, Oznobizhin, and Rzhevskii. Among the signatories of the Cherkasskii Petition were Semen Koisarov, Prince Danilo Druttskoi, Aleksandr Voznitsyn, Ivan and Petr Durnovo, Andrei Kologrivov, Ivan Nashchokin, Petr Lukich Voeikov, Semen Timofeevich Kishkin, and Stepan Lukich Vel'aiminov, all of whom can either be directly connected to Vladimir or Suzdal' or very likely came from established Vladimir-Suzdal' families. Vladimir-Suzdal' landlords who also signed the Trubetskoi petition, which requested the resumption of autoc-

racy, include Stepan Lukich and Nikita Vel'iaminov, Aleksei Zamyttskoi, Prince Fedor Vasil'evich Meshcherskii, Grigorii Obukhov, and possibly Andrei Stepanovich and Ivan Vasil'evich Zinov'ev. Korsakov, *Votsarenie*, pp. 22–48.

21. Raeff, *Plans for Political Reform*, p. 51; translation of Korsakov, *Votsarenie*, p. 275.

22. Raeff, *Plans for Political Reform*, pp. 50–51; translation of Korsakov, *Votsarenie*, pp. 271–72.

23. Kollmann, "Terminology about Society" and "Transformations."

24. Augustine, "Notes," p. 384.

25. J. M. Smith, "Culture of Merit," p. 97.

Bibliography

Archival Sources

Rossiiskaia gosudarstvennaia biblioteka (RGB) [Russian State Library],
   Manuscript Division, Moscow:
      RGB, fond 303, *Troitse-Sergieva monastyria kopiinaia kniga* [Trinity–
      St. Sergius Monastery Land Donation Book], no. 530.
Rossiiskaia natsional'naia biblioteka (RNB) [Russian National Library],
   Manuscript Division, St. Petersburg:
      RNB, Ermitazhnoe sobranie [Hermitage Collection], no. 343/2.
      RNB, fond 532, *Obshchee sobranie russkikh gramot i aktov* [General
      Collection of Russian Charters and Documents], nos. 77, 170, 302,
      315, 318, 348, 359, 360, 362, 368, 434, 447, 463, 486, 668, 684, 826,
      829, 890, 954, 985, 1000, 1041, 1046, 1061, 1062, 1085, 1103, 1717,
      1720, 1772, 1823, 1944, 2006, 2018, 2021, 2060, 2076, 2084, 2123,
      2143, 2144, 2285, 2360, 2383, 2596, 2724, 2728, 2749, 2874, 2895,
      2926, 2971, 3055, 3204, 3262, 3345, 3388, 3463, 3540, 3528, 3595,
      4652, 4653, 4738, 4781
      RNB, fond 178, *Muzeinoe sobranie* [Museum Collection], no. 1393
      RNB, fond 649, *Sobranie Rokotova* [Rokotov Collection], nos. 5, 15,
      16, 32,
      RNB, fond 299, *Sobranie Zinchenko* [Zinchenko Collection], nos.
      307, 393, 394, 444, 661, 1017, 1468, 1476.
Rossiiskii gosudarstvennyi arkhiv drevnikh aktov (RGADA) [Russian State
   Archive of Ancient Acts], Moscow:
      RGADA, fond 137, *Boiarskie i gorodovye spiski* [Boyar and Provincial
      Service Lists], *opis'* 1, Town of Galich, nos. 12, 28, 38.
      RGADA, fond 154, *Zhalovannye gramoty na votchiny, chiny i*

dvorianstvo [Grants of Land, Rank, and Gentry Title], *opis'* 4, *stolbtsy* 607, 628.

RGADA, fond 210, *Razriadnyi prikaz* [Chancellery of Military Affairs]:

   Belgorodskii stol [Belgorod Desk], *stolbets* 542.
   Bezglasnyi stol [Nameless bureau], nos. 70, 127, 177.
   Knigi zapisnye [Record books], book 11.
   opis' 4, *Dela desiaten'* [Muster Rolls], books 29, 291, 299, 302, 304.
   opis' 5, *Smotrennye knigi* [Service Attendance Books], no. 55.
   opis' 6A, books 12, 92.
   opis' 10, *Stolbsty Vladimirskogo stola* [Scrolls of the Vladimir Desk], books 11, 15.
   opis' 10, *Stolbtsy Vladimirskogo stola* [Scrolls of the Vladimir Desk], *stolbtsy* 4, 28, 32, 33, 40, 60, 63, 65, 70, 72, 73, 82, 84, 101, 115, 116, 132, 142, 146, 159, 186.
   opis' 18, *Rodoslovnye rospisi* [Genealogical tables], nos. 26, 29, 48, 53, 54, 134, 155, 157.
   Stolbtsy Moskovskogo stola razriada [Scrolls of the Moscow Desk of the Chancellery of Military Affairs] nos. 22, 106.
   Stolbtsy Prikaznogo stola [Scrolls of the Chancellery Desk], *stolbtsy* 17, 22, 36, 44, 51, 161, 167, 273, 314, 384, 516, 561, 585, 686, 702, 740, 784, 786, 819, 863, 993, 1151, 1181, 1431, 1434, 1513.

RGADA, fond 286, *Gerol'dmeisterskaia* [Ministry of Heraldry], nos. 241, 241A.

RGADA, fond 1112, *opis'* 1, *Vladimirskaia prikaznaia izba* [Vladimir Provincial Administration Office], nos. 2, 3, 4, 5, 10, 11, 12, 15, 17, 19, 41, 44, 47, 51, 55, 56, 57, 59, 60, 62, 63, 67, 68, 69, 70, 72, 74, 77, 81, 83, 84, 89, 90, 92, 93, 95, 99, 101, 103, 106, 107, 108, 109, 111, 114, 116, 121, 122, 123, 130, 131, 133, 138, 139, 141, 142, 154, 161, 163, 164, 165, 166, 688.

Sanktpeterburgskii filial Instituta rossiilskoi istorii RAN (SPbFIRI) [St. Petersburg Branch of the Institute of Russian History of the Russian Acadamy of Sciences], St. Petersburg:

   SPbFIRI, fond 21, *Kollektsiia V. Borisova* [Borisov Collection], nos. 11, 37, 45, 70, 74, 77–79, 81, 82, 83, 84, 97–101, 103–7, 123, 128, 129, 135, 136, 141–44, 147, 155, 158, 167, 169, 184, 185, 187–89, 201, 204, 211–19, 232–34, 237, 241, 251, 252, 257, 264, 281, 310, 313, 315, 317, 320, 330, 356, 370, 372, 377, 379, 382, 393, 396, 398, 399, 400, 433–35, 442, 462, 477, 482, 483, 487, 494–96, 500, 510, 516, 530, 534, 553, 556, 557, 569, 606–9, 626, 643, 650, 654, 668, 669.
   SPbFIRI, fond 62, *Kollektsiia Kablukova* [Kablukov Collection], nos. 13, 16, 17, 18, 22, 24, 25, 27, 30, 31, 36, 39–44, 47, 48, 51–57, 61, 63, 65, 99, 100, 115, 117, 119, 122, 126, 127, 129, 137, 138, 142, 146, 149, 151, 155, 159, 162, 167, 168, 169, 170, 173, 181, 183, 186, 187,

188, 191, 192, 195–200, 203, 206, 208, 210–13, 216, 218, 221, 222,
225, 228, 234, 241, 242, 243, 245, 248, 249, 252, 257, 258, 260, 261–
65, 267, 269, 273, 275, 276, 277, 278, 280, 283, 293, 294, 298, 303,
304, 306, 309, 323, 324, 325, 332, 333, 334, 336, 337, 339, 340, 342,
343, 347, 349.
SPbFIRI, *Sobranie Artem'eva* [Artem'ev Collection], no. 2.
SPbFIRI, *fond* 252, *Suzdal'skie akty* [Suzdalian Documents], nos. 2,
13, 15–17, 20, 26, 27, 34, 42, 45, 168, 243, 245, 257, 258, 265, 267,
269, 273, 276, 283, 293, 294.

Published Primary and Secondary Sources

Abrams, Philip. *Historical Sociology.* Ithaca, 1982.
Adrianova-Perets, V. P., ed. *Russkaia demokraticheskaia satira XVII veka* [Russian Democratic Satire of the 17th Century]. Moscow, 1977.
Akty istoricheskie, sobrannye i izdannye Arkheograficheskoiu kommissieiu (AI) [Historical Documents, Collected and Published by the Archeographic Commission]. 5 vols. and index. St. Petersburg, 1841–42.
Akty iuridicheskie ili sobrannye form starinnogo deloproizvodstva (AIu) [Juridical Documents or Collected Models of Ancient Record Keeping]. St. Petersburg, 1838.
Akty Moskovskogo gosudarstva. Izdannye Imperatorskoiu akademieiu nauk (AMG) [Documents of the Muscovite State, Published by the Imperial Academy of Sciences]. 3 vols. N. A. Popov, ed. St. Petersburg, 1890–1901.
Akty, otnosiashchiesia do iuridicheskago byta drevnei Rossii, izdannyia Arkheograficheskoiu kommissieiu (AIuB) [Documents Relating to the Juridical Life of Ancient Russia, published by the Archeographic Commission]. 3 vols. and index. St. Petersburg, 1857, 1864, 1884, 1901.
Akty, sobrannye v bibliotekakh i arkhivakh Rossiiskoi imperii Arkheograficheskoiu ekspeditsieiu Imperatorskoi Akademii nauk (AAE) [Documents Collected in Libraries and Archives of the Russian Empire by the Archeographic Expedition of the Imperial Academy of Sciences]. 4 vols. and index. St. Petersburg, 1836, 1838.
Alef, Gustave. "The Crisis of the Muscovite Aristocracy: A Factor in the Growth of Monarchical Power." *Forschungen zur osteuropäischen Geschichte* 15 (1970), pp. 15–58.
———. *The Origins of Muscovite Autocracy: The Age of Ivan III.* Published as *Forschungen zur osteuropaischen Geschichte* 39 (1986).
Aleksandrov, V. A. "Pamflet na rod Sukhotinykh (XVII v.) [Pamphlet on the Sukhotin Clan (17th C.)]." *Istoriia SSSR* [History of the USSR], no. 5 (1971): 114–22.
Aleksandrov, V. A. and N. N. Pokrovskii. "Mirskie organizatsii i administrativnaia vlast' v Sibiri v XVII veke [Communal Organizations and Administrative Authority in Siberia in the Seventeenth Century]." *Istoriia SSSR* [History of the USSR], no. 1 (1986): 47–68.
Alekseev, Iu. G. "15-rublevyi maksimum po sluzhiloi kabale: sluzhba s zemli i feodal'naia renta [15 Ruble Maximum According to Service Bond-

age Agreements: Service from Land and Feudal Rent]." In N. E. Nosov, et al., eds., *Issledovaniia po sotsial'no-politicheskoi istorii Rossii: Sbornik statei pamiati V. A. Romanova* [Research into the Social-Political History of Russia: A Collection of Articles in Memory of V. A. Romanov], (Leningrad, 1971), pp. 110–17.

———. *Agrarnaia i sotsial'naia istoriia severo-vostochnoi Rusi XV–XVI vv. Pereiaslavskii uezd* [Agrarian and Social History of North-Eastern Russia, 15th–16th Centuries]. Moscow and Leningrad, 1966.

Alekseev, Iu. G. and A. I. Kopanev. "Razvitie pomestnoi sistemy v XVI v. [Development of the *Pomest'e* System in the 16th C]." In Pavlenko, et al., eds., *Dvorianstvo i krepostnoi stroi Rossii*, pp. 57–69.

Alfavitnyi ukazatel' familii i lits, upominaemykh v boiarskikh knigakh, khraniashchikhsia v 1-m otdelenii Moskovskogo arkhiva Ministerstva Iustitsii [Alphabetical Index of Surnames and Individuals Mentioned in the Boyar Books, Preserved in the First Section of the Moscow Archive of the Ministry of Justice]. Moscow, 1853.

Anderson, Benedict. *Imagined Communities: Reflections on the Origin and Spread of Nationalism*. London, 1983.

Anderson, Perry. *Lineages of the Absolutist State*. London, 1979.

Andreev, A. I. "Kratkaia opis' gramot, khraniashchikhsia v Rukopisnom otdele Rossiiskoi publichnoi biblioteki [A Short Guide to the Documents Preserved in the Manuscript Division of the Russian Public Library]." In *Letopis' zaniatii Imperatorskoi Arkheograficheskoi Kommissii za 1919–22 gg.* [Chronicle of the Proceedings of the Imperial Archeographic Commission for 1919–22] 22 (1923): 1–46.

———. *Kratkii otchet o novykh postupleniiakh za 1947–1949 gg. [GPB]* [Short Report about the New Acquisitions of GPB (State Public Library) for 1947–1949]. Leningrad, 1952.

Andreev, I. L. "'Sil'nye liudi' Moskovskogo gosudarstva i bor'ba dvorian s nimi v 20–40-e gody XVII veka ['Strong People' of the Muscovite State and the Gentry's Struggle with Them in the 20s–40s of the 17th Century]." *Istorii SSSR* [History of the USSR], no. 5 (1990): 77–88.

———. "'Sluzhilyi gorod' v politicheskoi bor'be XVII veka [The 'Service Town' in the Political Struggle of the 17th Century]." In V. Iu. Popov, ed., *Chteniia pamiati V. B. Kobrina. Problemy otechestvennoi istorii i kul'tury perioda feodalizma* [Readings in Memory of V. B. Kobrin. Problems in the History and Culture of the Fatherland in the Period of Feudalism]. Moscow, 1992.

———. "Urochnye leta i zakreposhchenie krest'ian v Moskovskom gosudarstve [Fixed Years and the Enserfment of the Peasants in the Muscovite State]." *Istorii SSSR* [History of the USSR], no. 1 (1982): 142–48.

Armstrong, John A. "Old-Regime Governors: Bureaucratic and Patrimonial Attributes." *Comparative Studies in Society and History* 14 (1972): 2–29.

Arendt, Hannah. *On Violence*. New York, 1970.

Augustine, Wilson R. "Notes toward a Portrait of the Eighteenth-century Nobility." *Canadian Slavic Studies* 4 (1970): 373–425.

Avrich, Paul. *Russian Rebels, 1600–1800.* New York, 1976.

Aylmer, J. *An Harborowe for faithfull and Trewe subjectes.* Strasbourg, 1559.

Baehr, Stephen. *The Paradise Myth in Eighteenth-Century Russia: Utopian Patterns in Early Secular Russian Literature and Culture.* Stanford, 1991.

Baker, Keith Michael, ed. *The Political Culture of the Old Regime.* Oxford, 1987.

Bakhrushin, S. V. "Moskovskoe vosstanie 1648 g. [Moscow Uprising of 1648]." In *Nauchnye trudy,* [Scholary Works] vol. 2 (Moscow, 1954), pp. 46–89.

Baron, Samuel H., ed. *The Travels of Olearius in Seventeenth-Century Russia.* Stanford, 1967.

Barsukov, A. P. *Spiski gorodovykh voevod i drugikh lits voevodskogo upravleniia Moskovskogo gosudarstva XVII stoletiia* [Lists of Town Governors and Other Individuals of the Gubernatorial Administration of the Muscovite State in the 17th Century]. St. Petersburg, 1902.

Bazilevich, K. V., ed. *Gorodskie vosstaniia v Moskovskom gosudarstve XVII v. Sbornik dokumentov* [Urban Uprisings in the Muscovite State in the 17th C. A Collection of Documents]. Moscow and Leningrad, 1936.

Beik, William. *Absolutism and Society in Seventeenth-Century France: State Power and Provincial Aristocracy in Languedoc.* Cambridge, Eng., 1985.

Beliaev, I. D. *Lektsii po istorii russkogo zakonodatel'stva* [Lectures on the History of Russian Legislation]. 3rd ed. Moscow, 1901.

Berry, Lloyd E. and Robert O. Crummey, eds. *Rude and Barbarous Kingdom: Russia in the Accounts of Sixteenth-Century English Voyagers.* Madison, 1968.

Bien, David D. "Aristocracy." In Francois Furet and M. Ozouf, eds., with D. Baczko, *Dictionnaire critique de la Révolution française.* Paris, 1988.

——. "The Army in the French Enlightenment: Reform, Reaction and Revolution." *Past and Present,* 85 (1979): 68–98.

——. "Offices, Corps, and a System of State Credit: The Uses of Privilege Under the Ancien Régime." In Keith Baker, ed., *The Political Culture of the Old Regime.* Oxford, 1987.

——. "The *Secrétaires du Roi*: Absolutism, Corps, and Privilege Under the Ancien Régime." In Albert Cremer, ed., *Sonderdruck aus vom ancien Régime zur Französischen Revolution: Forschungen und Perspektiven.* Göttingen, 1978.

Blum, Jerome. *Lord and Peasant in Russia from the Ninth to the Nineteenth Century.* Princeton, 1961.

Bogoiavlenskii, S. K. "Prikaznye d'iaki XVII veka [Chancellery Secretaries of the 17th Century]." *Istoricheskie zapiski* [Historical Notes] 1 (1937 [Reprint, Wiesbaden, 1968]): 220–39.

Bogoiavlenskii, S. K. and S. B. Veselovskii. "Mestnoe upravlenie [Local Administration]." In A. A. Novosel'skii and N. V. Ustiugov, eds., *Ocherki istorii SSSR. Period feodalizma. XVII veka* [Outlines of the History of Russia. Period of Feudalism. 17th Century]. Moscow, 1955.

Bogoslovskii, M. M. "Issledovaniia po istorii mestnogo upravleniia pri Petre Velikom [Research into the History of Local Administration under Peter the Great]." *Zhurnal Ministerstva Narodnogo Prosveshcheniia* [Journal of the Ministry of Popular Education] 9 (1903): 45–144.

———. *Zemskoe samoupravlenie na russkom severe v XVII v.* [Civil Self-Administration in the Russian North in the 17th C.]. 2 vols. Moscow, 1909, 1912.

Bolotov, A. T. *Zhizn' i prikliucheniia Andreia Bolotova, opisannye samim im dlia svoikh potomkov* [The Life and Adventures of Andrei Bolotov, Described by Himself for His Descendants]. 3 vols. Moscow and Leningrad, 1931.

Bonfield, Lloyd. *Marriage Settlements, 1601–1740: The Adoption of the Strict Settlement.* Cambridge, Eng., 1983.

Borisov, V. A., ed. *Opisanie goroda Shui i ego okrestnostei* [Description of the Town of Shuia and Its Environs]. Moscow, 1851.

———, ed. *Starinnye akty, sluzhashchie preimushchestvenno dopolneniem k Opisaniiu g. Shui i ego okrestnostei* [Ancient Documents, Serving Primarily as a Supplement to the Description of the Town of Shuia and Its Environs]. Moscow, 1853.

Bourdieu, Pierre. *Outline of a Theory of Practice.* Richard Nice, trans., Cambridge and New York, 1977.

Braddick, Michael J. "State Formation and Social Change in Early Modern England: A Problem Stated and Approaches Suggested." *Social History* 16 (1991): 1–17.

Brown, Peter Bowman. "Early Modern Russian Bureaucracy: The Evolution of the Chancellery System from Ivan III to Peter the Great, 1478–1717." Ph.D. diss., University of Chicago, 1978.

———. "Muscovite Government Bureaux." *Russian History* 10 (1983): 269–330.

Buganov, V. I. "O sotsial'nom sostave uchastnikov moskovskogo vosstaniia 1662 g. [Of the Social Composition of the Participants of the Moscow Uprising of 1662]." *Istoricheskie zapiski* [Historical Notes] 66 (1960): 312–17.

———. *Moskovskie vosstaniia kontsa XVII veka* [Muscovite Uprisings of the End of the 17th Century]. Moscow, 1969.

———. *Moskovskoe vosstanie 1662 g.* [The Moscow Uprising of 1662]. Moscow, 1964.

Burke, Edmund, III. "Reactionary Rebels? Janissaries, Artisans and the Roots of Anti-Modern Protest in the Eighteenth Century Ottoman Empire." Paper presented to the Social Sciences Seminar, Institute for Advanced Studies, Princeton University, 1990.

Bush, M. L. *The English Aristocracy: A Comparative Synthesis.* Manchester, 1984.

———. *Rich Noble, Poor Noble.* Manchester and New York, 1988.

Bushkovitch, Paul A. "The Epiphany Ceremony of the Russian Court in the Sixteenth and Seventeenth Centuries." *Russian Review* 49 (1990): 1–17.
———. *Religion and Society in Russia: The Sixteenth and Seventeenth Centuries.* Oxford, 1992.
Bychkova, M. E. "Idei vlasti i poddanstva v genealogicheskoi literature (Russkoe gosudarstvo i Velikoe kniazhestvo Litovskoe v kontse XV–XVI vv.) [Ideas of Authority and Citizenship in Genealogical Literature (The Russian State and the Grand Princedom of Lithuania from the End of the 15th through the 16th Centuries]." 1991. Typescript.
———. "Iz istorii sozdaniia rodoslovnykh rospisei kontsa XVII v. i Barkhatnoi knigi [From the History of the Creation of the Genealogical Lists of the End of the 17th C. and of the Velvet Book]." *Vspomogatel'nye istoricheskie distsipliny* [Auxiliary Historical Disciplines] 12 (1981): 90–109.
———. *Rodoslovnye knigi XVI–XVII vv. kak istoricheskii istochnik* [Genealogical Books of the 16–17th Centuries as a Historical Source]. Moscow, 1975.
———. *Sostav klassa feodalov Rossii v XVI v. (Istoriko-genealogicheskoe issledovanie)* [The Composition of the Class of Feudal Lords of Russia in the 16th Century (A Historical-Genealogical Investigation)]. Moscow, 1986.
Campbell, Ira Lynn. "The Composition, Character and Competence of the Assembly of the Land in Seventeenth-Century Russia." Ph.D. diss., University of Illinois at Urbana-Champaign, 1984.
Cherepnin, L. V. *Zemskie sobory Russkogo gosudarstva v XVI–XVII vv.* [Assemblies of the Land of the Russian State in the 16–17th Centuries]. Moscow, 1978.
Cherepnin, L. V., ed. *Knigi moskovskikh prikazov v fondakh TsGADA. Opis'. 1495–1718 gg.* [The Books of the Moscow Chancelleries in the Collections of TsGADA. Inventory. 1495–1718]. Moscow, 1972.
Cherniavsky, Michael. "The Old Believers and the New Religion." *Slavic Review* 25 (1966): 1–39.
Chernov, A. V. *Vooruzhennye sily Russkogo gosudarstva v XV–XVII vv.* [The Armed Forces of the Russian State in the 15–17th Centuries]. Moscow, 1954.
"Chernovaia chelobitnaia tsariam Ioannu i Petru Alekseevicham o zakhvate chuzhoi votchiny s krest'ianami [Draft Petition to Tsars Ioann and Petr Alekseevich about the Seizing of Other People's Estates and Peasants]." In *Sbornik starinnykh bumag, khraniashchikhsia v muzee P. I. Shchukina* [Collection of Ancient Papers Preserved in the P. I. Shchukin Museum]. Pt. 2, 1897.
Chicherin, B. N. *Oblastnye uchrezhdeniia v Rossii v XVII-m veke* [Provincial Institutions in Russia in the 17th Century]. Moscow, 1856.
Chistiakova, E. V. *Gorodskie vosstaniia v Rossii v pervoi polovine XVII veka (30-40e gody)* [Urban Uprisings in Russia in the First Half of the 17th Century]. Voronezh, 1975.
———. "Volneniia sluzhilykh liudei v iuzhnykh gorodakh Rossii v seredine XVII v. [Disturbances among the Service People in the Southern Towns of

Russia in the Middle of the 17th Century]." In N. V. Ustiugov, Iu. A. Tikhonov, P. T. Iakovlev, eds., *Russkoe gosudarstvo v XVII veke: Novye iavleniia v sotsial'no-ekonomicheskoi, politicheskoi i kul'turnoi zhizni. Sbornik statei* [The Russian State in the 17th Century: New Developments in Socio-Economic, Political and Cultural Life. Collection of Articles] (Moscow, 1961), pp. 254–71.

Chteniia v Obshchestve istorii i drevnostei rossiiskikh pri Moskovskom universitete. Sbornik (ChOIDR) [Readings in the Society for the History and Antiquities of Russia at Moscow University]. 264 vols. Moscow, 1845–1918.

Collins, Samuel. *The Present State of Russia: In a Letter to a Friend at London.* London, 1671.

Cooper, Frederick. "The Dialectics of Decolonization: Nationalism and Labor Movements in Post-War Africa." 1994. Typescript.

Cooper, J. P. "Patterns of Inheritance and Settlement by Great Landowners from the Fifteenth to the Eighteenth Centuries." In J. Goody, J. Thirsk, and E. P. Thompson, eds., *Family and Inheritance: Rural Society in Western Europe, 1200–1800* (Cambridge, Eng., 1976) pp. 192–327.

Crummey, Robert O. *Aristocrats and Servitors: The Boyar Elite in Russia, 1613–1689.* Princeton, 1983.

——. "Court Groupings and Politics in Russia, 1645–1649." *Forschungen zur osteuropäischen Geschichte* 24 (1978): 203–21.

——. "Court Spectacles in Seventeenth-Century Russia." In Daniel C. Waugh, ed., *Essays in Honor of A. A. Zimin.* Columbus, Ohio, 1983.

——. "Origins of the Noble Official: The Boyar Elite, 1613–1689." In W. M. Pintner and D. K. Rowney, eds., *Russian Officialdom: The Bureaucratization of Russian Society from the Seventeenth Century to the Twentieth Century* (Chapel Hill, N.C., 1980), pp. 46–75.

——. "Reflections on *Mestnichestvo* in the Seventeenth-Century." *Forschungen zur osteuropäischen Geschichte* 27 (1980): 269–81.

Das, David. "History Writing and the Quest for Fame in Late Muscovy: Andrei Lyzlov's *History of the Scythians.*" *Russian Review* 51 (1992): 502–9.

Davies, Brian L. "The Politics of Give and Take: *Kormlenie* as Service Remuneration and Generalized Exchange, 1488–1725." Paper presented at the NEH Conference, Cultural Identity in a Multicultural State: Muscovy, 1359–1584, Los Angeles, March 1994.

——. "The Role of the Town Governors in the Defense and Military Colonization of Muscovy's Southern Frontier: The Case of Kozlov, 1635–1638." Ph.D. diss., University of Chicago, 1983.

Davis, Natalie Zemon. *Fiction in the Archives: Pardon Tales and Their Tellers in Sixteenth-century France.* Stanford, 1987.

Demidova, N. F. "Gosudarstvennyi apparat Rossii v XVII veke [State Organs of Russia in the 17th Century]." *Istoricheskie zapiski* [Historical Notes] 108 (1982): 109–55.

——. "Prikaznye liudi XVII v. (Sotsial'nyi sostav i istochniki formirovaniia) [Chancellery Personnel in the 17th Century (Social Composition and

Sources of Formation)." *Istoricheskie zapiski* [Historical Notes] 90 (1972): 332–54.

———. *Sluzhilaia biurokratiia v Rossii XVII v. i ee rol' v formirovanii abso-liutizma* [The Service Bureaucracy in 17th-Century Russia and Its Role in the Formation of Absolutism]. Moscow, 1987.

Denisova, M. M. "Pomestnaia konnitsa i ee vooruzhenie v XVI–XVII vv. [The *Pomest'e* Cavalry and Its Armament in the 16th–17th Centuries]." *Trudy gosudarstvennogo Istoricheskogo muzeia* [Works of the State Historical Museum] 20 (1948): 29–46.

Derzhavina, O. A. and E. V. Kolosova, eds. *Skazanie Avraamiia Palitsyna* [The Tale of Avraamii Palitsyn]. Moscow and Leningrad, 1955.

Dewey, Horace W. "Charters of Local Government under Ivan IV." *Jahrbücher für Geschichte Osteuropas* 14 (1966): 10–20.

———. "Old Muscovite Concepts of Injured Honor (*Beschest'ie*)." *Slavic Review* 27 (1968): 594–603.

———. "Trial by Combat in Muscovite Russia." *Oxford Slavonic Papers* 9 (1960): 21–32.

Dewey, Horace W., comp., trans., and ed. *Muscovite Judicial Texts, 1488–1556*. Ann Arbor, Mich., 1966.

Dewey, Horace W., and Ann M. Kleimola. "Coercion by Righter (*Pravezh*) in Old Russian Administration." *Canadian-American Slavic Studies* 9 (1975): 156–67.

Dewey, H. W., and A. M. Kleimola, trans. and ed. *Russian Private Law XIV–XVII Centuries*. Ann Arbor, Mich., 1973.

Ditiatin, I. I. *Rol' chelobitii i zemskikh soborov v upravlenii Moskovskogo gosudarstva* [The Role of Petitions and of Assemblies of the Land in the Administration of the Muscovite State]. Rostov-on-the-Don, 1905.

Dmytryshyn, Basil, ed. *Imperial Russia: A Source Book, 1700–1917*. 3rd ed. Fort Worth, Tex., 1990.

"Dokumenty Razriadnogo prikaza. Boiarskie knigi, boiarskie spiski, zhiletskie spiski, dela desiaten . . . [Documents of the Chancellery of Military Affairs. Boyar Books, Boyar Lists, *Zhiletskii* Lists, Provincial Muster Rolls . . .]." In *Opisanie dokumentov i bumag, khraniashchikhsia v Moskovskom arkhive Ministerstva iustitsii* [Description of Documents and Papers, Preserved in the Moscow Archive of the Ministry of Justice], 9: 1–161. Moscow, 1894.

"Dokumenty Razriadnogo prikaza. Stolbtsy raznykh stolov . . . Vladimirskogo stola [Documents of the Chancellery of Military Affairs. Scrolls of Various Desks . . . of the Vladimir Desk]." In *Opisanie dokumentov i bumag, khraniashchikhsia v Moskovskom arkhive Ministerstva iustitsii* [Description of Documents and Papers, Preserved in the Moscow Archive of the Ministry of Justice, 11: 446–509. Moscow, 1896.

"Dokumenty Razriadnogo prikaza. Stolbtsy razriadnykh stolov. Prikaznogo stola [Documents of the Chancellery of Military Affairs. Scrolls of Various Desks . . . of the Chancellery Desk]." In *Opisanie dokumentov i bumag, khraniashchikhsia v Moskovskom arkhive Ministerstva iustitsii* [Description of Documents and Papers, Preserved in the Moscow Archive of the Ministry of Justice]. Vols. 15, 16. Moscow, 1908, 1910.

Dolgorukov, P. V. *Rossiiskaia rodoslovnaia kniga.* 4 vols. St. Petersburg, 1854–57.

Dopolneniia k aktam istoricheskim, sobrannye i izdannye Arkheograficheskoiu kommissieiu (DAI) [Supplements to Historical Acts Collected and Published by the Archeographic Commission]. 12 vols. and index. St. Petersburg, 1846–1975.

Duara, Prasenjit. *Culture, Power, and the State: Rural North China, 1900–1942.* Stanford, 1988.

Dvortsovye razriady, po vysochaishemu poveleniiu (DR) [Lists of Court Service Postings by the Highest Decree]. 3 vols. St. Petersburg, 1850–52.

Dykstra, Robert R. and William Silag. "Doing Local History: Monographic Approaches to the Smaller Community." *American Quarterly* 37 (1985): 411–25.

Eisenstadt, Shmuel Noah. *The Political Systems of Empires.* London, 1963.

Ellersieck, Heinz Eberhard. "Russia Under Aleksei Mikhailovich and Feodor Alekseevich, 1645–1682: The Scandinavian Sources." Ph.D. diss., University of California, Los Angeles, 1955.

Ermolaev, S. L., comp. *Borovskii uezd v XVII veke (Materialy dozora 1613 goda)* [Borovskii Province in the 17th Century (Material from the Survey of 1613)]. Moscow, 1992.

Eroshkin, N. P. *Istoriia gosudarstvennykh uchrezhdenii dorevoliutsionnoi Rossii* [History of State Institutions of Pre-Revolutionary Russia]. 3rd ed. Moscow, 1983.

Ethington, Philip J. *The Public City: The Political Construction of Urban Life in San Francisco, 1850–1900.* New York, 1994.

Fletcher, Giles. "Of the Russe Commonwealth." In Lloyd E. Berry and Robert O. Crummey, eds., *Rude and Barbarous Kingdom: Russia in the Accounts of Sixteenth-Century English Voyagers.* Madison, Wis., 1968.

Flier, Michael S. "Breaking the Code: The Image of the Tsar in the Muscovite Palm Sunday Ritual." In Michael S. Flier and Daniel Rowland, eds., *Medieval Russian Culture,* vol. 2 (Berkeley and Los Angeles, 1994), pp. 213–42.

———. "The Iconology of Royal Ritual in Sixteenth-Century Muscovy." In Speros Vyronis, Jr., ed., *Byzantine Studies: Essays on the Slavic World and the Eleventh Century* (New York, 1992), pp. 53–76.

Fomin, N. K. "Sotsial'nyi sostav zemlevladel'tsev Suzdal'skogo uezda [The Social Composition of the Landholders of Suzdal' Province]." In V. T. Pashuto, ed., *Rossiia na putiakh tsentralizatsii* (Moscow, 1982), pp. 89–94.

Fonvizin, Denis I. *The Minor.* In Marvin Kantor, trans. and ed., *Dramatic Works of D. I. Fonvizin.* Frankfurt, 1974.

Geiman, V. G. and E. E. Granstrem. *Katalog drevnerusskikh gramot, khraniashchikhsia v Otdele rukopisei Gosudarstvennoi publichnoi biblioteki im. M. E. Saltykova-Shchedrina v Leningrade, 1647–1660* [Catalog of Old-Russian Documents Preserved in the Manuscript Division of the

M. E. Saltykov-Shchedrin State Public Library in Leningrad, 1647–1660]. Leningrad, 1960.

Giddens, Anthony. *Capitalism and Modern Social Theory: An Analysis of the Writings of Marx, Durkheim and Max Weber.* Cambridge, Eng., 1971.

Giesey, Ralph E. "Rules of Inheritance and Strategies of Mobility in Pre-revolutionary France." *American Historical Review* 82 (1977): 271–89.

———. "State-Building in Early Modern France: The Role of Royal Official-dom." *Journal of Modern History* 55 (1983): 191–207.

Golitsyn, Kn. N. N. *Ukazatel' imen lichnykh, upominaemykh v dvor-tsovykh razriadakh* [Index of Personal Names Mentioned in the Lists of Court Service Postings]. St. Petersburg, 1912.

Golombievskii, A. A. "Stoly Razriadnogo prikaza [Desks of the Chancellery of Military Affairs]." *Zhurnal Ministerstva Narodnogo Prosveshcheniia* [Journal of the Ministry of Popular Education] 270 (1890): 1–17.

Golombievskii, A. A. and N. N. Ardashev. "Prikaznye, zemskie, tamozhnye, gubnye, sudovye izby moskovskogo gosudarstva. Obzor dokumentov XVI–XVII vv. v delakh XVIII v., peredannykh v Moskovskii arkhiv Ministerstva iustitsii iz uprazdnennykh v 1864 g. uchrezhdenii [Chancellery, Local Tax-Collecting, Customs, *Guba*, and Judicial Offices of the Muscovite State. Survey of Documents of the 16–17th Centuries in Cases of the 18th Century, Given to the Moscow Archive of the Ministry of Justice from Institutions Abolished in 1864]." *Zapiski Moskovskogo Arkheologicheskogo Instituta* [Notes of the Moscow Archeographic Institute] 4 (1909): 1–86.

Goody, Jack. *The Development of the Family and Marriage in Europe.* Cambridge, Eng., 1983.

———. "Inheritance, Property and Women: Some Comparative Consider-ations." In J. Goody, J. Thirsk, and E. P. Thompson, eds. *Family and Inheritance: Rural Society in Western Europe, 1200–1800* (Cambridge, Eng., 1976), pp. 10–36.

Goody, Jack, Joan Thirsk, and E. P. Thompson, eds. *Family and Inheritance: Rural Society in Western Europe, 1200–1800.* Cambridge, Eng., 1976.

Got'e, Iu. V. *Istoriia oblastnogo upravleniia v Rossii ot Petra I do Ekateriny II* [History of Regional Administration in Russia from Peter I to Catherine II]. 2 vols. Moscow, 1913 and 1941.

———. *Zamoskovnyi krai v XVII veke. Opyt issledovaniia po istorii ekonomicheskogo byta Moskovskoi Rusi* [The Zamoskovnyi Region in the 17th Century. An Effort at Research into the History of Economic Life of Muscovite Rus']. Moscow, 1906.

Got'e, Iu. V., ed. *Akty, otnosiashchiesia k istorii zemskikh soborov* [Documents Concerning the History of Assemblies of the Land]. Moscow, 1909.

Gradovskii, A. D. *Istoriia mestnogo upravleniia v Rossii* [History of Local Administration in Russia]. 2 vols. St. Petersburg, 1868.

Gramotki XVII-nachala XVIII veka [Private Documents of the 17th and Early 18th Century]. Moscow, 1969.

Gramsci, Antonio. *Selections from the Prison Notebooks of Antonio Gramsci.* Quinton Hoare and Geoffrey Nowell Smith, trans. and eds. New York, 1971.

Grossman, Joan Delaney. "Feminine Images in Old Russian Literature and Art." *California Slavic Studies* 11 (1980): 33–70.

Guha, Ranajit. "The Prose of Counter-Insurgency." In Ranajit Guha and Gayatri Chakravorty Spivak, eds., *Selected Subaltern Studies.* New York and Oxford, 1988.

Habermas, Jürgen. "Hannah Arendt's Communications Concept of Power." *Social Research* 44 (1977): 3–24.

———. *The Structural Transformation of the Public Sphere: An Inquiry into a Category of Bourgeois Society.* Thomas Burger with Frederick Lawrence, trans. Cambridge, Mass., 1989.

Hall, John, ed. *States in History.* Oxford and New York, 1986.

Hammond, Vincent Elwood. "The History of the Novgorodian Pomest'e: 1480–1550." Ph.D. diss., University of Illinois, 1987.

Harding, Richard. "Corruption and the Moral Boundaries of Patronage in the Renaissance." In G. F. Lytle and S. Orgel, eds., *Patronage in the Renaissance* (Princeton, 1981), pp. 47–64.

Haxthausen, August von. *Studies on the Interior of Russia.* S. Frederick Starr, ed., Eleanore L. M. Schmidt, trans. Chicago, 1972.

Hay, Douglas, et al. *Albion's Fatal Tree: Crime and Society in Eighteenth-Century England.* New York, 1975.

Hellie, Richard. "Commentary on Chapters 3–6 of the *Ulozhenie.*" *Russian History* 17 (1990): 65–78.

———. *Enserfment and Military Change in Muscovy.* Chicago, 1971.

———. "Material Culture and Identity in Late Mediaeval and Early Modern Russia." Paper presented at the NEH Conference, Cultural Identity in a Multicultural State: Muscovy, 1359–1584, Los Angeles, March, 1994.

———. *Slavery in Russia, 1450–1725.* Chicago, 1982.

———. "Ulozhenie Commentary—Preamble." *Russian History* 15 (1988): 181–224.

Hellie, Richard, trans. and ed. *The Muscovite Law Code (Ulozhenie) of 1649.* Pt. 1: *Text and Translation.* Irvine, Calif., 1988.

Hellie, Richard, comp. and trans. *Readings for Introduction to Russian Civilization: Muscovite Society.* Chicago, 1967.

Henshall, Nicholas. *The Myth of Absolutism: Change and Continuity in Early Modern European Monarchy.* London, 1992.

Herrup, Cynthia, *The Common Peace: Participation and the Criminal Law in Seventeenth-Century England.* Cambridge, Eng., 1987.

Hughes, Lindsey. *Russia and the West: The Life of a Seventeenth-Century Westernizer, Prince Vasily Vasil'evich Golitsyn (1643–1714).* Newtonville, Mass., 1984.

———. *Sophia, Regent of Russia, 1657–1704.* New Haven, 1990.

Iablochkov, M. *Istoriia dvorianskogo sosloviia v Rossii* [History of the Gentry Estate in Russia]. St. Petersburg, 1876.

Iakovlev, A. I. *Prikaz sbora ratnykh liudei, 1637–1653 (146–61) gg.* [Chancellery for the Conscription of Soldiers, 1637–1653 (146–161)]. Moscow, 1917.

Iakovlev, A. I., ed. *Namestnich'i, gubnye i zemskie ustavnye gramoty Moskovskogo gosudarstva* [Namestnik, Guba and Zemskii Charters of the Muscovite State]. Moscow, 1909.

Ikonnikov, N. F. *NdR, La Noblesse de Russie,* 2nd ed. 25 vols. Paris, 1957–66.

Iushkov, A. *Akty XVII–XVIII vv, predstavlennye v Razriadnyi prikaz predstaviteliami sluzhilykh familii posle otmeny mestnichestva* [Documents of the 17th–18th Centuries Presented to the Chancellery of Military Affairs by Representatives of Service Families after the Abolition of Mestnichestvo]. 2 pts. Moscow, 1898.

Ivanchin-Pisarev, N. "O starinnoi sluzhbe russkikh dvorian [Of the Ancient Service Practices of the Russian Gentry]." In *ChOIDR* vol. 22, book 9, *Smes'*, pp. 305–6. Moscow, 1848.

Ivanov, P. I. *Opisanie gosudarstvennogo Razriadnogo arkhiva* [Description of the State Archive of the Chancellery of Military Affairs]. Moscow, 1842.

Jefferson, Thomas. *The Writings of Thomas Jefferson.* P. L. Ford, ed. 10 vols. New York, 1892–99.

Kaiser, Daniel H. *The Growth of the Law in Medieval Russia.* Princeton, 1980.

——. "Women, Property and the Law in Early Modern Russia." Grinnell College, 1988. Typescript.

——. "Women's Property in Muscovite Families, 1500–1725." Grinnell College, 1988. Typescript.

Kalachov, N. V., ed. *Akty, otnosiashchiesia do iuridicheskogo byta drevnei Rossii, Izdannye Arkheograficheskoiu kommissieiu* [Documents Relating to the Juridical Life of Ancient Russia, Published by the Archeographic Commission]. 3 vols. and index. St. Petersburg, 1857–1901.

Kalinychev, F. I. *Pravovye voprosy voennoi organizatsii Russkogo gosudarstva vtoroi poloviny XVII veka* [Legal Questions of the Military Organization of the Russian State in the Second Half of the 17th Century]. Moscow, 1954.

Kantorowicz, Ernst H. *The King's Two Bodies: A Study in Mediaeval Political Theology.* Princeton, 1957.

Kashpirev, V. *Pamiatniki novoi russkoi istorii. Sbornik istoricheskikh statei i materialov* [Texts of Modern Russian History. A Collection of Historical Articles and Sources]. Vol. 1, pt. 1. St. Petersburg, 1871.

Keenan, Edward L. "Muscovite Political Folkways." *Russian Review* 45 (1986): 115–81.

Keep, John H. L. "Bandits and the Law in Muscovy." *Slavonic and East European Review* 35 (1956): 201–22.

——. "The Muscovite Elite and the Approach to Pluralism." *Slavonic and East European Review* 48 (1970): 201–32.

——. *Soldiers of the Tsar: Army and Society in Russia, 1462–1874.* Oxford, 1985.

Kelley, Robin D. G. "An Archaeology of Resistance." *American Quarterly* 44 (1992): 292–98.

———. " 'We Are Not What We Seem': Rethinking Black Working-Class Opposition in the Jim Crow South." *Journal of American History* 80 (1993): 75–112.

Kettering, Sharon. *Patrons, Brokers, and Clients in Seventeenth-Century France*. New York, 1986.

Khilkov, Grigorii, ed. *Sbornik kniazia Khilkova* [Collection of Prince Khilkov]. St. Petersburg, 1879.

Khodarkovsky, Michael. "The Stepan Razin Uprising: Was It a 'Peasant War'?" *Jahrbücher für Geschichte Osteuropas* 42 (1994): 1–19.

Kiselev, E. A. "Feodal'noe zemlevladenie Iaroslavskogo uezda serediny XVI–pervoi treti XVII v. Po pistsovym knigam [Feudal Landholding in Iaroslavl' Province from the Mid-16th through the First Third of the 17th Century]." Abstract, Candidate diss., Moscow State University, 1978.

Kishlansky, Mark A. *Parliamentary Selection: Social and Political Choice in Early Modern England*. Cambridge, Eng., 1986.

Kivelson, Valerie A. "The Devil Stole His Mind: The Tsar and the 1648 Moscow Uprising." *American Historical Review* 98 (1993): 733–56.

Kizevetter, A. A. *Mestnoe samoupravlenie v Rossii. IX–XIX st. Istoricheskii ocherk* [Local Self-Administration in Russia. 9th–19th Centuries. A Historical Essay]. 2nd ed. Petrograd, 1917. Reprint, The Hague and Paris, 1970.

Klapisch-Zuber, Christiane. *Women, Family, and Ritual in Renaissance Italy*. Lydia G. Cochrane, trans. Chicago, 1985.

Kleimola, Ann M. "In Accordance with the Canons of the Holy Apostles: Moscovite Dowries and Women's Property Rights." *Russian Review* 51 (1992): 204–29.

———. "Military Service and Elite Status in Muscovy in the Second Quarter of the Sixteenth Century." *Russian History* 7 (1980): 47–63.

———. "Status, Place, and Politics: The Rise of *Mestnichestvo* During the *Boiarskoe Pravlenie*." *Forschungen zur osteuropäischen Geschichte* 27 (1980): 195–214.

———. "Up Through Servitude: The Changing Condition of the Muscovite Elite in the Sixteenth and Seventeenth Centuries." *Russian History* 6, pt. 2 (1979): 210–29.

———. "Who We Are or Who We Wish We Were: Genealogy, Kinship and Identity Among the Riazan' Elite." Paper Presented at the NEH Conference, Cultural Identity in a Multicultural State: Muscovy, 1359–1584, Los Angeles, March, 1994.

Kliuchevskii, V. O. *Boiarskaia duma drevnei Rusi* [The Boyar Duma of Ancient Rus']. 5th ed. Petersburg, 1919.

———. *A Course in Russian History. The 17th Century*. Natalie Duddington, trans. Chicago, 1968.

———. *Istoriia soslovii v Rossii. Kurs chitannyi v Moskovskom universitete v 1886 godu* [The History of Estates in Russia. A Course of Lectures Read at

Moscow University in 1886]. 3rd ed, Petrograd, 1918. Reprint, Gulf Breeze, Fla., 1969.

———. *Kurs russkoi istorii* [A Course in Russian History]. 5 vols, 1904–21. Reprint, Moscow, 1937.

———. "Sostav predstavitel'stva na zemskikh soborakh drevnei Rusi [The Composition of the Representatives to the Assemblies of the Land of Ancient Rus']." In his *Sochineniia v deviati tomakh*, vol. 8 (Moscow, 1990), pp. 277–374.

Kniaz'kov, S. E. "Sudnye prikazy v kontse XVI-pervoi polovine XVII v. [Judicial Chancelleries from the End of the 16th through the First Half of the 17th Century]." *Istoricheskie zapiski* [Historical Notes] 115 (1987): 268–85.

Knigi razriadnyia, po ofitsial'nym onykh spiskam [Military Postings According to the Official Lists]. 2 vols. plus index in 1 vol. St. Petersburg, 1853.

Kobrin, V. B. "Iz istorii pravitel'stvennoi politiki v oblasti kniazheskogo i votchinnogo zemlevladeniia v XV–XVI vv. (Zakony 1551, 1562 i 1572) [From the History of Governmental Policy in the Area of Princely and *Votchina* Landholding in the 15th and 16th Centuries (The Laws of 1551, 1562 and 1572)]." *Istoriia SSSR* [History of the USSR], no. 1 (1984): 172–84.

———. *Vlast' i sobstvennost' v srednevekovoi Rossi* [Power and Property in Medieval Russia]. Moscow, 1985.

———. "Zemlevladel'cheskie prava kniazhat v XV - pervoi treti XVI v. i protsess tsentralizatsii Rusi [Property Rights of the Princes in the 15th through the First Third of the 16th Century and the Process of Centralization of Rus']." *Istoriia SSSR* [History of the USSR], no. 4 (1981): 33–49.

Kochin, G. "Pistsovye knigi v burzhuaznoi istoriografii [Cadaster Books in Bourgeois Historiography]." *Problemy istochnikovedeniia* [Problems of Source Study] 2 (1936): 145–86.

Kolechenikova, V. N. "K voprosu o sosediakh kak sotsial'noi kategorii [On the Problem of Neighbors as a Social Category]." In N. V. Ustiugov, Iu. A. Tikhonov, and P. T. Iakovleva, eds. *Russkoe gosudarstvo v XVII veke. Novye iavleniia v sotsial'no-ekonomicheskoi, politicheskoi i kul'turnoi zhizni. Sbornik statei* [The Russian State in the 17th Century: New Developments in Socio-Economic, Political and Cultural Life. A Collection of Articles] (Moscow, 1961), pp. 201–7.

Kollmann, Nancy Shields. "The Boyar Clan and Court Politics: The Founding of the Muscovite Political System." *Cahiers du monde russe et soviétique* 23 (1982): 5–31.

———. "Consensus Politics: The Dynastic Crisis of the 1490s Reconsidered." *Russian Review* 45 (1986): 235–66.

———. "Honor and Dishonor in Early Modern Russia." *Forschungen zur osteuropäischen Geschichte* 46 (1992): 131–46.

———. *Kinship and Politics: The Making of the Muscovite Political System, 1345–1547*. Stanford, 1987.

———. "Pilgrimage, Procession, and Symbolic Space in Sixteenth-Century

Russian Politics." In Michael S. Flier and Daniel Rowland, eds., *Medieval Russian Culture,* vol. 2 (Berkeley, 1994), pp. 163–181.

———. "Terminology about Society in Early Modern Russia." Paper presented at the NEH Conference, Cultural Identity in a Multicultural State: Muscovy, 1359–1584, Los Angeles, March 1994.

———. "Transformations in Muscovite Political Culture, 1602–1690's." Paper presented at the AAASS Conference, Honolulu, November 1988.

———. "Women's Honor in Early Modern Russia." In B. E. Clements, B. A. Engel, and C. D. Worobec, eds., *Russia's Women: Accommodation, Resistance, Transformation.* Berkeley, 1991.

Konopczynski, W. "Une Antithèse du Principe majoritaire en droit polonais." In Paul Vinogradoff, ed., *Essays in Legal History Read Before the International Congress of Historical Studies in London in 1913* (Oxford, 1913), pp. 336–47.

Konshina, E. N., and N. K. Shvabe, comps. and eds. *Kratkii ukazatel' arkhivnykh fondov Otdela rukopisei [GBL]* [A Short Guide to the Archival Collections of the Manuscript Division of GBL]. Moscow, 1948.

Korsakov, D. A. *Votsarenie Imperatritsy Anny Ioannovny* [The Accession to the Throne of Empress Anna Ioannovna]. Kazan', 1880.

Kosheleva, O. E. "Kollektivnye chelobit'ia dvorian na boiar (XVII v.) [Collective Petitions of the Gentry against the Boyars (17th Century)]." *Voprosy istorii* [Questions of History] 12 (1982): 171–77.

Kozachenko, A. I. "K istorii zemskogo sobora 1653 g. [Toward a History of the Assembly of the Land of 1653]." *Istoricheskii arkhiv* [Historical Archive] 3 (1957): 223–27.

Kozliakov, V. N., comp. *Iaroslavskii arkhiv dvorian Vikent'evykh XVII veka. Sbornik dokumentov* [The Iaroslavl' Archive of the Gentry Family, the Vikent'evs, in the 17th Century. A Collection of Documents]. Iaroslavl', 1989.

Kudriavtsev, I. M., ed. *Muzeinoe sobranie rukopisei. Opisanie* [The Museum Collection of Manuscripts. Description]. Moscow, 1961.

Kurdiumov, M. G. "Opisanie aktov, khraniashchikhsia v arkhive Imperatorskoi Arkheograficheskoi Kommissii. Tri kollektsii V. Borisova [Description of the Documents Preserved in the Archive of the Imperial Archeographic Commission. Three Collections of V. Borisov]." In V. G. Druzhinin, ed., *Letopis' zaniatii Imperatorskoi Arkheograficheskoi Kommissii za 1913 god* [Chronicle of the Proceedings of the Imperial Archeographic Commission for 1913], vol. 26. St. Petersburg, 1914.

Kuznetsov, V. I. "Svetskoe feodal'noe zemlevladenie Kolomenskogo uezda poslednei treti XVI–XVII vekov (po pistsovym i perepisnym knigam) [Secular Feudal Landholding in Kolomna Province in the Last Third of the 16th and 17th Centuries (According to the Cadaster Books)." Abstract, Candidate diss., Moscow State University, 1983.

Latkin, V. N. *Zemskie sobory drevnei Rusi* [Assemblies of the Land of Ancient Rus']. St. Petersburg, 1885.

Latkin, V. N., comp. and ed. *Materialy dlia istorii zemskikh soborov XVII stoletiia* [Materials for the History of Assemblies of the Land of the 17th Century]. St. Petersburg, 1884.

LeDonne, John P. "Ruling Families in the Russian Political Order, 1689–1825." *Cahiers du monde russe et soviétique* 28 (1987): 233–322.

———. *Ruling Russia: Politics and Administration in the Age of Absolutism, 1762–1796.* Princeton, 1984.

Levin, Eve. *Sex and Society in the World of Orthodox Slavs, 900–1700.* Ithaca, 1989.

———. "Women and Property in Medieval Novgorod: Dependence and Independence." *Russian History* 10 (1983): 154–69.

Levy, Sandra. "Women and the Control of Property in Sixteenth-Century Muscovy." *Russian History* 10 (1983): 201–12.

Liutkina, E. Iu. "Gosudarstvo, tserkov' i formirovanie statusa patriarshikh dvorian i detei boiarskikh v XVII veke [State, Church and the Creation of the Rank of Patriarchal Gentrymen in the 17th Century]." In *Sosloviia i gosudarstvennaia vlast' v Rossii, XV-seredina XIV vv. Mezhdunarodnaia konferentsiia—Chteniia pamiati akad. L. V. Cherepnina. Tezisy dokladov* [Estate and State Power in Russia, 15th through Mid-17th Centuries. An International Conference of Readings in Memory of Academician L. V. Cherepnin]. Moscow, 1994.

Lockridge, Kenneth. *On the Sources of Patriarchal Rage: The Commonplace Books of William Byrd and Thomas Jefferson and the Gendering of Power in the Eighteenth Century.* New York, 1992.

Loewenson, Leo. "The Moscow Rising of 1648." *Slavonic and East European Review* 27 (1948), 146–56.

Lotman, Ju. M., and B. A. Uspenskij. "The Role of Dual Models in the Dynamics of Russian Culture (Up to the End of the Eighteenth Century)." In their *The Semiotics of Russian Culture.* Ann Shukman, ed., (Ann Arbor, Mich., 1984), pp. 3–35.

McNally, Susanne Janosik. "From Public Person to Private Prisoner: The Changing Place of Women in Medieval Russia." Ph.D. diss., SUNY at Binghamton, 1976.

Major, J. Russell. "Crown and Aristocracy in Renaissance France." *American Historical Review* 69 (1964): 631–45.

———. *The Estates General of 1560.* Princeton, 1951.

———. "Noble Income, Inflation, and the Wars of Religion in France." *American Historical Review* 86 (1981): 21–48.

Mann, Michael. *The Sources of Social Power.* 2 vols. Cambridge, Eng., and New York, 1986.

Margeret, Jacques. *The Russian Empire and Grand Duchy of Muscovy: A 17th-Century French Account.* Chester S. L. Dunning, trans. and ed. Pittsburgh, 1983.

Marker, Gary. *Publishing, Printing, and the Origins of Intellectual Life in Russia, 1700–1800.* Princeton, 1985.

Marriott, McKim. "Small Communities in Indigenous Cultures." In McKim Marriott, ed., *Studies in the Little Community.* Chicago, 1955.

Martin, Janet. "The Novokshcheny of Novgorod: Assimilation in the 16th Century." *Central Asian Survey* 9 (1990): 13–38.

Masonov, I. F. *Bibliografiia Vladimirskoi gubernii*. Vladimir, 1905.

Meehan-Waters, Brenda. *Autocracy and Aristocracy: The Russian Service Elite of 1730*. New Brunswick, N.J., 1982.

Merelman, Richard M. "The Political Uses of Territoriality." *Environment and Behavior* 20 (1988): 576–600.

Mikhnevich, N. P. and A. K. Il'enko. "Glavnyi shtab. Istoricheskii ocherk. Komplektovanie vooruzhennykh sil v Rossii do 1802 g. [Central Command. A Historical Essay. The Mobilization of Military Forces in Russia until 1802." In *Stoletie voennogo ministerstva 1802–1902* [A Century of the Ministry of War, 1802–1902]. Vol. 4, pt. 1. St. Petersburg, 1902.

Miliukov, P. N. *Ocherki po istorii russkoi kul'tury*. 3 vols. St. Petersburg, 1900.

Mousnier, Roland. *Social Hierarchies 1450 to the Present*. Peter Evans, trans. Margaret Clarke, ed. New York, 1973.

Nazarov, V. D. "Genealogiia Koshkinykh-Zakhar'inykh-Romanovykh i predanie ob osnovanii Georgievskogo monastyria [The Genealogy of the Koshkins-Zakharins-Romanovs and the Legend about the Foundation of the Georgievskii Monastery]." *Istoricheskaia genealogiia* [*Historical Genealogy*] 1 (1993).

Newey, Walter. "Vegetation and Soil." In Archie Brown, John Fennell, Michael Koser, and H. T. Willetts, eds., *The Cambridge Encyclopedia of Russia and the Soviet Union* (Cambridge, Eng., 1982), pp. 40–43.

Nikol'skii, Nikolai K., ed. "Rifmovannoe poslanie dvorianina k dvorianinu XVII veka [Rhythmic Letter of a Gentryman to a Gentryman in the 17th Century]." *Bibliograficheskiia zapiski* [Bibliographic Notes] 4 (1892): 279–81.

Nosov, N. E. *Ocherki po istorii mestnogo upravleniia russkogo gosudarstva pervoi poloviny XVI veka* [Essays on Local Administration of the Russian State in the first Half of the 16th Century]. Moscow and Leningrad, 1957.

———. *Stanovlenie soslovno-predstavitel'nykh uchrezhdenii v Rossii. Izyskaniia o zemskoi reforme Ivana Groznogo* [The Establishment of Estate-Representative Institutions in Russia. Investigations of the *Zemskii* Reforms of Ivan the Terrible]. Leningrad, 1969.

Nosov, N. E., ed. *Zakonodatel'nye akty Russkogo gosudarstva vtoroi poloviny XVI–pervoi poloviny XVII veka. Teksty* [Legislative Acts of the Russian State in the Second Half of the 16th–First Half of the 17th Century. Texts]. Leningrad, 1986.

Novitskii, V. I. *Vybornoe i bol'shoe dvorianstvo XVI–XVII vekov* [The Select and Great Gentry of the 16–17th Centuries]. Kiev, 1915.

Novombergskii, N. Ia. *Slovo i delo gosudarevy* [Sovereign's Word and Deed]. Vol. 1 of 2. Published as *Zapiski Moskovskago arkheologicheskago instituta* [Notes of the Moscow Archeological Institute], vol. 14. Moscow, 1911.

Novosel'skii, A. A. "Feodal'noe zemlevladenie. Boiarstvo, dvorianstvo i tserkov' [Feudal Landholding. Boyars, Gentry and Church]." In Novosel'skii and Ustiugov, eds., *Ocherki istorii SSSR*, pp. 139–63.

——. "Kollektivnye dvorianskie chelobit'ia po voprosam mezhevaniia i opisaniia zemel' v 80-kh godakh XVII v. [Collective Gentry Petitions on Questions of Surveying and Surveying Lands in the 1680s]." *Uchenye zapiski RANION* [Scholarly Notes of RANION] 4 (1929): 103–8.

——. "Kollektivnye dvorianskie chelobitnye o syske beglykh krest'ian i kholopov vo vtoroi polovine XVII v. [Collective Gentry Petitions about the Search for Runaway Peasants and Slaves in the Second Half of the 17th Century]." In Pavlenko et al., eds., *Dvorianstvo i krepostnoi stroi Rossii*, pp. 303–43.

——. "Pobegi krest'ian i kholopov i ikh sysk v Moskovskom gosudarstve vtoroi poloviny XVII veka [Flight of Peasants and Slaves and their Recovery in the Muscovite State in the Second Half of the 17th Century]." *Uchenye zapiski RANION* [Scholarly Notes of RANION] 1 (1926): 327–54.

——. "Praviashchie gruppy v sluzhilom 'gorode' XVII v. [Ruling Groups in the Service 'Town' in the 17th Century]." *Uchenye zapiski RANION* [Scholarly Notes of RANION] 5 (1928): 315–35.

——. "Raspad zemlevladeniia sluzhilogo 'goroda' v XVII v. (po desiatniam) [The Disintegration of the Landholding of the Service 'Town' in the 17th Century (According to Muster Rolls)]." In N. N. Ustiugov, ed., *Russkoe gosudarstvo v XVII veke. Novye iavleniia v sotsial'no-ekonomicheskoi i kul'turnoi zhizni. Sbornik statei* [The Russian State in the 17th Century: New Developments in Socio-Economic, Political and Cultural Life. A Collection of Articles] (Moscow, 1961), pp. 231–53.

——. *Votchinnik i ego khoziaistvo v XVII veke* [A Landlord and His Economy in the 17th Century]. Moscow and Leningrad, 1929.

Novosel'skii, A. A., ed. *Razriadnyi prikaz (nachalo XVI v.–1711 g.). Opis' stolbtsov dopolnitel'nogo otdela arkhivnogo fonda No. 210. Krainie daty dokumental'nykh materialov 1576–1716 gg.* [The Chancellery of Military Affairs (Beginning of the 16th Century through 1711): An Inventory of the Scrolls of the Supplemental Division of Archival Collection Number 210, with Documents Dating between 1576 and 1716]. Moscow, 1950.

Novosel'skii, A. A. and N. V. Ustiugov, eds. *Ocherki istorii SSSR. Period feodalizma. XVII v.* [Outlines of the History of the USSR. Period of Feudalism. The 17th Century]. Moscow, 1955.

Ogloblin, N. N. "Proiskhozhdenie provintsial'nykh pod'iachikh [The Origins of the Provincial Clerks]." *Zhurnal Ministerstva Narodnogo Prosveshcheniia* [Journal of the Ministry of Popular Education] 9 (1894): 118–50; 10 (1894): 219–41.

Opisanie dokumentov i bumag, khraniashchikhsia v Moskovskom arkhive Ministerstva iustitsii [Description of Documents and Papers Preserved in the Moscow Archive of the Ministry of Justice]. 21 vols. St. Petersburg and Moscow, 1869–1921.

Orlov, A. S. "Voprosy sotsial'no-ekonomicheskoi istorii v knige 'Evoliutsiia feodaliszma v Rossii' [Questions of Socio-Economic History in the Book *Evolution of Feudalism in Russia*]." *Istoriia SSSR* [History of the USSR], no. 3 (1982): 149–61.

The Orthodox Study Bible: New Testament and Psalms, King James Version. Nashville, Tenn., 1993.

Ortner, Sherry B. "Resistance and the Problem of Ethnographic Refusal." *Comparative Studies in Society and History* 37 (1995): 173–93.

Pagden, Anthony, ed. *The Languages of Political Theory in Early-Modern Europe*. Cambridge, Eng., 1987.

Pamiatniki delovoi pis'mennosti XVII veka. Vladimirskii krai [Texts of Practical Writing of the 17th Century: The Vladimir Region]. Moscow, 1984.

Pamiatniki russkogo prava (PRP) [Texts of Russian Law]. 8 vols. Moscow, 1952–63.

Parker, David. "French Absolutism, the English State and the Utility of the Base-Superstructure Model." *Social History* 15 (1990): 287–301.

———. "The Social Foundations of French Absolutism, 1610–1630." *Past and Present* 53 (1971): 67–89.

Paul of Aleppo. *The travels of Macarius, extracts from the diary of the travels of Macarius, patriarch of Antioch, written in Arabic by his son Paul, archdeacon of Aleppo, in the years of their journeying, 1652–1660. Translated into English and printed for the Oriental translation fund, 1836*. Lady Laura Ridding, comp. and ed. London, 1936.

Pavlenko, N. I., et al., eds. *Dvorianstvo i krepostnoi stroi Rossii XVI–XVIII vv. (Sbornik statei, posviashchennyi pamiati Alekseia Andreevicha Novosel'skogo)* [The Gentry and the Serf System of Russia, 16th–18th Centuries: A Collection of Articles Dedicated to the Memory of Aleksei Andreevich Novosel'skii]. Moscow, 1975.

Pavlov-Sil'vanskii, N. P. *Gosudarevy sluzhilye liudi: liudi kabal'nye i dokladnye* [The Sovereign's Servitors]. 2nd ed. St. Petersburg, 1909.

Perrie, Maurene. *The Image of Ivan the Terrible in Russian Folklore*. New York, 1987.

Petrikeev, D. I. *Krupnoe krepostnoe khoziaistvo XVII v. Po materialam votchiny boiarina B. I. Morozova* [Large-Scale Serf Economy in the 17th Century, According to Materials from the Estate of Boyar B. I. Morozov]. Leningrad, 1967.

Petrov, P. N. *Istoriia rodov russkago dvorianstva*. St. Petersburg, 1886.

Pintner, Walter McKenzie and Don Karl Rowney, eds. *Russian Officialdom: The Bureaucratization of Russian Society from the Seventeenth to the Twentieth Century*. Chapel Hill, N.C., 1980.

Pipes, Richard. *Russia Under the Old Regime*. New York, 1974.

Pitt-Rivers, Julian. *The People of the Sierra*. London, 1954.

Plavsic, Borivoj. "Seventeenth-Century Chanceries and their Staffs." In Pintner and Rowney, eds., *Russian Officialdom*, pp. 21–45.

Pocock, J. G. A. "Virtue, Rights, and Manners: A Model for Historians of Political Thought." In his *Virtue, Commerce, and History: Essays on Po-

litical Thought and History, Chiefly in the Eighteenth Century (Cambridge, Eng., 1985), pp. 37–50.

Poe, Marshall T. " 'Russian Despotism': The Origins and Dissemination of an Early Modern Commonplace." Ph.D. diss., University of California, Berkeley, 1993.

Pokrovskii, N. N. "Nachal'nye chelobitnye tomskogo vosstaniia 1648–1649 gg. [The First Petitions of the Tomsk Uprising of 1648–1649]." In E. K. Romodanovskaia, ed., *Literatura i klassovaia bor'ba epokhi pozdnego feodalizma v Rossii* [Literature and Class Struggle in the Epoch of Late Feudalism in Russia] (Novosibirsk, 1987), pp. 70–105.

——. "Sibirskie materialy XVII–XVIII vv. po 'slovu i delu gosudarevu' kak istochnik po istorii obshchestvennogo soznaniia [Siberian Materials of the 17–18th Centuries on 'Sovereign's Word and Deed' as a Source for the History of Social Consciousness]." In N. N. Pokrovskii, ed., *Istochniki po istorii obshchestvennoi mysli i kul'tury epokhi poznego feodalizma* [Sources on the History of Social Thought and Culture from the Epoch of Late Feudalism] (Novosibirsk, 1988), pp. 24–61.

Polnoe sobranie zakonov Rossiiskoi imperii [Complete Collection of Laws of the Russian Empire]. 45 vols. St. Petersburg, 1830–43.

Polnoe sobranie zakonov rossiiskoi imperii [Complete Collection of Laws of the Russian Empire]. 45 vols. St. Petersburg, 1830–43.

Potter, Cathy J. "The Russian Church and the Politics of Reform in the Second Half of the Seventeenth Century." Ph.D. diss., Yale University, 1993.

"Povest' ob Ul'ianii Osor'inoi [Tale of Iuliainia Osor'ina]." In L. A. Dmitriev, ed., and D. S. Likhachev, ed. and comp., *Pamiatniki literatury drevnei Rusi. XVII vek* [Literary Texts of Ancient Rus']. Bk. 1. Moscow, 1988.

Pozdniakov, S. V. "Sluzhilaia korporatsiia Maloiaroslavetskogo uezda [The Service Corporation of Maloiaroslavets Province]." Candidate diss., M.G.I.A.I., 1982. Abstract.

Presniakov, A. E. "Moskovskoe gosudarstvo pervoi poloviny XVII veka [The Muscovite State in the First Half of the 17th Century]." In V. V. Kallash, ed. *Tri veka. Rossiia ot smuty do nashego vremeni. Istoricheskii sbornik* [Three Centuries: Russia from the Time of Troubles to Our Time. A Historical Collection], vol. 1 (Moscow, 1912–13), pp. 4–84.

Pskovskaia sudnaia gramota [Pskov Judicial Charter]. In M. Vladimirskii-Budanov, ed., *Khrestomatiia po istorii russkogo prava* [Anthology on the History of Russian Law] (St. Petersburg and Kiev, 1889), pp. 132–78.

Putevoditel' po arkhivu Leningradskogo otdeleniia instituta istorii [Guide to the Archive of the Leningrad Branch of the Institute of History]. Moscow and Leningrad, 1958.

Raeff, Marc. *Origins of the Russian Intelligentsia: The Eighteenth-Century Nobility.* New York, 1966.

——. *Plans for Political Reform in Imperial Russia, 1730–1905.* Englewood Cliffs, N.J., 1966.

——. *The Well-Ordered Police State: Social and Institutional Change* through Law in the Germanies and Russia, 1600–1800. New Haven, 1983.

Ransel, David L. "Bureaucracy and Patronage: The View from an Eighteenth-Century Letter-Writer." In Frederic Cople Jaher, ed., The Rich, the Well-Born, and the Powerful: Elites and Upper Classes in History (Urbana, Ill., 1973), pp. 154–78.

———. "Character and Style of Patron-Client Relations in Russia." In Antoni Maczak, ed., Klientelsysteme in Europa der frühen Neuzeit (Munich, 1988), pp. 211–31.

———. The Politics of Catherinian Russia. The Panin Party. New Haven, 1975.

"Riadnaia rospis' pridanomu, 1679 goda [Marriage Agreement Concerning a Dowry, 1679]." In Sbornik starinnykh bumag, khraniashchikhsia v muzee P. I. Shchukina, vol. 2 (1897): 269–70.

Romanovich-Slavatinskii, A. Dvorianstvo v Rossii ot nachala XVIII veka do otmeny krepostnogo prava [The Nobility in Russia from the Beginning of the 18th Century to the Abolition of Serfdom]. St. Petersburg, 1870.

Rosen, Lawrence. "Alternative Courts and the Concept of Community. A Review Article." Comparative Studies in Society and History 29 (1987): 558–65.

Rosenberg, Hans. Bureaucracy, Aristocracy and Autocracy. Cambridge, Mass., 1958.

Rossiiskaia Assotsiatsiia Nauchno-Issledovatel'skikh Institutov Obshche-stvennykh Nauk (RANION) [Russian Association of Scholarly Research Institutes of the Social Sciences], Moscow.

Rowland, Daniel. "The Artist's View of Politics: The Golden Palace," University of Kentucky. Typescript.

———. "Biblical Military Imagery in the Political Culture of Early Modern Russia: The Blessed Host of the Heavenly Tsar." In Michael S. Flier and Daniel Rowland, eds., Medieval Russian Culture, vol. 2 (Berkeley, 1994), pp. 182–212.

———. "Did Muscovite Literary Ideology Place Limits on the Power of the Tsar (1540's–1660's)?" Russian Review 49 (1990): 125–55.

———. "The Problem of Advice in Muscovite Tales about the Time of Troubles." Russian History 6, pt. 2 (1979): 259–83.

Rozhdestvenskii, S. V. Sluzhiloe zemlevladenie v Moskovskom gosudarstve XVI veka [Service Landholding in the Muscovite State in the 16th Century]. St. Petersburg, 1897. Reprint, The Hauge, 1966.

Rozhkov, N. A. Sel'skoe khoziaistvo Moskovskoi Rusi v XVI veke [The Agriculture of Muscovite Rus' in the 16th Century]. Moscow, 1899.

Rummel', V. V., and V. V. Golubtsov, Rodoslovnyi sbornik russkikh dvorian-skikh familii. 2 vols. St. Petersburg, 1886–87.

Russ, Harmut. Adel und Adelsoppositionen im Moskauer Staat. Wiesbaden, 1975.

Russkaia istoricheskaia biblioteka (RIB) [Russian Historical Library]. 39 vols. St. Petersburg-Leningrad, 1872–1927.

Sabean, David Warren. *Power in the Blood: Popular Culture and Village Discourse in Early Modern Germany*. Cambridge, Eng., and New York, 1984.

Sakharov, A. M. "O termine 'gorod' v istochnikakh XVI v. [Of the Term 'Town' in Sources of the 16th Century]." In *Obshchestvo i gosudarstvo feodal'noi Rossii. Sbornik statei, posviashchennyi 70-letiiu Akademika L'va Vladimirovicha Cherepnina* [Society and State of Feudal Russia: A Collection of Articles Dedicated to the 70th Birthday of Academician Lev Vladimirovich Cherepnin] (Moscow, 1975), pp. 62–66.

Sbornik starinnykh bumag, khraniashchikhsia v muzee P. I. Shchukina [Collection of Ancient Papers Preserved in the P. I. Shchukin Museum]. 10 vols. P. I. Shchukin, ed. Moscow, 1890–1902.

Scott, James C. *Domination and the Arts of Resistance: Hidden Transcripts*. New Haven, 1990.

——. *Weapons of the Weak: Everyday Forms of Peasant Resistance*. New Haven, 1985.

Sedashev, V. N. *Ocherki i materialy po istorii zemlevladeniia Moskovskoi Rusi v XVII v.* [Essays and Sources on the History of Landholding in Muscovite Rus' in the 17th Century]. Moscow, 1912.

Selifontov, N. N. *Ocherk sluzhebnoi deiatel'nosti i domashnei zhizni stol'nika i voevody XVII stoletiia, Vasiliia Aleksandrovicha Daudova* [An Essay on the Service Activities and Domestic Life of a *Stol'nik* and *Voevoda* of the 17th Century, Vasilii Aleksandrovich Daudov]. St. Petersburg, 1871.

Sergeevich, V. I. *Drevnosti russkogo prava* [Antiquities of Russian Law]. 3 vols. 3rd ed. St. Petersburg, 1903–9.

Shakhmatov, M. V. "Chelobitnaia 'mira' moskovskago tsariu Alekseiu Mikhailovichu 10 iunia 1648 g. [The Petition of the Muscovite 'Community' to Tsar Aleksei Mikhailovich on 10 June 1648]." *Věstník královské české společnosti nauk. Třida filosoficko-historiká: Ročnik 1933* (Prague, 1934), pp. 1–23.

Shumakov, S. A. *Sotnitsy, zapisi i gramoty*. 7 vols. Moscow, 1902–13.

Shumilov, V. N., comp., and L. V. Cherepnin, ed. *Knigi moskovskikh prikazov v fondakh TsGADA. Opis' 1495–1718 gg.* [Books of the Muscovite Chancelleries in the Collections of TsGADA. An Inventory of the years 1495–1718]. Moscow, 1972.

Shvatchenko, O. A. *Svetskie feodal'nye votchiny Rossii v pervoi treti XVII veka* [Secular Feudal Estates in Russia in the First Third of the 17th Century]. Moscow, 1990.

Skocpol, Theda. "Bringing the State Back In." In P. Evans, D. Rueschemeyer, and T. Skocpol, eds., *Bringing the State Back In* (Cambridge, Eng., 1985), pp. 3–37.

Slater, Miriam. *Family Life in the Seventeenth Century: The Verneys of Clayton House*. London and Boston, 1984.

Smirnov, P. P. "Chelobitnyia dvorian i detei boiarskikh v pervoi polovine XVII veke [Petitions of the Gentry in the First Half of the 17th Century]." *ChOIDR* 254, no. 3 (1915), pt. 1, pp. 1–73.

——. "Neskol'ko dokumentov k istorii Sobornogo Ulozheniia i Zemskogo

Sobora 1648–1649 godov [Some Documents on the History of the Assembly of the Land Law Code and the Assembly of the Land of 1648–1649]." *ChOIDR* 247, no. 4 (1913), pt. 4, pp. 1–20.

——. "O nachale Ulozheniia i Zemskogo sobora 1648–1649 gg. [Of the Beginning of the *Ulozhenie* and of the Assembly of the Land of 1648–1649]." *Zhurnal Ministerstva Narodnogo Prosveshcheniia* [Journal of the Ministry of Popular Education] 47 (1913): 36–66.

Smith, Jay Michael. "The Culture of Merit in Old Regime France: Royal Service and the 'Old' Nobility, 1600–1789." Ph.D. diss., University of Michigan, 1990.

Smith, Sir Thomas. *De Republica Anglorum.* Mary Dewar, ed. Cambridge, 1982.

Sobranie gosudarstvennykh gramot i dogovorov. (SGGiD) 5 vols. Moscow, 1813–28.

Solov'ev, S. M. *Istoriia Rossii s drevneishikh vremen: v piatnadtsati knigakh* [History of Russia from the Most Ancient Times: In 15 Books]. 29 vols. in 15 bks. Moscow, 1959–66.

Starkey, Thomas. *A Dialogue Between Pole and Lupset.* T. F. Mayer, ed. Camden Fourth Series, vol. 37. London, 1989.

Stashevskii, E. D. *K istorii dvorianskikh chelobitnykh* [Toward the History of Gentry Petitions]. Moscow, 1915.

——. *K istorii kolonizatsii Iuga. (Velikii boiarin Ivan Nikitich Romanov i ego slobody v eletskom uezde)* [Toward the History of the Colonization of the South. (The Great Boyar Ivan Nikitich Romanov and his Settlements in Elets Province)]. Moscow, 1913.

——. *Ocherki po istorii tsarstvovaniia Mikhaila Fedorovicha. Pt. 1: Moskovskoe obshchestvo i gosudarstvo ot nachala tsarstvovaniia Mikhaila Fedorovicha do epokhi Smolenskoi voiny* [Essays on the History of the Reign of Mikhail Fedorovich. Pt. 1: Muscovite Society and State from the Beginning of Mikhail Fedorovich's Reign until the Epoch of the Smolensk War]. Kiev, 1913. Reprint, The Hague and Paris, 1969.

——. "Sluzhiloe soslovie [The Service Estate]." In M. V. Dovnar-Zapol'skii, ed. *Russkaia istoriia v ocherkakh i stat'iakh* [Russian History in Essays and Articles], vol. 3 (Kiev, 1912), pp. 1–33.

——. *Smeta voennykh sil Moskovskogo gosudarstva v 1663 godu* [Estimate of the Military Forces of the Muscovite State in 1663]. Kiev, 1910.

——. *Zemlevladenie moskovskogo dvorianstva v pervoi polovine XVII veka* [Landholding of the Muscovite Gentry in the First Half of the 17th Century]. Moscow, 1911.

Staves, Susan. *Married Women's Separate Property in England, 1660–1833.* Cambridge, Mass., 1990.

Steindorff, Ludwig. "Donations, Charity, and Commemorations as Expressions of Identity." Paper presented at the NEH Conference, Cultural Identity in a Multicultural State: Muscovy, 1359–1584, Los Angeles, March 1994.

Stevens, Carol B. "Belgorod: Notes on Literacy and Language in the Seventeenth-Century Russian Army." *Russian History* 7, pts. 1–2 (1980): 113–24.

Stone, Lawrence. *The Crisis of the Aristocracy, 1558–1641.* Abridged ed. New York, 1967.

Stone, Lawrence and Jeanne C. Fawtier Stone. *An Open Elite? England 1540– 1880.* Oxford, 1984.

Storozhev, V. N. "Opis' desiaten XVI–XVII vv. [Inventory of Muster Rolls of the 16th-17th Centuries]." In *Opisanie dokumentov i bumag, khrania-shchikhsia v Moskovskom arkhive Ministerstva iustitsii* [Description of Documents and Papers Preserved in the Moscow Archive of the Ministry of Justice], vol. 7 (Moscow, 1890), pp. 64–175.

Storozhev, V. N., ed. "Dva chelobit'ia (K bibliografii materialov dlia istorii russkogo dvorianstva) [Two Petitions (Toward a Bibliography of Materials for the History of the Russian Nobility)]." *Bibliograficheskiia zapiski* [Bibliographic Notes], pt. 1 (1892): 7–15.

———. *Materialy dlia istorii russkogo dvorianstva* [Materials for the History of the Russian Nobility]. 2 vols. Moscow, 1908.

Subtelny, Orest. *Domination of Eastern Europe: Native Nobilities and Foreign Absolutism, 1500–1715.* Kingston and Montreal, 1986.

Suny, Ronald G. *The Revenge of the Past: Nationalism, Revolution, and the Collapse of the Soviet Union.* Stanford, 1993.

Terdiman, Richard. *Discourse/Counter-Discourse: The Theory and Practice of Symbolic Resistance in Nineteenth-Century France.* Ithaca, N.Y., 1985.

Thirsk, Joan. "The European Debate on Customs of Inheritance, 1500– 1700." In Goody, Thirsk, and Thompson, eds., *Family and Inheritance*, pp. 177–91.

Thompson, E. P. *Whigs and Hunters: The Origins of the Black Act.* New York, 1975.

Tikhomirov, M. N., and P. P. Epifanov, eds. *Sobornoe Ulozhenie 1649 goda: Uchebnoe posobie dlia vysshei shkoly* [The Assembly of the Land Law Code of 1649: A Text Book for Higher School]. Moscow, 1961.

Tikhonov, Iu. A. "Podmoskovnye imeniia russkoi aristokratii vo vtoroi polovine XVII - nachale XVIII v. [The Estates of the Russian Aristocracy in the Moscow Area in the Second Half of the 17th-Beginning of the Eighteenth Century]." In Pavlenko et al., eds., *Dvorianstvo i krepostnoi stroi Rossii*, pp. 135–58.

Tikhonravov, K. V., ed. *Vladimirskii sbornik* [Vladimir Collection]. Moscow, 1857.

Torke, Hans-Joachim. "Continuity and Change in Relations between Bureaucracy and Society in Russia, 1613–1861." *Canadian-American Slavic Studies* 5 (1971): 457–76.

———. *Die staatsbedingte Gesellschaft im Moskauer Reich: Zar und Zemlja in der altrussischen Herrschaftsverfassung, 1613–1689.* Leyden, 1974.

Tregubov, M. I., comp., and A. V. Selivanov, ed. *Alfavitnyi spisok dvorian-*

skikh rodov Vladimirskoi gubernii s ukazaniem vazhneishikh dokumentov, nakhodiashchikhsia v delakh o dvorianstve raznykh familii Arkhiva Dvorianskogo Deputatskogo Sobraniia [Alphabetical List of Noble Clans of Vladimir *Guberniia* with Indication of the Most Important Documents Located in the Papers about the Nobility of Various Families of the Archive of Assembly of Deputies of the Nobility]. Vladimir, 1905.

Troitskii, S. M. *Russkii absoliutizm i dvorianstvo v XVIII v. Formirovanie biurokratii* [Russian Absolutism and the Nobility in the 18th Century: The Formation of the Bureaucracy]. Moscow, 1974.

TsGADA. Putevoditel' [*TsGADA*. Guide]. 2 pts: Pt. 1 edited by S. K. Bogoiavlenskii; Pt. 2 edited by A. I. Iakovlev. Moscow, 1946–47.

Ukmylova, T. K., ed. *Kratkii otchet rukopisnogo otdela za 1914–1938 gg. so vstuptel'nym istoricheskim ocherkom* [A Short Account of the Manuscript Division for the Years 1914–1938, with an Introductory Historical Essay]. Leningrad, 1940.

Uroff, Benjamin Phillip. "Grigorii Karpovich Kotoshikhin, *On Russia in the Reign of Alexis Mikhailovich*: An Annotated Translation." Ph.D. diss., Columbia University, 1970.

Vazhinskii, V. M. *Zemlevladenie i skladyvanie obshchiny odnodvortsev v XVII veke (Po materialam iuzhnykh uezdov Rossii)* [Landholding and Composition of the Commune of Single-Householders in the 17th Century (By Materials of the Southern Provinces of Russia)]. Voronezh, 1974.

Verba, Sidney. "Comparative Political Culture." In Lucian Pye and Sidney Verba, eds., *Political Culture and Political Development* (Princeton, 1965), pp. 512–60.

Veselovskii, S. B. *D'iaki i pod'iachie XV–XVII vv.* [State Secretaries and Clerks of the 15th–17th Centuries]. Moscow, 1975.

——. *Feodal'noe zemlevladenie v severo-vostochnoi Rusi* [Feudal Landholding in Northeastern Rus'], vol. 1. Moscow and Leningrad, 1947.

——. *Issledovaniia po istorii klassa sluzhilykh zemlevladel'tsev* [Investigations into the History of the Class of Service Landholders]. Moscow, 1969.

——. *Issledovaniia po istorii oprichniny* [Investigations into the History of the *Oprichnina*]. Moscow, 1963.

——. *Prikaznyi stroi upravleniia Moskovskogo gosudarstva* [The Chancellery System of Administration of the Muscovite State]. Kiev, 1912.

——. "Smety voennykh sil Moskovskogo gosudarstva, 1661–1663 [Estimates of the Military Forces of the Muscovite State, 1661–1663]." *ChOIDR* 238 (1911), pp. 1–60.

——. *Soshnoe pis'mo: Issledovanie po istorii kadastra i pososhnogo oblozheniia Moskovskogo gosudarstva* [Cadasters: Research into the History of the Cadaster and the Land-based Tax of the Muscovite State]. Moscow, 1915–16.

Vladimirskiia Gubernskiia Vedomosti [Vladimir Provincial News]. Vladimir.

Vladimirskii-Budanov, M. F. *Obzor istorii russkogo prava* [Survey of the History of Russian Law]. 6th ed. St. Petersburg, 1909.

Vodarskii, Ia. E. *Dvorianskoe zemlevladenie v Rossii v XVII-pervoi polovine XIX v. (razmery i razmeshchenie)* [Noble Landholding in Russia in the 17th through the First Half of the Nineteenth Century]. Moscow, 1988.

———. *Naselenie Rossii v kontse XVII-nachale XVIII veka (Chislennost', soslovno-klassovyi sostav, razmeshchenie)* [The Population of Russia at the End of the 17th–Beginning of the 18th Century (Numbers, Estate-Class Composition, Distribution)]. Moscow, 1977.

———. "Praviashchaia gruppa svetskikh feodalov v Rossii v XVII v. [The Ruling Group of Secular Feudal Lords in Russia in the 17th Century]." In Pavlenko et al., eds., *Dvorianstvo i krepostnoi stroi Rossii*, pp. 70–107.

———. "Sluzhiloe dvorianstvo v Rossii v kontse XVII-nachale XVIII v. [The Service Gentry in Russia at the End of the 17th–Beginning of the 18th Century]." In V. I. Shunkov, ed., *Voprosy voennoi istorii Rossii XVII i pervaia polovina XIX vekov* [Questions of the Military History of Russia in the 17th and First Half of the 19th Centuries] (Moscow, 1969), pp. 233–38.

Volkov, M. Ia. "Ob otmene mestnichestva v Rossii [About the Abolition of Mestnichestvo]." *Istoriia SSSR* [History of the USSR], no. 2 (1977): 53–67.

Vorob'ev, V. M., and A. Ia. Degtiarev. *Russkoe feodal'noe zemlevaldenie ot "Smutnogo vremeni" do kanuna petrovskikh reform* [Russian Feudal Landholding from the Time of Troubles to the Eve of the Petrine Reforms]. Leningrad, 1986.

Vremennik Imperatorskogo obshchestva istorii i drevnostei rossiiskikh pri Moskovskom universitete (Vremennik OIDR) [Annals of the Imperial Society for Russian History and Antiquities at Moscow University]. 25 vols. Moscow, 1849–57.

Vysotskii, D. A. "Kollektivnye dvorianskie chelobitnye XVII v. kak istoricheskii istochnik [Collective Gentry Petitions of the 17th Century as a Historical Source]." *Vspomogatel'nye istoricheskie distsipliny* [Auxiliary Historical Disciplines] 19 (1987): 125–38.

Weber, Max. *Economy and Society: An Outline of Interpretive Sociology*. Guenther Roth and Claus Wittich, eds. 3 vols. New York, 1968.

Weickhardt, George G. "Due Process and Equal Justice in the Muscovite Codes." *Russian Review* 51 (1992): 463–80.

———. "The Pre-Petrine Law of Property." *Slavic Review* 52 (1993): 663–79.

Whittaker, Cynthia H. "The Reforming Tsar: The Redefinition of Autocratic Duty in Eighteenth-Century Russia." *Slavic Review* 51 (1992): 77–98.

Wrightson, Keith. *English Society, 1580–1680*. London, 1982.

Zabelin, I. E. "Bol'shoi boiarin v svoem votchinnom khoziaistve (XVII-yi vek) [A Great Boyar in His Estate Economy (17th Century)]." *Vestnik Evropy* [Messenger of Europe], no. 1, pp. 5–49, no. 2, pp. 465–514, (1871).

Zagoskin, N. P. *Istoriia prava Moskovskogo gosudarstva* [History of the Law of the Muscovite State]. 2 vols. Kazan', 1877 and 1879.

———. *Stoly Razriadnogo prikaza po khraniashchimsia v Moskovskom arkhive Ministerstva iustitsii knigam ikh. Otchet o zaniatiiakh v arkhive osen'iu 1878 goda* [The Desks of the Chancellery of Military Affairs According to Their Books Preserved in the Moscow Archive of the Ministry of Justice. A Report of the Proceedings of the Archive in Fall 1878]. Kazan', 1878.

Zaozerskaia, E. I. "Pomeshchik Zhukov i ego khoziaistvo [Landlord Zhukov and His Economy]." In Pavlenko et al., eds. *Dvorianstvo i krepostnoi stroi Rossii*, pp. 213–26.

Zaozerskii, A. I. "K voprosu o sostave i znachenii zemskikh soborov [On the Question of the Composition and Significance of the Assemblies of the Land]." *Zhurnal Ministerstva Narodnogo Prosveshcheniia* [Journal of the Ministry of Popular Education] 21 (1909): 299–352.

——. *Tsarskaia votchina XVII v.* [The Tsar's Landholdings in the 17th Century]. Moscow, 1937.

——. "Zemskie sobory [Assemblies of the Land]." In V. V. Kallash, ed., *Tri veka. Rossiia ot Smuty do nashego vremeni. Istoricheskii sbornik* [Three Centuries: Russia from the Time of Troubles to Our Time. A Historical Collection], vol. 1 (Moscow, 1912), pp. 115–62.

Zenkovsky, Serge A., ed. *Medieval Russia's Epics, Chronicles, and Tales.* Revised and enlarged ed. New York, 1974.

Zimin, A. A. "O politicheskikh predposylkakh vozniknoveniia russkogo absoliutizma [Of the Political Preconditions of the Rise of Russian Absolutism]." In N. M. Druzhinin, ed. *Absoliutizm v Rossii (XVII–XVIII vv.). Sbornik statei k semidesiatiletiiu . . . V. V. Kafengauza* [Absolutism in Russia (17th-18th Centuries). A Collection of Articles for the 70th Anniversary . . . of V. V. Kafengauz]. (Moscow, 1964), pp. 18–49.

——. *Reformy Ivana Groznogo. Ocherki sotsial'no-ekonomicheshkoi i politicheskoi istorii Rossii serediny XVI v.* [The Reforms of Ivan the Terrible. Essays on the Socioeconomic and Political History of Russia in the Middle of the 16th Century]. Moscow, 1960.

——. "O slozhenii prikaznoi sistemy na Rusi [Of the Establishment of the Chancellery System in Rus']." In *Doklady i soobshcheniia Instituta Istorii (Akademii Nauk)* [Reports and Communications of the Institute of History of the Academy of Sciences] 3 (1955): 164–76.

——. "Sostav boiarskoi dumy v XV–XVI vekah [The Composition of the Boyar Duma in the 15th-16th Centuries]." In *Arkheograficheskii ezhegodnik za 1957 god* [Archeographic Year Book for 1957]. Moscow, 1958.

Zimin, A. A., ed. *Tysiachnaia kniga 1550 g. i dvorovaia tetrad' 50-kh godov XVI v.* [The Thousand Book of 1550 and the Court Register of the 1550s]. Moscow, 1950.

Index

In this index an "f" after a number indicates a separate reference on the next page, and an "ff" indicates separate references on the next two pages. A continuous discussion over two or more pages is indicated by a span of page numbers, e.g., "57–59." *Passim* is used for a cluster of references in close but not consecutive sequence.

Library of Congress Cataloging-in-Publication Data

Kivelson, Valerie A. (Valerie Ann)
Autocracy in the provinces : the Muscovite gentry and political
culture in the seventeenth century / Valerie A. Kivelson.
    p. cm.
Includes bibliographical references (p.) and index.
ISBN 0-8047-2582-9 (cloth : alk. paper)
    1. Russia—Politics and government—1613-1689. 2. Gentry—Russia—
History—17th century. I. Title.
DK114.K55 1997
947'.046—dc20
96-14634 CIP

⊗ This book is printed on acid-free paper.

Last date below indicates year of this printing:
05 04 03 02 01 00 99 98 97 96